# Freedom to Freelance

Beginning the fight against IR35

Philip Ross

Freedom to Freelance...
Beginning the fight against IR35

by Philip Ross

Copyright © Philip Ross 2012. All rights reserved.
ISBN 978-1-4717-7149-1

Extracts with permission from *Shout99.com*

(Short Edition)
Third edition, November 2012

All reasonable efforts have been made by the author to contact the copyright holders of work reproduced in this volume. The author will be pleased to make good any omissions or rectify any mistakes brought to his attention at the earliest opportunity.

www.Lulu.com

02/11/2012 14:34

## About the Campaign and IR35

"I think you're quite a vocal lot and have seriously terrified figures in Whitehall."
*Lord Haskins (Labour Peer and Head of the Better Regulation Task Force)*

"The second congratulations are due to the Professional Contractors Group. I have never encountered such a literate, persuasive series of letters. Ministers have received something like 2,000 letters. I have received many dozens. The noble Lord, Lord Jenkin, has received a number. They are literate, well spelt, well argued, persuasive letters (and wrong)" *Lord McIntosh (Labour Peer to the Lords)*

"The hon. Gentleman should explain why he is prepared to support a group of workers whose companies their own advisers describe as tax havens. Why should they be allowed to continue to cheat honest taxpayers?"
*Dawn Primarolo (Paymaster General to Parliament)*

"We have awarded the new personal service company rules a score of 30 out of 100. This is a poor result". *Francesca Lagerberg ICAEW*

"The Tax Faculty believes that the IR35 proposals are fundamentally unfair. We believe the rules affecting personal service companies are unnecessary".
*Tax Faculty*

"Andy [White] deserved a special mention in the Elected Representative Awards. Even though this was intended for MPs, MSPs and councillors, such was the depth of support for Andy that we felt that his sterling effort to show what would happen with IR35 deserved to be recognised". *New Statesman New Media Awards Judge*

"I'm a very strong admirer of what you have done and I am very keen to see you do even more in the immediate future." *Sir John Harvey-Jones*

"[IR35] fails to understand that knowledge and skills are commodities that are traded today just as manufactured goods have been traded in the past".
*Philip Ross - to the Labour Conference*

"The members of PCG did more than talk about the injustice of it - they formed a group, put their hands in their pockets and sent a message to the Government saying 'we're not going to take this, we're going to do more about it than moan, you've got a fight on your hands and we're not going away".
*Andy White PCG Founder*

Foreword to this Edition ................................................................. 12

Preface ........................................................................................... 13

About the Author ........................................................................... 15

# PART 1 - FORMING THE PCG ..................................................... 16

## Chapter 1 ...................................................................................... 17
Becoming a contractor ....................................................................... 17
But why go contracting? ..................................................................... 17

## Chapter 2 ...................................................................................... 21
Budget Day 9th March 1999 ............................................................... 21
IR35: Press Release – 9 March 1999 ................................................... 23
Engineerjob.com ................................................................................. 25
No sympathy for contractors .............................................................. 26
Red Dawn ............................................................................................ 28

## Chapter 3 ...................................................................................... 30
The Revenue gets their way after all .................................................. 30
The British Computer Society ............................................................. 31
Travel Allowances ............................................................................... 32
BCS when IR35 broke .......................................................................... 33

## Chapter 4 ...................................................................................... 37
Fairness in the Tax System ................................................................. 37
1981 – PRIDE ....................................................................................... 38
The Architects of Doom ...................................................................... 39
Why don't contractors work as self-employed? ................................. 42

## Chapter 5 ...................................................................................... 43
United we stand? ................................................................................ 43
Recruitment Industry led alliance ....................................................... 43
An industry alliance against the tax? .................................................. 44
Enquiries to the Inland Revenue ......................................................... 47

## Chapter 6 ...................................................................................... 48
22nd April 1999 – The full plans laid open ......................................... 48
Speaking up for contractors ................................................................ 48
Creation of the Professional Contractors Group: ............................... 50

## PART 2 - PARLIAMENTARY BATTLE ........... 53

### Chapter 1 ........... 54
Any minute now the Minister will be calling me ........... 54
Shopping Hours Reform Team get settled in ........... 55
ICCG goes for Compromise ........... 55
Backdoor Legislation ........... 57
Foot in the Door – Talking to the Revenue ........... 58
Friday to Monday working – Winning the argument ........... 58
Lord Weatherill becomes PCG Patron ........... 58

### Chapter 2 ........... 60
Raising the Profile ........... 60
Write to Your MP ........... 60
How MPs Reply to Letters ........... 62
Meeting your MP ........... 63
What MPs Said ........... 64
Parliamentary lobbying ........... 65

### Chapter 3 ........... 66
Small Business Minister ........... 66
Meeting with the Small Business Minister ........... 67
After the DTI ........... 70

### Chapter 4 ........... 72
A war of facts and figures - Full Consultation? ........... 72
Employees on paper, businesses in reality ........... 72
Facts, Figures, Evidence to no avail ........... 73

### Chapter 5 ........... 75
The Parliamentary Battle Begins ........... 75
$4^{th}$ May 1999 ........... 75
$16^{th}$ May 1999 ........... 76
$17^{th}$ May 1999 ........... 76
PCG Democracy ........... 81
9th June 1999 ........... 81
10th, 11th June 1999 ........... 82
Government took shortcuts in IR35 consultation, says CIOT ........... 83
IR 35 Time to make our mind up ........... 85
$9^{th}$ June 1999 ........... 86
$10^{th}$ June 1999 ........... 86
$16^{th}$ June 1999 ........... 87
$28^{th}$ June 1999 ........... 88

29th June 1999 .................................................................................. 90

## Chapter 6 ............................................................................................. 92
More MP Lobbying .................................................................................. 92
20th July - House of Lords Debate ........................................................ 92
Lord McIntosh's Seminar ....................................................................... 93
Second Meeting with Michael Wills ..................................................... 93
Taking Stock ............................................................................................ 94
Aberdeen Chapter .................................................................................. 94
PCG Membership is growing to 3,000 ................................................. 95

## Chapter 7 ............................................................................................. 96
Secret Meetings – Divide and Conquer ............................................... 96
Think Tank Report – 'An inflexible friend' .......................................... 97
Letter to the Prime Minister ................................................................. 98
Politicians and the reshuffled .............................................................. 99
The Revenue Meeting ............................................................................ 99
PCG-for the future ............................................................................... 100

## Chapter 8 ........................................................................................... 101
23$^{rd}$ September – Revised Proposals - Son of IR35 ........................ 101
What next? ............................................................................................ 103
Public Response to the reformed IR35 ............................................. 104
Thursday 23$^{rd}$ September .................................................................. 104

## Chapter 9 ........................................................................................... 106
IR35 Speech to the Labour Party Conference .................................. 106
27$^{th}$ September .................................................................................... 106
Knowledge Based Economy ............................................................... 110
Compositing ......................................................................................... 110
Meeting with Dawn Primarolo ........................................................... 114
Mail on Sunday .................................................................................... 117
Knowledge Based Economy Debate ................................................. 118
Other Meetings .................................................................................... 119
Conservative Party Conference ......................................................... 119
The BBC and IR35 ................................................................................ 120

## Chapter 10 ......................................................................................... 123
Preparing for the big battle ................................................................ 123
A new Regulatory Impact Assessment (RIA) ................................... 124
Situation Update .................................................................................. 125
House of Lords Reject the Clause ..................................................... 127
House of Lords Debate ....................................................................... 127
What happens now? ............................................................................ 130

| | |
|---|---|
| Dawn's Response | 131 |
| Early Day Motion | 134 |

## Chapter 11 .................................................................................................. **136**
| | |
|---|---|
| Mass Lobby on Parliament / Flash Mob | 136 |
| Monday 1st November 1999 | 138 |
| Tuesday 2nd November | 139 |
| Final Call for Mass Lobby | 140 |
| Contractor Wednesday – 3rd November | 141 |
| Thursday 4th November | 145 |
| Conservative leader William Hague | 146 |
| What happens next? | 146 |

## Chapter 12 .................................................................................................. **149**
| | |
|---|---|
| Back to the House of Lords - 8th November 1999 | 149 |

# PART 3 – JUDICIAL REVIEW ........................................................... **151**

## Chapter 1 .................................................................................................... **152**
| | |
|---|---|
| What has just happened? | 152 |
| Judicial Review | 155 |

## Chapter 2 .................................................................................................... **156**
| | |
|---|---|
| Revenue Issues Guidance | 156 |
| Raising the Profile with Presentations | 157 |
| Going abroad and Fast Track visa | 158 |
| Unpicking the new Proposals | 159 |
| Legal opinion – there is no case law | 160 |

## Chapter 3 .................................................................................................... **162**
| | |
|---|---|
| First ever e-Petition | 162 |
| Alan Duncan helps with e-Petition | 163 |
| Sunday Times cover IR35 | 165 |

## Chapter 4 .................................................................................................... **166**
| | |
|---|---|
| Agencies don't care about IR35 | 166 |
| Comparison with nurses | 168 |
| PCG Grows and Defines more clearly what it does | 169 |

## Chapter 5 .................................................................................................... **171**
| | |
|---|---|
| PCG Meeting the Paymaster General | 171 |
| The meeting | 173 |
| Dawn's version of events to Parliament | 178 |
| Our final response | 180 |

## Chapter 6 .................................................................................................. 182
The Stephen Timms fiasco .................................................................... 182

## Chapter 7 .................................................................................................. 184
Seminars... spreading the word ........................................................... 184
Andy's New Year's Campaign Review ................................................. 186
Opening up new fronts ......................................................................... 190
Dawn comes under pressure from her own MPs ............................... 190
William Hague increases the pressure ................................................ 191
Pressure on e-Minister increases ......................................................... 191
E-Envoy adds his voice .......................................................................... 191
Treasury under Siege ............................................................................ 192
ATSCo in the Times ............................................................................... 193
2$^{nd}$ February – Final Guidance issued by Revenue ............................ 194
Ground laid for a legal battle ............................................................... 194

## Chapter 8 .................................................................................................. 196
The Phoney War Begins ........................................................................ 196
Revenue Approves PCG contract ......................................................... 197
2$^{nd}$ April – PCG Growth Figures Revealed ........................................... 197
Andy White hands over the PCG to its members ............................... 198
*Shout99.com* Launched – Mouthpiece for Contractors ..................... 199

## Chapter 9 .................................................................................................. 201
Budget 2000 – No joy for contractors ................................................. 201
IR35 estimates doubled to £900m ....................................................... 201
FTVs gathers pace ................................................................................. 202
Agency Misinformation ........................................................................ 202

## Chapter 10 ................................................................................................ 204
IR35 - See you in court .......................................................................... 204
Inland Revenue spin doctors go to Newsnight .................................. 204
*Shout99.com* tocsin bell rings! ............................................................ 205
Newsnight Affair – The tocsin bell rings ............................................. 205
IR35 confuses at Prime Ministers Question Time ............................... 207
Lucky Aussies drop IR35 equivalent .................................................... 207

## Chapter 11 ................................................................................................ 209
The final parliamentary battle ............................................................. 209
Hague and Portillo keep enterprise on the agenda ........................... 209
12th June 2000 - Final parliamentary fight ......................................... 209
5% debate .............................................................................................. 214

## Chapter 12 ................................................................................................ 217
Professional bodies all come out to say it is no good ........................ 217

Accountants slam the Government over IR 35 .................................................. 218
The ICAEW Score Card ..................................................................................... 219

## Chapter 13 ................................................................................................... 223
IR35 is not the only fruit .................................................................................. 223
RIP Bill ............................................................................................................. 223
Fast Track Visas ............................................................................................... 224
Agency legislation ........................................................................................... 224

## Chapter 14 ................................................................................................... 225
Office of Fair Trading (OFT) ............................................................................. 225
Is there anyone out there? Susie makes a desperate call .............................. 225
Summer time .................................................................................................. 226
Revenue asks agencies for contactor details ................................................. 227
There is no case law says Revenue inspector ................................................. 228
Lord Report on e-Commerce .......................................................................... 229
PCG launch their Gone Abroad Page .............................................................. 232

## Chapter 15 ................................................................................................... 233
The e-Envoy .................................................................................................... 233
Guardian interview the e-Envoy ..................................................................... 234
New Statesman Award .................................................................................... 235
Meeting with the e-Envoy ............................................................................... 236

## Chapter 16 ................................................................................................... 240
The e-Minister ................................................................................................. 240
Hewitt dodges questions on IR35 ................................................................... 241
Govt Report opens a door on IR35 ................................................................. 243

## Chapter 17 ................................................................................................... 244
Tories and IR35 ............................................................................................... 244

## Chapter 18 ................................................................................................... 247
Media training course for directors ................................................................ 249
Joint Letter to the Financial Times ................................................................. 250
July Forum Flaming! ........................................................................................ 250
October – High Court agrees that PCG has a case ......................................... 251
Account of the proceedings ........................................................................... 252
Media is mad for IR35 ..................................................................................... 254
The Evening standard ..................................................................................... 254
The Times wrote .............................................................................................. 255
York AGM and Conference .............................................................................. 256
Sir John Harvey-Jones on Sky News ................................................................ 258
December – ATSCo fight with Jobserve .......................................................... 258
ATSCO interview Sarah Walker ....................................................................... 260

Downing Street Forums close down ............................................................. 260

**Chapter 19** .................................................................................................. **262**
January 2001 – I stand down from PCG board ............................................. 262
FI offers £1,000 bounty on contractors ........................................................ 263
Dawn says that contractor who are leaving are silly .................................. 264
Final Justifications ....................................................................................... 265

**Chapter 20** .................................................................................................. **267**
March 2001 – Judicial Review ...................................................................... 267
What is a judicial review? ........................................................................... 268
The legal process ......................................................................................... 268
The PCG's Case ............................................................................................ 268
Tuesday 13th May 2001 – Morning Session ................................................ 271
JR 2: Judge 'sympathetic only to uncertainty over IR35' ............................. 273
Judicial Review Session Three – Wednesday 14 March 2001 ..................... 275
Who was who in court? ............................................................................... 278
The War Room – PCG take over the Cheshire Cheese ................................ 278
Thursday 15th March ................................................................................. 282
Morning of Monday 19th March ................................................................ 283
The Judicial Review – Day 4 – Monday19th March .................................... 284
Waiting for the ruling .................................................................................. 286
Taking a last political shot .......................................................................... 288
Andy's view ................................................................................................. 289
The Register's View ..................................................................................... 290
The Ruling ................................................................................................... 291

**Chapter 21** .................................................................................................. **294**
Revenue says Pay Up! ................................................................................. 294
PCG's Response ........................................................................................... 295
PCG Press Statement .................................................................................. 295
Press Reaction ............................................................................................. 299
Dawn responds in Parliament ..................................................................... 300
Sarah Walker Speaks ................................................................................... 301
PCG offers discounted tax insurance .......................................................... 306

**Chapter 22** .................................................................................................. **308**
June 2001 - General election ...................................................................... 308
Aftermath .................................................................................................... 308

APPENDIX .................................................................................. 310

Nominations for the New Statesman Award....................................311

Glossary of Organisations ............................................................319

Glossary of terms........................................................................320

INDEX......................................................................................... 323

# Foreword to this Edition

This edition of *Freedom to Freelance* covers three of the eight parts that I have written. These are:

*Part 1 - Forming the PCG - the original formation of the PCG following the announcement of IR35*

*Part 2 - The Parliamentary Battle - the initial Parliamentary battle in both the House of Commons and the House of Lords*

*Part 3 - Judicial Review - how we raised the money and took the Government to the High Court for a judicial review hearing over IR35*

This is not the full story you need to read all eight parts for that. It has proven difficult to find any division but being the first phase in the development of the PCG when the movement was very much united I find this the clearest place to divide and the part that would interest people the most.

Parts 4 - 8 deal with what followed after the judicial review hearing and in my personal opinion are even more interesting.

*Part 4 - Political Engagement - how we sought to engage in the broader political process*

*Part 5 - Fast Track Visas - how we successfully fought the Home Office on the issue of work permits for non-EU workers as the system was being abused and UK workers were losing their job as a result*

*Part 6 - Agency Regulations - the new agency regulations threatened to redefine contractors as temporary workers for employment purposes just as IR35 had done for tax purposes.*

*Part 7 - Appeal and Case Law - the follow up judicial review and the subsequent case law strategy implemented.*

*Part 8 - Thermidor - the founders of the PCG leave, including myself*

The Preface is from the original eight part book which I have left in unaltered.

I hope that having read parts 1-3 you will also be keen to read parts 4-8.

All comments are welcome at my blogspot:

http://freedomtofreelance.blogspot.co.uk/

PER
July 2012

# Preface

This is the story of the birth of Britain's first on-line trade association, its founding members and the use of technology to revolutionise political lobbying and representation. It tells how they were formed from nothing and within two years had over 14,000 members. It is about how they turned themselves from a single-issue pressure group into a fully functioning trade association that was able to leverage the power and the pocket of their members to battle with the Inland Revenue over IR35 and the Home Office over the issue of fast track visas.

The story should appeal to anyone who was involved in the campaign at the time, the 14,000 members of the Professional Contractors Group and perhaps the other 120,000 contractors who were affected by IR35. It should also appeal to anyone with an interest in politics and the battles with the Government and the Inland Revenue. Thirdly it should appeal to anyone interested in e-democracy and the use of the Internet to develop, grow and manage a pressure group or an organisation.

This is partly a story of how a group of plucky IT contractors banded together and took on the Government. It is a story of sacrifice and endeavour, of valour and of great deeds and successes. It is one of the first examples of crowd-funding, High Court drama and the biggest post 1997 lobby on Parliament, which many have described as the world's first flash mob, and the first e-petition presented to Parliament. Also perhaps of the only on-air apology transmitted on Newsnight.

It is the story of two campaigns. The first campaign is surrounding IR35 where we would take on the Government in a direct confrontation. The second campaign is where we would use more gentle persuasion and diplomacy to defeat fast track visas and the agency legislation that threatened to turn contractors into temps. The second campaign was only possible due to winning the first. This book covers only the first campaign, that of taking on the Government against IR35.

Overlaying the whole drama is the narrative of a revolution. It may have been an online revolution but it is predominately a story about people.

This is the story of my time with the PCG and considers the period between 1999 and 2002. Many of the original Internet links for documents and sources are no longer available so I am relying on both memory and checking facts through *Shout99.com*. Fortunately I kept a box file of original cuttings and I apologise in advance for shamelessly rehashing some of these documents. If I have forgotten to mention anyone I apologise and also if my memory has contained factual errors which will be corrected in future editions. I was at the heart of the campaign and fought hard for contractors and believed in the cause. I have included many documents and press notices which were either sent to me at the time or I use with the kind permission of *Shout99.com*.

IR35 created a huge division between freelancers and the previous Labour Government and a bitter campaign was fought on both sides. The Government thought they could just force the measure through, pay lip service to consultation while dealing roughly with any opposition. The biggest irony of IR35 is that a poll taken just after its release showed that the majority of those affected had elected New Labour in 1997.

Contractors themselves looked up from their coding and development work and although many wrote thoughtful and intelligent letters some angry and bitter letters were sent out too. This resulted in angry letters to the Paymaster General as well as bitter and antagonistic letters to MPs. The Opposition parties embraced the campaign. At the time of high poll ratings for the Government it was one of Labour's first real identifiable mistakes. Tory leader William Hague would make it a central plank of his election manifesto and I would find myself as a Labour supporting member of an increasingly Conservative leaning trade association. Not only Labour supporting but I would soon find myself as a parliamentary candidate for Labour Party at the 2001 General Election.

This is the story of how I navigated my way through the campaign, helped establish the PCG as a force and became its first Campaign Director. How I then left to fight the General Election for the Labour Party who were pro-IR35, only to return after the election to win the contract to provide PCG's public affairs. We would then undertake the almost impossible campaign against the issue of fast track visas which brought in labour from abroad resulting in contractors becoming unemployed. IR35 would be about whether contracting was financially viable, fast track visas would be about whether there was any work and agency legislation about whether we were to be reclassified as temporary workers,

Looking through the PCG website or any of their materials you will have to look long and hard to find any mention of Andy White, Susie Hughes or myself and the role we played in establishing the PCG. It is almost as if we are non-persons, as Trotsky was in Stalin's Russia, air brushed out of photographs and history so that now we have been forgotten.

At best we are noted as radicals like the Jacobins were in France, blamed for the excesses of the revolution and considered to be mavericks. The truth is we were radical; we were bold and we were audacious as were much of the membership. That is what got us results and is how the PCG was founded. I am happy with the Jacobin tag for myself as I am proud of my part in the history and pleased at now being able to tell it.

# About the Author

Philip Ross was one of the founding members of the Professional Contractors Group and played a leading role in the fight against IR35. He was elected as their first external affairs director. He left the group to stand for Parliament later returning in an executive capacity running their external affairs function. He led the PCG's successful campaign against Fast Track Visas.

After leaving the PCG he went to run the parliamentary office of Tony McWalter MP. He decided to return to IT contracting but in the interim took a part job on the tills at John Lewis. He made it back into IT as a permanent employee in Dunstable after which he returned to work in London in 2006.

On the political front he became Mayor of Letchworth Garden City from 2007-9. He continues to write political articles on freelancing and small business for Progress and for Shout99.com. He has also become an international speaker on the topic of Garden Cities.

He now works for a consultancy in London called Alpheus in which he is a shareholder. Though no longer a contractor he is still committed to the cause.

# Part 1 - Forming the PCG

# Chapter 1

## Becoming a contractor

This is the story of a real 'dot-com' revolution, or to be more precise a revolution that occurred during the dot-com boom and the consequences of which could limit our chances of having another one. Like all revolutions it begins with remarkable pace and energy, endures great travails, makes considerable progress – little of which was acknowledged at the time – and ends as most revolutions do, with the movement destroying its founders and key players, losing some of it old vitality and recasting its self in a different mould.

This is in part the story about the birth and growth of the Professional Contractors Group, a trade association representing freelance workers that was to grow from zero members to a little over 14,000 in just over two years. Above all else it is the story as I see it, the story through my own eyes, how I experienced it, how I remember it and how I felt at the time and how I feel now.

It is estimated that around 20% of the UK's workforce are self-employed or run a small business which includes freelance workers or contractors. Unfortunately the Government doesn't collect any real statistics on this so freelancers are as an invisible workforce and are disregarded by policy makers. Industry figures estimate that in 1999 there were around 150,000 freelance IT contractors working in the UK.

To tell you about my role in it I need explain why, like so many others, I decided to go contracting, what my motivation was and what the economic climate was as the time.

In the mid to late 1990's there was a great convergence of demand for information technology. Firms were becoming worried about the millennium bug, redundant COBOL programmers who were happily retired were dusting off their keyboards and were coming back to work for great rewards. On the continent the Euro was about to become a reality and the worlds investment banks needed to update their systems to cope with a major new currency and the abolition of old ones. It also saw the birth and growth of the Internet and the dot-com boom coming into full swing, which meant that skilled IT professionals were suddenly in great demand.

## But why go contracting?

Working as an IT contractor had become a respectable career in the 1990s. The previous recession had changed traditional thinking about a job for life. The Conservative Government led by example in the late 1980s as central and local authorities contracted out services on a grand scale. This also led employers to look closely at hiring people only when needed rather than having them permanently on the books.

Employers also halted their training and recruitment so the combination of revived projects, the year 2000, the creation of the euro currency and developments such as intranets brought a shortage of trained and experienced people, the shortfall was thought to be around 50,000. Training and the hiring of raw recruits started again but the desperation to meet the year 2000 deadline, the revival of postponed projects and the pace of new technology developments forced IT departments to turn more and more to contract staff.

The number of contractors was thought to have doubled to around 50,000 during the 1990s. This was partly due to people being made redundant and partly due to average contract rates of £1,000 a week, which proved highly attractive at a time when people could be assured of a new contract well within a month of the last one ending. At the same time employment agencies desperate for new people were offering everything from starter guides to discounted or even free training schemes.

'Most organisations use contractors these days,' said Mike Cullen, chairman of the BCS Independent Computer Contractors Specialist Group (ICCG) during an interview in 1998. 'In addition to the estimated 50,000 contractors there are 120,000 people in outsourcing companies, which could be regarded as a half-way house towards full contracting for people transferred from the client companies. '

He add that 'Most permanent staff now have a realistic idea of what is involved in becoming a contractor, because they work alongside contractors every day.' He noted that the market in the late 1990's was by no means perfect and there had been loud complaints from agencies about contractors walking out on clients when better offers came along, also from contractors about contracts being heavily weighted in favour of the agency and the client. Some things never change.

To counter this he explained that the ICCG had developed a code of practice for contractors. This was formally accepted by the BCS and work was begun on a standard contract to help cut disputes. While the ICCG was open to all contractors, not just BCS members, these did tend to be the bulk of the membership. The code of practice stated in particular that contractors must not walk out on contracts, although it suggested that all sides benefit if a contract is even handed. Other issues included making a stand if asked to do something which broke the law or the BCS code of conduct. At that time the trade body of IT agencies was the Federation of Recruitment and Employment Services (FRES)[1] who introduced stricter entry requirements on their side.

Mike Cullen explained that "As well as going through business vetting - both the company and its directors - a job agency now had to advertise its intention to join and invite comments from clients and job applicants. New members went through a probationary year. A complaints procedure was set up with publicised expulsion as

---

[1] The current equivalent body is known as Recruitment and Employment Confederation (REC)

the ultimate sanction, not that any of it seemed to make any difference to the way some agencies treated their contract staff."

Mike was optimistic that these early efforts had "helped to turn contracting from a stop-gap between permanent jobs into a full-time career for thousands of IT specialists." He noted that people considering taking the plunge still needed to consider all the issues.

Pay was one of the biggest attractions, especially for contractors who had reached a cross roads in their careers. They were being asked to move from being technically minded to management if they wanted to make more money, which is something of a British disease and misconception. The best engineers don't make the best managers and vice versa, a fact I can confirm having worked in several places where the poor programmers and engineers are those that slipped into management. Unable to cut the mustard doing the coding or development they would perform administration orientated tasks which allowed them to slowly climb the management ladder.

He explained that "Going contracting, or starting any business is not the same as working for anyone else. No holidays, no sick pay, no promotion, no fringe benefits. In the good times more cash, but also new expenses: forming a limited company (agencies generally only take on contractors operating in this way[2], otherwise they can face tax liabilities); accountants fees (accountants not only draw up accounts but can advise on how to cut tax and save national insurance by taking the best combination of salary and dividends from the limited company); VAT; training; perhaps equipment.

Once established, contractors have to look after their own development. If they go for training they lose twice: they pay for the training and lose paid work while on the course. But for me all the new skills that I had acquired during my career had been through my own hard work in the evenings and weekends, it would then be my employer who would gain. Time, self-discipline and a tidy mind are needed for administration, keeping the books and staying in touch with agencies to get the next contract. Changing contract every six, 12 or 18 months is like starting a new job every time, with all the pressures that creates, especially if it involves living away from home, in a bedsit or in digs. And each time the expensive hired hand is expected to be productive very quickly".

His final tips were that "there is job insecurity and the real prospect of working away from home, the need to steer clear of office gossip, possible exclusion from social events, and even resentment from permanent staff." I felt that although you have job insecurity, you have a certain degree of certainty; you know you will be out of contract in six months time. With my contract time ticking away, I embraced

---

[2] Though in 2011 we see more contractors working through 'umbrella' companies

my uncertainty with both hands, whereas my permanent colleagues would worry on a day to day basis as redundancy threatened but never came.

# Chapter 2

### Budget Day 9th March 1999

After the Chancellor, Gordon Brown, closed his Red Box on the year's budget the 'minor' announcements - not worthy of verbal explanation at the Dispatch Box - were published. The Inland Revenue's 35th such announcement (hence IR35) explained in a press release the Government's intention to target a particular type of 'tax avoidance', the so-called Friday-to-Monday scenario.

The Inland Revenue wanted to stop people leaving - sometimes under pressure from employers - their jobs on a Friday, setting up their own companies over the weekend; and returning to the same job, at the same place, doing the same work on a Monday - only now as a 'small business' rather than an 'employee'.

I actually remember the budget day well. Gordon Brown gave a marvellous budget speech. I had just come back from working at Labour's HQ in Millbank Tower where I had an annual contract to process electoral data for the party. I never really made any money from doing it as I'd earn less there than I could at the investment bank at which I was working, but I got to help the party and I still thought it was kind of cool to be working at Millbank Tower.

When I first went to work there I thought I would be bumping into Tony Blair or Gordon Brown at the coffee machine, or even in the bathroom, but in the all the years I worked there I hardly ever saw any politicians. I once saw Frank Dobson MP when he was running for Mayor of London, looking worried and intense sneaking out of the back of the building with Margaret McDonagh[3], but I only saw him because I was having a cigarette there. John Prescott did call by one day and thanked everyone for what they were doing, but I was late in on that day and missed him by about 5 minutes.

As far as I was concerned on Budget Day Gordon Brown had given a fantastic speech, everything was positive, there were no negative elements in the budget at all. As a Labour supporter I was very pleased and was thinking about how I would feed this into my election materials for the local elections. I remember going for lunch in the cafeteria the next day with fellow contractors Jerry Hone and James Mitchell. I actually remember Jerry saying to us 'what are your thoughts on the budget then guys?' I answered 'not much in it for us, a new rate of corporation tax for small business…' Or so I thought.

Before I had become a contractor I had worked for a software house in Stevenage. I had not really enjoyed it; the management seemed to believe that because you worked there they owned you totally. There was a great deal of bullying of staff and personal verbal attacks on them – standard management stuff. I hated it but was preoccupied with helping the Labour Party fight the General Election in mid

---

[3] Then General Sec. of the Labour Party

Bedfordshire. Every Sunday morning we would be out knocking on doors in leafy suburban streets to be greeted with disdain, enthusiasm, lies (I haven't decided yet) and worst of all to be ignored. You'd see the TV on in their lounge but your knocking on the door would be ignored. Of course it wasn't always helped by the fact the Jehovah's Witnesses were also doing the rounds. So I lived to help fight the elections and my manager professed himself an admirer of Michael Portillo.

We were told by Millbank[4] that we should be evangelical to friends, family and work colleagues about the need for a new government, so that is what I did. I slowly persuaded many of my IT friends about the need for a Labour Government. They tolerated my ramblings and who knows, I may have got through to some of them.

A couple of days after the budget I received an email from one such friend, Justin Connaughton, saying "looks like Labour plans to abolish contracting".

I couldn't believe it. It pointed to a website called engineerjob.com so I went and had a look at it.

---

[4] New Labour offices. Millbank was short hand for the New Labour management and leadership. Now in 2011 Labour had moved offices and David Cameron's Conservatives have offices there.

# IR35: Press Release – 9 March 1999

The Chancellor announced today that changes are to be introduced to counter avoidance in the area of personal service provision. This move underlines the Government's commitment to achieving a tax system under which everyone pays their fair share.

There has for some time been general concern about the hiring of individuals through their own service companies so that they can exploit the fiscal advantages offered by a corporate structure. It is possible for someone to leave work as an employee on a Friday, only to return the following Monday to do exactly the same job as an indirectly engaged 'consultant' paying substantially reduced tax and national insurance.

The Government is going to bring forward legislation to tackle this sort of avoidance. The Inland Revenue will be discussing the practical application of new legislation with interested parties and will work with representative bodies on the production of guidance. The new rules will take effect from April 2000.

## DETAILS

1. The Government is committed to encouraging modern businesses which develop and build on the strengths and commitment of their workforce. The aim of the proposed changes is ensure that people working in what is, in effect, disguised employment will, in practice, pay the same tax and national insurance as someone employed directly.

2. Businesses employing their workers directly say that they are unable to compete with those encouraging the avoidance at which the new legislation is aimed. As a result, ordinary workers can find they are unable to compete for jobs with those willing to participate in such arrangements. But those who do participate often have to pay a price in terms of loss of protection under employment law. They may find their terms and conditions altered - perhaps losing entitlement to sick pay or maternity leave. They may even lose their jobs without entitlement to notice or redundancy pay. They will usually have no right to any claim for unfair dismissal and may lose their entitlement to social security benefits through a failure to make adequate contributions.

3. The proposed changes are aimed only at engagements with essential characteristics of employment. They should affect only those cases where these characteristics are disguised through use of an intermediary - such as a service company or partnership. There is no intention to redefine the existing boundary between employment and self-employment.

4. Legislation is to be introduced to address the problem with effect from April 2000. However, a primary concern is to minimise any impact of these changes on ordinary businesses not involved in avoidance. To this end, the Inland Revenue will over the next few months be working with representative bodies on aspects of the practical application of the new rules and on the production of guidance. Any groups interested in contributing to this process should write to:

Elaine Carey
Personal Tax Division
Inland Revenue
New Wing
Somerset House
LONDON
WC2R 1LB

NOTES FOR EDITORS

These changes buttress the new measures to support small and medium sized companies. Without the changes it would be very difficult to target support at genuine entrepreneurial activity - making such measures less effective and more costly.

Engineerjob.com

Ex contractor Andy White ran a successful recruitment agency in Southampton. He had used his earnings as a contractor hovercraft engineer to build up this new business and in March 1999 he was regarding the Internet with interest and was a planning his 'dot com play'. Then IR35 struck. Andy realised that with these new rules in place he would never have been able to have started his recruitment business and other ventures. The proposals struck him as profoundly unfair. He had a domain name registered - engineerjob.com - that was going to be used for an on-line recruitment agency. Instead he turned it into an information resource about IR35.

I remember the initial days after IR35 had been announced, I was surfing the web to find out anything about the new proposals but there was nothing on the IT or accounting websites. Only engineerjob.com mentioned anything about it and included many opinions and information. These plans were too outlandish to be true surely? Freelance informer, silent, FRES, silent. By encouraging contractors to register for email updates it sowed the seeds then for what would become the Professional Contractors Group and *Shout99.com*. With the Internet still in its infancy with regards to use, I have to say that it was the first site I ever registered with for anything.

The website read:

The Chancellor announced in the March 99 Budget that changes are to be introduced to counter avoidance in the area of personal service provision. Effective from April 2000.

The objectives of this website are to:-

- Act as a focal point for information and opinion on this key issue with regard to Contractors in the IT and Engineering Sectors.

- Provide informed and independent analysis of the situation as it develops.

I noticed on the main pages of the site that it talked about the proposals from 'New Labour'. I emailed Andy and suggested that he changed it to the 'Inland Revenue'. "Let's keep politics out of it" I said. Andy complied and changed the text.

I wasn't alone; contractors all over the country were hitting on the engineerjob.com website. Of all the disparate groups of people in the country, the most Internet savvy and most connected were IT people and word about the new site passed from person to person like wild fire. I remember a few years ago some girl had had an indiscretion with her boyfriend and was a little too candid with him in an email, he forwarded to a friend who forwarded it on and very soon it had worked its way round most companies in the UK and was off over the Atlantic. The poor girl became a television and newspaper story and was even forced to change her name. Well news of IR35 and of engineerjob.com swept through the contractor community with similar speed.

In theory the IR35 legislation wasn't limited to any specific group, industry or sector. In general terms it was aimed at what has become known as the 'knowledge-based contractor', that is a person working in his or her business selling their knowledge rather than manufacturing a product.

However, the reality of the measure was that the prime group targeted were IT contractors. For reasons I have already explained this group of people was at the cutting edge of the new media, Internet, email, social networking, e-forums. All accepted and used in today's world by school children and grannies alike, but in 1999 this was the brave new world of the elite few. Not only were IT contractors highly proficient in the new technology, in many cases these were the men and women who were developing it and trail-blazing its use.

It short, the Government had chosen to attack the one group of individuals who could come together and collectively use the Internet as their lobbying tool. To use the clichés, books were being rewritten, goal posts were being moved and frontiers were being rolled back.

The one advantage this group had over the rest of the country, including the Government, was the ability to use the development of modern media and the Internet for unparalleled communication, research and co-ordination.

A new form of lobbying had just been born - and the Government had chosen the one group of people who knew how to use it.

Andy White found himself at the centre of the spread of information. Tired of replying to the same questions on email, hundreds of times, he turned engineer job.com into a basic information exchange resource.

The site went live on Saturday 13$^{th}$ March, by Wednesday 17$^{th}$ March it had received 1,500 hits and by a week later on Wednesday 24$^{th}$ March it was receiving 40,000 hits a day.

As contractors we quickly became informed of what was going on, but was there anything we could do about it? We were outraged but until now powerless to act. Over the coming weeks a few letters graced the pages of the computing press, no one really understood what was going on anyway and no one had any real sympathy for these "overpaid contractors".

## No sympathy for contractors

One of the things that had astonished me when working as a permanent employee was the way that contractors were able to arrange their tax affairs. Typically they would be earning a rate of three times what I earned, which is fair enough as they had chosen to work freelance, but they wouldn't earn the money directly themselves, it would go to a limited company of which they were shareholder as would be their spouse or other relatives. Magazines and advice dispensed explained that to be most tax efficient contractors should pay themselves the lowest possible PAYE wage. Such advice would come back to haunt the contractor community. Around £65/week was the suggested amount and then to withdraw the rest of the income as dividends which they could split between the shareholders.

The 'husband and wife' scenario (or Section 660 as it later became known) was at the time, a normal way of operating and would be recommended by accountants and also the Government-supported Business Links website, until the Government realised what it was doing and removed it. The spouse would often not work and would be able to be absorbed in dividends at a lower rate of tax. On top of this contractors would claim for every possible expense through the company. One contractor I met had all his children as shareholders as well as his wife. The Inland Revenue understandably frowned upon such arrangements. These people were not acting within the spirit of the law but the letter, but the letter of the law was all that mattered according to tax consultants. Not everyone acted like this though. A large number paid themselves a working wage commensurate with the job they were doing. For instance, I paid myself the same wage that I had earned when a permanent employee.

In 1999 Y2K was in full swing and the euro was being introduced as a real currency, combined with the dot-com boom rates for contract staff were going through the roof. Contractors weren't doing themselves any favours either; stories abounded about contractors terminating jobs early to go somewhere else for more money. IT companies saw their moderately paid but highly trained, skilled and experienced staff jacking in their jobs and going off contracting. They were not happy. The skills shortage itself contributed to this. Firms were forced to use contract staff while their own staff were trained, their staff soon learnt how much the contractors were earning for doing pretty much the same job as they were and so soon followed suit. Body shop firms - suppliers of trained staff for projects - soon found they were faced with the same problem. Body shop firms would soon be hiring contractors themselves and then would be selling them on. Quite a chain would be built up, the contractor would invoice their agency, the agency the body shop and the body shop the client and often the client again, their end client. Margins were down, body shops thought about the good old days when they paid their staff £25,000 a year and hired them out for £75,000. Contractors seeing a gap in the market were going it alone charging only £50,000. Agencies would take their 15-30% (or even more). Costs were rising. Why? Because the people that did the actual work were taking a larger cut of the profits made from their work. This didn't ring right in some circles. Profits are supposed to be made by exploiting labour, not from doing the actual work. IT firms felt aggrieved. They did have a genuine reason too as they were training up the staff, giving them the right experience and then they were leaving to go it alone. Something had to be done.

Meanwhile in the Treasury, Chancellor Gordon Brown found himself hemmed in. He'd promised to stick by Tory spending plans for the first two years of office, promised also not to raise taxes including national insurance, but desperately needed to raise extra taxes to fund much needed improvements to the public services. I can almost imagine him asking his officials 'how can we raise extra revenue without putting up taxes?' Mandarins in the Treasury scuttled off and dusted down an old box file for a tax proposal that they had first put together in

1981 targeting freelance workers. It had been rejected in 1981 but they brought it back out and showed it to Ken Clarke when he was chancellor. He'd considered it but rejected it, I understand, on the basis that it could have a detrimental effect on the market. Under Blair's government businessman and entrepreneur Geoffrey Robinson MP was the first Paymaster General and I understand that the proposals first graced his desk but events were to intervene. The Mandelson home loan scandal broke and for some reason Geoffrey Robinson, who was quite blameless, (all he'd done was lend a friend some money), was forced to resign too. His replacement would be the tough Dawn Primarolo and when the plans graced her desk she decided to implement them. Had Geoffrey Robinson still been in post his attitude towards entrepreneurial small businesses and the knowledge-based economy might have been somewhat different from 'Red Dawn's'.

### Red Dawn

Dawn Primarolo had become a junior Treasury Minister after the 1997 General Election and when her appointment was announced to Parliament members of the Opposition were said to have been totally aghast. This, in many respects for me was a good reason to like her. She had been known as 'Red Dawn' and as 'Dim Prawn', she had voted against the first Gulf War – but not the second. She had become an MP in the 1980's as part of the militant intake ousting out a more moderate candidate in her constituency. I remember her name being mentioned on the Tony Benn diary tapes when she was his constituency party secretary.

Her appointment as Paymaster General was a surprise to many. At the time The Guardian described her as a 'former hell-raiser with a radical past'. Ironically, she was not a stranger to direct action against taxation measures that she objected to. She had been one of the poll-tax refusniks ending up in Bristol magistrate's court where she represented herself, dismissing the proceedings as a sham.

Dawn was someone who had had to endure the high years of the Tories in office. She had had to sit there powerless while botched privatisations were voted through Parliament, while our public services were run down, while inflation and unemployment rocketed and while the country divided down the lines of rich and poor, north and south. I am sure that in her opinion after 18 years of Tory misrule it was time to get on and put things right. Of course she had sat opposite the Thatcher Government who never consulted anyone on their policies and never listened to criticism. Imitation is the best form of flattery.

However, her own abilities as a minister were later questioned. Tony Blair revealed in his autobiography 'A Journey' that he did not think she was "right for government" but had to give her a job because she was one of Gordon Brown's key allies. Conservative political commentator Danny Finkelstein argued that she was "contender no. 1" for title of "Labour's worst minister". Outside of IR35 she was responsible for the implementation of the tax credits system which was considered to be a botch. (She blamed IT failures, perhaps it was the lack of skilled staff?) The system was intended to provide working families with financial support. However, the administration of this system was rubbish and received significant criticism, including allegations that some families have been left less well off as a result. I certainly suffered because of it, I was overpaid one year and then the following year when I was out of work I was forced to repay it. In 2003 a Treasury select committee member accused her of "losing control of [her] department" after it became known that the Inland Revenue buildings had been sold to tax-haven companies. Inland Revenue staff walked out in protest against the pressure they were being placed under when implementing her tax credits system. Yet despite all this she was the longest serving Paymaster General in history, which is a strong defence.

# Chapter 3

## The Revenue gets their way after all

The Inland Revenue had their eyes on the freelancing, small business and self-employed sector for some time. Generally speaking small firms were an annoyance to the Inland Revenue; it was far more expensive to collect tax from them than if they all work for one big employer. In other Whitehall departments they would prefer to engage one big American or Indian company to run their IT projects than have to fiddle about engaging many small businesses to do the same job.

So poor was the link between enterprise and taxation that there was no thought as to why people arranged to do business through a limited company, or any other vehicle, to the tax man. It was just about tax. The starting point for them was an assumption of guilt that they must be tax avoiders or evaders and their role was simply to determine how much.

The Inland Revenue and Contributions Agency had, for a number of years, acted jointly to challenge "self-employed" individuals and consultants who they considered to really be employees. Revenue had been lost as a result of a more liberal regime for expenses, avoidance of national insurance by payments of dividends and the payment of wages to spouses for sometimes purely nominal duties. It had always been difficult for the Inland Revenue and Contributions Agency inspectors to challenge arrangements with companies, albeit single individual companies, because the "consultant" remained an employee.

Politically, Labour wanted to introduce a new reduced corporation tax rate for small firms and later, according to Dawn Primarolo, introduce IR35 as a way of ensuring it was correctly targeted. She said IR35 was made so they could "introduce tax policies which encourage and support small business - such as the 10% corporation tax rate… But we were faced with a situation where people who were not small businesses in the accepted sense". The 'accepted sense' of a small business to them wasn't contracting.

This opened the way for a smash and grab raid on freelance workers. Some of it would claw back legitimate lost tax revenues but it would ignore the balance between wealth creation and taxation. It would be severing the roots of the entrepreneur tree, the results of their actions wouldn't be immediately visible but the tree would wither and wane while those responsible would be long gone.

Those in the accounting profession told us that it didn't need to be like this. The Inland Revenue could have clearly expressed that it would be 'frowning' on large dividend and low salary arrangements, that is normally enough to scare people into compliance. Most local or smaller accountants would recommend a modest wage be paid and that it was important to be trading 'reasonably' but the growth of large factory accountancy practises didn't do this and needed bringing into line. The Government could have done some proper consultation on what was the best model for contractors to work through. At this same time the Government introduced limited liability partnerships which helped the legal and accountancy profession who found that their status as partnerships needed the protection of limited liability. Labour had no shortage of lawyers in its ranks to complain about problems facing highly paid barristers and solicitors, though not so many or any contractors. I suggested at one stage to a government minister why didn't they have limited liability self-employed or something similar? But it wasn't to be.

The disparate IT contractors were basically an unrepresented group - partly no doubt because it appealed to the very sense of 'going it alone' which had driven them to contracting in the first place. Although several worthy bodies existed to represent industry or small firms, none sat well with this new breed of business, the one-man-band contractor. As such, there would be a void to be filled by anyone capable of, as Andy White often described it, 'herding cats'.

## The British Computer Society

When I was thinking about going freelance in 1997, I was chatting to one of the contractors who worked for me; he had decided to become a Member of the British Computer Society (BCS) when he started as a contractor so that he had "something behind him". The BCS is the professional body representing IT workers in the UK. The BCS had only gained its Royal Charter in the early 1980's, but if accepted as a member you could put the post nominal letters of MBCS after your name. I had been a student member years before and at one stage tried to join as a full member when I approached the BCS stand at an exhibition, but was basically laughed at by some academic with elbow pads on his jacket and told to come back in 5 or 6 years time when I had gained more experience. Of course I got on fine without being a BCS member and didn't really think I needed to join up, but now I was having second thoughts. I went through the tortuous application procedures and gathered up references from previous jobs. It struck me that the process was more geared to someone who worked in academia or had worked for some large IT company for their whole career, not someone like me who had swapped and changed and moved around working for smaller firms, but the difficulty in getting in gave it some value.

I finally managed to join in 1997. It didn't do me much good as a contractor, though it embarrassed the management where I was working as a project leader. The management came from sales and not IT backgrounds but were managing the IT projects with varying degrees of success. I not only became a chartered member of the BCS but also became a Chartered Engineer, which enabled me to place the post nominal letters of MBCS CEng after my name. I was always and still am more proud of the CEng than the MBCS, partly because it has greater recognition.

After the 1997 election, where I failed to be elected as a County Councillor, I was reading the BCS's monthly journal where there was a call for new members for the council. 'New blood' was called for. I applied. The BCS HQ managed to arrange for the necessary nominations for me as I didn't know any members. Successfully nominated I was asked to write a short election manifesto, which is exactly what I did. I didn't realise that the normal procedure was to write some text detailing how *worthy* you were for election to the council. The usual thing would be 'I started as an IBM operator in 1962 using ALGOR and then did x, y and then became an academic at the university... I am worthy of election'. I didn't understand or even realise that such a protocol existed, so instead I wrote a mini-election manifesto detailing what I would do if elected. I said I wanted the BCS to stand up for contractors, I wanted to see the Society opened up, recognise non-academic exams such as MCSE's and Novell Certifications and be the body representing all IT workers. Really, up until then – and still at the present though it is getting better – it was an exclusive club for academics and semi-worthies. It didn't represent many IT workers in the private sector at all. Everyone could progress their career in IT quite happily without being a member. Instead, as far as employers were concerned it stood for nothing at all. If you were an engineer and were 'Chartered' it would stand for something and improve your job prospects, but as a Member of the British Computer Society it could almost suggest you were a bit crusty. I believed in the Society and still do. I believe that there is the need for more professionalism in the industry. At the time I felt that it needed to reflect more the current market and those professionals working in IT. For instance, it needed to support those working freelance too. In a way it did, there was a specialist group called the Independent Computer Contractors Group (ICCG) run by Mike Cullen, it had a few hundred members and did support work for the group and had represented freelancers to the government in the past.

### Travel Allowances

A little over a year before IR35 struck the Inland Revenue decided to look at expenses claims. If you work for yourself, or indeed any company, you can claim for legitimate business expenses and travel costs. For instance, if you lived in Kent and worked in London then you may be eligible to claim back the travel expenses for going into London to work for your client. If you had many clients and/or made regular or irregular business trips then it is quite legitimate that you should be able to claim these costs back, after all you are not travelling there for your own pleasure. Conversely, employees cannot claim back the cost of their daily commute to work whether it is by bus, train or car. The Inland Revenue therefore looked very closely at travelling costs. For contractors, some of whom were working for the same clients for years, the Inland Revenue looked upon these costs as really commuting costs. It was their real place of business and the expenses they were claiming were really commuting costs. But if you could demonstrate that your real place of business was your home or office where you did more than just print off invoices, then you could legitimately say that your travel costs to your client were business expenses.

Once I hit on hard times and unable to secure an IT contract I took a Christmas job working for John Lewis as a selling assistant. Only earning £5.70 / hour I would catch the train to work, which cost me £5.35 return. I thought to myself on those miserable journeys that when I was a contractor earning 10 times as much I was able to claim back the cost of this journey tax free, but now as a lowly paid temporary worker I was having to pay for it out of my taxed income. It would take me over an hour to earn back the cost of my travel. I was working for over half a day a week just to earn back the cost of getting there. I thought why shouldn't commuters, especially low paid ones, be able to at least get their travel expenses tax free? That is not to say that freelancers shouldn't be able to claim back the costs, they do, but obviously it needs to be clearly defined. One contractor I knew worked for the same client for seven years doing the same job and had claimed back all his travel costs. London is a sticky wicket because people are travelling there for work anyway, but if I took a contract in Glasgow it would be quite legitimate for me to charge my travel costs for going there once a week and my accommodation during that time as a business expense. Just the same as if I took a daily commute from say Hitchin to Ipswich every day for a certain period it can be considered business travel, but over a period of time it can become just commuting.

On behalf of the ICCG, Mike Cullen had negotiated with the Inland Revenue with regards to travel costs. When the IR35 rules were announced Mike told a round table meeting of interested parties[5] that "the BCS has an excellent relationship with the Inland Revenue." He also said that he felt that the Inland Revenue had been very good to contractors. The Inland Revenue had begun by applying rules that were 106 years old, back to an age when no one worked outside their village. Such a use of old fashion rules for a bygone age would be one of the hallmarks of IR35. On this occasion they agreed that this was unfair and changed the rules for one-man limited companies. The agreement was that contractors working on an engagement for two years or less, with an expectation of working for less than two years, would be able to claim back their travel costs. This victory had not needed a mass email campaign or a judicial review; it had just been negotiated by Mike on behalf of contractors. However, contractors in general were not impressed or they just took it for granted. One of my work colleagues in 1997, Brian, was a member of the ICCG and he evangelised about it to other contractors who basically dismissed him asking why should they spend £30 a year (or whatever it was) when the group was already doing the job? Besides as contractors they had left behind things like unions etc. You could say that on the whole they were quite a selfish lot, but either way I remember Brian warning us back then that for our own safety contractors should band together, because next time the Inland Revenue came along the ICCG might not be able to stand up to them. Indeed the travel expenses may have turned out to be just a probe to determine the strength of contractors, or if not from undertaking that work they understood more about how they worked and considered them to be unorganised.

### BCS when IR35 broke

When news of the tax broke, council members of the BCS debated the issue by email. Unfortunately the feeling from BCS council members (very few of whom had experience of non-salaried work) was not to get involved directly. In the end it was decided to mandate the ICCG to campaign, not the BCS itself.

One senior member xxx said: '

---

[5] 360 Group organised Open Forum Meeting 14th April 1999

Given the above dilemma I feel that it would be impossible for the Society to adopt any form of position that suggested that we support tax avoidance. In making statements about the issue the BCS must support the existing laws and any moves by the Chancellor to introduce legislation for the benefit of UK as a whole, whether in the interests of a group in our Society, or not.

Another member replied urging action:

> I would not have thought that there was any dilemma in helping to prevent badly worded/constructed legislation that could, by dint of the legislators not being aware of all concerns, possibly injure the ability of a significant section of our IS/T community to carry out their business.
>
> I am surprised and concerned that the BCS is not at least prepared to consider voicing their disquiet over possible poorly phrased/contrived legislation as has been seen to have happened many times in the past.

But an ex-president of the BCS suggested:

> I'm inclined to agree with xxx that this is potentially a difficult area for the BCS. The BCS must be concerned primarily with professional issues - it should not be lobbying for or against specific tax breaks or contractual relationships, unless it compromises the standards or ethics of the individual's performance in some way. I think it is perfectly acceptable for the ICC to lobby on this cause and I'm happy with Mike's statement that we "ought to state that the ICC are the lead body within the BCS in dealing with this, and will be participating fully in the consultation exercise."

I joined in the exchange and said:

> Colleagues, as a new member of BCS Council, and a contractor, I was elected last year on a platform to promote the interests of younger and newer members of the society. The dynamism of the UK computer industry is oiled by the contracting market, the quick transfer and movement of skills. This is a growth sector in the market and is the future and as such will be the source of new members in future years. Many of our younger members (late 20's/early 30's) are opting for the contract route. When encouraging people to join the society they often ask what can they do for me? Promote the professional and protect our interests as professionals, is the answer I give. If ever there was a case for BCS involvement this is it.
>
> We need to make a clear stand.
>
> As far as being one-man corporations is concerned, it is not the contractor who chooses to become incorporated but the agencies and clients insist on it, otherwise they would become liable for employers NI after two years. As far as being 'employees in disguise' I suspect that in some places this is the case, but for instance, at the bank where I contract we are not eligible for bonuses, cut-rate mortgages, training, pensions or use of company facilities (gym etc). In other companies there may be little difference between permanent and contract staff. Presumably contractors who move around at least every two years should have nothing to fear.

> Everyone should pay their fair share of tax and national insurance, contractors included. We cannot support, or be seen to support, tax avoidance but any changes made must be fair and be good for the profession and I believe, defend the independent contracting market.
>
> The society needs to take a constructive stand on this issue, defending our members and the profession and I thus support xxx proposal that the BCS is involved in the consultation - with maximum publicity - and encourages the ICC to do likewise.
>
> Regards
> Philip Ross

So the BCS opted out of it in a very wet English way. This reasoning didn't stop the CIOT or the ICAEW from getting involved and representing their members. I was annoyed with the BCS's consultative council, not that we even debated it at a council meeting that I can remember, but somehow a huge issue had broken and the Society had managed to opt out of even debating it properly. It was as if it had never happened. The council had been packed full of academics and public sector workers who, generally speaking, were the people who could get time off to go to the meetings. At a later meeting I tried to support a deal where AEEU[6] union members could cross-join into the BCS for a reduced fee. The ideas was to help build up the membership of the BCS but this was talked down by the same people. They complained about the sums of money that some engineers were able to earn while building the Jubilee Line and Dockland Light Railway. I said, "so what? Can't they earn good money?" I was warned that as a union they could 'go on strike and that wouldn't look good for the BCS to be involved with such people'. What is wrong with people going on strike if they are treated badly? A minute ago you were telling me it was because they were over paid and now it is because they are might strike? Which is it?

I can't remember how it finished off, there was real debate taking place so it was closed down quite quickly. I think the arrogant academic wasn't used to having his opinions challenged. Needless to say he wasn't an elected member of the BCS council. The conclusion was that the plans were put 'on hold', which was a small victory because it meant the proposals weren't voted out, just kicked into the long grass. I wanted them to stand because I wanted to follow this up with a scheme that would allow PCG members to join up in a similar way[7]. Instead I had witnessed first-hand the unadulterated prejudice of some Southampton academic that had looked down upon me as some jumped-up school boy.

It is strange isn't it that when normal people can earn good money through their profession, whether they are electrical, oil and gas or IT engineers, that there is righteous outrage. 'It is not right that these sorts of people can earn that sort of

---

[6] Now a part of UNITE

[7] It wouldn't be until 2005 that such a scheme was finally implemented

money!' Yet when vast sums are being paid to barristers or solicitors, there is not a murmur of dissent. Hidden in there is a degree of snobbishness and as contractors we were falling victim to this from both here and elsewhere. We weren't part of the old boy's network that ran things and in their eyes we were riding roughshod over many unknown rules and protocols.

Later on the BCS and in particular their old-boys-network, also known as the 'Elite Management Group', would have no problems campaigning in favour of the fast track visa system[8] and pushing work offshore, but when it came to supporting contractors they weren't interested. I was told that the reason was that "one was in the interests of the industry as a whole and the other was just in the interest of a few individual shareholders". To which I thanked them for their honesty and added that they shouldn't be too hard on themselves, to which they blustered that I had got it the wrong way round. No, I had understood it perfectly well.

---

[8] A scheme to bring foreign IT workers into Britain. In one letter in their magazine the marketing director criticised UK IT workers for not having or investing in the right skills, though to be fair this wasn't the view of many of the membership and some BCS members helped to bring it down, but the marketing director of the BCS seemed to come out in favour of the scheme.

# Chapter 4

## Fairness in the Tax System

Perhaps the writing had been on the wall, Labour had been swept into power in 1997 campaigning hard against "22 Tory tax rises". The fact is that the Tories had talked about Labour's "tax bomb shell" in 1992 to scare people away from voting for them only to have to implement it them themselves. In the end it was calculated that their tax rises had cost average earners about £1000 each[9]. What upset people the most was that they were now paying higher taxes, not for better public services but to pay for the cost of economic failure[10]. Worse public services endured, crime was rising as were primary school class sizes and the NHS was crumbling. Following the ERM debacle they lost people's trust in their ability to run the economy.

Many of us in the Labour Party would privately reflect on how fortunate it was that we never won in 1992. Had we won we probably would have had to implement the same tax rises as the Tories, though at that time John Smith as chancellor would probably have been more up front about it and put rises straight on national insurance or income tax. Instead the Tories set the tone of creating new taxes, which they would later term themselves as 'stealth taxes'. VAT on fuel and duty on insurance. Our view was that Labour had often been elected in the past inheriting the collapsing Tory economy only to reap the worst of it, implement the hard measures to put it right only to be voted out again once it had turned the corner. But in 1992 the script went wrong. John Major hadn't read it, they got elected and had to do their own dirty work. People talk about 1997 as being the greatest election victory ever, but secretly I think 1992 was. John Major, abandoned by his party with only Chris Patten for support effectively campaigned alone, pulling out his soap box and winning the hearts of the people. Cashing in the last of their goodwill and personal vote they scraped home.

As a Labour movement we were unhappy about the tax avoidance schemes in operation. The fact that the rich would move all their money offshore and would have lots of schemes to avoid it was considered grossly unfair. Later, as a PCG member I would witness discussions on the merits of taxation. Many angry members would declare that the role of the tax system should not be used for 'social engineering', whatever that is, but simply as a means for government to raise revenue to run the necessary services of the state and that new Labour had no right to meddle with the tax system to do more than that. Of course I disagreed with this. I don't know quite what is meant by social engineering but the tax system is used by a Labour Government as a method of redistributing wealth, by taking from the wealthy who can afford to pay more and spending it on good

---

[9] Hansard 22nd November 1995, pt 620 Column 642, based on 21 tax rises

[10] 2011 - Some things never change

public services to bridge the gap between the haves and the have not's. The policy of first class public services, for all the people, is socialism in action.

However, where I and many others differed from Gordon Brown was in the method by which this principle is applied. I favoured rises in the underlining rate of income tax as opposed to all these stealth taxes like IR35, but it was still electoral suicide to propose this.

## 1981 – PRIDE

Professional Register of Independent Design Engineers

When Andy White first launched his engineerjob.com website highlighting the likely effects of IR35 he included a note on the front page criticising 'New Labour'. I recognised that if this campaign was to be at all successful it needed to be non-political. As noted I had emailed Andy and suggested that he removed the words 'New Labour' and replaced them with 'Inland Revenue'.

Andy obliged and changed the text. I couldn't believe that my Labour Government would want to attack entrepreneurs; surely those of us in the vanguard of the new knowledge based economy couldn't be the target of this attack? I was actually right, the plan wasn't one dreamt up Labour, Gordon Brown or Dawn Primarolo, it was an Inland Revenue plan they had been trying to get in since 1981, if not before.

Andy was contacted at the time by some contractors who then had formed a group to fight the proposals. They had called themselves: - PRIDE -Professional Register of Independent Design Engineers. Just like now the plans then were incorporated into Clause 34 of the 1981 Finance Bill -workers supplied by companies through agencies. This was thrown out and after a review over the following year.

On 4th June 1981, Hansard recalled Hertfordshire Conservative MP Richard Page as saying:

> "I have grave doubts about whether they have accurately hit the target of drawing into the tax net people who have evaded taxation without hurting those who have legitimately paid tax.
>
> For some time I have been puzzled by the approach of the Inland Revenue in trying to solve the problem. I have concluded that there were two strands of thought behind its activities. There was the Machiavellian approach, in which, while asking for a whole loaf, it might be satisfied with half a loaf as the scheme was watered down slightly.
>
> The second strand of thought I can only liken to a commando leader being called in and told that 12 terrorists have to be eliminated at all costs. They are attending the Wembley Cup final, so the commando leader hijacks a B52, flies over Wembley Stadium at 4.30 PM, drops a bomb and reports to his leader to say: "Mission accomplished, sir, twelve terrorists destroyed.

Mark you there have been one or two minor side effects" "

In reply Barry Sheerman, Labour MP for Huddersfield, talked about these *"tax fiddlers"*. He is still an MP and ironically became the Chair of the Education and Skills Select Committee.

> "They are not people who are short on money, short of food, or short of accommodation. They are the well-heeled Tory payers and members of their constituency parties"

Even the press releases at the time, such as "Industry fight back" and "The Inland Revenue and many M.P's do not understand the nature and the value to the economy of Agency workers, and should check their facts before issuing insulting and defamatory statements" echoed the statements made about IR35.

So, why did PRIDE succeed and the PCG fail?

Was it the campaign approach adopted?

Was it the fact that we had a Labour rather than a Conservative Government?

Was it that in 1981 the change was put through as primary legislation and was debated properly, whereas in 1999 it was slipped in as an appendix to the budget statement?

Was it that the fact that tens of thousands of people now worked in this way?

All of these reasons combined I suspect. The fact was that freelancing was now a huge industry especially in IT in the wake of the Euro, Y2K and the dot-com boom. Instead of freelancers going to their small accountant down the road they were being signed up by huge factory style accountancy firms with products and plans in place that minimised the tax that the freelancers would pay. People were entering the market in great numbers and most contractors that I knew understood very little about their tax affairs and just left it to the accountants. Of course the accounting firms were acting in accordance with the law, delivering up to contractors the best possible tax package. The large number of contractors, the extreme tax packages being implemented, (my local accountant for instance dissuaded me from a tiny salary, large dividends were set up), and the fact that we now had a Labour Government meant that this way of working caught their eye again. This time the Paymaster General was sympathetic to the Inland Revenue's plans.

### The Architects of Doom

So contrary to popular opinion the architects of IR35 were not Gordon Brown or Dawn Primarolo, they were the ministers who had the political will to implement it. The proposals themselves probably underwent many revisions since 1981 as they passed by Ken Clarke. This proposed version of the tax was not the makings of the poor Elaine Carey or even Sarah Walker, but is widely held to have been the work of someone who had previously been Inland Revenue status inspector and later an Assistant Director.

Much of my information comes from a contractor who had called and chatted to him and gained information on his plans.

> "Dear xxxx! Was, and is, a push over on the telephone. Providing you give him the odd carrot, he will talk away, happy as a bird about his pet subject. This is why XXXX has been pushed on to new things, because he is an Intel operators dream for us and a leaky nightmare for the Revenue. Because of the way he let slip so much thinking behind IR35 in the 70 mins or so I had him on the phone in March."

> xxxx is believed to have designed IR35 in several phases. He carefully investigated the background to contracting during a case they successfully prosecuted against someone for site based working. Against the odds they won against a single man company who commuted from Bedford to Croydon over several years. They won this case and realised that they had the opportunity to get thousands of other one man companies. I understand that XXXX was the negotiator for the travel expenses issues. So they put together a team of around seven people and spent the next two years plotting.

> They engaged in conflict with one of the big contracting accountants – JSA – over the issue of home office expenses and eventually a compromise was agreed if the JSA would make all their contractors pay an additional few hundred pounds each, which they did.

> Indeed the Civil Service manual prior to Site Based Working clearly states that site based expenses are valid for up to 1 year, at the moment the employment is likely to go over one year (contract renewal) the expense payment becomes a benefit in kind.

> The JSA investigation was thought to be the driving force for IR35 because by this time the team was in place, and so was a receptive Paymaster General. Xxx and his bunch were given a mandate to remove 70,000 NON business which where interfering with the PAYE system.

> The Revenue had two targets in their sights - IT and Oil/Engineering but would or could not say that. Instead they passed the issue over to the press officers or 'spin doctors' who talked about Friday to Monday working (where someone leaves as an employee on the Friday and comes back as a contractor on the Monday) and competition issues over Kitchen Fitters!

> Apparently limited company kitchen fitters were competing with established Kitchen fitting firms who couldn't compete because of the dividend and NI benefits of being in business for one's self. Therefore they were losing bids for work against gangs who were organising the fitters into teams. "

This was code. Substitute kitchen fitters for IT/Engineering contractors and EDS, or similar, for established kitchen fitting firms and you have the picture but the Inland Revenue continued to deny this; indeed in a fax to Andy White of engineerjob.com on the 26th March they continued to deny that it was targeted at the IT sector.

The gangs were not really individual contractors but the buoyancy of the market. The fact that agencies could supply 10 C/++ programmers at a stroke and there was no need for clients to go to the more expensive body shop firms such as Andersons or EDS. I did a contract at one of the big investment banks. They had spoken to an agency and said 'we need 20 contractors next week to work on our Y2K project, can you supply?' Normally it is only body shop firms that can do this, but they went out, got us, interviewed us and technically tested us, and all the people were good.

Indeed the super agents were giving the likes of EDS a rough time, as were the DSS, because they could point to their contractor staffed Job Seekers Allowance (JSA) project which was brought in on time and to budget, it also worked.

As Xxxx talked he is alleged to have referred to large consulting companies and went on to highlight that they could not train graduates to undertake skilled IT tasks then to have them depart as trained contractors, or threaten to leave to gain an increase in salary.

The belief was that one of the persuading factors behind IR35 was that one or more of the larger consultancy companies lobbied the Inland Revenue specifically mentioning the lower tax advantages of small independent consultancy companies. This is particularly ironic as in the 1999 financial year EDS, a large American consultancy group, paid approximately 10% of their turnover in tax. The average small consultancy paid approximately 20-25% of their turnover in tax.

What the large consultancies failed to mention however was that when people leave their companies and set up their own businesses they become direct competitors to their ex-employers and are able to offer the same services and skills as before but at significantly reduced cost to the client. That, after all, is what competition is about. This was about large consultancies who failed to pay their staff appropriately for the skills that they had and lost them because of that. Had they a blank piece of paper they couldn't have framed better legislation to put their small competitors out of business.

The Inland Revenue's plan however didn't stop here.

Xxxx is alleged to have suggested that the Inland Revenue would like to merge employees NI with income tax. IR35 was the first step towards solving avoidance within Incorporated Business; - *they don't like partners receiving salary or dividends*[11]. It was suggested by many that family owned business were next on the chopping block.

---

[11] The Inland Revenue did target this later on with Section 660

But this detailed analysis was completely one sided. When IR35 broke, Mike Cullen emailed me and said:-

> "I was contacted by Mark Nellthorpe of the Inland Revenue yesterday, and asked to represent [IT] Contractors in the discussions with the Inland Revenue (I think he's fairly cheesed off with individual Contractors ringing him up to discuss matters...)"

He went on to say:-

> "I did point out to Mark that Directors were specifically excluded from many of the benefits which their national insurance contributions would entitle them to if they were employees. He was unaware of this and is looking into this aspect as a matter of urgency. Vastly increased contribution with no benefit is hardly equitable..."

What is astonishing is how badly the plans were thought through and how little they understood the industry. The official brought in to implement this new tax would be Sarah 'Scary' Walker.

## Why don't contractors work as self-employed?

This was something I had always wondered. Why can't I work as self-employed? My father was self-employed and hadn't had to go through all the rigmarole of setting up a limited company. Apparently it was because of an earlier hash of legislation.

Previously all contractors had worked as self-employed but when legislation was introduced to regulate recruitment agencies they agreed that they could exclude businesses who found work through agencies, which is exactly what contractors did, they were businesses who found work through agencies. It was recognised then, I suspect, that they weren't temporary workers but were different. So it was enshrined that individuals operating through limited companies would not be eligible to acquire employment rights from clients, either directly or via an intermediary, such as an agency, therefore all contractors were forced to incorporate to continue operating in the market. It was impossible to find any contract work if you were not in a limited company.

The irony was that agencies twisted the arms of their clients saying that if they didn't employ their contractors through them then they would be liable for employment rights, which would be true if it was a receptionist or a secretary, but not a limited company contractor. This FUD –fear, uncertainty and doubt – was, and still is very prevalent in the contracting industry and was successfully used to discourage institutions and firms from engaging contractors directly, thus preserving the 15-30% commission for agencies.

# Chapter 5

## United we stand?

Andy's engineerjob.com website had raised awareness of the implications of the new tax directly among contractors. Though slow to action, other groups became alerted to the dangers of the tax, to both the competitiveness of the IT economy as a whole and also the future viability of the contracting industry. The BCS had decided that it was not appropriate that they got involved with such an issue and many contractors would feel betrayed by them for this. Instead the BCS mandated the ICCG to take up the issue. I had attended many BCS meetings at which they talked about 'initiatives' to grow membership and here was a cause on which they could have spoken out on and seen IT professionals rally to them, but instead the BCS sat on the side-lines and watched 14,000 IT professionals flock to the newly-formed Professional Contractors Group. The many academics on the BCS board understood little about freelance working and so the opportunity was missed.

There then came to pass on the 14$^{th}$ April an important meeting of the worried parties in the cause.

The contracting market, however, was not just about contractors; it was wider than that consisting of agencies, tax consultants, clients and contractors. Would everyone stand together? Would there be an industry alliance against the tax or would vested interests prevail?

### Recruitment Industry led alliance

At the end of March the recruitment industry decided to launch a group called Forum 2000 to take responsibility for fighting the proposals. It was fronted by the accounting firm, Giant.

On their website Giant stated:-

> "At Giant we believe that there needs to be a strong and consistent voice within the contracting industry. The best way of doing this is to form a pressure group representing end users, agencies, advisors and contractors to make representations to government and to influence their decisions."

They proceeded to reassure contractors further:

> "Giant has established Forum 2000 and are inviting key industry figures to action. Our first meeting will be arranged shortly. The aim of this first meeting is to: plan how to develop the industry response to the Revenue's proposals, and develop a strategy for influencing public and political opinion to ensure support for the legitimate ambitions of contractors. As well as senior figures from the top 25 agencies and the contracting media the chairman of FRES will be attending together with representatives from the CBI's taxation committee and leading accountants and lawyers with interests in the debate."

At the time Andy commented to contractors in a newsletter –

'the last thing we need is a fragmented approach to the issue and with Forum 2000 taking responsibility for campaigning on this issue I wish them the best of luck'

But by the next day, Andy was already starting to lose faith with the 'leave it with us' approach suggested by the agencies and accounting firms and pressed for a place at the table for contractors. He wrote the following to contractors:

From their web site 25th March referring to the planned mtg:"As well as senior figures from the top 25 agencies and the contracting media the chairman of FRES will be attending"

But by the 27$^{th}$ March the FRES chairman had better things to do and it appeared that he wouldn't be attending. Andy wasn't happy.

Their web site 27th March: "representatives from........FRES"  What, no Chairman!

Read this, clipped from a press article provided by Giant, sent to the Freelance Informer:

"We recommend that existing contractors leave the worrying to others. They should continue to take advantage of the benefits contracting brings whether commercial, fiscal and in terms of empowerment. And those who are considering going the contracting company route should press ahead in the knowledge that under the current arrangements they cannot lose."

I would be interested to know if that is a view shared by the Agencies. Some independent Accountants would argue, in face of the likely guidelines, that advice such as this gives credence to the Tax avoidance argument presented by the Inland Revenue. As such is this the most effective route for presenting a case against these proposals? Wait and see would be my advice. I have asked for an invitation to the meeting on the 21st so will keep you posted.

Andy decided he needed to get more involved.

## An industry alliance against the tax?

On the 14$^{th}$ April 1999, the 360 Accounting Group hosted an open forum meeting of interested parties, politicians and trade groups to discuss the new tax.

In attendance were John Redwood (Conservative MP and shadow DTI spokesman), Dr Vincent Cable MP (Lib Dem DTI), representatives from the CSSA (now Intellect), the FEI, the IAP (Institute for Analysts and Programmers), Mike Cullen from ICC (and BCS), Andy White from engineerjob.com along with members of leading agencies, end users and accountants

The minutes of the meeting which survive on the Internet are interesting because at the time there was a chance that the industry would stand together. What is also interesting is the non-political advice offered by the two politicians, who instead of trying to enflame the situation offered sound advice.

Brian Keegan (MD 360 Groups) advised the group of the basis for the changes and the discussions that had been taking place with the Inland Revenue. He confirmed that the measures as proposed would affect approximately 80% of IT Contractors working through a Limited Company Structure

The Inland Revenue are going to implement the changes from April 2000; however, they will take the proposals before ministers within 3 weeks."

John Redwood, Shadow Trade and Industry secretary expressed his support "This meeting has highlighted some points that may be damaging to UK plc. I am very happy to take this case to Parliament when I know what the industry wants. The Government will give in under pressure when it knows there are real business issues at stake."

Iain Sutherland asked if there was anyone in the room who felt that the proposed regulations would be a positive move. He advised the group that 360 were told by the Inland Revenue that "the response from the industry so far is that the industry supports this measure". Those present did not support this opinion. (Interestingly enough contractors always suspected the CSSA as being one of movers behind IR35, but they were quiet on this occasion).

Christopher Kettle of Oldham and Thomkins commented on the differences between situations where you have a knowledge based contractor rather that a trade based contractor, be it on a long term contract, but still moving from contract to contract. He noted that there is an increase in the number of lower rate contractors being put through as limited companies. They are often doing fairly repetitive jobs and continue doing the same thing for 5 or 10 years under a limited company. This difference possibly distinguishes the lower skilled person working through limited companies who is possibly just hiding behind the corporate structure versus the professional.

Mike Cullen commented that they the meeting on Saturday (11/04/99) of the ICC had recognised that they had to recognise the legitimate arguments and tackle the abuses highlighted by the Government. He went on to say "this would ensure that the professional knowledge based sector is not wiped out."

Steve, an agency representative, commented, "I have been running an agency which has been dealing with aircraft engineers, nothing to do with IT. But what we have seen over the years is a move towards self-employed contractors. There was a situation that arose when the Government cancelled all subsistence and the engineers were no longer able to claim genuine expenses that were incurred in the course of their job.

Iain Sutherland commented that "we can move government and this has been demonstrated on similar issues in the past. However, this can only be done by working with the government to achieve a compromise, rather than taking a heavy handed approach."

Iain Sutherland highlighted the knock on effects of the proposed legislation and commented that "the revenue doesn't seem to think that there are any genuine IT contractors who are entrepreneurs."

He went on to ask Terry Harvey of Harvey Consultants to explain his company's history and thanked him for travelling from the North of England to be at the meeting. Terry Harvey went on to explain how he had worked for four years as a contractor in a limited company to save enough money to set up his agency. At this time he was then able to support 17 contractors, two part time staff and himself full time. The business grew over the following 8 years to a turnover of £15,000,000 - at which time he sold his company to an American company. The company has continued to grow and now has a turnover of £27,000,000. The money he gained from the sale of the company has been re-invested in UK based companies. Mr Harvey went on to say "had it not been for the limited company structure through which I was able to work, I would not have been able to expand the business and I would not have been able to have the impact on other businesses around me. Nor would I have been able to employ the numbers of staff that have benefited along the way" I think that this legislation will have a knock on effect.

An agency representative from Gatton commented, "There seems to be a lot of confusion as to where the DTI fit in and the national insurance issue". He made the point that "we should all pay our social contribution, however, legitimate business expenses should be allowed." He went on to say that we "should not try to take the government head-on because they will attack you back".

"It is therefore down to the service industry to lobby its case to the revenue. It would be naive to think that this legislation could be prevented altogether."

Interestingly enough later in the campaign I put Terry Harvey's argument to Patricia Hewitt MP, the e-Business Minister, about the damage this was doing to IT entrepreneurs, but she didn't take me seriously and believed the number of people involved was minimal. I told her that I used to live in the northeast and after the Consett Steel works closed one of the workers founded 'Phileas Fogg' the snacks company, here I suggested was one seed out of the thousands made redundant, but it took root. Given that it is so hard for businesses to succeed should we really be limiting the chances of future success stories? I told her too about a friend of my father who owned a really successful motor dealership. When he had one dealership he made a lot of profit and was worried about the amount of tax he had to pay. He asked my father how he could avoid paying the tax, my father told him to buy another dealership, invest the money further and grow the business, because the money hadn't been taken as profits and had been invested, no tax was paid. The next year both dealerships made a big profit so he bought two more and the following year the same again, so he bought four more and so on. My argument was that it was the same for contractors, we had our profits and we could choose to invest it in new opportunities. From those opportunities, from these tiny acorns great oaks could grow. She didn't agree and clearly didn't believe that 'proper businesses' would be founded by contractors. My real life experience was somewhat different. I felt that as I had generated this revenue I should have the chance to invest it to make it grow and the tax men would still get their cut, she felt differently, that government should take the money straight away and spend it on its priorities.

Back to the meeting... sage advice would be offered but none of it headed:-

> 'We should not try to take the government head-on because they will attack you back'

> 'It would be naive to think that this legislation could be prevented altogether.'

Instead of heeding this advice the PCG that would shortly be formed, like the miners a decade beforehand, would take the Government head on and believed that the legislation could be prevented altogether. I say this with the benefit of hindsight but was there truly any other way to fight the proposals? If we had all just stood there with signs saying 'I am really not very happy about this', would it have been more effective?

### Enquiries to the Inland Revenue

While 'industry groups', the beneficiaries of IR35 met with the Treasury to discuss the proposals, contractor groups sat out in the cold restricted to having to fax the Inland Revenue office. Individuals wrote in to the named Elaine Carey and were all sent back the same details which for many was a waste of time because the standard letter from Elaine Carey was already being displayed on the engineerjob.com website.

It had almost become a challenge among contractors to write a letter which would result in a variation on the standard reply. None were forthcoming. The Internet was allowing us to compare responses and find that we were being 'fobbed off' - collectively and individually. How else would a group of unconnected individuals from around the country writing different letters have known this? The Internet was becoming the tool of the revolution.

# Chapter 6

## 22<sup>nd</sup> April 1999 – The full plans laid open

The Budget announced the tax on the 22<sup>nd</sup> April, the Inland Revenue's Elaine Carey published the full proposals behind IR35, still insisting that they would not influence or impair entrepreneurial activity.

The cornerstone of the new proposals would be a 'simple test'. Anyone under the direction, supervision or control of their client would be caught. It was proposed that all contractors would have to register with the Inland Revenue and that the clients or agencies would be responsible for deducting the necessary tax and national insurance at source. This was a nightmare for agencies that would have to change all their procedures so that they could take off the tax and NI at source.

Included in the text were of a number of examples intended to illustrate how the tax might work. There were some specific IT examples:

A travel company has had a new computer system installed. The company hires an IT consultant to supply additional technical support and training for staff in the use of the new system. The consultant is taken on for a period of three months to undertake tasks as directed on a day by day basis by the IT manager. The new rules should apply here.

Contractors' worst fears had been realised as the Government's proposed that anyone operating under the 'direction, supervision and control' of a client or agent was a 'disguised employee' for tax and NI purpose. Rather than targeting the Friday-to-Mondayers, this would have made it virtually impossible for small businesses to operate and compete with the larger 'body-shops'

## Speaking up for contractors

But who was speaking up for contractors? At this time it was the ICCG and Andy White at engineerjob.com. Neither organisations could declare to be really mandated by contractors themselves and so lacked legitimacy. The ICCG obviously had the advantage of being already established, but engineerjob.com had the momentum. Meanwhile, the recruitment industry and some of the large super-agencies were declaring that they represented '20,000' contractors. Agencies are self-serving at the best of times, interested only in their own margins. I wouldn't trust them to negotiate my own contract, let alone represent me to the Government. It would be a bit like the CBI saying that they represented all the workers in British industry just because they employed them. On the other side was the 360 Accounting Group who had organised the forum. They were making good progress, but again it was someone acting for contractors, not contractors acting for themselves. On all sides it had to be decided whose interests were being served.

By the end of March www.engineerjob.com was attracting over 200,000 hits and had a subscriber base for a free email newsletter of some 2000 and was growing at over 250 each day. Government seemed to listen to big business and industry, contracting though disparate was a big industry but with no voice for contractors. For instance, when the proposals first broke the accounting firms and recruitment industry got together to form Forum 2000 and stated that they would invite 'senior figures from the top 25 agencies and the contracting media and the chairman of FRES'. No mention of anyone to actually represent the contractors. Andy's early plan was not only to give a voice to contractors but for it to equal in size and numbers that of a large business. If government plans were going to impact on a firm employing 3,000 or 4,000, let alone 14,000 workers, then they would listen and take heed.

Andy White was, however, not a well-meaning amateur. He had run a successful business and now reflected on the best way to go about campaigning on IR35. He took a professional approach and took advice. He spoke to his local solicitors, Bond Pearce in Southampton; they put him in touch with political lobbyist David Ramsden. He was an experienced political campaigner who was responsible for establishing and directing the Shopping Hours Reform Council which lobbied successfully for Sunday trading. He had links with all the political parties, but was principally linked with the Conservatives. David contacted Susie Hughes who was an ex-Downing Street press officer who had worked with him on the Sunday trading. Andy negotiated with him and put together a budget of how much it would cost to run a campaign against the changes. Having done this the next step was to obtain the necessary funding.

He chose to ask freelancers directly and sent out the now famous email to his engineerjob.com subscribers. He calculated he needed £100,000 and suggested if 2,000 contractors gave £50 each it could be up and running. Having sent off the email he went off mountain biking for the weekend. On his return, within four working days, two thousand and two contractors indicated their willingness and had pledged £50, myself included. The Professional Contractors Group was born.

## Creation of the Professional Contractors Group:

Over the past 10 days, we have sought the involvement of, not only Contractors, but also, Accountants and Agents. Although the objective of a concerted voice would appear admirable it has proven difficult to implement. This would perhaps reflect that each group has differing objectives.

For background to this see exchange of emails We therefore would like to receive your views on forming a campaign group that will be focused on the interests of the Contractors, in the IT and Engineering sector and to build on the work started by engineerjob.com. If this should go ahead at a future date, when our campaign is up and running, we will seek to involve the end-user and others, but the main aim will always be to protect the interests of the Contractor. Such a group would have one focus that of addressing the issues contained within ir35. Before we form the campaign and accept money we would like to gauge the likelihood of our being able to raise sufficient funds. (See http://www.pcgroup.org.uk/join.html for estimates).

We are looking for minimum contributions of £50 per contractor (please note any contribution made to engineerjob.com will be transferred across) we would be grateful if you would send a blank email message to join@ir35update.co.uk if you are in agreement that this Group should be formed.

We have set a target of 2000 emails by close of business on Tuesday May 4th to provide sufficient confidence that such a campaign will be properly funded.

Andy White
engineerjob.com
27th April 1999

## CONTRACTORS SIGN UP TO SAVE THEIR INDEPENDENCE

More than 2,000 contractors have joined the Professional Contractors' Group's campaign to ensure the Government's proposals to counter tax avoidance do not unfairly target legitimate independent contractors.

In the first four working days after the Professional Contractors' Group (PCG) called on contractors via the Internet to register their concern with them, 2,000 contractors from IT, engineering and other industries have contacted the Group to add their voices to the possible impact of the Government's so-called Friday-to-Monday proposals on their businesses.

In this year's Budget, the Chancellor Gordon Brown announced that he intended to introduce legislation to counter tax and NI avoidance in the area of personal service provision (IR35). He explained how someone who leaves employment on a Friday and returns on Monday to do the same job as an indirectly engaged 'consultant' pays substantially reduced tax and NI contributions.

However, many legitimate contractors believe that the legislation will be so wide-reaching that it will impact on them and create a situation where a limited liability company is treated as an individual temporary employee - with a only few limited exceptions.

Director of PCG, David Ramsden, said: "This is an example of the Government using a sledgehammer to crack a nut. We agree that there is a case to act on the Friday-to-Monday tax avoidance - but these proposals are a real danger to the legitimate contractor who has built up a business over time, having been encouraged by successive Governments to develop their entrepreneurial abilities in highly-skilled, competitive industries.

"We have already registered our interest with the Revenue and have been invited to a meeting in June to put our point of view across. We hope by then our membership will have increased significantly so that we can demonstrate to the Government the strength of support for our position."

Contractors who want to support the PCG's campaign can join by going to the website www.ir35update.co.uk

Notes to editors;

1. The PCG is a not-for-profit organisation. Its aim is to work with Government to ensure that the Friday-to-Monday proposals outlined in IR35 are proportionate in achieving their objective. PCG supports the Government's aim to counter blatant tax avoidance but believes any proposals must ensure that they do not unfairly disadvantage those contractors who have set up a company, abandoned their employment rights, paid their taxes and NI and provided for their retirement.

2. PCG's directors and guarantors are David Ramsden and Andy White. David Ramsden is an experienced political campaigner who was responsible for establishing and directing the Shopping Hours Reform Council which lobbied successfully for Sunday trading. He also sits on the Council of the Industry and Parliamentary Trust, a cross-Party organisation whose aim is to foster better understanding of the role of Parliamentarians and industry.

3. Andy White is a contractor who provides design services and through the commercial freedom and income provided from contracting has built up other business interests. He realised that after six years as an independent contractor, his business could be caught by the Friday-to-Monday proposals.

4. Bond Pearce Solicitors have been appointed to oversee the establishment and financial side of PCG and provide advice on tax and employment issues relating to IR35. Bond Pearce is based in Southampton and is one of the largest provincial law firms in the country.

# Part 2 - Parliamentary Battle

# Chapter 1

Any minute now the Minister will be calling me....

I'd thought long and hard before committing my £50 as I am sure others did. Andy had displayed a budgeted cost for the campaign which seemed to add up. Besides in the first instance I was only pledging my cash where Andy was taking a huge leap of faith. Once the pledges were in he had to then carry the cost of collecting the money and underwriting the organisation. We all wrote our cheques and sent them in, although not everyone was prepared to put up their money. Other contractors who I spoke to declined saying that their 'accountant is sorting it out,' (I wonder how they are getting on now). A new website was set up – ir35update.co.uk and discussion forums were established.

So, at a stroke contractors had organised themselves and now had a pool of over £100,000, not bad for a bunch of people who had never even met. Today we would call than 'crowd sourcing' or 'crowd financing' and it is another near first that the PCG can claim as it raised this money across the Internet with very little overheads and few resources.

I still felt a personal obligation to do something, after all I had been elected to the governing council of the British Computer Society on a platform to protect and promote contractors. I had lunch with a friend of mine who was politically active locally in Bedfordshire and now worked for Margaret Moran MP. He suggested that I put some notes together and send them in to my MP, or even to Margaret, though he said no MPs had even heard of this new tax. He also suggested that I wrote to the IT Minister and after some research he came back and told me that it was Michael Wills MP. There seemed to be no point in contacting Dawn Primarolo at the Treasury as we both expected the professional PCG team to already have this covered.

So that's what I did, I wrote a two page briefing paper on IR35, copying details down from the engineerjob.com website and embellishing it with details of my own and sent it to Margaret Moran MP, but as I wasn't in her constituency I didn't get a reply. I also sent a copy to the constituency office of Michael Wills MP, judging that I was writing to him as a Labour Party member as opposed to anything else. In my covering letter I naively stated that these Friday-Monday proposals aimed at kitchen fitters would impact on the thousands of people like me who were working freelance in IT. Surely it couldn't be the Government's intention to target us in the vanguard of the knowledge economy?

I sent the letter off and spoke to a contact at Millbank Tower[12] who suggested that I wouldn't get a reply. Meanwhile at work I joked with those around me that 'any minute now the minister will be ringing me up asking for a meeting'. When the

---

[12] Then the Labour Party HQ

phone would ring I would joke, 'that could be him now'. Imagine my utter surprise when it was – well his diary secretary anyway.

## Shopping Hours Reform Team get settled in

The team that Andy had assembled had a history of working together. They had run the 'Shopping Hours Reform Council' which basically campaigned for a reform of the Sunday opening hours and was funded principally by the DIY stores. Susie Hughes had been a Government Information Officer in the days before they were called 'spin doctors' - working in the Home Office, DTI and Number Ten. At Downing Street she had worked under Bernard Ingham while Maggie Thatcher was in power, she was very well connected and one of the best press officers in the country. The campaign against IR35 was to be almost a repeat run of the Sunday Trading campaign with the same tactics employed and the same barristers and accountants used, and in some respects the same paper results, but not the same conclusion.

On the technical side, programmer Simon Banton contacted Andy early in the campaign and offered his expertise. The website, discussions forums, email lists, petitions and the like would be the product of Simon's technical wizardry and deployment of open source code.

In addition, Andy would later bring in chartered accountant Kevin Miller as our finance director. He had the ability to absorb and understand the facts and figures and would prove to be our non-political person to send in to meetings. For technical meetings with Sarah Walker at the Inland Revenue we would send Kevin, for political meetings Andy and I would go.

The Sunday Trading campaign aimed to highlight the anomalies in the law, the fact that certain shops in certain places could open but others couldn't. It aimed to demonstrate that the law was an ass – well actually some good similarities with IR35 as it too was vague and would apply to some people and not others. From what I can understand shops would open up 'illegally' with the aim that they would be prosecuted by the local authorities and the case would serve as ammunition in a war of attrition against the law. The Reform Council wanted cases to be brought; money was no real object as they had huge financial backing. Ultimately they would carry the case through to a Judicial Review at the High Court —and would lose, but having won their case the Government had a change of mind and decided to legislate for Sunday trading anyway. While it may be disingenuous that the team turned up with a campaign in a box, very similar tactics would be employed in the fight against IR35.

## ICCG goes for Compromise

Forming the PCG provided a clear mandate to represent contractors and the funds to operate a campaign. The ICCG meanwhile lingered behind with a smaller mandate (about seven hundred contractors) and with no campaign budget. The PCG banner was raised, you could sign up and join on line but to join the ICCG was far more tortuous as it was all done by post. The PCG started to pro-actively raise the issue in the press and media. However, the more people that joined the higher expectations became and the less scope there would be for action. It was democratic and populous by its inception, with no clear or appointed leaders other than the founder Andy White. There grew a need to sustain the impetus of the organisation. The ICCG of course was more old fashion, hierarchical and staid. Like the BCS from which it had sprung, being pre-internet, in fact just being an established organisation it was controlled and led from the centre. Now as fresh young members of the PCG we revelled in the on-line revolution that we were now a part of. We had all registered with the online forums. It was e-democracy in action, contractors from all over the country united in discussion and debate. Mass debate was taking place in the online forums. It was wonderful. Academics had talked for ages about e-democracy and here it was in action. Up until this point e-democracy had just meant having a website, in fact Margaret Moran MP had launched a website entitled 'The Luton Democracy pages' but it had very little interaction aside from a form for people to fill in.

The PCG felt like the organisation that would solve our problems and what's more, we would be left with an organised group of contractors to truly represent the interests of freelancers and challenge the power and dominance of the agencies. The ICCG, however, could make decisions and negotiate without constant reference back to the members. As the PCG established itself there would become a zeal and dogmas that all members were expected to follow. Not by any decree but by the consensus enforced on its Internet forums by the louder and more opinionated members. The ICCG had no mob that it had to satisfy and operated to a large extent outside the constant glare of its members, like most mature organisations. As such they put together an action plan for IR35 which they called their six point plan.

The plan in part acknowledged that contractors would have to pay more tax. It recommended a minimum salary for contractors, in effect a salary-dividend split.

At a meeting in Bath in mid May attended by 60 contractors, the group voted almost unanimously to adopt the 6 point plan. How it would be forced on the bulk of contractors I'm not sure but the plan proposed that freelancers working through single person companies would pay themselves a statutory minimum wage of around £15,000.

Given that national insurance must be paid on wages, the scheme would end contractors' practice of avoiding the levy by paying themselves solely through lightly taxed company dividends.

Then the committee recommended freelancers join the Professional Contractors Group. Ideally, the PCG would lobby for this issue and at the end – given that the plan was that the PCG was disbanded – the members would be then scooped up by the ICCG. Indeed I saw a great deal of synergy between the BCS and the PCG. The PCG would be a lobbying and trade body and the BCS the professional body and contractors could be members of both. Indeed later on I tried to raise the issue with the BCS, but they were a bit sniffy at the idea.

This wasn't to be the end of the ICCG relationship with the PCG, though relations were to sour as the PCG were increasingly viewed as a maverick organisation following the more extreme actions by some of its members, the ICCG hoped to be the voice of reason and to steer a middle course.

## Backdoor Legislation

The Inland Revenue had learnt the lessons of 1981. Back then the decision to make a fundamental change to the way that small companies and freelance workers were taxed was considered to be important enough to be put through as primary legislation. In doing so it would face the full scrutiny of parliamentary debate and discussion. This time round it wouldn't even warrant a mention in the Chancellor's Budget speech and instead would be slipped out as a hidden appendix to the budget proper.

This time round the rushed Welfare Reform Bill, into which confusingly these plans would go, dictated that the power to decide how to implement it would be delegated to the Inland Revenue. It became termed as the most widespread (ab)use of "Henry VIII powers" that could be recalled. It meant that changes in future could be bought in without the scrutiny of our elected representatives. Considering these proposed powers it was even more important that genuine consultation took place. Some parliamentarians were concerned and it was noted that 'this process will need to be structured on a continuous basis to ensure that these enormous powers are used proportionately'.

The irony is that the amount of money targeted in 1981 was £40 Million, in 1999 they estimated that they would raise £450 million. That was an annual growth rate of 15% compared with a growth rate in the overall UK economy of 2.7%. The key question and the one the Government needed to answer was "Have tax abusers been 5 times more effective than the rest of the economy at growing their business?" or rather "Has the proportion of tax abusers remained constant and therefore this knowledge based sector grown 5 times faster than the overall economy?"

Andy suggested that

> If the former is correct then it implies gross incompetence on behalf of the Revenue. I do not believe this to be the case. If the latter is the case we need to ask another key question. *"Had the Revenue succeeding with Clause 34 in 1981, do we believe that this knowledge based sector would have outperformed the rest of the economy by a factor of five?"*

The fact was that we had a huge flexible workforce in IT and this had enabled much of our economic growth, which of course was largely driven by IT. Visit any large continental IT project and you would find it largely staff by UK freelancers. The reason? The ability to work as a one man company, as a freelancer never existed on the continent. The flexibility in the UK was present. The irony was that the UK's flexible market wasn't planned but was a consequence of earlier decisions not being implemented and a change in the political climate.

## Foot in the Door – Talking to the Revenue

The PCG and the ICCG managed to then get their foot in the door and were invited to meetings with the Inland Revenue in June. The absence of representatives of kitchen fitters and the like and the overwhelming presence of companies on the IT side clearly demonstrated the real targets of this legislation and the inclusion of these industry bodies was a tacit recognition by the Inland Revenue that their original talk about kitchen fitters was just a sham. What a way to go about delivering legislation, pretend it is targeted at a completely different set of workers, refuse to acknowledge the real target, pretend that it is someone else and talk in vague terms about what you are going to do. Even the reasoning for the legislation so-called Friday-Monday working, though common in industry and local government, it was certainly not the case in IT.

## Friday to Monday working – Winning the argument

An early PCG survey showed that hardly any IT workers[13] left their permanent jobs on the Friday only to come back on the Monday morning as a consultant; because in IT the financial reasons to go contracting were personal and not done to save the employer their national insurance stamp. For instance, a friend of mine's father had worked as a camera man for a TV company in the North East and I was told that he had indeed left on the Friday and returned on the Monday morning as self-employed. This was to benefit his employer principally, he may well have received a little extra cash as the employer was now saving about 12% in national insurance payments. It was also common practise in higher education. It was in fact exploitation, give up your employment and pension rights, holiday entitlement and sick pay, save us some tax payments and you can come back as a consultant, work on a flexible basis and we will pay you slightly more. The Inland Revenue's raison d'être for the tax was to counter Friday-Monday working, the PCG was confident that it could win this argument hands down.

Indeed the Inland Revenue would constantly lose the argument that this was about Friday-Monday working, or that it was about fairness and in comparing it with nurses. Initially the PCG even described the issue as the 'Friday-Monday' proposals. If this was the real target of the legislation then we should have had nothing to fear, but the purpose of the legislation wasn't about fairness or even-handedness, it had a darker purpose, it was about tax and collecting more taxes.

## Lord Weatherill becomes PCG Patron

Lord Weatherill, former Speaker in the House of Commons and current convenor of the Cross Bench Peers in the House of Lords, threw his support behind the aims of the Professional Contractors Group and became their patron in early June. David Ramsden had used his influence to get Lord Weatherill to act the PCG's patron. Why we needed a patron I am not sure, but I have to say that in these early days it

---

[13] About 5% of those surveyed in May 1999

added an immediate amount of respectability to our organisation and the campaign, and of course made us news worthy. David justified the decision by stating "His Lordship is a highly respected politician of long standing and his support underlines the serious intent behind our aims".

This was true and in many respects it added the required respectability to the fledgling organisation and helped it to grow in members, his support reassured potential members that this organisation wasn't a scam and that they could be trusted.

The press notice at the time said "Lord Weatherill, whose support for small business is well known would be concerned if the proposals contained in IR35 had the effect of driving small enterprises out of business."

"The Government should be doing all it can to encourage small businesses", said Lord Weatherill, "over burdensome and unnecessary legislation should be avoided at all costs".

# Chapter 2

## Raising the Profile

The way things would work is that after Kevin Miller had done analysis on the facts, figures and the legislation he would pass it to the campaign manager David Ramsden. Alongside David worked Susie Hughes, an ex-Downing Street press officer now working for Vane-Percy Associates. If David could press buttons in Parliament, then Susie would make sure the press found out about it. The biggest difficulty at this stage was that no one had heard of the tax. It was an obscure Section 70 of the Welfare Reform Bill, nothing to do with tax or small business, hence it was difficult to engage the interest of journalists. Susie persevered and used her contacts and slowly but surely the press started to understand some of the issue. Of course they still had to go through the process of putting it into plain English so their readers could understand it.

Fortunately the Government's own arrogance would gift us our first break. After their election in 1997 the Government agreed to issue Regulatory Impact Assessments (RIA) for all new legislation. (This is standard practise in Europe). On paper a tax like IR35 should be exactly what RIA had been designed for, but they forgot to do one for IR35 and on being found out, wrote one in a hurry. The hastily written RIA would prove to be the breakthrough for us. Written originally in haste, it made glib assumptions about how businesses and individuals would behave when the new tax rules were implemented and suggested that it would lead to 66,000 'businesses' closing down, manna from heaven for a press officer like Susie Hughes.

A few days later the front page of the Daily Telegraph ran the story that new tax plans would lead to the closure of 66,000 small businesses. The Times also picked up the story and ran a back page story on the general topic in the business section. They would run a number of stories on the topic.

Despite the fact that even the PCG's own survey had shown that the majority (90 %+) of contractors were male runs the press used a case study of Jane Akshar, a City contractor. Jane featured with her picture and a fairly accurate article detailing the shambolic nature of the new plans. (Jane would later become a leading player in the PCG and its third chairman).

## Write to Your MP

One of the first plans to be put into operation by the new public affairs team was a letter writing campaign to MPs. Very few MPs understood what IR35 was all about, especially given that the chancellor hadn't even announced the changes in his budget speech and instead had hidden it away as minor appendices. As a result it was viewed as just an obscure change, but surely any change that hopes to net an annual revenue of £475m should have been worthy of a mention in the budget speech?

When I say the PCG started to co-ordinate a letter writing campaign, what they really did was try to encourage people to take part, huge numbers were already writing intelligent and thoughtful letters, some not so thoughtful and some very irate to their MPs.

Indeed during the first debate in Parliament on IR35 Jackie Lait MP stated:

> "My hon. Friend was not the only person who received irate e-mails within 24 hours of the measure being announced. I, too, had an irate constituent. "

Now having worked for an MP myself I know what sort of post they are used to receiving. Volume does indeed matter, as do thoughtful well written objective letters. Some people will write to their MP as the first port of call for anything, some write in desperation as the last port of call and some of course are somewhere in between.

Some wrote nice letters objectively putting their case. Some wrote abusive, threatening letters. The same is true with phone calls and of course it is likely to be the MPs staff fielding those. One contractor set up his fax machine to send his MP a fax every five minutes of a picture of a rabbit with a huge sledgehammer cracking a nut. It may have been quite amusing the first or even the second time, but the police had to intervene to stop it. Another contractor wrote some abusive statements about Tony Blair in Arabic on emails and notes online which resulted in Special Branch being notified. So, which type of letters to your Labour MP/Government Party are the most effective?

Clearly if you wrote to your MP saying what a disaster 'New Labour' is/was and that you never would/did vote for them in a thousand years and then add a PS 'you disgust me'[14], then you are not really motivating your MP to work for you. (Such a letter minus the PS could of course be manna from heaven for an Opposition MP).

Some replies were positive even from Labour and others from Conservatives were a real let down. The worst being from Richard Page MP, the previous hero for talking down IR35 Mark 1, he wrote back to a constituent to say:

> 'In view of the huge majority the Labour Government has, there is nothing that can be done to reverse this situation and as a former Small Business Minister, I know exactly what damage this proposal will cause.'

This prompted people to remark that in that case, what's the point of voting Conservative if they can't do anything, noting that they'd be better off with a Labour MP.

A flood of letters went to MPs, some directed by the PCG and David Ramsden and some just sent off in anger. Alongside this the PCG's online forums were now in operation and many contractors were using it to vent their anger. Some worry that

---

[14] I actually received a letter like this when I was working for an MP (though not on IR35)

the same tone is being sent to MPs, Andy notes that contractors are angry. Then before we knew it the measure has passed through the House of Commons, buried in the Welfare Reform Bill and is now due to be debated in the House of Lords. How do you lobby a member of the House of Lords, what is their constituency and accountability? I wrote to Baroness Joyce Gould, who I knew from my time on the board of computing for Labour, I had also written to Andrew Miller Labour MP, who was the president and other letters were sent out.

## How MPs Reply to Letters

On the whole there was dissatisfaction with the replies received from MPs. This was in part the fault of MPs and in part the result of the new Internet age exposing their working practises. The way it works knowledgeable MPs will write their own responses that come through on every subject under the sun, others will get their research staff to draft the letters for them, and there is nothing wrong with that. The key to being a good parliamentary researcher/case worker is the same as being a good PA – you should know the mind of your boss – and in many respects be able to write letters in his style or know ones written before.

When a letter arrived from a constituent we would automatically send them a post card acknowledging the receipt of the letter once the letter had been logged either on paper or into a database. Some letters would require further information from a minister and would be forwarded to the appropriate government minister with a short note from the MP. When the reply came back from the minister it would simply be forwarded on to the constituent with an invitation to write in again if they have any further queries.

A standard reply letter could be used for some constituents with a special note added on. For instance, a thoughtful letter detailing the MPs stance on an issue, such as the Iraq war, doesn't need to be rewritten for every constituent but a paragraph can be added to answer any specific points raised by the constituent and not already covered by the standard letter. Some MPs will not write their own thoughtful replies and would simply pop down to the Parliamentary Labour Party Office/Conservative Resource Centre/Lib Dem Office and get a standard letter prepared centrally by the party which they could just send out. These would tend to be government/party propaganda and would say how wonderful Gordon Brown/Tony Blair, etc. were and what a great job the Government was doing – or not as the case may be.

Now the IR35 letters went through this process. Some constituents received individual replies from their MPs and some received a telephone call from them. Some received a standard letter from their MP, some had their letter forwarded to Dawn Primarolo at the Treasury and received the standard response from the Treasury and some received the PLP propaganda letter. Some, instead of getting letters from Dawn Primarolo received letters back from the Inland Revenue, which none of them were happy about. One thing about being in business is that you don't want to draw the attention of the Inland Revenue.

Ordinarily, people all over the country receiving the same bog standard response from the Treasury or the Inland Revenue and their MPs would go unnoticed, but introduce the Internet and discussion forums and the ability for people to post up copies of the letters received and suddenly you have exposed the whole system.

This is of course what happened. People were outraged that they had taken the time to craft their worries in detail about the new plans only to receive the standard response from the Inland Revenue's Elaine Carey. Some friends of mine who were Labour Party members actually resigned in protest at the plans. They duly wrote a letter to Margaret McDonagh, the party's General Secretary (the equivalent of Chief Executive). Margaret's office, I assumed, forwarded these to the Treasury who forwarded them to the Inland Revenue who directed them to Elaine Carey who sent them photocopied details about why the legislation was being brought in. Details that you had already seen because that's what had been sent to everyone else. So after twenty years in the party, hours and hours of delivering soggy leaflets in the rain, knocking on doors and attending boring meetings they received the reward of a letter from the Inland Revenue. I don't think it was the deliberate policy of the party to do this, but this is what happened.

Meeting your MP

Take a group of highly educated, motivated workers and point them at their MPs and the results could be startling. While some did indeed rant at the MPs, others prepared well thought out letters and at constituency surgeries delivered professional presentations detailing how and why the tax would affect them. Contractors would deliver well prepared presentations, often to quite perplexed Labour MPs. For most of them it was the first real contact any of them had had with politicians and they were pleasantly surprised to discover that they were real people, normal people who weren't totally divorced from reality. The MPs for their part, particularly the Labour MPs, found it quite hard to consolidate the view put forward by the Treasury that these people were money grabbing tax dodgers who weren't paying their fair share. One typical case would be an IT worker made redundant in the 1980's, out of work, retrained in IT and started working freelance. He put aside cash to carry him through bad times between contracts and out of his earnings put aside cash to keep his training up to date and was then being told via IR35 that he couldn't.

Though many contractors were good advocates of the freelancers cause, some were very poor. Some used MPs surgeries to rant at the Government and the need to pay any tax. One very influential MP, who had been a small businessman before, had a constituent come and rant and rave at him – the object of his rage? – The fact that because of IR35 he wouldn't be able to finance his private yacht. A Surrey based Conservative MP may be sympathetic to this, but a Labour MP whose next constituent could be someone who is on the minimum wage and is about to be evicted would not be, and in this case the support of this MP was lost.

We had PCG members in almost all the English constituencies and the majority of the Scottish and Welsh too. They wrote to their MPs and went to see them at their local constituency surgeries while the PCG supplied them with facts, figures and briefing notes.

## What MPs Said

Simon Banton organised the setting up of a special online database that allowed us to work out who lived in which constituency so that members could log who had written to which MP. We had members in nearly every constituency, the only place we didn't seem to have someone in was Sedgefield, which was Blair's. I even floated the idea of renting a flat there so we could get to see him, though it was rejected and suggested that we probably wouldn't get to see him anyway.

We did have a few people in Gordon Brown's constituency. One such person was Alec Jordan, who created email systems for companies, so he trudged along to see him. Brown probably assumed this was just a southern tax and wouldn't affect anyone where he lived. He was wrong. However, when Alec raised the subject as a constituent Brown got very angry with him. He then said that he had heard how contents of letters and discussions had been recorded on the PCG's website. He thought that was wrong and said that he wasn't prepared to discuss the issue except through a written submission.

This is the Chancellor of Exchequer who has introduced a new tax threatening thousands of small businesses, he hasn't done a white or green paper, he hasn't even announced it as primary legislation; he didn't mention it in his budget speech and didn't debate it in the Finance Bill. It was to slip into the Welfare Reform Bill. Now when asked about it directly he refuses to even discuss it with one of his constituents.

He told Alec that he could talk and he would listen but not reply, so that's what happened. Alec explained in this very intimidating atmosphere how the tax affected him, how he was a genuine business and believed in paying a fair share of tax but that this measure was unfair. While he was speaking he reported that Brown used the opportunity to read and write on some other papers.

It was clear that they didn't like the PCG campaign and its digital nature. Years later David Cameron would accuse Brown of being 'an analogue politician in a digital age'. It resonated with the public and even with me, though I still voted for him.

Other members reported good friendly meetings with Anne Campbell, Robin Cook and even Alistair Darling. Tony McWalter, the Labour MP for Hemel Hempstead, was very supportive. Years later he would host a fringe meeting for us at a conference and I would become his Parliamentary Researcher.

With the Tories and the Lib Dems was a lot of support and they urged contractors to send them as much information as they could. Sir Robert Smith MP said he welcomed letters on the subject, he said letters gave him the 'bullets to fire at the Government'.

## Parliamentary lobbying

In politics, as in war, speed is of the essence. If you can fall upon your enemies while they are disorganised or in disarray then your chances of success are far greater. In politics time can really be the enemy. Politicians don't like to lose face or retreat from positions. Fluidity is the key, as soon as things are written down and published and positions are taken then the more difficult it is to move them. While contractors had moved like lightening and had organised themselves into a formidable trade body, raised funds for a campaign and were engaging with public opinion, MPs and Inland Revenue officials, they hadn't engaged the Government. Members of Parliament and the Government aren't the same thing. Looking back now it is astonishing to think that post budget with the plans starting to take shape that the PCG never managed to get a representative to meet directly with the Paymaster General. I don't know that Dawn Primarolo would have changed her plans but as the days ticked by during March, April and May the chances of changing her plans slipped further and further away. As the PCG was formed and hiring of a professional lobbyist and press officer had not made the difference, the parliamentary links they had were primarily with the Conservatives, not Labour. If Andy White made a mistake it was now, he needed to have hired a lobby team that could have got him in front of the Paymaster General for a personal meeting at that early stage.

This is where I entered onto the stage.

# Chapter 3

### Small Business Minister

The small business minister in 1999 was Michael Wills MP, or to give him his correct title – Parliamentary Under Secretary of State for Small Firms. He was a Swindon MP and had previously run his own TV independent production company, Juniper, for whom he acted as the producer/director until elected to Parliament in 1997. Someone who not only sympathised with small business but had actually run one, he was noted to be a friend of both Gordon Brown and Peter Mandelson, which was a surprising combination.

I had been in contact with Michael Wills' constituency office and in my letters to him I had stressed my Labour Party credentials and suggested that I wanted to stop this issue becoming political and damaging the Government, which was true. I didn't want the Conservatives to be able to gain any points from this but I was as surprised as anyone to have actually got the call to go in and see him and a date a few weeks away was arranged. I was out of my depth. A meeting with a Government minister was unfamiliar territory for me at the time. I emailed the PCG team and suggested that I could go alone but really would like some help. No reply ever came. I chased them up but no reply ever came. I assumed that with meetings with Inland Revenue officials planned and the assumption that ministers were already being met I considered my meeting to be a side show. I assumed that they were already in at the Treasury meeting with the Paymaster General. I didn't worry too much about it as I happened to work only 15 minutes away from the DTI and could easily attend the meeting, then I got a phone call from the minister's office asking for the names of the people who I would be bringing with me. I felt too embarrassed to say – 'just me!' So I said I'd get back to them. I tried to contact David Ramsden again but got no reply. Now, to be fair to David at this time he was getting deluged with emails and messages from contractors putting in their two pennyworths about what they should be doing and I think my mail just got lost in the mix.

The day drew closer and I felt obliged to put together a team for the meeting. I thought of three friends, Chris Ireland, one of the best IT programmers and analysts I have ever worked with, Elaine Rae, my daughter's godmother who worked as a freelance network engineer and Graham Hoyle, who started as freelance web designer and had grown his business to employ other web designers. All were potential victims of IR35. I chose Chris because we had worked together for two years and had done countless number of business meetings together and we could communicate with a look and a nod, there was a tremendous amount of synergy between us, but the main reason for choosing them was that I knew them and trusted them all. Graham dropped out a day or so before because of child care commitments.

By chance Elaine was working on contract in Sandy, both Chris and I lived in Bedfordshire so we met up the night before at my house. I had spent days working out what we should and shouldn't say, lines of attack and defence. We went through it and it was agreed that I would lead the meeting. We wouldn't focus on the tax side of the proposals but on their impact on our competitiveness. We would talk out the need for us to operate as freelancers and the benefits to the economy. We would also focus on the criteria for 'direction, supervision and control' and that this didn't fit with IT contracts and knowledge based work. Chris had prepared some thoughts on how you would implement standard systems development methodologies and that these were incompatible with direction, supervision and control. The problem with IT is that it is still an art as opposed to a science. Clients don't know exactly what they wanted at the start of a project, but they do know the skills required to do it, therefore contractors and consultants are often engaged on a time basis. Very often on IT projects the first part of the project has been defined, the requirements and specification defined and you work on that while at the same time the requirements for the next stage are being drawn up.

## Meeting with the Small Business Minister

Department of Trade and Industry, 1 Victoria Street

We arrived in good time at the DTI building in Victoria Street. I was working for Salomon Brothers International just above Victoria station so it was easy for me to get there. We met up at the reception area, gave in our names and waited. After ten minutes we were collected from reception and taken into the inner bowels of the Department of Trade and Industry. Inside the DTI there are a number of lift shafts, we were taken up high to the ministers floor and deposited in a small waiting area. Time ticked by, the minister was running late. Our 45 minutes slot had now shrunk to 30 minutes. Eventually we were collected and carried through to an empty meeting room. We waited again and then a harassed Michael Wills appeared and filed into the room with his entourage a note taker and two officials, Stuart Balthrope and Guy Hooper who was the senior of the two. Apologies were given for being late and we could sense that the minister was keen to push onto his next appointment and we were really a bit of an inconvenience.

My Labour Party friend, Karl, had warned me that they will compare me to the dirt on their shoe and it would be up to me to convince the minister otherwise. I have to say that in subsequent meetings with ministers and officials this hasn't always been the case, but it is a good frame of mind to go in with. He advised me that we should aim to make a good enough impression so that we would be invited back, so that was our objective.

The minister sat laid back in his chair flanked by his advisors while we sat eagerly on the edge of our seats. I accepted the offer of tea, though it was a distraction. Though appearing disinterested and nonchalant the minister was not offensive or threatening, he was open to discussion.

He thanked me for the briefing paper that I had sent and said:

"We are amazed at the amount of lobbying and correspondence that we've received on this subject, as are the Inland Revenue."

Indeed, he added, the Inland Revenue is now referring callers to the engineerjob website for more information about IR35.

(At this time the Inland Revenue only had a very basic website and were really found lacking when faced with the engineerjob site. The PCG system had been put together with open source Perl code by Simon Banton and his team and was being updated on a daily basis).

I talked about the difference between knowledge based work like IT and engineering and other types of work and said that these measures which were out to target tax avoidance were going to unintentionally impact the IT industry. The 'leave on a Friday and come back as a consultant on the Monday' was not true of IT.

My colleagues affirmed this point. I said that in the survey commissioned by the PCG it showed that only 4% of applicants had done this.

I said also that plans to target work if it was 'controlled or supervised' didn't work for IT as that was all work. They were trying to differentiate between contract *for* service and contracts *of* service, i.e.: you can sign up to do a project as a fixed cost thing, but not sign up on a time basis to work on a project and this isn't how IT works.

Chris talked about the DSDM methodology, which time-boxes work and is in use at the MOD and other government departments, and said using this methodology would exempt the use of freelance contract staff.

The minister listened with some interest as we went through these points, but still sat laid back in his chair.

"The result of these measures, which I think you are more interested in", I said making eye contact with him, "is that these plans would pose a restriction on trade and make it harder for us to work as independents."

"The larger body shop firms with whom we compete for work would gain a huge commercial advantage"

The minister sat forward in his chair we had engaged him.

"Why would it favour them?" he demanded.

It was getting hostile now. They flashed points and issues at us on issues ranging from tax and evasion and about the need for regulation. I never expected such a hard time but I was so up for the meeting, so mentally prepared and in the right frame of mind and because of our co-operation and team work we pressed on fending off supplementary questions from him and Guy Hooper and refused to be drawn.

The "Supervision, direction and control clause would catch practically everyone and the need for us to be registered and for clients to deduct tax and national insurance at source would probably mean that would be too complicated to take us on for short contracts"

Guy Hooper said that the proposed certification scheme would be okay, wouldn't it, and would solve the problem?

"No", I said, "It would inhibit clients from engaging and also we are wary of this because it doesn't differentiate between different types of work."

"But it is just one phone and they can check that you are registered or not"

"Be realistic", I said, "you know what that will mean in practise".

They paused to consider this. They'd thrown criticism and argument at us but we had held our ground. They were impressed.
We talked about Graham Hoyle and others and explained how they had grown their businesses on the back of IT contracting and we also mentioned Andy White's business too.

"Look", I laboured, "these plans will dampen entrepreneurial activity"

Further discussion followed and they rejected the idea that contractors could all leave and go abroad and that businesses would close. I said that this was most likely because revenues could get cut by up to 25%. They disputed this figure and I had trouble trying to explain it so I agreed I would get back with some calculations on this.

We seemed to reach a bit of an impasse then came the killer question from the minister:

"What is it that you want?" he asked.

To be fair, we weren't really prepared for this level of co-operation and were feeling a little uneasy as the minister considered us to be the official representatives of the PCG, although a member I wasn't mandated directly but power isn't something that is always given to you but something you take, so I assumed the mantle.

"We want the ability to trade freely in a fair market and have the ability to grow and develop the equity in our companies." I answered.

The minister exchanged glances with his advisors, he had expected us to go in and complain about tax and that is what they were ready to defend against, we had changed the game.

He sat back in his chair and murmured and considered what we had said.

"I started out as a one-man company and then grew it up" he said, "so I am sympathetic and I don't want small business to suffer on my watch."

He also knew about practises of laying costs off against expenses and also said that he didn't approve of paying non-working spouses, he also mentioned the known villain of self-incorporation, John Birt.

I said I wanted to see an RIA (Regulatory Impact Assessment) done on this. They said one was being done as part of the Welfare and Pensions Bill.

We also talked about the meeting coming up with the Inland Revenue and other bodies. We'd got a result now, the minister was on side – or at least sympathetic – so we drew the meeting to a close. I had never been in such a tough meeting where we had to work so hard and I'd never been in one with a good team. If ever any of us started to flag one of the others would interject and beat back their questioning. It was a victory.

The minister invited me back to see him after the meetings with the Inland Revenue had taken place to clear up any points that we were not happy with and also said they could lobby the Treasury for us on those if they agreed.

We shook hands, his advisors passed me their business cards and minutes later we were back out on the street basking in the spring sunshine. We dispersed fairly quickly as after all we were all contractors and were in effect losing money by not being at our clients. As I walked back down Victoria Street I felt very pleased with myself, we had successfully lobbied a Government minister and he had invited us back in to see him. I never realised then that this would probably be the most positive meeting ever that would be held on IR35, I considered it to be a side show. The real work was influencing the Treasury, but even so given how hard the meeting had been I resolved that if we went back in I would take David Ramsden from the PCG as by then the proposal for how we are to contract in the future will be on the table and we could pick off points. We were amateurs and the ironic thing is at this time I had tried hard to come across as a professional public affairs person, later on as I became a professional public affairs person I would try to define myself as just an IT contractor.

## After the DTI

I went onto the PCG forums and wrote up my report about the meeting. It was of course generally well received and those who logged their thanks as well as Andy would be the future directors of the PCG. I thought should I get some publicity for our visit? I contacted Susie Hughes, the PCG's new press officer, who suggested that The Times could be interested, but then I thought again. This had been a private, productive meeting, you need publicity to get your foot in the door to see the minister, but we were already in.

Andy got in touch with me by phone and was clearly impressed that I had managed to get in to see the minister and was also disappointed that he hadn't. I explained that I had been invited back to see Michael Wills and Andy pushed me to get him in there as quickly as possible. I half explained that my invitation was to go in after the new rules had been published but Andy was very insistent that he needed to go in. I suspect that Andy was a little annoyed that here he was running this great

Internet campaign and yet some guy from rural Bedfordshire writes a letter and gets in to see the minister. The trick is to write the letter and not to trust to lobbyists to conjure a meeting out of thin air. To be fair though, this was the early days of the Labour Government.

# Chapter 4

## A war of facts and figures - Full Consultation?

When the Government plans to make reform of any industry it usually consults with the industry, puts out a green paper, consults further, investigates the impact of the changes that it plans to make and then on the basis of consensus and political objectives, makes its decision. Look for instance at the 'Right to Roam' legislation. The political objective was to open up the countryside to the people, but they listened carefully to landowners and countryside groups before finally putting in place the final legislation. Plan to reform the brewing industry, green paper and discussion. Plan to reform 'widget' manufacture (workforce ~10,000 nationwide), green paper and discussion. Plan to reform freelance working and the impact on the IT infrastructure and competitiveness within the new knowledge economy, sneak a few paragraphs into the appendices of the budget. To be hard on the Treasury you could say that they just wanted to implement this by stealth, to be fairer you could say they never understood the importance of the freelance market place. So, plans to redefine self-employment that effect 250,000 workers in the UK gets no green paper and just a couple of meetings with those it will benefit on how to implement it. I think that freelancing is a hugely important part of our economy and was a dynamo that helped drive our competitiveness so I found it astonishing that such changes were planned without forethought or consultation. Of course changes to the way that freelancers work should not have come from the Treasury but should have been driven by the DTI, but the DTI was a junior partner in the Blair\Brown government. By driving the issue from the Treasury and not the DTI it affirmed that this was a tax raising measure, not an entrepreneurial one.

## Employees on paper, businesses in reality

The idea that the tax would collect £475m a year was fanciful and later on it would be claimed that it would collect £900m or even more. The fact is that there were no figures on the number of contractors or people working in this way, it was just a guess. Indeed in later years the Paymaster General would refuse point blank to give out any figures on how much extra tax it had collected so not only was it badly thought out, but there were no metrics to measure its revenue generation and success or failure. No way to measure how effective it was. Money doesn't disappear, it doesn't evaporate, in times of recession it just stops moving around and as money moves around it gets taxed and government generates income.

The original Regulatory Impact Assessment for the Welfare Reform Bill didn't contain any mention of this important tax plan. This was pointed out in Parliament by a Conservative MP and met by a mixture of blushes and a rolling of eyes on the government benches. By now we had a whole army of thousands of clued up and Internet savvy contractors who sliced their way through the Government's woeful online presence. One contractor discovered that

> "The original signed Alistair Darling MP, 8 Feb 1999, does not contain the RIA appendix of concern to us. Hence the evasion in the debate in the House on 20 May! Looks like our appendix was a main part of the update dated 21 May"

On May 21st a new rushed Regulatory Impact Assessment (RIA) of the Welfare Reform Bill appeared, tucked away inside this was the analysis of the effects of IR35. The assumption of this analysis was that ALL affected companies would close down and the individuals would go onto their client's payroll – it estimated this as 66,000 businesses. They did not expect any one-man companies to sign for their proposed certification scheme. They had no idea that contracting is a legitimate part of the economy. As far as they were concerned working through a limited company was only done to avoid tax. The whole freelancer equation was ignored. They assumed that the majority of freelancers were 'disguised employees' and that their clients would simply take them on as permanent employees and that the rates of pay would remain the same, but the taxes would now go to the Inland Revenue. It doesn't take a genius to see through the flaws in this argument but here it was, the justification and analysis of the biggest ever tax raid on small business.

It confirmed contractor's worst fears, the prize of higher tax revenues by punishing a group with no political allegiance to Labour and supporting big business was what was driving the Government. Indeed it is perhaps disingenuous to say government and more correct to say Treasury.

The PCG though, was driven by Andy White and Kevin Miller and their allegiance was to contractors. They compiled and published our own RIA to counter these arguments.

In opposition, Labour had been critical of how legislation had been implemented without enough forethought and consideration on how it would affect other areas. Indeed this theme was picked up by Will Hutton in his seminal work 'The State We're In'. Once in Government they commissioned and then published the Better Regulation guidelines and an early mantra was the need for more joined up government. In reality this just meant that the Treasury had more control over everything, in fact I was told that inside the Treasury they had teams shadowing the other ministries, for instance a shadow health team, a shadow transport team etc. There was a strong belief that the role of the other Ministries was simply to implement policy, not to think it up. "The Treasury will do the thinking, thank you."

### Facts, Figures, Evidence to no avail

What had motivated Andy White and other entrepreneurs who had come forward was that freelancing was the seed corn of their business success. Many businesses in the UK had come from contractors. Logica, one of the big IT consultancies, had started as a group of freelancers who had banded together to do a project. Many IT recruitment agencies and software houses had grown this way. This opportunity would be lost, the flexible workforce that we had would be lost. With a less flexible pool of labour firms would be forced to engage the larger consultancies to undertake their software projects but as this would prove a very expensive route so they would seek cheaper alternatives and take the work offshore instead. This would throw the UK's IT service industry into a cycle of decline, which is what happened.

Despite the fact that this was primarily a tax issue ministers didn't justify IR35 in revenue terms, instead they justified it in terms of 'fairness'. Fairness to who - the large IT consultancies who felt that they would benefit from this? The tax evasion/avoidance that was taking place did not need a sledge hammer solution. One accountant commented at the time that all the Inland Revenue had to do was declare that they would take a very dim view of a high ratio of dividends to salary and similar suggestions would later be made by the Tax Faculty. Had they done so it is suggested that industry would have fallen into line.

This was a smash and grab raid on freelancers which in the long term would weaken the industry reducing the number of freelancers in work. Many would work permanently and the tax avoidance would now be done by the corporations that employed them, many of them foreign, and using complicated tax structures.

Following a working party, which included the PCG and the Institute of Chartered Accountants for England and Wales (ICAEW), a powerful submission to the Inland Revenue was made. One of the main conclusions stated:

> "We believe that if the proposed rules are enacted there will be no significant financial gain to the Treasury. The operation of the rules will be extremely burdensome if not unworkable. This will impact on the entrepreneurs who have set up personal service companies and who are contributing successfully to the economy.

It added that:

> A particular hard hit area will be that of information technology ('IT') where such arrangements are common and are often insisted upon by clients. Many individuals working within IT are highly mobile and may well seek to take their skills and knowledge to other countries, thus depriving the UK of an invaluable skills base."

These long term arguments would be to little avail, governments, particularly the Treasury, greedily eyed the immediate tax that it thought it could get its hands on.

# Chapter 5

## The Parliamentary Battle Begins

### 4th May 1999

With IR35 having been hidden within the budget statement the biggest difficulty was getting the message out and then getting MPs to understand the issue. In many respects the short hand term of 'IR35' helped us to do this, it was easy to say and easy to remember, although the Government originally preferred to call it the taxation of personal service companies. In the late 1980s the Tories had tried to implement the 'community charge' which Labour renamed the 'poll tax'. Instead such was the farce at the time that Government ministers would refuse to answer any questions on the 'poll tax' and would only answer then on 'the community charge'. For a while Labour followed the same tactics with IR35, but to little avail.

John Whittingdale, the Conservative front bench Spokesman on Treasury, raised IR35 in Parliament for the first time on 4th May 1999, he said:

> "I have mentioned measures that have received publicity and are causing concern, but which do not appear in the Bill. One other measure, which may have provoked more letters from my constituents and those of my hon. Friends than almost any other, is not mentioned in the Bill at all. It was referred to in the press release accompanying the Budget documents--IR 35--which announces the Government's intention to deal with personal service companies.
>
> In certain professions, people choose to incorporate themselves as a personal service company and to undertake contracts of perhaps three or six months on behalf of companies.
>
> The change in the tax treatment of those people is causing a great deal of concern. Professionals in the IT industry, in large part, choose to form themselves into personal companies, and gain a tax advantage in terms of their equipment and training expenses. I understand that the Government are anxious to close loopholes and crack down on tax avoidance, but I do not regard that as an example of tax abuse.
>
> The importance of IT professionals to the economy is considerable, especially now that we are wrestling with the possible problems of the millennium bug and the Y2K issue. I would have thought that the Government would be anxious to encourage IT professionals rather than to disadvantage them through tax changes.
>
> The measure is provoking enormous concern, and I am sure that almost every hon. Member will have received, or will receive, letters from people in the industry. I understand that the measure will come into effect at the beginning of the next financial year.
>
> It is not mentioned in the Bill, however, and I understand that the Government do not intend to legislate until they introduce next year's Finance Bill. It is worrying

that the implementing legislation will not come before the House until after the measure has come into effect"

The concern being registered, in what was quite an even handed speech, was that this huge change in the taxation of personal service companies with its possible knock on effects on our industry was not going to be debated properly.

## 16$^{th}$ May 1999

We had a written question from Lib Dem spokesman Vince Cable to Alan Milburn criticising IR35.

Vince Cable asked the Chief Secretary to the Treasury (Alan Milburn MP) about IR35.

> Is the Chief Secretary aware that there is a great deal of concern in British business that, as a result of the Government's perfectly valid concern about tax avoidance, there could be a considerably increased tax burden on legitimate businesses, notably through Inland Revenue 35 as it is applied to the computing industry and through the application of value added tax on the internal transactions of banks? How much revenue does he propose to raise in that way, and what assurances is he giving to business that he will not penalise legitimate companies?

Milburn didn't really reply to the question directly, he just had a stock answer. The Red Book estimates at that time were £475m for IR35 though in the next budget it would almost double to £900m for some undetermined reason. It sounded as though they had just made it up.

> If the hon. Gentleman cares to look in the Red Book, he will see what the tax yield would be from that measure. As we have made clear in the Finance Bill Committee, no legitimate service businesses will be affected by this proposed measure

## 17$^{th}$ May 1999

One warm evening in May as MPs sat on the terrace, ate in the restaurants and glasses were filled in Strangers Bar and pool balls clinked in Annie's Bar, the day's parliamentary business was dragging on. Stephen Timms, Labour MP for East Ham, himself an ex-IT worker, was at the despatch box navigating through the Welfare Reform Bill. They were discussing new clauses that needed to be inserted into the Bill. At around 7:00pm they began to debate a clause entitled 'Excessive pension contributions made by persons who have become insolvent', which is the sort of subject you would expect in a Welfare Reform Bill, then at 9:00pm they began to debate the new clause 15 - Earnings of workers supplied by service companies etc.

What the 'etc' is I am not quite sure, I suspect it means –that sort of thing, but this was it, this was IR35.

**"Earnings of workers supplied by service companies etc**

4A--(1) Regulations may make provision for securing that where--

(a) an individual ("the worker") in any specified circumstances personally performs, or is under an obligation personally to perform, services for the purposes of a business carried on by another person ("the client"), and

(b) the performance of those services by the worker is (within the meaning of the regulations) referable to a contract between the client and a third party, relevant payments or benefits are, to the specified extent, to be treated for the purposes of the applicable provisions of this Act as earnings paid to the worker in respect of an employed earner's employment of his (where they would not be such earnings apart from the regulations).

The proposed tax changes had been hidden away in the Welfare Reform Bill – because of a procedural anomaly. According to Stephen Timms this was because "the responsibility for national insurance policy has been transferred to the Treasury through the Contributions Agency transfer legislation, which a number of us enjoyed debating not long ago. However, this is still a matter for social security legislation". So there you have it. The House was largely deserted of Labour members, who to be fair considered this to be just standard welfare reform issues. Of course they would all be back to pass through the lobbies and vote at the appropriate time.

The arguments put forward by Stephen Timms for plugging a loophole in the tax arrangements to the uninitiated sounded like reasonable ones. He persisted with the myth that it wouldn't affect IT workers specifically. He quoted two examples, one of an overseas hospital doctor who would get caught by the rules and one of an IT worker who leaves his place of employment on the Friday only to return on the Monday, but doesn't get caught by the rules. The example claimed that he would be returning to do a piece of fixed price millennium bug fixing. By this time a huge number of MPs, especially those in the south east had received letters from IT contractors, many of them PCG members, explaining how the new tax would affect them. Stephen Timms' charming little story about the plucky engineer in a medium sized manufacturing company who decided to 'go it alone' was designed to mislead.

A misunderstanding of how self-employment worked was evident in his open answers when he suggested that the client in his first example (of the overseas doctor) was that the hospital would now be responsible for their sick pay. A hastily scribbled note by a civil servant was hurriedly passed to him and a few minutes later he apologised for his error stating that:

> "My answer to the hon. Member for Christchurch (Mr. Chope) was wrong. For a doctor supplied by a service company, the arrangements for paying statutory sick or maternity pay, where the worker is paid by a certified agency, remain unchanged. The agency will be responsible for such payments. "

I've never worked on an IT contract where they have been paid sick pay or received it from an agency, but if he was confused about who exactly it would disadvantage and effect the one-man companies, he was clear on who it would benefit.

Because, in trying to justify the new rules, Stephen Timms let the cat out of the bag when he said:

> "The problem at the moment is that there is an uneven playing field, which is disadvantageous to major organisations"

We knew what sort of organisation would be disadvantaged from a contractor's conversation with a Director of the Inland Revenue. He had admitted that the tax was:

> '....drawn up to answer the complaints of the big employers who have complained that Ltd company contractors are distorting the employment market'.

What was laughable were the Government's estimates for implementing the new rules, £175,000 in the first year and then £55,000 per year after that. The PCG's future policy of aggressively fighting the rules through contesting cases and pushing them as hard as possible makes this figure totally laughable.

However, please do not make the mistake of thinking that this debate was taking place in front of a packed audience of MPs; the Labour benches were virtually deserted to the dismay of the Conservatives and Liberal Democrats present.

They were concerned that this piece of small business legislation was being sneaked through as the press release before it had been, but they were also concerned about the precedent that this legislation was having. The complications of how the new rules would be applied was missing from the Bill, instead it was proposed to simply legislate so that the powers would be delegated to the Inland Revenue.

Indeed Eric Forth MP noted:

> "It would appear that real people in real businesses were conned into believing that they were going to engage in some sort of consultation with the Government, and have been shocked to find that the Government are attempting--rather typically--to slip into this important Bill a crucial new clause, with no notice and, certainly, no consultation. "

The Government would play a clever device; in Parliament they would tell MPs that any consultation would be done at the regulatory stage and that all they needed to do was approve the principles. But at the regulatory stage during the consultation they would tell anyone who questioned or challenged the proposals, that these have already been approved by Parliament and they have to be implemented.

Eric Forth MP made some really telling comments about the plan, he said:

> "You and I know, Madam Speaker, that the real opportunity for proper debate, amendment and so on arises in the early stages of legislation.
>
> Once legislation has been set in terms of new clauses such as this, opportunities for consultation on the regulations will be--I will not say zero, but they will

certainly be minimal. Moreover, there will be no opportunity to amend the regulations, which will be presented on a take it or leave it basis."

On the regulations:

> "He said that some £200 million of additional revenue would result from the new clause--that was his estimate--and, in almost the same breath, went on to say that there would be no damage to business whatever."

Where this £200m figure came from I have no idea. As the debate proceeded it became clear that what worried the Opposition as much as the plans themselves was the way they were being implemented, with no debate in Parliament and no real chance that they would ever return to Parliament for a debate in the future. The substance is in subsection (9) which said that, whatever happens, whatever has been said it will be rewritten when the Government see fit to do so.

Mr. Forth added:

> "There is no attempt to limit or qualify what can be done. Use of such terms leaves the matter wide open, and it is at the discretion of the Treasury as to what can be done with the powers.
>
> The supremacy of the Treasury is here for all to see. There is no attempt to conceal it, and the Minister does not see why he should. That lays bare the motivation behind the measure--it is Treasury-driven regulation, designed solely for the purpose of making sure that the revenue take by the Government is maximised.
>
> This is a stealth tax if ever I saw one. It is dressed up as part of the Welfare Reform and Pensions Bill, but it is, in essence, a Treasury-driven measure that may or may not get the concurrence of the Secretary of State. "

There followed a debate with Andrew Miller, Labour MP, urging the Government to take a more positive line and consult properly to stamp out avoidance, but not to damage small firms. He quoted the Public Contractors Association, and this is also picked by Sir Robert Smith MP (LD) though a Public Contractors Association does exist, it is quite possible he did mean the Professional Contractors Group. Andrew Miller was the President of Computing for Labour and I had written to him on the subject telling him of the PCG's concerns, but once he had spoken he left the chamber.

A very positive contribution was made by Vince Cable MP (Liberal Democrat) and on the Conservative side, Iain Duncan Smith and John Bercow. They were furious because the measures were being introduced without any real debate. This debate simply gave the Treasury powers to do as it wished in the future.

> "the new clause is breathtaking. I have never seen anything quite like it. It moves from being a Henry VIII clause to being a Louis XIV clause--absolute power to the absolute monarch--before any consultation. "

At the time we were generally assured by the PCG team that these were just the opening shots and indeed the fact that the rules were going to be defined by secondary legislation gave us more of a chance to modify them. Reading this debate again now in retrospect I am quite impressed with the Opposition members who spoke on the issue, you could see in everything that they said the letters of PCG members. The power of writing in early to key members of Parliament was self-evident. Opposition members of course are keen to pick up any issue with which they could attack the Government, but getting those key letters in allowed key points to be communicated. MPs are not experts. Having worked for one myself constituent letters detailing their grievances, especially if there are several of them detailing the same point, make it an issue in the post bag to be addressed and also one that you can get the MP to focus on. During my time as a researcher at the House of Commons we received a considerable number of letters on the new Licensing Bill.

The revelation from the debate was positive through an angry contribution made by Iain Duncan Smith MP, who had risen considerably in my own estimation. I say revelation because when he was party leader and was asked about IR35 by *Shout99.com* he appeared as a rabbit in the headlights unsure even of what the tax was, let alone whether he would revoke it.

The Bill passed this stage in the House of Commons to a more or less empty chamber. Few Government MPs heard the debate though 375 returned to the chamber to vote it through with some 182 voting against, so a regular split between Government and Opposition MPs, there was no great rebellion or any rebellion here.

What was significant was the precedent of making massive changes to how small firms operate and secondly, moving this out of primary legislation to let the Treasury make any changes that they saw fit with no future discussions to take place.

The Welfare Reform Bill, having passed its stages in the House of Commons would now move on to the House of Lords. The date set for the second reading in the House of Lords was Thursday 10th June.

David Ramsden made a plea with PCG members to write to Lords suggesting that if you had a former member of Parliament who is now in the House of Lords it was worth writing to them. "You should refer to the fact that you are a constituent in their former constituency and ask for their help. I have put an outline of such a letter on the member's website but you must make your letter as relevant to yourself as possible."

Before we had really noticed or got that organised the Welfare Reform Bill had passed its first reading in the House of Commons and was off to the Lords. The peers however, hopefully rallied by our new patron, Lord Weatherill, and with a sympathetic inbuilt Conservative element would be more sympathetic.

## PCG Democracy

As a new organisation the PCG, and in particular Andy, was conscious of its mandate to speak on behalf of contractors. He felt that it was important to involve them in strategy and policy to get their approval and buy-in. As such the PCG put its proposals on IR35 together for consultation and put them to the membership for a vote, a referendum for approval. That is the sort of the thing a new revolutionary organisation does. Older established groups certainly wouldn't do anything like that and the current PCG would have to be included in that. In 2011 its submission to the Government enquiry about IR35 failed to call for 'abolition of IR35'. The old PCG would have put its submission down to the vote but it was a new organisation then and had nothing to lose. What was different at the beginning was that the PCG did not have special discussion boards for the director or consultative council members and everything was done in the open. There was no representative democracy, it was just open and direct democracy with all its strengths and weaknesses.

## 9th June 1999

The Government's revised RIA was music to the ears of the PCG press office and a great press release was put out on the subject. Susie then pushed it hard in all the newspapers and the Daily Telegraph ran it as a front page story. I was so surprised by it that I never spotted it (though I am a Guardian reader), people came up to me at work and congratulated me on it and it was unbelievable. I then wrote a letter to the Telegraph in support of the article and they published it on their website. To their credit it says much about the Civil Service that they did write a fairly honest document.

The PCG press release read as follows:

### 66,000 SMALL BUSINESSES FACE CLOSURE

The Government's Regulatory Impact Assessment on the 'Friday-to-Monday' (IR35 - Budget) proposals reveals that 66,000 small businesses face closure as a result of the Government's proposals in the Welfare Reform Bill to target independent contractors.

The Professional Contractors Group, which represents the interests of several thousand contractors, believes that this Government figure could be a serious underestimation of the actual closure rate.

David Ramsden, director of the PCG, said: "The Government's initial attempt to introduce this proposal via the Welfare Reform Bill without proper consultation was an attempt to legislate through the backdoor. The appearance of the Regulatory Impact Assessment at the 11th hour is totally contrary to open and fair Government. It also seems incredible that the Government seems willing to endorse the closure of so many small, entrepreneurial businesses.

"The RIA is based on flawed concepts and ill-conceived assumptions without proper regard for the reality of the market-place or the actual numbers of people who will be affected.

"Tomorrow (June 10) we will be attending a meeting with the Revenue as part of the consultation process - but now we find that these incorrect assumptions mean that any discussion of the detail would be based on figures - as described by the Government in the RIA - which are 'subject to considerable uncertainty' " The Professional Contractors Group highlighted its concerns about the RIA, which included:

- The basic assumptions are, by the Government's own admission, 'uncertain';

- The Government's figure of 66,000 potential small business closures could be a considerable under-estimation;

- Many contractors will relocate overseas resulting in a skills shortage in an already stretched knowledge-based industry;

- The Government assumes that the contractors will become full-time employees - but this shows a lack of understanding of an industry which is often project-based and the companies do not have vacancies for permanent staff;

- The RIA fails to comply with all the procedures in the Better Regulation Guide;

- There is no mention of pension losses, redundancy payments, official winding-up costs, consequential losses to other businesses.

David Ramsden concluded: "This RIA and the legislation it assesses are fundamentally flawed, due to a profound failure to grasp the essentials of the high technology contracting sector. If this goes ahead in its present form, the damage to small businesses, individuals and the economy in general will be significant."

### 10th, 11th June 1999

We knew also from the 'so-called' discussions with the Inland Revenue that their consultation still hadn't finished, so how had they completed the legislative process before finishing the consultation? How does that work? Exactly as you see it!

This legislation was still only the secondary part of a set of 'mirroring legislation' and was still reliant on the final wording of the Finance Act 2000. The lobbying would continue both to the House of Lords and back to the Commons for the Finance Act in 2000, as the plan was that it wouldn't be implemented until April 2000, but the debate about it was taking place now.

So, the Inland Revenue continued to go on with the charade of consultation with interested parties. Am I being too harsh there? I think in hindsight that the Government was aware of its majority and knew it could get anything it wanted so the consultation was really just to sort out a few technicalities or just a technicality. In fact two years later the CIOT would publish a report accusing them of doing just that.

It would comment that:

A proper consultation process would have allowed the legislation to focus on the areas of abuse, it would also have been much easier to apply. The current IR35 regime is enormously complex.

An article on *Shout99.com* explained the stance of this respected tax body.

## Government took shortcuts in IR35 consultation, says CIOT

by Richard Powell at 16:51 01/08/01 (News on IR35) Shout99

The Chartered Institute of Taxation (CIOT) has accused the Government of taking shortcuts during the consultation process when introducing new regulation, including IR35, which it says has resulted in complex legislation that has wasted both time and money.

The accusation was made following the recent release of a CIOT survey entitled, 'The Good, The Bad and The Complex', which studied a selection of 73 tax consultations from May 1997 to January 2001.

The survey's section on the consultation of IR35 says...

'On 9 March 1999 the Chancellor announced that: "Changes are to be introduced to counter avoidance in the area of personal service provision" and that, "the Inland Revenue will, over the next few months, be working with representative bodies on aspects of the practical application of the new rules and on the production of guidance. Any groups interested in contributing to this process should write to [address supplied]."

Respondents were supplied with, inter alia, a document entitled: 'Summary of a possible approach' which was described as being, "for use as a basis for discussion, but is not a consultation document." The accompanying letter encouraged them, "to take this opportunity to provide additional written input on the practical application of the proposed new rules in response to the documentation attached." The letter indicated that, "issues with respect to the policy decisions underlying the Chancellor's announcement, "were not on the agenda." A summary of the new rules published on 23 September 1999 stated that they had been "developed following extensive consultation."

The CIOT's report found that: 'It is simply unsatisfactory to refuse to discuss 'whether' a highly contentious proposal should proceed, to require interested parties to make written requests in order to obtain a hearing and to deny that papers inviting comments were consultation documents'.

Thus, although the respondent to our questionnaire acknowledged that there were 'major changes' from the original summary, the process was described as a 'failure to consult properly' and the lowest possible mark was awarded to the question: 'Were the issues treated fairly?'

Anne Redston, Chair of the Personal Tax Committee of the CIOT, confirmed that the IR35 consultation process had been considered by the Institute as part of the background work on the paper.

Anne Redson said, "The original IR35 proposals were launched without any consultation at all, and although sustained pressure from many bodies, including the CIOT and the PCG, caused the Government to make changes, there remain many areas which are unduly complex, unfair and burdensome. A proper consultation process would have allowed the legislation to focus on the areas of abuse. It would also been much easier to apply. The current IR35 regime is enormously complex and wholly unsuitable for a one-person company. Ultimately, the Institute's clear conclusion is that the process was flawed."

John Whiting, President of the Chartered Institute of Taxation, said:

"We are asking the Government to avoid mistakes by taking more time to follow every stage of the consultation process. We would also like a full report back which explains what is going to happen and why particular options have/haven't been chosen. This emphasises that changing the tax system should be seen as a partnership between all sides- not just something to be imposed. Proper consultation produces better tax law and practice."

"We think there are three broad stages to a good consultation - consult on whether to make a change, then on how to make the change, then finally on the detail of the new rules. Recent problems over subjects such as Capital Gains Taper Relief, Double Taxation Relief and IR35 can be traced to one of the stages being omitted."

"If a consultation takes place, it is something of a puzzle why consultation sometimes shuts down part way through the process. In cases where there is a dramatic shift in departmental thinking after the consultation, the resulting legislation can bear little resemblance to the original proposals. If new options emerge then there should be further consultation rather than changes being shoehorned into the Budget/Finance Bill process. Publishing draft Finance Bill clauses on Budget day with a time limit for responses of a few days add insult to injury."

The Institute's report, generally found that tax consultation should extend more widely on the stance taken by the UK in relation to proposed EU legislation. It also requested that members of the public should have access to all consultations.

The report was prompted by the Consultations Code which was published in early 2000. It found that once a proposal is agreed there is often no consultation on the principles of implementation.

'Once implementation moves to the detail stage, the survey shows that there is proper consultation in only about 50 per cent of cases. Given the complexity of most tax issues, more time should be allowed for responses so that the 12-week 'standard minimum period' can be followed,' it advises.

So on the 10th and 11th June following submissions from interested parties, meetings were held at the Inland Revenue HQ in London.

As noted the Inland Revenue had been shamed into producing a Regulatory Impact Assessment with an appendix relating to IR35. This had been approved on 18th May and posted to the DSS web site on 21st May but the PCG countered it with their RIA. The Inland Revenue one had been done in a rush and the figures in it, as history would later show, did not add up. Indeed the Inland Revenue would later release a revised one that steered clear of actual figures. Years later they would admit that they hadn't monitored any of the figures for the tax and so didn't know how much money it had raised.[15] Andy White attended the meeting on behalf of freelancers along with figures from CIOT, IOD, ICAEW, ICAS, PCG, CBI, FRES, Forum 2000, Forum 35, FSB and a host of other individuals representing groups. FRES is the old version of REC (the agencies body) and Forum 35 and Forum 2000 were agency or accountant led groups. The only group actually representing people who would actually be paying the new tax were Andy White and Mike Cullen.[16] Without the PCG there would have been no one to represent contractors, it would have been just the great and the good dividing up the pie making sure that they were alright.

Andy White wasn't very happy about the presence of some of the groups at the meeting and noted:

> "From closer inspection some would appear to be nothing more than an individual Company "badged" as a representative body. Many will ask why should they have an unfair advantage over other Companies in hearing from the Revenue first hand, matters which may affect whether they will be able to stay in business. Further, are their submissions to be given equal weight to that of other, genuine representative bodies?"

Strangely enough there was no representative from the Kitchen Fitters Association, these were the Friday-Monday people that IR35 was supposed to clamp down on. By this time I think even the Inland Revenue had dropped that pretence.

Andy reported that the

> 'CIOT, following a meeting on 7th June, is taking a lead in organising a meeting on 23rd June to discuss and confirm the understanding of the position on this important issue. Following that the situation may become clearer.
>
> The PCG will not be issuing any news release about these meetings until after the 23rd June.'

## IR 35 Time to make our mind up

---

[15] On 6 Jan 2004 Dawn Primarolo was asked by Mark Prisk, MP, about additional revenue secured from investigations under IR35. She replied that "Establishing whether or not the intermediary legislation applies is undertaken as part of the Inland Revenue's Employer Compliance Review programme. As such it is not possible with any accuracy to isolate data relating solely to this legislation." She gave a similar answer when asked about administration and employment costs.

[16] That isn't to dispute the goodwill of the other representatives.

As can be seen in a newsletter sent to contractors at the time, Andy White had clearly been doing his homework as he had researched the issue back to the early 1980s and the team produced a detailed document on the implications of IR35.

> "Drawing together information contained in existing and recently published Government statistics, coupled with an analysis of the 1981 attempt by the Inland Revenue to put contractors out of business, the article offers evidence that this apparent failure to close a loophole in 1981 has, in fact, resulted in a booming knowledge based sector enabling New Labour to deliver on its election promises."

> It concludes "If Clause 34 (the 1981 attempt to close PSC down) had come in the UK would not be in the position today in which we lead the world in key knowledge based industries. The labour market flexibility, as we have turned from a nation of shopkeepers into a nation of contractors, coupled by the genuine entrepreneurial "grunt" of this live wire sector has helped deliver an economy to New Labour able to take care of the less fortunate. It is indeed a third way, a stepping stone for the entrepreneurial amongst us, without the benefit of inherited wealth, to make the move from the security and protection of genuine employment to the risks and excitement of business on our own account."

9$^{th}$ June 1999

Philip Ross met Michael Wills (as documented before)

10$^{th}$ June 1999

House of Lords Second Reading

As noted earlier, David Ramsden was able to work his magic and get the ex-speaker of the House of Commons to become our patron which Susie issued to the press.

## LORD WEATHERILL ADDS HIS SUPPORT TO PROFESSIONAL CONTRACTORS GROUP

Lord Weatherill, former Speaker in the House of Commons and now, convenor of the Cross Bench Peers in the House of Lords, threw his support behind the aims of the Professional Contractors Group.

Lord Weatherill, whose support for small business is well known, would be concerned if the proposals contained in IR35 had the effect of driving small enterprises out of business.

"The Government should be doing all it can to encourage small businesses", said Lord Weatherill, "over burdensome and unnecessary legislation should be avoided at all costs".

David Ramsden, Director of the PCG welcomed the support given by Lord Weatherill. "His Lordship is a highly respected politician of long standing and his support underlines the serious intent behind our aims".

16th June 1999

While the newly formed PCG was busy trying to save contractors, elsewhere people had spotted a business opportunity and set out to create a brand new market in tax avoidance with the creation of tax avoidance companies. Andy White and I were both appalled, we wanted to keep a contracting market based around limited companies. In the long term that isn't what happened but it was what we wanted to avoid.

Andy wrote to contractors warning them of the consequences and described what some so called business consultant had been offering to a member:

There is an alternative [to IR35]. ****-********** Management has developed a PORTABLE payroll facility specifically designed to meet the particular needs of Contract/Temporary workers. Through our facility YOU can continue to legally minimise the amount of tax you pay and enjoy more of YOUR Hard Earned Money in a portable, Hassle-Free System with NO ADMINISTRATION that you can take from Contract to Contract, Agency to Agency, Employer to Employer. The enclosed brochure provides a detailed explanation of the benefits of our facility.

The attached brochure describes that you would become a shareholder of an umbrella or composite company working on a

"contract for services".

The income would comprise a weekly PAYE salary and a dividend payment generated from your shareholding in one of the companies within their facility.

It sets out that those joining will increase their net earnings between 10% and 15%

Andy wasn't happy about this. He explained that engineerjob.com had run an article from a leading law firm on composite companies which stated that "no one who researched the issues fully could possibly recommend that a person trade through an umbrella Company" This company seemed to be saying that they would also get round IR35. Andy phoned them and said that this all seemed too good to be true. What were the risks? They said there were no risks with doing this.

Andy asked if they were sure it would get round any new rules. They stated they had been inspected by the Inland Revenue and there was no problem. They stated they had 1500 on their scheme so Andy asked the cost. They stated that it would cost 2% of the money paid out as Dividend, but when asked to confirm all this in writing they started to become uncomfortable. They eventually caught on and refused.

Andy was cross that these, and possibly other accountants, were actually insisting they will get round IR35 by using such schemes. It was a threat to the PCG as people said that their accountants would get them out it.

One of the consequences of IR35 would be the growth in this sort of service, composite companies and umbrella companies.[17] It would create a powerful lobby for retaining IR35 that would come into full force when the Coalition Government of 2011 considered abolishing it. Gordon Brown, as well as creating bad legislation had generated fear, uncertainty and doubt, and on top of that a further monster. There would be a huge growth in management service companies so much so that in the 2007 budget fresh legislation had to be introduced to restrict their use.

Andy would be proved right. IR35 would generate a whole new industry that would live off the earnings of contractors while nominally helping contractors circumnavigate the tax. So much so that when the Coalition through the Office of Tax Simplification examined whether to scrap IR35 in 2011 I imagine that there were strong vested interests committed to keeping it.

## 28th June 1999

The PCG had agreed its submission and consulted it members, gained a consensus and a mandate for action and then negotiated with the other trade bodies and together they issued the following declaration. (Just as an aside it was real democracy in action, none of this paternalistic rubbish where they spoke for contractors, they allowed contractors to speak through them. But then the PCG was at the heart of the online revolution, what they were doing was radical to some and maverick to others).

When reading this you need to remember what the Government was proposing at the time. They were going to introduce a scheme like that in use for casual construction workers. Tax and NI were all to be deducted at source and contractors would all be subjected to a control and supervision test and would have to register with the Inland Revenue. If under the control of the client then they would fail the test. The big push was to defeat this clause as it really would have meant the end of contracting.

This is what we said:

---

[17] There is a respectable part of the umbrella companies business that promotes convenience and is easy to use. That is part of the choice for contractors.

**Joint submission to the Inland Revenue from: Federation of Small Businesses, Professional Contractors Group, Independent Computer Contractors, and the Association of Temporary & Interim Executive Services.**

Reference: Recent meetings held on 10th and 11th June 1999 at the Inland Revenue, concerning proposals to change the fiscal regime for small businesses. Announced in press release IR 35.

We are writing as organisation who represents many of the businesses who find themselves at the "sharp end" of the legislation proposed by IR 35. We believe that our position to the present proposals was made clear at the meetings on 10 and 11 June. They are, in our view, unduly complicated, unworkable and disproportionate to the problem as outlined in the Press statement; IR35. Furthermore the potential economic and political consequences will be far greater than suggested by the Regulatory Impact Assessment

We believe the proposed "control" test for "disguised employment" is unreasonable and that it fails to take account of the realities of the modern knowledge based economy: it would result in real small businesses (many of them with ambition to be large businesses) being arbitrarily treated as if they were merely devices for tax avoidance. These companies, especially in the IT and engineering field, are an important engine of economic growth and it is surely counter to Government policy to discourage them, as this measure would do.

We should point out that adoption of such a narrow test would in fact change the definition of employment/self employment and contradict the statement in IR35 "There is no intention to redefine the existing boundary between employment and self-employment."

As such, a disproportionate number of small businesses, who do consider themselves engaged in "genuine entrepreneurial activity", will be disadvantaged when compared to their larger Competitors. We understand from the meetings that these changes have been Lobbied for and note a recent article in the Times (24 June) which states, when discussing the background to this issue "Nor does it go down well with the large IT consultancies such as EDS, for example. It was organisations such as these that first alerted the Government to what they perceived as a problem. They felt that if they could break up the tax advantages that individual consultants had it might bring down what they saw as the exorbitant rates charged by them"

We support the objective of IR 35 to achieve "a tax system under which everyone pays their fair share" and would support and assist in developing targeted and proportionate measures to tackle abuse of the existing system, however there is a growing concern that measures to target such abuse are being used by larger Companies, often with strong Government connections, to drive smaller competitors out of business

When this is coupled with the last minute amendment to the Welfare Reform Bill we are sure it will be appreciated that Government stating we are engaged in "genuine consultation" is treated with some suspicion. We already note that the Bill, which refers to a "Certification" scheme, would now appear to be contradicted by statements at the Revenue meetings that this should now be called "Registration"

We would ask that the Government engage in a proper consultative process to ensure targeted and proportionate measures are taken to meet the objectives set out in IR35.

Approved on 28th June 1999

Andrew White: Professional Contractors Group (PCG)
John Whiting: Association of Temporary & Interim Executive Services (ATIES)
Mike Cullen: Independent Computer Contractors (ICC)
Simon Sweetman: Federation of Small Businesses (FSB)

### 29th June 1999

Susie then did her magic and sent it out to the press.

## PROFESSIONAL CONTRACTORS' GROUP URGES RE-THINK TO SAVE TENS OF THOUSANDS OF BUSINESSES

The Professional Contractors' Group together with the Federation of Small Businesses (FSB), the Independent Computer Contractors (ICC) and the Association of Temporary & Interim Executives (ATIES) today (June 29 1999) urged the Inland Revenue to rethink its proposals which would lead to the closure of at least 66,000 small businesses.

In a joint submission to the Revenue, the groups highlighted the problems with the last minute amendments to the Welfare Reform Bill which were targeted at 'tax avoiders' but have the potential to seriously damage the knowledge-based economy.

David Ramsden, Director of the Professional Contractors Group, said: "We applauded the Government's original stated objective to target tax avoiders and welcomed the consultation period on IR35, the so-called Friday-to Monday scenario. However, the proposals outlined by the Revenue were disproportionate to their stated aims and which would lead, by the Government's own estimation, to the closure of 66,000 small businesses.

"This creates a no-win situation for all concerned. We now hope that in the Revenue report to Ministers they will highlight our concerns and that they will take this opportunity to rethink their position and bring forward suitable legislation which meets its objectives without destroying a vital part of the economy."

The submission from the four groups highlights:

• The current proposals are unduly complicated, unworkable and disproportionate to the problem outlined by the Chancellor, Mr Gordon Brown, at the time of the Budget;

• The potential economic and political consequences will be far greater than anticipated by the Regulatory Impact Assessment;

- The proposed 'control test' for 'disguised employment' is unreasonable and fails to recognise the realities of the modern knowledge-based economy;

- It would treat small entrepreneurial businesses as if they were merely tax avoidance devises;

- It would disadvantage smaller concerns compared to larger businesses.

David Ramsden concluded: "We would welcome a genuine consultative process which will make these proposals fair and proportionate. At the moment, they are neither."

# Chapter 6

## More MP Lobbying

All this time many members were writing to, and meeting with, their MPs. Here is another thoughtful report from a contractor about a meeting with an MP, this time with Gordon Brown's PPS. What I thought was great was that people weren't just going in to see their MPs with their angry hats on, but did so much preparation and put so much thought into it.

Subject: Don Touhig MP - PPS to Gordon Brown
Date: 27 Jun 99 13:52:32

I had a meeting with Don Touhig MP today. Don is Gordon Brown's parliamentary private secretary - i.e. right hand man. I prepared a small quality presentation prior to the meeting in readiness. Mr Touhig came across as a very intelligent man and open to all I had to say. I explained that the government initiatives on 10% start-up tax, grants for small businesses, shorter capital writing down periods, etc., were good news for the small businessman. I could only give analogies with the IT industry.

I then went on to talk about existing businesses and the control and direction test proposed by the Revenue. I used a chart that showed the relationships of company to company via an agency, and the relationship of employee to company based on the team I work in. I proved that not one of the companies or employees could pass the control and direction test. He agreed and showed his concern at how the government, acting in good faith for the small business, could end up with something that discourages the entrepreneurial nature of the IT industry. He wants the UK IT industry to be the best in the world and I really felt that he now understands how the direction and control test could cause serious problems

## 20th July - House of Lords Debate

The Welfare Reform and Pensions Bill had been in committee in The House of Lords for some three weeks when on Tuesday 20$^{th}$ July they reached the all important part of the Bill, Clause 70; the section which would require class one NIC to be paid by those workers supplied by service companies.

Briefing documents and speaking notes were sent to Lord Weatherill, our patron. The Earl of Kintore was asked to speak for us and speaking notes were provided by IT contractor Gareth Williams, who had been a parliamentary advisor long ago, and a personal briefing was given by Susie Hughes and David Ramsden. The Earl of Kintore was an Aberdeenshire-based cross-bench peer without a political axe to grind, however, he felt compelled to take up the case on behalf of freelancers particularly in the oil and gas sector which was prevalent in his local area.

The Government, clearly concerned about the issue did not allow The Under-Secretary of State, Baroness Hollis, to handle the debate but instead parachuted in The Deputy Chief Whip in the House of Lords, Lord McIntosh of Haringey.

According to David Ramsden "Peers recognised the appearance of the Deputy Chief Whip as a sign of how much importance the Government was attaching to this section." During the debate Lord McIntosh of Haringey said:

> "We have to remove the avoidance but the mechanics of how we remove the avoidance are not set in stone. If there is an alternative approach which business believes is more sympathetic and yet delivers our policy, we will consider it sympathetically"

This suggested that there was still much to play for. Previous to the above quote, Lord McIntosh said at column 924:

> "There are many important issues, particularly those identified by the noble Lord, Lord Goodhart, on which we have a great responsibility to respond to consultation and to report that response to the House before we come back on report. I am not making any promises, but there may be modifications to Clause 70 as a result."

Finally, Lord McIntosh offered to call a meeting in the parliamentary recess to discuss with interested parties the responses the Government intended following the consultations currently taking place.

As a result clause 70 and 71 were nodded through. David Ramsden assured us that this was nothing more than part of the parliamentary process and no doors had yet been closed. There was still the report stage when the House could be expected to divide on a number of issues.

### Lord McIntosh's Seminar

Andy had always been convinced that if we could just get access to politicians, MPs and Peers, to put our case then the day would be won, they couldn't fail to see how important freelancing was to the knowledge economy. Ironically years later that opportunity would arise, but by then the freelancer movement would have split into factions[18] and I don't think they really got the message across.

Lord McIntosh's seminar would be held in the September, only the PCG's Kevin Miller turned up to watch it. Lord McIntosh couldn't have been very pleased because he clearly failed to convince his 'Lordships' and when they were to arrive back in October they would vote it out.

### Second Meeting with Michael Wills

Philip and Andy went to meet with Michael Wills who had said come back after the consultation if you are not happy, by then Patricia Hewitt was e-Minister and Alex Allen was the e-envoy.

---

[18] The All Party Parliamentary Small Business Group did an investigation into freelancing in 2003

Taking Stock

We were all pretty exhausted and during this time I wasn't working for the PCG or drawing a wage from them, I was also doing my day job as an IT contractor working at Salomon Brothers International in Victoria. At home I had a two year old daughter and did my best to balance home life, the PCG and work. I was also still heavily involved in my local Labour Party where I was chairman of the local branch.

The big question was could we keep up with the process. Fortunately we had Andy running the show. He approached it as a businessman and did things properly by bringing in Susie, David, Kevin and Simon, so we had professionals on our side who knew their way around and Andy kept members up to date with a series of emails.

Aberdeen Chapter

The pretence that this measure was aimed at bathroom or kitchen fitters had now pretty much been dropped by the Inland Revenue, though it is good sport now, years later, to bring it up. IT contractors were one large target group but another was oil and gas workers in Aberdeen. As a consequence a special Aberdeen Chapter of the PCG was established for these workers.

In mid July about 250 oil and gas contractors attended an open meeting in Aberdeen organised by the Chapter to discuss the impact that IR35 would have on their businesses.

Members of the audience expressed their concern about the Treasury's measures which could put them out of business and have a damaging effect on the oil and gas industry in Aberdeen.

David Ramsden reported that: "The livelihood of tens of thousands of contractors is at risk by these proposals, and this is particularly true in Aberdeen where there are so many engineers and oil and gas contractors. If these Inland Revenue proposals go through, there will be significant damage to individuals, the industry and the economy of the region. We know through the concern of our membership that oil and gas is only one of the many industries which will suffer as well as many small businesses."

Other speakers at the meeting who expressed their concern at the proposals included the Earl of Kintore, Sir Robert Smith MP for Aberdeenshire West and Kincardine and Cliff Grover, a contracting engineer and Leigh Mount, who would become the active link person in the PCG for oil and gas workers.

> The threat of a 'brain drain' was never more evident anywhere than it was in the oil and gas industry. These specialised contractors could work on an oil rig in Azerbaijan as easily as they could in Aberdeen. They had a very marketable and exportable skill set. The Earl of Kintore, an 'old-school' Peer and clan chief, stood up for his oil and gas 'constituents'. He later told the House of Lords during an IR35 debate that:

"The threat of IR35 being enacted has already caused a trickle of entrepreneurs to go abroad. If the provision is enacted as Clause 70, there is a danger of the trickle becoming a flood. If the seven or eight contractors--young, smart, articulate and interested--who were listening to the debate with me in another place last Wednesday (Commons) are a representative sample of the group, we should be fighting tooth and nail to keep them in this country, and not treat them like unwanted raffle prizes."

When he died in 2004, Susie wrote a tribute on Shout99. She concluded "I met him on several occasions and he genuinely felt that, although he technically didn't have a constituency, someone had to speak up on behalf of the contractors in the Aberdeen area."

## PCG Membership is growing to 3,000

By mid July the PCG had grown by a third, its membership was now nearly 3,000.

With the summer approaching the PCG signed up a leading think tank to write an analysis of the tax and then prepared for some time off before the battle commenced again in the autumn. PCG members were urged to send letters in to Dawn Primarolo, Lord McIntosh, Alistair Darling (as Secretary of State for Social Security) as well as their MPs. It was suggested that contractors compared the tax they paid to the 11% tax paid by EDS as a proportion of their turnover. This 11% figure had been taken from an analysis of EDS's accounts. Also, contractors were urged to impress upon their MPs that they were a genuine business and that they looked to the Government to help them stay that way.

Andy also wrote to contractors and said:

> 'Remember, three months ago no one had heard much about IR35, now barely a day goes by but one paper or another carries a story. This is largely down to you and Susie. Keep up the pressure, we are making a difference'.

# Chapter 7

## Secret Meetings – Divide and Conquer

It wasn't going very well for the Government or the Inland Revenue, the consultation meeting hadn't really worked and all the submissions were against, so they must have decided that it was best to go back to those behind the plans and ask them what to do next, which is exactly what the Inland Revenue did but unfortunately for them we found out about it.

They held secret meetings with bodies who wanted the tax (I still don't know who they were exactly, but I think you can guess).

The PCG wrote in and complained to Dawn Primarolo while also putting out a press release to that effect. The problem was that up until this point the Government hadn't wanted to appear unreasonable but at the same time engaged in some dirty tricks and as they got exposed they looked more and more shabby. Good news? Not really, ultimately it meant they knew they were already damned so they might as well press on anyway and get the money from IR35. We told the press:

> "It has been reported that at least one secret meeting has been held at which alternative proposals were released to certain representative groups which have been commenting on the IR35 proposals. The Treasury chose not to include PCG despite the fact they are the representative group of the people the legislation will affect. "

In the letter to Primarolo, David Ramsden, as Campaign Director of PCG said:

> "We have sought to ensure that the Government is totally informed on the way we work in the knowledge based sector. If the Government choose to ignore Professor Burton's research and our reasoned approach we will draw the inevitable conclusion that this measure has more to do with raising tax and benefiting certain favoured large companies than promoting fairness and the protection of worker's rights."

David added:

> "The government's current approach appears to be in direct contravention of the Better Regulation Guide which states that those affected should be consulted. PCG's requests for a genuine consultative process appeared to have been ignored which raises the question of how many other secret meetings have taken place. "

There was a lot of general embarrassment from the Inland Revenue and ministers about the secret meetings. Unfortunately for them, attendees at the secret meetings had let it slip to journalists who were then calling Susie for our reaction.

> "We were asked by journalists to comment on the next 'secret meeting' with the Revenue, scheduled for Friday September 17. As we had not been invited we re-iterated the points about transparent consultation and workable solution."

Then the Inland Revenue caved in and decided to hold a separate meeting with contractor groups, presumably in the interests of fairness, but the meeting was probably arranged by the public relations department to counter bad press reports.

> "On Friday afternoon, PCG was invited to a meeting with the Revenue this Wednesday. Kevin Miller will be attending on behalf of the PCG. The attendance list appears to be restricted to the ICCG and PCG, (Chris Steggles a PCG committee member will be attending on behalf of the ICC) together with representatives from the Contractors accountants; 360 group, Forum 35 and Forum 2000. Other groups such as FSB and FRES expressed surprise that they had not been invited."

Think Tank Report – 'An inflexible friend'

Now we could all say that IR35 was a disaster, was badly thought through and should be dropped or amended, but we would say that wouldn't we?

Despite the fact the Institute of Chartered Accounts of England and Wales (ICAEW) and Chartered Institute of Taxation (CIOT) may be saying similar, as were the Federation of Small Business (FSB) and others, that didn't count. As far as the Government was concerned they were probably misinformed, besides this was something that they shouldn't be making a fuss over.

I don't know if you have ever seen the episode of 'The Thick of It' where they are discussing education reform and Malcolm Tucker says, 'Well my expert says the opposite'. 'Who is your expert?' was the reply. 'Well, I haven't got one yet but I could probably get one in about half an hour'. It is a Westminster game.

Try as they might, the Government could find no experts to speak up for them. No doubt the CEO's of EDS and the members of the big four management consultancies would speak out, but that would reveal the truth of who was really behind it. The other exponents of the tax, at least those who saw opportunities behind to create new umbrella or composite companies, where ironically pretending to be on the side of contractors.

The PCG and contractors weren't having much trouble in this area. They hired in a professor from the Adam Smith Institute think tank to do a report and then in an effort to be helpful sent a note to Dawn Primarolo asking her to rethink her plans and to let her know about this helpful report that was being written. Though at the time my feeling was that the Adam Smith Institute was a Conservative leaning group and we could all predict what they would say, 'they would say that wouldn't they' would be the reaction. If we could have got DEMOS or a left leaning group to write such a report then it could have changed opinions or at least got noticed by Downing Street. In a press release in early September it was announced that:

> "The Professional Contractors Group announced today that it has commissioned a leading economist, Professor John Burton of Birmingham University, to look at the impact of the IR35 proposals and urged the government to await the findings of this research before rushing into any further knee jerk regulation. "

97

The PCG commissioned the report, but it was supported by sponsorship from FSB, ICAEW, CIOT, ATIES and FRES.

The report would be published just as the Inland Revenue released its new proposals, this meant that they could later say that all the issues raised in it had been addressed by the reformed IR35.

Guy Hooper, tax advisor to the DTI, wrote to me in the November and said:

> 'I have seen a copy of Prof. Burton's paper, thank you. My main thought was that his concerns had been largely addressed by the $23^{rd}$ September announcement.'

No they hadn't.

Incidentally, Professor John Burton was no stranger to our team. He had worked closely with David, Susie and PCG's lawyer Tony Askham as the lead economist on the Sunday trading legal cases.

## Letter to the Prime Minister

Andy White then wrote a letter to Prime Minister Tony Blair expressing PCG's concern at the lack of real consultation by Treasury ministers despite the guidelines in the Better Regulation Guide; the flawed assumptions in the Regulatory Impact Assessment; the Treasury's failure to understand the entrepreneurial spirit within the knowledge-based sector; and that, in its current form the main beneficiaries would be international IT companies, like EDS, at the cost of home-grown entrepreneurs. He concluded by suggesting self-regulation could be considered and asked the Prime Minister to ensure there was consultation in line with the approved guidelines, clear proposals are issued with a full RIA and all relevant interested parties are included in the process.

I was never convinced that Blair really understood what IR35 was all about, nor do I think he cared much. I doubt that he even read our letter. It was very much Gordon Brown's plan and Blair was probably happy to let him suffer the consequences. Besides, Gordon's other tax clangers had to be sorted out, such as giving pensioners just a 75p a week rise, putting up petrol excise when oil was rising and years later abolishing the 10p tax rate.

For my part I went to a Labour Party meeting and one of the speakers was Charlie Falconer, I decided that if Andy had done the PM then I would do his best friend. Charlie Falconer was in the House of Lords but rumour had it that he couldn't get selected as an MP. As he left the meeting I walked out with him and chatted with him for ten minutes in the lobby of the building, gave him directions to the train station and a copy of my briefing paper to read on his journey. Of course I don't know if he read it or if it had any effect but the door stepping that I had just done was being repeated up and down the country by members whenever they saw their MPs.

## Politicians and the reshuffled

With the Brownite Treasury having declared war on the IT freelance sector with IR35 and provoking lots of complaints that the Government didn't understand IT or freelancing, elsewhere in government the Blairites were keen to try and establish their trendy IT and enterprise credentials.

Tony Blair set some new broad objectives on e-government for Britain to take a lead in this field, whereas the Treasury undermined the workers who would help do that.

Andy reported to members about:

> "The appointment of an e-envoy (Alex Allan); an e-Minister (Patricia Hewitt) and the Prime Minister's continued praising of the IT sector together with his own desire to become more IT-literate, led to a flurry of letters from PCG members pointing out the irony of these moves. The PCG took onboard the advice about e-commerce and can announce you can now join and pay via our secure server using your credit card. This will allow instant access to the PCG member's area"

On hearing the news of her appointment I despatched a letter off to Patricia Hewitt's office and asked for a meeting.

It was almost a classic Blair-Brown confrontation. They conversation could have run as 'I am going to build an e-Economy' said Blair. 'Not with my help' replied Brown introducing IR35.

If we thought Labour was clueless about IR35 then the Lib Dems did little better. They try to be friends to everyone but in a BBC online interview, Lib Dem leader, Charles Kennedy, was asked about IR35 and he professed ignorance. Within minutes the forum started buzzing; several members told of the previous correspondence they had received from him supporting their stance and the briefing letters he had received on the subject. Mr Kennedy then became the target of a concerted letter writing drive reminding him of what he already knew. A Lib Dem leader caught with his 'pants down'.

## The Revenue Meeting

The PCG inclusion at the next meeting with the Inland Revenue came to pass and the PCG representatives with little notice were ushered into a special meeting about IR35. Obviously they weren't really that welcome, the Inland Revenue had been shamed into holding this meeting with contractor representatives. The chairman watched in silence as they were conveyed in. Some brief announcement was made and the discussion kicked off.

Then a red faced Inland Revenue official pushed into the meeting and whispered something into the chairman's ear. It appeared that there had been another cock-up.

So, half way through discussing new proposals the chairman suddenly suspends discussions and says that it doesn't matter because the new proposals have already been announced. Poor Kevin Miller from the PCG was mid-sentence explaining the problems with the plans. Some consultation!

The announcement was supposed to have come after the meeting not during it. The reports that I got back were that the Inland Revenue were bored with the discussions and were just doing it to go through the motions and then it seems they got fed up. I thought that at least they could have pretended to consult, but no.

The new reformed IR35 announcement was timed to pour cold water on the research done by the Adam Smith Institute and in time for the party conference season.

### PCG-for the future

I think we were a little wrong footed about this, our focus had been on the future of the PCG. Instead of being wound up at the end of the campaign, we believed that it should be retained and built up as a trade association ready to represent and fight for freelancers in the future. Andy had put up proposals to create us as a permanent body and arrangement for an online vote to agree to it or not.

He added the reason why he felt it was important that the PCG stayed together:

> "The PCG Executive and the Committee have prepared a paper for review by members which looks at the first three months and puts forward a proposal to broaden the services so that it can act as a proper Independent representative body for Contractors in the IT and engineering sector, rather than just a Lobbying body. In addition, we need to send a message to Government that we are not going to go away. The paper and Internet ballot are available on the member's site, see links at the end of this newsletter. The closing date for Votes is Friday 24th September at 1600 hours. "

As it turned out it happened just in time. The Inland Revenue had hoped to spin that the new reformed changes meant that contractors could all now go home, back to their keyboards, and leave the politics and economics to them.

A bit like at the end of the Peasants Revolt when King Edward seemingly agreed to all the demands of Wat Tyler and co. only to see the peasants return home where upon he reneged on all the promises and oversaw the executions of some 7,000. I am not sure if the Inland Revenue planned to create a Witchfinder General as well as a Paymaster General, but there could certainly have been echoes of 'villiens ye are and villiens ye remain', to 'temps you are and temps you will remain'.

98% of members voting in the ballot via the Internet agreed to turn the PCG into a representative body to look after the interests of contractors in the IT and Engineering sector.

After the vote Andy said:

> "The Group will remain focused on IR 35 issues and more detailed proposals on how the changes are to be implemented will be provided to members for consideration. "

# Chapter 8

## 23$^{rd}$ September – Revised Proposals - Son of IR35
**NEWSFLASH IR 35**

"Son of IR 35" announcement.

At a meeting yesterday afternoon with the Inland Revenue, at which Kevin Miller of the PCG was present, the Revenue officials stated that ministers had agreed that an announcement would be made as soon as possible. There would be no further discussion except into the detailed implementation of the revised proposals.

It would appear that the request of representative groups such as the PCG, the Federation of Small Businesses (FSB), The Chartered Institute of Taxation (CIOT), FRES (agency body looking after the small to medium sized agencies), ICAEW, ATIES, CBI, IOD and the Engineering Council, for consultations on these wide ranging proposals has been ignored. It also became apparent that the Inland Revenue considers that compromise proposals from groups such as the 360 Group, a firm of accountants and ATSCo, a new body representing the large agencies, are evidence that "consultation" has taken place. The compromise proposals put forward by these groups involved raising the requisite tax by contractors agreeing to pay more salary and take less dividend. They have been rejected outright by the government.

Overall summary of proposals

1. The Treasury ministers were determined to stop the avoidance of tax and NIC by means of disguised employment. They regarded it as unfair and intended to take steps to stop it.

2. Ministers had taken on board the many comments received and were taking steps to ensure that contractors could still work through their own companies if they wanted to. Hence they were dropping the certification requirement.

3. All end users/agencies could pay the contractor's company gross. It was up to the contractor's company to ensure compliance with the new rules, where applicable.

4. The tests to be applied were those already established in tax law and practice for distinguishing employment and self employment.

5. Where a contractor works for a client under conditions which equate to employment then they would be required to take their remuneration from that client in a form subject to PAYE and NIC, after deducting certain expenses.

6. These expenses would include contributions to approved pension schemes, PI premiums and expenses which were allowable under schedule E. In addition there would be an allowance, yet to be agreed, for the running costs

of the business such as meeting statutory requirements. A figure of 5% has been suggested but nothing has yet been decided.

7. After deduction of these expenses all remaining income derived from disguised employment contracts would have to be paid out as salary subject to PAYE and NIC. Compliance with this requirement would be based on tax years not accounting periods.

8. The timetable was that the report stage of the Welfare Reform and Pensions Bill would be passed on 11 October and it should get Royal Assent by late November. Detailed regulations for the NI aspects of IR35 would be out in January. The tax aspects of IR35 would be dealt with in the Finance Bill after the budget next spring year but would be retrospective to April 2000. Meanwhile the Inland Revenue would want to work with all interested parties to develop guidance on the application of the new rules.

What did it all mean? Well the large complicated salary/dividend split from the ICCG Group and other alternatives proffered to the Government were all turned down and they had come up with a new scheme, which was basically to treat all contractors as if they were self-employed and let case law status tests for self-employment determine whether they should be caught by IR35 or not. For the maintenance cost of a limited company they offered a 5% salary split.

The control and supervision test and the registration requirements that we had all feared had gone. The idea of the agencies removing tax and NI at source had gone, contracting could continue and people could continue to use their limited companies to trade with. Initially when I had heard that they had watered down their plans for IR35 from being a scheme similar to construction workers to the new one I had been pleased as they had ditched the control test and the need to be paid through the agency. But it was just like the budget statement it looked glossy and good but when you looked at the detail you realised it wasn't. It had just gone from being a totally unworkable system (they had appreciated that) to just a bad one, (which they didn't appreciate).

Of course it meant ministers could go around saying 'yes, yes' we have listened and made changes. Of course they didn't go far enough but were an improvement. Many industry groups and company representatives were soon giving themselves pats on the back and taking credit for the change. ATSCo had said that it had been a good result for *their* members.

Our lobbying of the DTI; of ministers and of MPs had paid off. It was a success and some sage voices suggested that we accepted it as such and folded up the organisation. We could disperse the funds to charity as promised. It was suggested to Andy that he could leave as a hero with his head held high[19], but Andy would

---

[19] At this point the PCG had only two shareholders – Andy and David. There was no reason why they couldn't have pocketed all the money and walked away

have none of it. As far as Andy, David, Susie and I were concerned the fight went on. The members would not have accepted anything less. When others were urging us to claim success, with some justification, we felt that the line had been drawn in the sand. We would not dilute our stance that the principle was wrong. Ironically, when the Government did finally look at abolition ten years on, the PCG did not back repeal and opted to support a compromise proposal.

Instead of trying to work out what the new proposals meant for us personally, Andy brought in an expert to do it. He hired Anne Redston from Ernst and Young; she was the Vice Chair of Chartered Institute of Taxation.

She produced a detailed report that covered the following:

- Can you pass the new test
- Hints on Contracts.
- What happens if you are caught by the new rules.
- Income and expenses
- Travel expenses
- Calculation and payment of Tax/NIC

It was published on the PCG website for members to share.

## What next?

Andy wrote to contractors and said

> "We believe this is the first comprehensive analysis of the new rules. It is written by a top tax expert and cost the PCG a thousand pounds. For members that represents 28p each. An example of how a representative group can and will reduce the compliance cost for these burdensome regulations. In addition after members have studied we will be inviting Anne Redston and other Key legal and accounting advisers to respond to questions from those attending the on-line conference."

Anne Redston remains one of the leading and respected experts in IR35.

We were less impressed with the response from other industry bodies, many of which were commercial firms who wrote to their members telling them how they alone had saved the day and had persuaded government to change its mind.

ATSCo, the body representing the large agents told the Financial Times on the 24th September that they:

> "welcomed the announcement. In my opinion it is a very good result for our members".

Who were/are its members? Agencies, not contractors.

Andy said:

> "Members also commented on the forums that some had received emails from Parity quoting the benefits of PAYE "temping". I met with David Ramsden and Kevin Miller yesterday and our view was somewhat different."

## Public Response to the reformed IR35

Andy clearly wasn't convinced by the new proposals, but if you think about it, the Treasury hardly put us in a nice place to accept them. If Dawn had called us in and sat down and said I am trying to do my best here, what do you think? Well then the initial response would have been a lot better, especially if it had looked like she would work with us, but that wasn't the case at all.

## Thursday 23$^{rd}$ September

Susie put our press release together on the premise that the Government had just been paying lip service to concerns.

### IR35 - A CONSULTATION OR A FABRICATION?
### PCG Reaction to Revenue's proposals

The Professional Contractors Group accused the Government of paying lip service to holding genuine consultation on the IR35 proposals, which will affect tens of thousands of small companies in the UK.

The Revenue's revised IR35 proposals published today (September 23) show 'astonishing naiveté' of the knowledge-based entrepreneurial sector and tip the balance in favour of large US companies at the cost of small British enterprises.

Andy White, Chairman of the PCG, said: "Inviting people to sit around a table and then tell them what the Revenue intends to do regardless of their opinions is not genuine consultation by anyone's standards. And it's certainly not consultation as spelt out in the Government's own Better Regulation Guidelines.

"The process has been a sham. There have been poor proposals; ignored letters, false promises and no genuine consultation, Gordon Brown and Dawn Primarolo have repeatedly ignored the people who will be affected by this. Now they have replaced the unworkable with the illogical.

"The consequences of their actions will be to kill the enterprise culture and the fine words about promoting enterprise and appointments of an e-czar, an e-Minister and are not going to change that.

"They have shown astonishing naiveté in dealing with a part of the economy that generates added value the size of a small country. The only winners in this are the large foreign companies who compete with our members and the losers are the genuine British entrepreneurs who have set up their own businesses. The American multi-nationals will be laughing all the way to the bank as the British Government destroys their home-grown competition.

"The irony is that at the end of the day, the proposals are unlikely to generate a penny extra tax and are more likely to reduce overall tax revenue."

After repeated requests, the PCG was invited to a meeting at the Revenue yesterday (September 22) as part of the so-called consultation process. At the meeting they were told by Revenue officials that Treasury Ministers had already reached a decision and an announcement was imminent.

The proposals have replaced the 'direction and control test' with existing tests for self-employment which do not take into account the actual workings of the knowledge-based sector. They also deprive entrepreneurs of the ability to retain profits to grow their businesses and are a body blow to enterprise culture.

The PCG has set up an on-line conference for its 3,500 members to comment on the Government proposals.

The Adam Smith Institute is publishing a report 'Inflexible Friend' by Professor John Burton this week which analyses the impact of the Revenue proposals. Despite requests to await its publication, it would appear the Government has come to its decision before seeing the evidence contained in it.

# Chapter 9

## IR35 Speech to the Labour Party Conference

## 27th September

Serendipity is a great thing. It just so happened that in 1999 I had been selected by my local Labour Party to be their constituency party delegate for the annual conference. I'd tried to be the delegate in 1997, but someone else won the vote (yes, we voted for conference delegate) and then in 1998 it had to be a female delegate. So come 1999 it was my chance and off I went. This was still the early days of New Labour and conference still had some meaning, one thing you were able to do as delegate was to have the chance to take along your own resolution and put it to conference, which is what I did. Of course I persuaded my constituency party to do one on IR35. Now it is pretty tricky to describe IR35 to someone with no understanding of the tax system. Most Labour members were ex-teachers and public sector workers but there were a few of us with an interest in it. Back at the PCG we had realized that it made sense to wrap IR35 in clothes of the knowledge based economy. It allowed us to talk about contracting in a positive light, as something new, cool and trendy. Of course Labour was all for being new, cool and trendy (remember cool Britannia?). So I wrote a resolution on the knowledge based economy which included a few damning references to IR35 as not being the right way to go about it.

I didn't really understand how the resolution stuff worked at conference. Given the fact that most delegates are newbies to the conference it makes it easy for the party staff to run rings around them and get what they want, but I had the resolution and at least I could flourish it where necessary. Kerry McCarthy (now a Labour MP for Bristol) gave me some advice but largely it was a case of play it by ear.

Half in hope I had written a speech before I had left for conference, standing in front of my tape recorder I had it timed down to the second. You only had three minutes and if you ran over they'd boot you off. I'd been to a conference delegates training session, so in fact I should withdraw some of my remarks about it all being a stitch up. They had given us tips on public speaking and we'd even done some practice ones. They gave advice in what to wear – something distinctive – that would allow the chair to pick you out of the crowd. For women red wasn't the best option as all the women wore red jackets.

'You in the red jacket, no, no... next to, no... no, no the next one'.

Women were told to wear a distinctive scarf or similar.

Monday was the day of the economy debate, which is fine except I'd arrived at conference on the Sunday and had bumped into my best friend from school who was there as a journalist for the Mail on Sunday. We gate crashed a few parties and had some good nibbles at the Independent party where we saw Peter Mandelson and Janet Street Porter. I'd seen Tony Blair at the Eastern Region bash, he came in and gave a quick private speech, cracked a few jokes, 'apparently, this is going to be my hardest conference ever… since the last one'. He moved effortlessly through the room in a way that he was to shake a lot of hands but avoid actually talking to anyone. This of course was when he was popular. I got to bed late after a lot of drinks but managed to force myself up in the morning and down to the conference hall.

The fringe events, particularly the social ones (and there are many) are compulsory for journalists and lobbyists who rub shoulders with the politicians, while the corporate lot get to show their hospitality and hopefully, impress a few MPs or ministers en-route. Susie and David were veteran conference goers from their Sunday trading lobbying. They were on a mission to 'work the rooms', but I had my own mission.

The next morning I picked up the conference newspaper, it had a big picture of Gordon on the cover with the bold headline 'Trusted on the economy'.

The economy debate began, Gordon Brown came in and a gave a rousing speech about how great everything was with a few hidden notes about how he should really be in charge. We had been told at the training session the floor would then be open to speakers. It was, sort of, except then the next two speakers were trade union leaders. Were they really chancing it, just like the rest of us?

A few speakers from the floor were picked and it wasn't looking good for me, so I left my seat mid-way back in the hall and slipped passed the security and went to the front rows of the conference usually reserved for the trade union barons and their supporters.

'Time for one more speaker', said Margaret McDonagh the chair for this session and there I was at the front with my jacket off standing with my new bright red shirt jumping up and down shouting 'pick me, pick me!'.

Then to my utter amazement she did just that. I pulled my jacket back on and climbed the steps. Seconds later the green light in front of me came on and I was on.

Out there in front of me I knew there were about 3,000 people plus thousands at home and hopefully somewhere Andy and Susie would be watching too.

'Conference, Philip Ross, delegate from Mid Bedfordshire CLP…'

I had nodded to Gordon as I had climbed the steps and had a faint disinterested smile in return but over the next three minutes I would wipe that smile from his face and replace it with some red angry cheeks and lots of head shaking as I explained how IR35 was contrary to what we believed in and could close down thousands of companies. I urged conference to support me in asking the Government to think again. This is some of what I said:

> '[IR35] fails to understand that knowledge and skills are commodities that are traded today just as manufactured goods have been traded in the past".
>
> "For example these plans imply that a small company that invests in a van is a genuine business. But one that invests in knowledge is a disguised employee! This can't be right."
>
> "Under these rules, small companies will NOT be able to retain profits to grow their business. Small companies will NOT be able to claim the same expenses as their larger competitors"
>
> "These plans betray the principle, ' that the Workers should have the Right to reap the fruits of their own labour by hand or by brain'. These plans imply that I cannot work for myself"

When it was over I descended from the platform and waved to Gordon who was now looking not disinterested but absolutely furious.

The wave disconcerted him because he started to wave back and then stopped himself. I walked through the hall towards the back as the morning's session was closed by the chairman. It had been a good speech though, given that most people didn't understand what IR35 was I had a good reception from people who smiled and nodded at me. Basically I'd had a go and people respected that. This is the Labour Party where it is almost de rigour to be critical. You need to do it to prove your credentials. It has its pluses and minuses and is of course what kept them out of office for 18 years.

As I marched down the hall I realised that my jacket collar was creased. In my rush to get onto the stage I had just yanked my jacket on with the result that the collar was twisted. Hence over the new few hours not only would I be asking people what they thought of the speech but also if they noticed the thing with the jacket, which some would be swift to point it out. I point it out because I was as self-conscious about the jacket as I was proud of the speech and a little reticent about telling my mother about my triumph on the TV as she would be sure to spot the jacket. Indeed my brother said 'It was a good speech but your jacket wasn't on properly'.

At the back of the hall I bumped into the delegate from Brighton Pavilion CLP[20]; she congratulated me on the speech and didn't mention anything about the jacket.

---

[20] CLP – Constituency Labour Party

Her speech had preceded mine and had been a broadside against PFI and PPP projects. She said that they would cost the taxpayers millions and probably won't work and cited a new project that was being undertaken on the London Underground. You could see all the suits from the Ministry shaking their heads and suggesting that she didn't know what she was talking about, 'what did a girl from Brighton know about economics? It was far too complicated, etc'. As with IR35 the girl from Brighton was absolutely right. The PFI scheme announced with Metronet and others not only cost the tax payers millions but collapsed as costly failures.[21]

As we left the secure part of the hall the media scrum descended upon us, or more so on her, but I was there and played my part.

'Wait.. wait... wait', I said, 'let's do this properly. We are happy to answer questions on both the IR35 and PFI fiasco's,'

'Tell us your name and paper and then we will do what we can'

I then chaired an impromptu press conference accompanied with admiring looks from the Brighton delegate. Sadly every question that came in from the Mail, Express and Telegraph was on PFI. They were trying to get her to say something more critical of Gordon Brown. I whispered a caution to her on this and we kept our criticism to the policy. 'It is reheated Tory policy; we should be doing it properly'. I'd add on to the end of each question a note about IR35:

'don't forget IR35, it could close 66,000 businesses'

'IR what mate?'

'35, IR35...'

'Never heard of it....love, turn give us a smile'

The snappers went to work on the attractive girl from Brighton and successfully kept both my image and comments out of the frame, but I had done it, an IT contractor from Bedfordshire had stood up in front of the chancellor and taken him to task on his economic policy - or at least, one part of it - and had the audacity to do it publicly and in the heart of the party conference. The girl from Brighton might have received the media attention, but my speech had been picked up in other quarters and was not well-received. I was on the radar as I was about to discover.

Outside the hall I bumped into the boss of IT at the Labour Party, Roger Hough.

'Good speech, Philip', he said, 'but did you know your collar was up...'

---

[21] http://www.tfl.gov.uk/corporate/modesoftransport/londonunderground/management/5500.aspx

I found Susie and Andy who didn't mention the collar as presumably they had been listening to the words. Susie was really pleased, Andy couldn't believe it. They knew I had written a speech but couldn't actually believe that I had delivered it.

'How did you manage to get up there?'

I didn't really know - just sheer audacity, the same audacity that had got me in to see the Minister Michael Wills and the very same audacity that had built and created the PCG. I was in good company being with Susie and Andy.

## Knowledge Based Economy

It was only Monday but we had manage to achieve our objective of raising IR35 at the Labour Conference and now I could spent the rest of week focusing on some more generic left-wing clauses closer to my Labour party heart, though I should add of course that I had the full backing of my constituency party to pursue the IR35 issue. I felt mandated and successful.

Andy got some coffees in and then I chatted with him and Susie. Susie began fielding calls on her mobile. Some to journalists others from media friends who were asking if that was her guy, 'yes it was', she beamed.

I was in the process of reliving the moment and punching the air demonstrating a few metaphorical body blows that I dreamt I may have inflicted when suddenly a strangers voice cut through the air...

'Philip Ross? Philip Ross?'

'Errrr.... Yes' I said lowering my arms and looking up.

Three party apparatchiks stood there with their party passes on, one of whom I vaguely recognised.

My God, they've come for me, I am in trouble. I felt that I had been caught throwing stones at the windows and was about to be sent to the headmasters study.

But no, fortunately, or unfortunately, I was either not that important or the Labour Party wasn't that organised.

Had I submitted a motion on the knowledge based economy? Yes.

I needed to go to a compositing session with a number of other delegates to create a motion for debate on Wednesday. Could I go to Room XYZ at 6:00pm? Yes, ok.

## Compositing

To get a motion debated at the Labour Party conference isn't easy. There are few opportunities for it and allegedly even less so under New Labour. The party machine was terrified of returning to the conferences of the 1980's. The Conference in 1980 had been more a show trial against the defeated Labour

Government with delegate after delegate mounting the platform to say how they had been betrayed and let down.

New Labour had introduced a new consultation process with constituency parties called 'Partnership into Power' to ensure this never happened again. Workshops and meetings were held by local parties to discuss issues around health, education, business and industry (mainly industry), foreign policy, transport, etc. From these issues for debate at conference were selected, but there remained a slim chance to debate something fresh as a 'contemporary issue', so I submitted a motion on IR35 and the knowledge economy as a contemporary issue. It was titled 'Knowledge Economy at Serious Risk'.

To get it debated it needed to be accepted as a 'contemporary issue'. I managed to do that. Constituency delegates would then vote on which contemporary motion would be debated.

So I created a flyer with both the motion text on it and a leading letter from me and at all the early reception drink parties I went to I asked people to support it. It was good actually because it gave me a reason to go up and talk to everyone.

The motion slammed IR35 and called for a genuine consultation. It wouldn't survive the composite meeting in tact (and I am embarrassed to say 10 years on I don't have the composite text but this is what we started with…)

"A knowledge based economy is a key issue for Labour given our manifesto commitment to build a high wage, high technology Britain. The phrase 'people are our greatest assets' is becoming a reality, the information revolution is already underway.

"The knowledge based economy is booming in Britain thanks largely to the growing number of small businesses in IT and engineering that sell their skills and knowledge. Such entrepreneurs pollinate other businesses with knowledge, ideas and experience; they are the chrysalises of the new knowledge-based economy. But this small business revolution is now at risk and the future is shifting towards big business.

"Plans submitted by the Treasury in document IR35, to tackle 'disguised employment' will inadvertently affect these new knowledge-based companies. These plans threaten to remove their right to trade as legitimate liability companies and will confine small business development and destroy their competitiveness, leaving the market unfairly balanced in favour of larger companies.

"We reaffirm that 'to give the workers by hand or by brain the full fruits of their labour' remains a priority for the party as we enter the information age.

Conference calls upon the party to reconsider these plans and put them out to genuine consultation so that they won't affect our fledgling knowledge-based economy. Conference wants to see a dynamic, innovative future where knowledge and skills belong to the community and the individual".

Now you have to admit that it is pretty good and reading it now after all these years I am very proud of it. In it is the case for using contractors, the case for small firms and freelancing as being a model that should belong to Labour. I still believe that Labour should be the party of small business.

I had cunningly criticised the Treasury, not the party of government as a whole which is an astute political line to follow as you are focusing your opposition clearly to one policy and issue. Over the years I think the PCG had trouble with this and Labour didn't really help them by introducing fast track visas and other changes, but I'd always felt that the miners' strike went wrong when Scargill moved from attacking mining policy and called it a strike to bring down Thatcher.

Anyway I don't think anyone had really read my motion, perhaps they had just looked at the title and thought 'knowledge economy', yes that's trendy, we want some of that.

I went to the composite meeting, there had been another delegate who had done a knowledge economy motion but they hadn't turned up. However, the AEEU trade union had also done one. Maybe I had been able to raise a few votes on the topic but it was now clear that Ken Jackson, President of the AEEU, had dropped his union's votes in for it, which no doubt counted for a few million.

I couldn't quite help but think that this was the Labour 'party' conference, not the union conference and they had theirs with the TUC a few weeks before, but they would insist on trying to dominate this one too.

The union delegate was a good guy. It was Tom Watson, who would later become an MP and help to bring down the News of the World. We got on well, it was clear that he was used to doing these every year, it was my first time and I didn't understand the rules or what to do. The party apparatchiks who were there supervising presented me with a pre-prepared composite motion, which was pretty much the motion that the AEEU had written. They said if I could sign that then we could all leave and go to the bar.

I realised that the only card I had to play was not to sign.

'No thanks', I said' I'm not signing that, where has all my stuff gone?'

A debate ensued and the longer it went on the better I got at understanding the rules. I realised that the contemporary motion had been agreed ages ago between the party and the AEEU. By chance I had stepped on the grass and was now an unexpected and inconvenient part of it. A semblance of democracy existed still in the party and I could exploit that.

'I want to speak. I want more text in there about the importance of small business. I want IR35 included'

They wouldn't go for this and then showed they had done their homework when they said I had spoken on that this morning.

'I want to see the Minister, Dawn Primarolo, about IR35.'

They suggested I wrote to her.

'You are having a laugh. We're all going to be here ages….I want you to get me a meeting'.

'Why do you need us to do it?'

'Because those are my terms…'

They went off and huddled, Tom gave me a nod while they were talking and congratulated me on my negotiation skills.

They came back…. 'OK, she will meet with you'

'When?'

'Tomorrow.'

'She has a meeting on tax credits in the morning, after that?' I said

'Yes, yes' they said.

'How do you know?'

'Because we are telling you she will'

I didn't believe them.

'How do you know she will meet me?'

'She just will, trust us'

I lifted up the pen and went to sign and then held back and said,

'and I want to second the motion from the platform'

'For f*** sake…'

'?'

'Ok then'

'and I can say whatever I want….'

'yes you can say whatever you want, now sign…'

So I signed the motion and it went onto the order papers for Wednesday's proceedings. I don't think anyone ever read or referred to it again, but I had a second shot at speaking at conference and this time I wouldn't let my jacket be creased.

## Meeting with Dawn Primarolo

The words Party Conference can be rearrange to read 'conference party'. The whole thing is a bit of a beer and party fest and despite staying up late celebrating my conference speech the following morning I found myself at the conference building at a 'breakfast' meeting on tax credits which was to be hosted by the Paymaster General, Dawn Primarolo.

As I was struggling with the coffee pot and my hangover wondering if I really would get to see Dawn I suddenly heard an angry voice behind me saying, 'How dare you!' Sensing that some commotion was taking place I turned to look only to discover that the voice was being directed at me.

It was Dawn Primarolo.

'How dare you! How dare you stand up on the stage and criticise the Government!'

There was clear rage and anger in her eyes. Ah, someone had heard my speech.

'Absolutely dis....'

'What!!!' I shrieked in return.

I haven't had time to think this through at all, but I am not having it, I will not be spoken to like this.

'How dare you...'I said raising my arm at her raised fist

'How dare you speak to me like that, I have every right....'

'NO you do not'

'Yes I bloody well do. I am mandated', I said, as if it really mattered, 'I am mandated and delegated to speak on these issues by my constituency party'.

I thought this was an important thing to say besides I had been principled enough to go and get the mandate as I thought it was the right thing to do. Dawn presumably had thought I had been just talking off my own bat.

I had the advantage now and pressed it...

'How dare you tell me what I can say? This is our conference, a conference for delegates not ministers, our chance to have a say....'

This is absolutely what they had told us at the pre-conference training day.

'She is the minister...' said a voice from the side rushing to her defence; it was her researcher or special advisor.

'I don't care who she is....'

'I wrote to you...' said Dawn

'Yes you did'

'... a nice letter...'

'...it was'

'We have reformed the proposals...'

'...but not enough...'

>> 'Minister we need to start...' she was tugged away.

'Let's talk afterwards' I offered

'I'm not talking to you' was the retort.

I caught her assistant before she left and told her of yesterday's agreement; it appeared that she knew about it, which amazed me. 'That' I said 'was not the meeting'.

'I'll see what I can do',

What followed was a presentation by Dawn on the new Working Families Tax Credits plan; it seemed to be an idea that had come across from the US Democrats and Bill Clinton. I asked a question on a point of interest and had a glaring look from Dawn, who now had to be nice to me in front of the rest of the audience.

The meeting ended and the audience departed while I remained there smiling and waiting and Dawn busied herself tidying up and avoiding eye contact. I did make eye contact with her assistant who went over to Dawn and whispered something to her.

'WHAT!'

Dawn glanced at me and her assistant assured her that this was correct.

I took this as my cue to speak so I got up and walked over.

'I am sorry we got off to a bad start, I just want to help'

'Yes' she said, accepting my olive branch, 'but I can't see why you are helping these Tories...'

'They are not all Tories' I said, 'at our CLP there were two other people directly affected by the tax.'

I had her attention.

'Let me tell you where it puts me', I continued, 'they [the contractors] criticise me because they think I am on Labour's side, you think I am on the Tories' side, the side I am on is that of the contractor who pays his fair share of tax. I am stuck in the middle and am getting shot at by both sides, it is not a nice place to be but I am not budging'

'I appreciate that' she said, 'but we have reformed the tax, we have listened and changed it and given you what you wanted, what's the problem now?' she stormed.

'You have reformed it, true, it is better but it is not us contractors you listened to, the PCG haven't met you formally, but we know you had all those secret meetings with others'

'No, we did meet with the contractor representatives too'

'Agencies aren't contractors' representatives; it is like saying that the CBI represents all workers...'

'No' she insisted, 'contractor groups were there...'

'We would like to meet with you directly'

She refused that request.

'Look' I said, 'I have spent years pounding pavements and knocking on doors to get Labour elected, so I haven't come here to score political points or to undermine the Government I just want you to get it right'

'Ok.... But you still haven't told me what's wrong with the new changes...'

'...well they are based on case law...'

'...what's wrong with that?'

'...let me finished... the problem is that case law is out of date...'

'How so?'

'Basically you are relying on Schedule D[22] case law for IT work, but because IT work hasn't been subjected to case law there is none to act as a precedent. '

'I don't think that is true, if you can't stand as self-employed what are you?'

'People can't go as self-employed because they source work through agencies, but as far as the tests go, that is what I have been told... if you want to seriously engage with it why don't I send you proof of that'

'Send what?'

---

[22] Schedule D – rules that define self-employment, as opposed to Schedule E which are rules covering employees

'I could send you some case studies that show that the Schedule D stuff doesn't work'

'Ok do that'

I thanked her and complimented her on the new tax credits system and we parted on cordial terms. I felt that I'd held my ground and in doing so gained some respect from her. Now we knew each other and of course that made it harder for me to stomach anything personal against Dawn. Indeed I would intervene on the PCG forums and demand that people withdraw anything personal against her, I wasn't prepared to stand for it and most people agreed and withdrew stuff. Others took it as evidence that I was too pro-Labour, but I don't like personal politics.

That was my response to the meeting with her, I don't know what hers was except that a couple of days after returning from conference I got a letter from the Inland Revenue telling me that my company was under a compliance investigation for national insurance payments. I hope that this was a coincidence.[23]

We put together a number of case studies and sent them to Dawn with explanations as to why they didn't work. In the November we would have an exchange of letters.

## Mail on Sunday

The following day I met up with a journalist friend and managed to convince him that IR35 was an issue of note. Adam was my oldest and best friend from school. I introduced him to David Ramsden and told him also about the think tank report. Adam went to work on it and uncovered a story where Peter Mandelson was pouring scorn on Gordon Brown over the issue. He wrote a piece for the Mail on Sunday that portrayed Mandy pouring a bucket full of figures over Gordon Brown's head. Of course the real story here was the enmity between Brown and Mandelson, not IR35 per se.

Adam also followed me to a little side room off the conference hall which was full of computers and delegates writing their speeches. I explained to him that this was where you wrote your speeches and that party staff were on hand to help and you could also rehearse them as well as get tips and tricks. There was absolutely no censorship, just help. Adam may be my best friend and I have known him since we both were 13, his parents are among the people who really inspired me, however, when we were 17 and cycling in France my bike had a puncture and he left me to walk home alone in the pitch black through rural France for three hours, so I knew I couldn't trust him. While I got him to write a good piece on IR35 he also wrote a piece about this office with a suggestion that speeches were censored.

---

[23] I got a relatively clean bill of health from them in the end, mainly because I had multiple clients and paid myself the same salary as I had when I was employed. In the end I paid some extra tax as it was cheaper than taking time off to sort it out.

They used it as a centre page spread in the Mail on Sunday. I wasn't too pleased about it and neither was Adam because in the end the editor took the by-line for himself.

Jumping ahead a little bit - on the Wednesday night at the conference I went to meet Adam at the Bath Hotel. Drinking down in the bar as the evening stretched on it became a who's who of British media as I drifted in and out of conversation with the entire aristocracy of the British political media and their editors. Steve Bell, Rebecca Wade, Nick Cohen, Grant from Eastenders, David Yelland, Charlie Whelan and others besides. Steve Bell was the best and most entertaining. It was a heavy night and in the morning I caught up with Adam again briefly, he was much the worse for wear and it would be some years before he fully remembered the evening, which was just as well since after he had gone to bed I had charged many drinks to his room bill.

## Knowledge Based Economy Debate

There isn't that much to say here. I had taken a shot at the Government on the Monday, spoke to the minister on the Tuesday and attempted to build some bridges. Now on the Wednesday did I need to have another go at the Government about IR35? Perhaps not, at least that was my decision at the time so I wrote a speech that praised contracting and freelancing and highlighted its importance to the economy and then had a few small pops about IR35.

I seconded the motion on the Knowledge Economy that Ken Jackson, the head of the AEEU, had proposed. Somehow he managed to link the knowledge based economy to manufacturing and old industrial jobs, whereas I linked it to new sunrise jobs and the New Labour Government thought it had something to do with new .COM businesses. After I had spoken, a business 'entrepreneur' came on stage and showed a flashy film about websites and how fast moving and flashy the future would be. This entertainment had been the whole reason behind the debate to show Labour was ready for the 21$^{st}$ century; my part had been just filler.

My speech had gone well, the only problem I had was that Ken Jackson had an auto-cue, which meant that somehow words were projected into the air in front of me, invisible to the audience but the Labour party staff had forgot to turn it off and it was a bit of a distraction for me. If I was doing the speech now I would simply say to the conference as a whole, 'can you turn off this auto-cue', but then I was too worried to do that. It is not easy speaking in front of thousands of people.

For the last night of conference we went to a party hosted by the East of England region, my region. Standing at the bar with friends I bump into someone and turned around to apologise and make conversation. Two minutes later her friend came over to join us; it was Dawn Primarolo, my new friend.

'I nearly had another go about IR35 today,' I said

'I couldn't believe it when I saw you mount the platform, I thought oh no not again!'

'It was ok though wasn't it? Not too bad'

'It was ok' she said.

We chatted a bit about the conference in general and the band that was playing. The band came from Bristol where Dawn was an MP. Kerry McCarthy, who was with me, said 'have you been talking about your tax thing'. 'Yes'. In one of those strange coincidences Kerry became Dawn's neighbouring MP in Bristol in 2005.

## Other Meetings

David Ramsden had been busy at the Labour Conference too. Though a known Conservative himself he was still respected by the Labour hierarchy, mainly because he never abandoned talking to them during Thatcher's time. He told me that Neil Kinnock had said to him that when back in power 'we will remember our friends'.

I had briefed James Purnell (a later minister) who was then Blair's researcher on the knowledge economy. He didn't get IR35 or want to get it though. David also got to see Lord McIntosh and reported that he was generally annoyed that we had objected to the concessions while everyone else supported them and thought that the Government had gone further than was necessary.

## Conservative Party Conference

I had enjoyed conference and it had been an incredibly packed week with the think tank report, the reformed IR35 proposals and then my conference speeches followed by some celebratory drinking.

Susie, Andy and David had travelled to the Tory conference, they asked me to go too but I respectfully declined. I knew that as a lobbyist you had to do all the parties, but to me it felt like going to Mordor.[24] Besides, as a contractor I needed to return and start earning some money again.

The Tories were sympathetic to the PCG and what a disaster IR35 would be, or rather here was one issue that could unite them when they were split on everything and still engaged in lots of acrimonious in-fighting. Besides, up until this point Blair had proved to be Mr Telflon, nothing seemed to stick to him and anything that came close was simply knocked off by just blaming the Tories.

David Ramsden was able to 'doorstep' a number of Conservative MPs and shadow cabinet members to get the point across. William Hague (then their leader) knew all about it and said that it was an 'ill thought out piece of legislation'. Ken Clarke said his view was that you are either self-employed or you are not, which was true but did the definitions of self-employment work for knowledge based workers?

---

[24] The home of the baddy Sauron in Lord of the Rings

Francis Maude, who was then Shadow Chancellor, said in his conference speech –

> 'And he's (Brown) designing a new tax on entrepreneurs too. It'll cost £500m, put thousands out of business and send thousands more overseas. That's his philosophy........Britain needs these entrepreneurs, if we are to lead the world in the New Economy'

This was all good stuff. Quentin Davies, Dawn's opposite number for the Tories, was also briefed. In 2007 he defected to Labour, although that didn't seem to do us any good.

## The BBC and IR35

To the BBC IR35 was some complicated story, the real story for conference must be education or transport or health, surely?

They put up a summary story on their website about the Labour Conference and what had happened. They invited comments and received more on IR35 than anything else, but still they refused to run it as a story and much to my annoyance didn't report my conference speech.

A friend at the BBC later told me that they hated it whenever they put up a story about technology as they would be flamed on IR35, but the BBC bosses[25] (who had been tax avoiders with their own personal service companies) still wouldn't run it as a proper story. This is what posters said:

Gordon Brown's claims to be supportive of enterprise, small business, technology and research are simply not compatible with the recently confirmed tax changes of IR35.

I run a small business offering consultancy in clinical research in the pharmaceutical industry. Under IR35, from next April my income will fall by 30%. I will be forced to close my business and re-enter the crowded employment market.

Many other businesses, especially in the research and technology sectors, will be similarly affected. These punitive measures will destroy the livelihoods of many thousands of entrepreneurs.

Why is the government not listening to us, and how can their actions be compatible with their claims? *Ruth xxxxxx, Nottingham*

Question:

When is a business not a business?

Answer:

a) When it is in arguably the fastest growing industry sector (IT)

---

[25] John Birt worked for the BBC through a personal service company

b) When the entrepreneurs are those who risked their 'comfortable' permanent jobs for the relative insecurity of running their own enterprise - and have made a huge success of it!

c) When these risk takers are seen by the Inland Revenue as 'disguised employees' and supposedly 'evade' (or is it avoid?) tax.

d) When you (Government) can be influenced that such a small organisation can be a threat to a much larger consultancy company who can then be exempt from the stifling rules applied to their smaller competitors.

The Prime Minister seems happy to embrace the 'E-world' of the 21st Century, whilst his Chancellor and Ministers seem intent on alienating the creative talent that could put Britain at the forefront of the next Industrial Revolution.

What on earth is going on? Is this the reality behind New Labour - for the many and not the few?

PS - Maybe it should be pointed out that the minister responsible for this proposal was a poll tax defaulter in 1991!

Maybe she could send us all some tips on tax avoidance! *Paul, London*

When I helped them into power at the last election, I was impressed at New Labour's commitment to potentially controversial & unpopular legislation in the interests of giving the consumer and small business a fairer deal.

Now, as a victim of their IR35 steamroller, I find myself deeply concerned at New Labour's willingness to discretely bypass the democratic process to put expedience before fairness. Small businesses have been effectively eliminated from any consultative process for IR35 by evasive and uncooperative contact with the Inland Revenue.

We are left with an IR35 implementation that will bias knowledge-based sectors towards large foreign corporations at the expense of our home-grown small businesses, thus slashing profits. Ironically, IR35 also prevents those small businesses from using more than a small fraction of their profits to expand. The rest must be processed as salary, with income tax and national insurance deducted at source.

I fear that as New Labour hones its stealth skills, this may just be the tip of the iceberg. *Tim xxxx, Barnsley*

The Treasury and the Inland Revenue claim that the driving force of the so-called IR35 regulations for personal service companies is fairness. What is fair about making all my business's income subject to PAYE after expenses when large American consultancies are exempt? These measures will drive members of the fledgling knowledge based economy overseas. *Douglas xxxx, Berkshire*

Labour promises to make the UK a world leader in E-commerce and the Internet.

IR35 (Inland Revenue's tax avoidance through personal service companies press release) means that small consultancy firms that are usually involved at many stages of Internet related development (we need to be - our skills are very rare in a corporation) will be unable to compete with the large IT consultancies. Nearly all Internet companies have started small, and grown. We could be about to prevent one of the most important steps in forming a successful Internet company - the one-man/woman consultancy.

Large consultancies whose workers are not shareholders will be able to retain any net profits they make. Smaller consultancies (like mine) will only be able to retain 5% of profit from IR35 related income; the rest must be paid to the consultant as salary. I and many of my colleagues are not in this just for personal gain, I want my companies to be successful and enable my staff and myself to retire early! How do I pay my other staff, set aside capital for bad cash-flow months and start up new businesses without any bank loans when I only have 5% of my profits to reinvest into my company?

New Labour needs to see that we must promote our (rare) Internet skills, keep them here and make the UK a truly "wired" country. Not force them abroad to tax friendly competitors, where we can compete on more equal terms.

I will be part of the new "geek-leak" if this legislation becomes law - taking my corporation tax, VAT, NIC and income tax with me. *Andy xxxx, Bristol*

The government promise full consultation on a wide range of issues, including fox hunting, the transport industry, Europe, Sterling, IR35, to name but a few.

But, after promising this consultation, they then proceed to steamroller their flawed views into law without ANY of the promised consultation.

When will this government cease their undemocratic behaviour, and actually find out what the people REALLY want? *Adrian xxxx, London/Liverpool*

How can Tony Blair say that he supports small businesses and entrepreneurs when his government brings in legislation (IR35) which makes us uncompetitive with the rest of Europe?

Perhaps what he really means is the he supports small businesses and entrepreneurs from outside of the UK. New Labour bangs another nail in the coffin of British business. *Andrew xxx, Portsmouth*

When this government came into power, Tony Blair promised that a Regulatory Impact Analysis would be carried out for all legislation. Why was this not done for the forthcoming IR35 legislation? *Tim xxxx, Swindon*

# Chapter 10

## Preparing for the big battle

After the conference season and with the new reformed proposals on the table, we tried to make sense of it all, but we weren't the only ones.

The new e-Minister Patricia Hewitt, who I had already had some email correspondence with, said that she 'welcomed' the Treasury's redrafting of IR35 which gave contractors concessions including a tax exemption on five per cent of their income. (I had to email her to put her right on that). Computing newspaper reported that she told the press.

"I shall be looking at it in detail, and have no doubt the IT industry will make representations," she said, having earlier told the audience of a Labour conference fringe meeting that she welcomed all comments to her email address. However, the PCG said about 20 of its members have tried emailing the minister at least once regarding IR35 - and none has yet received so much as an acknowledgement[26]

Andy wrote to members to keep them informed of developments:

> "PCG attended all the political conferences which concluded with the Tories in Blackpool this week.
>
> The main objectives were to raise awareness of the issue, dispel the myths, rally support for the forthcoming legislative debates, explain the damage to the knowledge-based sector and the UK's ability to compete internationally and identify and educate supporters and opponents. The detailed messages we put through were the lack of proper consultation, which led to a lack of understanding of the sector, which led to a proposal which tries to use tests which have never been applied to this sector. We are consequently left in a black hole.
>
> In summary, the Labour Party is convinced it has gone far enough (in some cases, there is a belief that the Revenue has gone too far in its 'concessions'). There is also a feeling that 'if you can't pass the self-employment tests, the point is proved that you aren't really self-employed'.
>
> Despite letters, briefings and meetings, there is reluctance within Government and backbench Labour MPs to understand the detail of the specific problems, particularly as many other organisations are telling them they've got it right.
>
> This combination of arrogance which comes with a huge majority and ignorance which comes from listening only to people who say what they want to hear means realistically that there is little support within Government."

As for the Tories he said

---

[26] Read more: http://www.computing.co.uk/ctg/news/1817626/opposition-leader-set-help-contractors-ir35-battle#ixzz1fxAIoqZT

> "The Conservatives, on the other hand, are significantly on-side. They generally understand the situation and are prepared to oppose it.
>
> The Conservatives will use us for political capital. It is in their interests to criticise a Government policy which taxes entrepreneurs in order to show that that Government doesn't understand business.
>
> Labour will therefore take a counter political view and accuse the Conservatives of being the party which supports 'tax evaders' as the genuinely self-employed can pass the test.
>
> Once political battle-lines have been drawn the Government will not back down and with a majority of nearly 200 doesn't need to. Some within the Labour party however will ask questions why a supposedly genuine Consultation exercise has resulted in such negative fall-out and the provision of political capital to the opposition parties."

Andy's analysis would prove correct that 'Once political battle-lines have been drawn the Government will not back down'. IR35 became not just a PCG issue but a political issue too. When we campaigned on fast track visas this was one of the lessons that we'd learnt and applied it successfully in that campaign.

I'd seen the film Clockers with Harvey Kietel about a ghetto in the US and the key phrase he made in the film to the young criminals was 'we play you, you don't play us'. I took this up as a motto and put forward the risk that the Tories would try to play us while we need to be sure that we played them.

This was, generally speaking, a losing battle. Everyone hated Labour now and wanted to help the Tories and I couldn't blame them, but the advantage of having me as a Labour supporting member was that I could provide a different perspective to things. We had to try and keep in with the Government and not become an off-shoot of the Tory party.[27]

## A new Regulatory Impact Assessment (RIA)

In opposition, Tony Blair promised that for each new piece of legislation introduced they would carry out an impact assessment or as it became known a 'regulatory impact assessment' (RIA), basically a compulsory assessment. Its aim was to provide a detailed and systematic appraisal of the potential impacts of a new regulation in order to assess whether the regulation is likely to achieve the desired objectives. To put it more simply; what was it trying to do, would it work and at what cost?

For IR35 the plan was to raise more tax, the impact they thought was that people would just pay it. Of course they didn't think it was a proper piece of legislation; to

---

[27] In 2011 I wrote an article for Shout99 and Progress damning the PCG for being too close to the Tories. They had failed to call for the abolition of IR35 at the very moment the Tories were ready to consider it. They had become too close politically.

them it was just some additional plumbing of the tax system except that it was supposed to raise £900m (a claim Labour later made)[28], surely a huge piece of tax legislation?

IR35 was either so big or so obscure or unimportant that they forgot to do an RIA on it, then they rushed one out stating that some 66,000 businesses would close. The PCG and Susie had a good laugh with this as did I raising it at the Labour Conference (to gasps from the audience).

Eventually they realised that the 'back of a fag-packet' RIA that they had hastily produced was no good and not even the famed Westminster spin machine could defend it, so they dropped it and released a new one.

This new version was still significantly flawed but this time it made no attempt to put a figure on the number of companies that would close and suggested it would be in the region of 25 to 75 per cent.

Kevin Miller managed to review the RIA and prepare an initial briefing paper.

## Situation Update

As we entered the first week of October Andy wrote to contractors outlining where he felt we were.

**Our Current position**

We have secured three major advances over the original proposals.
1). The removal of the requirement for Registration. Registration was being actively lobbied for by the larger agents (ATSCo). It would have forced Contractors to be paid net of PAYE and NIC whilst leaving the agent free to receive their income Gross.
2). The Contractor will be responsible for NICs and PAYE. This will remove the current obstacle for new contracts, direct with end users.
3). The change from the test of supervision, direction and Control to the wider self employment tests (Schedule D) allows more PCG members to demonstrate they are genuine businesses.

A major concern remains however. We have been prevented from working as self-employed for over 20 years (due to Agency legislation). As a result the Schedule D rules that have evolved through case law have therefore not taken account of the knowledge-based sector. This could result in a 5-year vacuum as case law is developed, during which time many PCG members will be forced out of business and the UK will lose its lead in this key sector. Our task is now to concentrate on a simple, clear and unambiguous set of rules which are capable of being met by PCG members working in the knowledge based sector.

---

[28] In future Budget notes and during the 2001 general election

It is ironic to note that in the USA a Bill is in front of the Senate that states a method of demonstrating such a genuine business relationship would be to have a Ltd Company and a written Contract! Just as we are about to throw out a method of working that has delivered a thriving economy, the USA are about to adopt this way of working.

The 5 year vacuum that Andy referred to in his note has proved to be optimistic despite a few High Court wins of high profile. As for the US Bill, I don't know what happened with that.

One thing that did emerge from the week was a general hatred of the ATSCo trade association who represented large IT agencies and appeared to have betrayed contractors. Of course they weren't there to represent contractors but to represent agencies. As every contractor knows an agent will pretend to be your best friend while happily exploiting you and taking a large margin off your work.

Andy, himself owning a large agency, had sparked the anger with ATSCo and now tried to calm it down:

> "Despite the unhelpful comments from ATSCo, it is important that we work with Agents and Clients, in partnership, to ensure that our members can stay "in business on their own account." Our Lawyers are drafting a specimen contract to follow, which would tend to show that the member is in self employment. This will incorporate feedback from the detailed discussions between the PCG and the Government. We have also prepared briefing papers for both Agents and Clients and would ask that members download and send out."

We produced an agent's briefing paper and a client's briefing paper which were to be distributed but at the investment bank where I was contracting I couldn't quite see who would be interested in reading it, their interest in IR35 ended once they realised they weren't liable for it.

This was the same for the agencies; they were happy with the new IR35 ("a good result of our members") as it wasn't their concern anymore it would just affect the contractors. Neither the end-client nor the agency now had any interest in ensuring that a contract was outside of IR35. Why should they care?

The agents could keep their retention fees on the contractor and their temp-to-perm fees and the client could be happy that they wouldn't become liable for employment rights. On the new IR35 the only people who really cared now were the contractors and now we really did stand alone.

We did our best to bring agents onside and Andy and Susie released plans to allow them to join the PCG as associate members. Of course they wouldn't be joining the fight now but they would be there for marketing purposes.

> "To facilitate this further we have opened up the PCG to associate membership from Agents, End users, Accountants, Lawyers and Representative bodies. Although not having an Internet vote in PCG matters it will allow access to all PCG commissioned reports and model contracts. "

## House of Lords Reject the Clause

The House of Lords had an early reading of the new clauses on the 7$^{th}$ October and Kevin Miller helped to brief them on this. Lord McIntosh did hold his seminar for the Lords and Kevin also observed, the only representative to do so. Of course the others no longer cared.

IT consultant and PCG member, Gareth Williams and others beavered through the nights preparing briefing notes for our supporters in the Lords. We were just hoping for some fresh mentions on the tax and how bad it was having decided that we should fight for every inch of ground.

Then something amazing and quite unexpected happened, the House of Lords rejected it, we won a parliamentary vote!

Just before midnight on October 13, after an hour-long heated exchange in the House of Lords, their Lordships walked through the lobbies and voted out the IR35 section of the Welfare Reform Bill (Clause 71-72) by 84 votes to 66.

## House of Lords Debate

The debate was effectively between the Government (Lord McIntosh), who felt that the proposals had already been significantly watered down, and Lords Higgins, Jenkin and Kintore who put forward the case for PCG.

McIntosh opened by getting his retaliation in first - mainly taking on board the PCG's objections and dealing with them before they could be raised. He supported the consultation process during the summer and explained the changes which had resulted, including change of obligation on to the intermediary, the use of the self-employment tests and the expense deduction.

He made a strong point of attacking the IT industry:

> "Let us consider the case of two people sitting side by side in the computer department of a big company. One is an employee of the company, the other works for his own service company. They might have been there for the same length of time; they are both part of the same team and work under the same team leader, doing the same kind of work. It has been argued that because one worker has chosen to set up a service company, he is somehow an entrepreneur and deserves to pay less tax and NIC, and that because applying the normal rules to distinguish employees from self-employed would result in taxing both in the same way, there must be something wrong with those rules. I do not think his colleague at the next desk would agree."

He did not believe much of the PCG's case, although frequently (and with more annoyance) referred to PCG.

> "We do not believe that the payment of a fair level of tax and NICs will wipe out the IT industry or that IT workers will leave the UK en masse as a result of those changes."

> "If it is argued, as it has been argued by the IT industry, that that puts them at a disadvantage compared to the large and, in particular, foreign companies which provide consultancy, I can only say that that is based on a misconception. One company which is other than a one-person service company cannot use the loophole of paying its principals in dividends."

Having felt that he had dealt with the objections and dismissed PCG's case before it was raised, he seemed to look confident. That confidence diminished in direct proportion to his anger rising as a number of speakers took his arguments apart, and Civil Servants sitting nearby sent hand-scribbled notes with more and more urgency.

Lord Goodhart was more circumspect than some of the later speakers as he acknowledged that:

> "There has been a high-pressure lobbying campaign by some organisations, notably the PCG, to retain the status quo....At the same time we accept some of the complaints from the PCG and others."

He went on to explain that the existing tests for self-employment need to be reassessed. He detailed his specific concerns and was highly critical of the Government's attitude to 'brushing off' the PCG with phoney consultations.

> "The PCG plainly represents a large number of those people who have created personal service companies in the IT industry. It has a very strong view. As I have made clear, I do not, by any means, agree with everything it says but it is directly affected by this legislation and its voice needs to be heard by the Government."

The heavy guns then came out with Lord Higgins opening his speech by describing the proposals as 'half-baked'. He made a case for the IT and oil and gas sectors criticised the self-employment tests, he said they would have an adverse effect on entrepreneurial companies and concluded by attacking the Government and Revenue for the manner in which it had tried to introduce these clauses with no consultation with the people who mattered.

Lord Jenkins followed on saying that the case had already been 'blown out of the water' and that the Government had underestimated the concern felt by the IT industry and others. He quoted extensively from letters from contractors which he had received.

He concluded by saying:

> "This is one more example of the Government saying one thing - 'we want to encourage e-commerce; we want to encourage private enterprise and entrepreneurs' - and then doing something that seeks to destroy them both. We should not allow this clause to pass into the Bill."

The Earl of Kintore, who had been closely associated with the PCG, delivered a fine explanation of the damage this could do to the Aberdeen oil and gas sector. He was supported by Lord Campbell of Troy. He said:

> "During my journey back to Scotland on Friday after our sadly curtailed Sitting, I read an article in the Evening Standard of which I should like to quote the first sentence: 'Shortly after becoming Chancellor of the Exchequer, Gordon Brown decided to find out why there are so few entrepreneurs in Britain'.
>
> "I think I can now assist the right honourable gentleman. The threat of IR35 being enacted has already caused a trickle of entrepreneurs to go abroad. If the provision is enacted as Clause 70, there is a danger of the trickle becoming a flood. If the seven or eight contractors--young, smart, articulate and interested--who were listening to the debate with me in another place last Wednesday (Commons) are a representative sample of the group, we should be fighting tooth and nail to keep them in this country, and not treat them like unwanted raffle prizes. "

The Government started to retaliate. Lord Hughes of Woodside described the concerns about Aberdeen as 'bunkum'.

Lord McIntosh took the opportunity to wind-up the debate and to address the issues that had been raised. He was clearly annoyed. First he dealt with the process, rejecting suggestions that it would have been possible to introduce amendments earlier, then he went on to defend the nature of the consultation and pointed out that the PCG was the only group to object then, which was somewhat contradicting himself that the PCG was content with the consultation. He dismissed any problems with the self-employment tests.

> "These tests have been built up by the courts over many years. They are not new to anybody, or to anybody like me who has run a small business."

Interestingly, he seemed to imply that if the clause was voted out it would not reappear...

> "That would certainly be the effect if this clause was removed from the Bill. It would not be considered at Third Reading, and I am not sure that it would ever come back again. We would have to introduce it another way."

He then tried to draw comparisons with IT contractors and market researchers whom he had employed. By the time he concluded his temper was running high:

> "All this talk we have heard about the IT industry, the North Sea oil industry and all this emotional stuff is way outside the scope of the amendment. We really have no case to answer here. We are doing a simple thing to get rid of tax avoidance. We are doing it in a way which, after consultation, has received the approval of virtually everybody who has been consulted, and the idea that we should back down now on the arguments we have heard is simply not acceptable."

At this point the Division Bell rang and the House divided. The Opposition benches which had been gradually filling up throughout the debate filed into their lobby. The Government benches, which had about 12 people listening, suddenly filled as Lords and Ladies downed their drinks and left their meals to file into the Chamber.

The amendment was defeated by 84-66 votes which meant we had won! IR35 had been removed from the legislation, albeit temporarily.

What happens now?

We were in unexpected territory. I never thought in a million years that we could have won a vote. It is a big thing for the Lords to throw something back to the Commons and I think that this was the first time it had happened to Blair's government. Of course the newspapers couldn't quite work out what it was all about, but then again it was the Welfare Reform Bill that contained a tax from the Finance Bill!

I wrote a letter to Dawn asking if I could help build some bridges and compromise. I didn't get a reply, there was to be no compromise from her.

There were a number of options for what could happen next:

1. The Government could try to reintroduce something when the Commons consider Lords amendments in a few weeks. If they do, the Lords have another opportunity to look at it and there is a danger (to the Government) that time will run out.

2. There could be a clause in next session's Finance Bill.

3. The Government could now have proper consultation with the PCG who are willing to help them achieve their objectives without damaging the enterprise sector.

Option three was only a dream that they could have a proper consultation although the Tories in 2011 did just that with the Health Bill and with their plans for the Forestry Commission.

All we could do was carry on fighting we had unexpectedly gained some ground and we should make them fight if they wanted to win it back. With the parliamentary process still on-going, David Ramsden wrote to our members:

**Advice on Lobbying your MP**

Following the events of Wednesday 13th October 1999 in which the IR35 Clauses in the House of Lords were deleted from the Welfare and Pensions Reform Bill there are two scenarios:

1. The Government will attempt to reintroduce clauses 71/72 in the House of Commons at the time of "Consideration of Lords Amendments".

2. They will abandon the Welfare Reform and Pensions Bill, as far as we are concerned and, introduce the IR 35 legislation, in total, in the Finance Bill 2000.

In either case, our attention must now swing back to members of Parliament. We would ask that all Contractors now write to their MP. Even if not a member of the PCG your views could make a difference.

Lord McIntosh cited, in the House of Lords the case of two workers sitting side by side which we believe demonstrates a fundamental misunderstanding of how we work.

We have prepared a comprehensive brief for your local MP. We believe that it clearly demonstrates the difference between the relationship of the directly employed, the Consultancy employed and, the small business.

Therefore the task is now to:-

You write to them at:-

The House of Commons,
London,
SW1A 0AA

You write a letter saying who you are, what you do for a living and, how you believe IR 35 will have the effect of putting your business at risk.

Include the briefing document and ask them to complete the attached questionnaire;

- Offer a meeting if they need a personal briefing to understand the issue.

- You can say that the matter of ir35 could well be coming back to their House, how would they vote?

- Ask for as written reply and, if one is not forthcoming within 10 days, phone them up in The House of Commons. 0171 219 3000 and ask when you might expect to receive a reply (you probably will not get the MP, more likely a secretary or researcher).

- If by the end of a further 5 days you still have not received a reply write a second letter asking for a reply to the original.

Keep a copy of any response, as we will be modifying the web site to allow you to record these. They will remain as a permanent record until the next election.

At this stage, please, do not write to the House of Lords.

### Dawn's Response

Instead of writing to the PCG or even meeting with us, Dawn chose to engage and communicate with us through the media. Our media strategy had been done in part to get in to see her; her strategy seemed to be somewhat different. This is the letter that she wrote:

A lot has been written about the changes we announced in the Budget to stop avoidance of tax and NICs [National Insurance Contributions] by people using personal service companies. I want to explain why we acted.

The problem arises where an individual is doing a job in circumstances which would normally make him an employee of a large business. For instance, he may work in the offices of that business, for a set number of hours a week, as part of a team led by an employee of the business. But this individual has set up a one-man company. That company has a contract with the business (his client) to provide the services of the individual. The client can then pay the company a fee, without deducting tax or National Insurance Contributions, or paying employer's NICs. The individual can take money out of his company in a variety of forms: he can pay his wife a salary, he can claim[29] a wide range of expenses, and he can take the rest out as dividends on which no NICs are payable. This way of working is common in the IT industry, though it also happens in other industries as well.

The result is that the worker pays a lot less in tax and NICs than he would if he were an employee of the client. In some cases no NICs at all. We don't think that is fair to the other taxpayers who have to pay more as a result.

Legislation to introduce the new rules is included in the Welfare Reform and Pensions Bill, which is about to return to the Commons from the House of Lords. The Government was defeated in the Lords on this, but the Chancellor and I believe it is important that we should press on. That is why we intend to reinstate this measure in the House of Commons.

Some groups in the IT and engineering industries have campaigned against the measure. One of the groups says that its members earn an average of 45 pounds an hour - that's about 1,800 pounds a week. Yet they can pay no NICs at all - less than a nurse, a teacher, or a self-employed plumber. Let me answer some of their arguments.

They say that we haven't consulted them.

We have in fact conducted an unusually extensive consultation. We announced the measure a year in advance. We sent out over 1,700 copies of our proposals, and the Inland Revenue held meetings attended by 38 representative bodies. And we have listened to what people were saying by announcing changes to the proposals in September which met the main concerns expressed during the consultations. The only people who are now complaining about the consultation process are those who want us to let them continue to avoid tax and NICs and are disappointed that we have not backed down.

They say that this measure will destroy the IT industry.

This is not just about the IT industry; there are plenty of people in the IT industry who do not use service companies, just as there are many people in other industries who do. Our support for the IT industry is on record. And we have put in place many measures, such as the 10p starting rate of Corporation Tax, to support genuine small businesses. What we are doing with this measure is ensuring that people who meet the accepted definition of employee pay tax and NICs on the same basis as all other employees.

---

[29] While the Brownites were painting contracting as a male-run affair, the Blairites were trying to promote IT for Women.

But we have listened to argument put to us that the flexibility provided by service companies was valuable. Our revised proposals therefore made sure that this flexibility could continue, as long as the workers paid a fair share of tax and NICs.

They say that consultants who work for short periods for different employees should be treated as self-employed.

What they are asking for is in fact more favourable treatment than either the self employed or employees. But our proposal would apply the same rules to consultants as are already applied to a whole range of other workers, including other temporary or casual workers, to decide whether they are employed or self employed. They are based on the courts' decisions in a series of real life cases. If, using those rules, the worker would be self-employed, he will not be self-employed, he will not be affected by our legislation.

They say that the proposals will favour big foreign firms over small UK businesses.

The proposals will prevent a form of avoidance which is only available to workers who control their own service companies and can use them to decide the form in which they take their income to minimise tax and NICs. This is not an issue for big companies which cannot be used by employees to manipulate the form of their income. Where there is evidence of tax avoidance by large companies we are just as ready to act against it. The real competition we should be concerned about is the competition between people who are employees, and others doing substantially the same job but using a service company to pay much less in tax and NICs. That is unfair and we shall stop it.

They say that the measure will cost the UK economy 8 Billion pounds.

One of the IT groups has commissioned research which claims that the cost to the UK economy will be huge. But the way in which this figure has been calculated doesn't bear a moment's scrutiny. They have asked their members how much extra they would like to be paid if they had to change their way of working in response to the legislation. They have then just multiplied the answer by their estimate of the number of workers affected. It's not surprising that the result is a big number. They have not attempted to find out whether the clients would be prepared to meet these demands.

Most of the responses we received from the consultation process this summer acknowledged that there was a problem, and that it was legitimate for the Government to tackle it. There were criticisms of the method we originally proposed, and we have listened and made changes. What we now propose is fair, targeted and proportionate. It allows the flexible market for skilled labour to continue, using service companies, but ensures that those concerned pay a fair share of tax and NICs.

Apparently our figures didn't bear 'a moments scrutiny', five years later Dawn would be explaining to the House of Commons that she didn't know how much money IR35 had helped to collect and then later figures would show it to be derisory low. (It would be as contractor websites pointed out because lots of contractors were now operating through tax avoidance schemes like umbrella companies).

Dawn had put the ball in Susie's media court allowing her to take the moral high ground and express regret and indignation on behalf of the PCG that a minister chose to conduct consultation through the media rather than directly. In responding to Dawn Primarolo's claim that there was no damage to the IT industry, she invited the Paymaster General to the spate of leaving parties which were taking place around that time as contractors packed their bags and headed to new challenges.

Susie's response was[30]:

Responding to criticisms within Primarolo's letter, Susie Hughes of the Professional Contractors' Group said: "We find it unfortunate that the paymaster general has decided to address our genuine concerns in an open letter to the press, rather than respond to the many requests we have put for a meeting.

"We genuinely believed that the government wanted to consult. We fail to understand why they won't meet us so we can work together."

Hughes said the Group still wanted to meet Primarolo tomorrow, at her convenience.

On specific points in Primarolo's letter, Hughes said that the consultation offered to the Group consisted of a meeting during which the final proposals arrived from ministers.

On whether IR35 will destroy the IT industry, Hughes said this is already happening. "If she doesn't believe this, then she can come along to some of the leaving parties."

On the question of whether big businesses had lobbied for IR35, Hughes said Revenue officials have confirmed this and on whether the Group's figures are accurate, Hughes said its estimate that the Revenue will actually lose 750 million pounds through introducing the measure was made by a top UK accountant.

"We find it quite amazing that the chancellor can be talking about enterprise on Monday, and on Tuesday the paymaster general has this letter coming out," Hughes concluded.

### Early Day Motion

EDM number 964 in 1998-99, proposed by Robert Smith on 01/11/1999.

In Parliament Robert Smith MP (LD, West Aberdeenshire & Kincardine), who had been a good friend to the PCG, laid down an early day motion on IR35. Basically an EDM is a little petition that MPs can sign to express support for a cause for concern about an issue. Often MPs would sign an EDM and then write to their constituents and tell them about it. MPs can sign EDMs condemning an issue but

---

[30] http://www.computing.co.uk/ctg/news/1855297/government-dismisses-contractor-fears-ir35

then vote it through later under the Government's whip. EDMs can act as early warning systems to Government about concern on an issue.

This one of Robert Smith's had 40 signatories to it. The majority were Lib Dem but with a few surprise Labour signatories too. A handful of Tories, but generally speaking members tended to only sign EDMs from their own party unless they felt strongly about an issue.

The EDM read:

> That this House notes with concern the Government's proposals, commonly referred to as IR35, to counter tax avoidance by some one-person company contractors which should be curbed, the present proposals are potentially very damaging to United Kingdom industry, particularly in the areas of information technology, engineering and offshore contracting; and calls on Her Majesty's Government to consult more intensively with industry representatives on the detailed proposals and to review the proposals in light of the genuine concerns of those affected.

# Chapter 11

## Mass Lobby on Parliament / Flash Mob

We had hoped, beyond hope really, that Dawn would reconsider the plans in light of them being rejected by the Lords. On the contrary, I suspect she was even keener than ever to push the plans through and we as the contractors were becoming more than just an annoyance. As someone who had long believed in the supremacy of the Commons and wanted to see the Lords abolished, I could suddenly see the value of the House, not so much of the hereditary peers but of a second chamber, but the mandate the Lords had was simply to send the clause back to the Commons for them to consider it afresh; they couldn't stop it altogether.

Would Dawn reconsider the clause as the Lords had suggested? Not a chance.

News came through that the date the Commons were going to debate the clause again was to be Wednesday 3$^{rd}$ November. Of course they didn't want to give us much of an advantage and it was only on the Friday before that we found out.

With only four days now until the final reading the PCG sat around fairly dismayed. We had such a responsibility to the members and contractors at large. We had won a huge victory by winning concessions and had now won a vote in the House of Lords. How can we top that, how we capitalise on these victories? We can't let the members down.

What shall we do?

Let's lobby Parliament.

But we'll never get the word out!

We can't be organised in such a short time.

Oh yes we can, said Andy.

So they did.

Susie and David came up with a little-known parliamentary lobbying device - 'the green card'. At the time any constituent could walk into the House of Commons, go to central lobby, fill in a green postcard, hand it to one of the Sergeants-at-Arms and request a meeting with their MP. If he or she could be found, and was in the building, a polite little chat could ensue in central lobby. The parliamentary officials dealt with a handful of these requests.

We decided to organise a 'green card lobby' in four days time.

So using the Internet we created what must be one of the world's first ever flash mobs, although we didn't know it at the time. On the Friday afternoon an email was put together urging contractors that if they could, to come to Parliament on Wednesday to lobby their MPs.

Perhaps a few would turn up but these were contractors that we were talking about, would any of them sacrifice any rate-time to travel to Parliament? I was sceptical, but that didn't mean we shouldn't do it.

David Ramsden duly let the parliamentary authorities know that 20-30[31] contractors may turn up to lobby their members on Wednesday. He told contractors that letters should still be written and faxes and emails should be sent.

During the French Revolution the armies of the Duke of Brunswick threatened to come to Paris and murder all the revolutionaries if the King was not restored to his 'proper place' and accorded proper respect. He was only three days march from Paris but instead of quelling the revolution it gave it a spark and people took up arms to defend their new won liberty.

One of my heroes, Danton, gave a great speech when he said:

> The tocsin that will ring will be no mere signal for alarm; it will sound the charge against the enemies of the nation.

He added that

> Pour conquérir nos ennemis, il nous faut de l'audace et de plus en plus de l'audace, alors la France sera victorieuse

This means if we are bold we will win.

The PCG were now going to be bold and were going to win. Danton had spoken of the tocsin bell ringing. We would now ring that metaphorical bell as they had done in Paris as an alarm and call to arms our members. Instead of the tocsin ringing it would be the ping of 10,000 incoming emails on computers from Land's End to John O'Groats. It was about to prove another defining moment for the PCG as we would call people into action.

Peers opposing the IR35 clauses indicated they would not vote against the measure again after it was debated in the Commons, meaning that Wednesday's debate was likely to make the moves introduction the following April a near-certainty.

What had we to lose?

We were all fired up and David sent out his call to arms that Friday afternoon to some 4,000 PCG members and an additional 6,000 contractors, so 10,000 in total. Our 'call to arms' read:

---

[31] If memory serves me correctly

Newsflash - Calling all Contractors

**Mass Lobby of Parliament**

The Government have announced that it will re-introduce Clauses 71 and 72 (IR 35) into the Welfare Reform and Pensions Bill on Wednesday 3rd November 1999.

Now is the time for you to take positive action. As many Contractors as possible should go to the House of Commons on Wednesday afternoon to both Lobby your MP and attend a meeting.

We are finalising arrangements for a senior opposition spokesman to address this meeting at the House of Commons at around 1430 on that day.

We are telling you this now so that you can make the necessary arrangements. The action you should take is as follows:

1) If possible arrange to go to London on Wednesday 3rd November

2) For those who can go; you should write to your Member of Parliament. You should tell him/her that you are coming to a meeting concerning IR 35 in the House of Commons on that day and that you will put a "Green Card" in and you hope they will be able to meet with you.

You need send this letter so it arrives by Monday.
The address is: Your Member of Parliament (put MP after their name)

House of Commons
London
SW1A 0AA

As soon as the detail of the speaker and the meeting room is concerned we will send a further briefing which will include full details of the action to be taken on the day.

Kind regards
David Ramsden, Campaign Director
Professional Contractors Group

Maybe some people would turn up?

**Monday 1$^{st}$ November 1999**

The response had been good, it now looked as though we could get 100 people so David sent out a fresh email and let the House of Commons authorities know.

The Tories got their act together and put out a briefing note accusing the Government of saying one thing and doing another to entrepreneurs and imposing measures that would leave contractors uncertain over their fiscal status. It said "IR35 is a stealth tax on the self-employed".

Our next communication:

Mass Lobby; 3 November 1999

We sent out a newsletter on 29th October and asked you to attend a mass lobby on 3rd November. In addition we can now confirm that Quentin Davies MP (Shadow Paymaster General) has arranged a public meeting for 1430 in the Jubilee Room of the House of Commons on the same day.

The meeting will be restricted to 100. To register for this meeting on a "first come, first served basis.

If you cannot attend the meeting or if it is full, we would still hope you will Lobby your MP. This can start at 1430 and runs on until 2200. Please note; Prime Ministers Question Time is from 1500 until 1530. During this time it is unlikely that MPs' will be available to come to the Lobby.

We would ask that if you are attending that you complete the registration form so we can gain an idea of coverage.

For details of the last newsletter, the meeting, how to "green card" and Lobby your MP, including map of the House of Commons together with briefing information for your MP, please go to: http://www.pcgroup.org.uk/lobbying.html.

Kind regards

David Ramsden

## Tuesday 2$^{nd}$ November

We now had more than 100 contractors registered to go to the lobbying meeting in the House of Commons. I was impressed though the Commons authorities were less so, they didn't like mass lobbies turning up without much notice.

Contractors all like a drink so we decided to set up and meet at the Red Lion pub. It is across the road from the Treasury and is their local as it were. This was my idea, a friend of mine told that that the Ministry officials all liked to go for a drink, so I thought we will take that ground too to annoy them. Apparently it did.

Susie knew the place as a journalist/politico haunt from her days as a Government press officer. It even had a division bell so MPs who had popped out for a swift half could dash back across the road in the event of an unexpected vote. As a precaution we reserved the small downstairs room as a rendezvous point. Part of the issue was that we didn't know how many would turn up but we hoped a couple of dozen would show on the day but equally, we didn't know anyone and they wouldn't recognise us. To this point in time, with very few exceptions, there had been no face-to-face meetings among the membership. All correspondence had been conducted over the Internet and email and in most cases, as is the vogue on Internet forums, people were posting under pseudonyms. Many conversations started, 'Hello, I'm John Smith but you'll know me as Red Dragon' or something similar. The low-tech solution of sticky badges with space to write real names and 'forum names' was the answer.

With Conservative help we also managed to get a room inside the Palace of Westminster room W1. We sent a note to Dawn Primarolo cordially inviting her to come and meet contractors face to face. I can just imagine how that went down. However, on my side if she had turned up she would have to be met with respect and would gain a considerable amount of it.

I got the feeling though she didn't like the PCG. Of course she was used to being the good guy fighting the evil Tories, now to have a group against you isn't nice so we added a note to the letter also inviting her for a drink at the Red Lion.

Now this may sound exciting but at the time we didn't know what was going to happen. We knew we wouldn't win the vote but wanted to go down fighting and so it seemed did the entire contractor community. There was plenty of spirit and movement that day. What would happen to the PCG at the end of this day? Would the movement end or fizzle out? We didn't know and so lived for the moment and in a way the day was sort of a festival for the PCG as much as it was our storming of a Bastille.

### Final Call for Mass Lobby

**Final details: Mass Lobby of House of Commons**

Meeting 1430 until 1500. Jubilee Room

To clarify; this is a meeting organised by the Conservatives to which we have been invited to say a few words. There may also be some other speakers, as well as the press in attendance. Be aware that it is likely to be a scrum getting into the meeting as other Groups and companies have been telling people to come. We have emailed the 100 who registered on the internet form with separate instructions.

**Lobby your MP**

For us this is the main point of the day. This is the chance to come and have your say to your representative. As this is a key Bill the House will be full. Your MP will be there. Even if you have not written you can "green card" your MP on the day. There will be no guarantee that they will come out to see you, but if they fail to do so we will ensure that their local media is alerted to this fact. Whatever the Party of your MP, get "on your bike" and get to Westminster. Lobbying can take place from 2:30 PM until 10:00 PM.

**Meeting points**

We have booked W1 (a smaller room at the House of Commons) from 2:00 PM until 4:00 PM. David Hopkins will be holding the fort and after you have met (or not) with your MP, come up and report your discussion. Myself, Andy White, Susie Hughes and Kevin Miller will be in and around during this time. We have also invited Dawn

Primarolo to attend so that she can talk to the "person at the sharp end" for a change. As yet she has not responded.

For those arriving early and for a central point for Contractors to meet up, we have booked a function room downstairs at the Red Lion. A well-known Whitehall Pub, it is 5 minutes walk from the House of Commons. It is on Parliament Street going towards Trafalgar Square, opposite the Treasury. (If DP cannot meet us in W1 maybe she will join us for a drink!) This is booked from 12:00 until 3:30 and then from 5:30 until 11:00 PM. (The main bar is open all day.) The room only takes 40, but the weather forecast looks good and we can always spill over into the street.

Look forward to seeing you

Kind regards, David Ramsden

## Contractor Wednesday – 3rd November

This was the Contractor's Bastille Day. Ten years later the new PCG would celebrate 'National Freelancers Day' on the 23rd November, they got the day wrong it should have been on the 3rd November, the day that the PCG literally stormed Parliament, our Bastille Day. On second thoughts maybe it is because they wanted to distance themselves from such a confrontational history and this can, in part, be understood. It would be one of the first ever flash mobs to be mobilised.

Below is Susie's report on the day:

Over the weekend of 30th and 31st October, PCG posted details of its lobby of Parliament, intended to educate and inform individual MPs about the ramifications of their actions during the vote on IR35. It was clear the Government intended to reintroduce the Clauses -which had earlier been removed by the Lords- during the final stages of the Welfare Reform Bill in the Commons. It was also clear that - in order to ensure the Bill didn't run out of time - the Government would 'guillotine' the debates. The guillotining provision received as much criticism as the controversial clauses on disability and IR35.

Shadow Chancellor Francis Maude and Shadow Paymaster General Quentin Davies invited PCG members to a meeting in the Commons prior to Wednesday's debate.

Originally a room was booked for 20 people, but after some encouragement by PCG a room, which could hold 100 was organised. Even this proved to be an underestimation as several hundred contractors crowded into the room and the meeting had to be moved to a larger room which was under decoration at the time.

Francis Maude, David Willetts (Shadow DSS) and Lord Higgins[32] put forward the reasons why the Opposition disapproved of IR35. Andy White, Chairman of PCG,

---

[32] He was given a standing ovation by contractors when he introduced

explained how the PCG had been born and the strength of feeling among contractors who had been motivated to take on the Government over these proposals.

The meeting was immediately followed by Prime Minister's Question time - the weekly opportunity for Hague to tackle Blair in a parliamentary head-to-head on a subject of his choosing. On Wednesday, it was IR35 with reference to PCG which dominated the questions, as Blair, for the first time, was required to make public comments on it.

In the meantime, hundreds of PCG members were forming queues to lobby their MPs. At one point, the weight of numbers threatened to overwhelm the House of Commons lobby system as policemen and members handed out 'green cards', the system whereby MPs are summoned to meet their constituents. In the first hour, 400 green cards were submitted - compared to the usual 25.

The response of MPs varied considerably, but all were better informed at the end of the meetings than they had been prior to it. The lobbying continued throughout the day, with one contractor still waiting to see his MP at midnight.

PCG had hired the downstairs bar at the 'politico pub' the Red Lion and members held informal meetings throughout the day with progress updates.

Andy White, David Ramsden and I were privileged to sit on the floor of the House of Commons to witness the debate on IR 35, limited by the Government to between 10pm and midnight. It was disappointing to see Dawn Primarolo leave the floor of the House at 10 pm and not be present to witness the debate. Stephen Timms, DSS Minister, outlined the case for the Government. With the exception of one Labour MP who sought clarification on a point, no-one from the Government's backbenches spoke. The rest of the two hour debate was dominated by Opposition MPs who, in the main, were working from PCG briefings, PCG members' letters and the lobbying from earlier in the day. Although the Government never had more than two dozen people on its benches when the Division Bell rang at midnight, IR35 was reinstated in the Bill by 345 votes to 203.

The Opposition MPs expressed their displeasure at the manner in which the Government had guillotined the debate and insisted on pushing the outstanding clauses to a vote until 1.30am. During this time several MPs came up to us to thank PCG members for their support.

It was unbelievable nearly 1,000[33] contractors had turned up at Parliament to lobby and green card their MPs. Most had never been to Parliament before or spoken to their MP, but they had heeded the call and come. I met some walking down the street that had flown in from Scotland just for day.

---

[33] 700 PCG members and 300 non-members

Parliament was overwhelmed and the authorities were furious with David Ramsden because they had to draft in extra security[34]. MPs were being green carded and were having civilised cups of tea and conversations with IT contractors. Most of the Labour MPs were confused, they had that morning been sent a briefing note from Dawn Primarolo warning them that they had been misled by the contractors group and make no doubt about it we were all a bunch of tax avoiders. A friend of mine who worked for a Labour MP leaked me a copy and we put out a rebuttal which we passed to members as they arrived.

Many Labour MPs also complained about the expenses that contractors could claim and said that it wasn't fair; that was the line I got from Margaret Moran's office. Interestingly Margaret Moran refused to come out when she was green carded and I chased her assistant but was told she never comes out on green card. Generally speaking though, MPs did come out.

William Hague used his quota of PMQ's to attack Blair on IR35. Though Blair looked as though he didn't even know what it was. You can imagine the briefing beforehand – 'what is this IR35 thing?', 'some stupid tax of Gordon's', 'not another one!'

Susie was watching from the public gallery and later said that an amusing by-product of our activities during Prime Minister's Questions was the number of green cards being passed up and down the rows of MPs as the officials of the Palace of Westminster tried to deliver the hundreds and hundreds of green cards which had come their way from contractors.

The sheer numbers that came through were truly incredible and we stood there in Central Lobby directing our forces as they marched through and into battle in the tea rooms with their MPs. The press were focused on the Welfare Reform Bill and its changes to disability allowances. Initially they got very excited about the numbers turning up but as it wasn't for what they expected they ignored it. Though I'd say it is hard to do, they had no trouble doing so.

In the following day's Guardian, parliamentary sketch writer Simon Hoggart showed how out of touch he was when he wrote:

> "Mr Hague had tried to work up some anger over IR35, a set of rules that will make people who employ computer experts pay more tax, but failed. Nobody is capable of caring about something called IR35, however vital it is. No one is going to go on a march chanting: "Dead or alive, I'll fight IR35!""[35]

---

[34] The lobbying of Members of Parliament caused so much chaos it was probably the reason Tony Blair brought in legislation to ensure it would never happen again by banning the assembly of a group of people without prior police permission within a mile of Parliament.

[35] http://www.guardian.co.uk/politics/1999/nov/04/thatcher.politicalnews

Presumably he must have watched it all on TV instead of actually being in Parliament, because what he laughed at and ridiculed is more or less what happened. Nearly 1,000 people had lobbied Parliament in protest against IR35. Indeed Parliament then woke up to the power of the Internet and the ability to hold mass lobbies, so then they became outlawed unless strict rules were followed.

I admit I found it a little strange as I saw lots of my left wing friends who assumed I was there for the disability stuff not the IR35 stuff. At the Jubilee Room I found myself in conversation with Conservative grandee Francis Maude who was telling me how bad Labour was and I wasn't sure whether to nod in agreement or not. The problem for me was that the Opposition were firing bullets at the Labour Government that I had helped to get elected but I reserved my anger for Labour as they had put me in this unhappy position.

Central Lobby was the battlefield and I saw Dawn Primarolo scoot across it firing dagger looks in my direction. It wasn't so much a lobby, it was an invasion and they were furious. Susie told me that they had received a note from Dawn's office regretting that she couldn't come to room W1 to meet contractors. I asked if she could make it for a pint though to which Susie couldn't help but suppress a laugh.[36]

At one point we saw a group of other suited men carrying bags through the lobby. They exchanged frightful glances with Andy. I asked who they were and was told that they were the Forum 2000 or similar. It was like a sketch from Monty Python where they had encountered the Judean People's Popular front when trying to kidnap Pilot's wife. "Shouldn't we be fighting the real enemy?" I was tempted to ask. "What, the Popular People's Front/ATSCo?" "No, the Romans/Inland Revenue".

It was a long hard day and people just kept coming and coming. Eventually I found myself at the Red Lion propping up the bar and enjoying a few drinks. It was like an election day when the polls had closed there was little more we could do now.

I stayed as late as I could and hung around Central Lobby watching the Labour MPs go in to vote for IR35, MPs I had helped to elect. I wasn't very happy with that but I was so proud of what we had created with the PCG.

Every contractor who attended felt that they had played their part in a peaceful yet assertive manner. They had received mixed receptions, some were taken for tea and a tour of the House; others were left sitting in Central Lobby for hours. As Susie was leaving much later in the evening she told me she had met one of 'our contractors' who was still waiting to see his MP. He had a copy of a letter confirming his immigration papers and new contract - in America. He was one of the technical experts at the cutting edge of computer mapping and sat nav development, and they said no-one would leave the country and our claims of a technical brain-drain were misleading! As far as I know he is still in the USA.

---

[36] This may have been on a separate day in Parliament, but it did happen

That sense of pride in what we had achieved went beyond me and to all those who had attended. It was our Bastille Day, or perhaps our Agincourt, because to quote Shakespeare's Henry V[37]:

This story shall the good man teach his son;
And Crispin Crispian shall ne'er go by,
From this day to the ending of the world,
But we in it shall be remember'd;
We few, we happy few, we band of brothers;
For he to-day that sheds his blood with me
Shall be my brother; be he ne'er so vile,
This day shall gentle his condition:
**And gentlemen in England now a-bed**
**Shall think themselves accursed they were not here**,
And hold their manhoods cheap whiles any speaks
That fought with us upon Saint Crispin's day.

For contractors everywhere those that were there still boast with pride their involvement in that day and those that weren't have no response.

In the forums and debates people even now refer with pride to their involvement on that day, and they are right to.

## Thursday 4th November

### CONTRACTORS MASS LOBBY OF PARLIAMENT AS GOVERNMENT REINTRODUCES IR35[38]

About 700 members of the Professional Contractors Group lobbied their MPs in Parliament yesterday (November 3) to protest about the reintroduction of the IR35 regulations which will close tens of thousands of small entrepreneurial companies.

Despite the information and education lobby of MPs, which went on from 2pm to midnight, the Government forced the proposals back into the Welfare and Reform Bill.

Andy White, Chairman of the PCG, said: "Yesterday we lost a battle, but we discovered a voice. The debate was clearly in our favour yet hundreds of MPs who weren't in the Chamber to hear the rational arguments put forward, voted to put our companies at risk.

"This measure has been lobbied for by big, usually foreign, businesses and has been further confused by mixed messages from accountants.

---

[37] Henry V Act 4 Scene III

[38] 700 PCG members and around 300 other contractors took part in the lobby

"Yesterday we chose to take our message into the heart of Government with reasoned and irrefutable evidence. We packed the lobbies and demanded to be heard. We made it clear that, despite the misinformation by some people that we are Porsche-driving, tax dodgers, we are legitimate businesses who are trying to protect our future and the future of the enterprise economy on which both we and the Government know our future prosperity depends."

The Welfare Reform Bill will return to the House of Lords on Monday (November 8) where the IR35 Clauses have already been rejected once.

## Conservative leader William Hague

Andy reported to members that

> On Thursday evening, the PCG were present in numbers at a dinner attended by the opposition leader. Andy White sat next to William Hague, who, during his after dinner speech, made four references to PCG and IR35, using it as an example of the 'Government's stealth tax'. Following the dinner Andy White said, "It was an excellent opportunity to brief the opposition leader on the knowledge based economy and the damage IR 35 could do to it.
>
> We would welcome the chance to carry out a similar briefing for Tony Blair and Charles Kennedy. We are confident that by continuing with our education process we will ensure that IR 35 is proportionate to the aims.
>
> As one of our members said, and it was quoted during the debate on Wednesday, - You cannot have a knowledge-based economy with an ignorance based Government"

I didn't go, I would have felt uncomfortable being with the Tories, that was my problem not theirs.

## What happens next?

Andy wrote out to contractors to explain the next steps. We were all fired up and ready to fight and so were the 1,000 contractors who had turned up that day for what was probably the first ever flash protest and certainly one of the largest mass lobbies of Parliament.

The Bill now returns to the House of Lords for considerations of the Commons action. While technically the Lords could vote the clauses out for a second time, it would be unusual for the Lords to take this action after the Commons have reinstated clauses.

The whole process will be repeated in April as the income tax element of the measure will need to be put forward in the Finance Bill.

The PCG will be carrying out the following.

1. Engage in the "consultation" concerning the guidelines to the new rules. A draft guidance paper is to be issued by the Inland Revenue and the Minister confirmed in the House that it would be "sent out to representative bodies -

the Professional Contractors Group and others" Kevin Miller our Accountant will be leading our team on this. As they say "the devil is in the detail" and if anyone is able to make sense of these complex rules it will be Kevin Miller who produced the PCG alternative RIA and has been involved since March on this issue.

2. Continue with the education of the Government and opposition parties as well as Clients, Accountants, Agents and other representative bodies. The members themselves, who have the benefit of our briefing papers and discussion forums to ensure they are fully briefed, will carry this out.

3. Provide an independent source of information to Contractors in the knowledge-based industries. Encourage them to join up and lend their support. To paraphrase Kennedy, if you join the PCG "ask not what PCG can do for you, but what you can do for the PCG".

4. Following confirmation of the new rules, provide briefing packs for our members including arranging seminars around the Country to ensure, as far as possible, members are fully briefed. We will not carry this out until we have certainty and would hope that this will take place sometime in January. Part of the process will be to work with other representative bodies and draft standard contracts. It will be important when a Contractor starts with a client in April -under a new contract that will demonstrate self employment- that the client has received the same contract from their representative body. The new rules will create great uncertainty and we must work hard to ameliorate the impact

5. Build on the web site and the organisation to ensure that, if required, we can again make our voice heard during the Finance Bill and in the run up to the next election. As Vincent Cable said to the House - "Some of us are beginning to receive postbags comparable to those on fox hunting" That is Unlike Frank Dobson's letters supporting his Mayoral campaign, there is not a form letter amongst them. The web site will also build into a permanent public record of the actions of individual MPs to allow contractors, come the next election, to check on their position on this issue. Contractors understand that if they do not perform, daily, then contracts are terminated and it is unlikely they will work for that client again. It is one of the differences compared to permanent employment. In Aberdeen it is common knowledge that the Client will write the following initials on a contractor's details -NBA- Not Back Again. On the ballot papers it will be easier, just a cross in a different box!

I could tell that both Andy and Susie were shattered, we all were, but we were not just physically worn out but emotionally drained too. It was so amazing that all these people had turned out, I found it hard to deal with as we now realised the weight of responsibility that rested on our shoulders. These contractors were real people not just email addresses. They were relying on us to get it right.

Andy said to contractors:

"Finally I would like to thank all those who attended the Mass Lobby on Wednesday. With only a few days notice, close to a thousand Contractors marched on the House of Commons, slipped past the media cameras, which quite rightly were focused on the disabled campaigners, and took our message direct to the people whom we elect to govern our Country. Our strategy has been and will continue to be; no fanfare or spin.

It is my belief that increasingly we will turn away from the "Orwellian" control of the media as exercised by this Government and look for a message with substance rather than style. Our web site and this newsletter allow us to communicate effectively with the target audience who we wish to influence –The Government and the Contractor.

We present the information raw and unfiltered; you then make up your own mind as to our case. The Internet cuts out the middleman - in this case the media and allows us to go direct. It was quite amazing to see Central Lobby overflowing with Contractors and MPs queuing to see their constituents.

William Hague told me that during PMQ his attention was drawn to the bundles of green cards being passed down the benches. To those who could not make it, many thanks for the messages of support".

# Chapter 12

## Back to the House of Lords - 8th November 1999

The parliamentary battle was really over but the Bill still had to go back to the House of Lords for final approval. That is the way it works. We asked our people in the Lords to reject it again but were told it was unlikely because that wasn't the protocol with an unelected chamber.

Susie reported as follows:

After the drama and controversy of the Welfare Reform Bill's ping-ponging between the two Houses of Parliament the Lords finally backed down and the Bill, with IR35 in it, entered the Statute Books.

After the debate was won and the vote was lost in the House of Commons, the Bill returned to the Lords on Monday 8th. Again their Lordships pushed the matter to a debate. The Earl of Kintore, who has been a staunch supporter of PCG, spoke from his personal experience of contractors and his involvement with PCG. He said: "If the seven or eight contractors - young, smart, articulate and interested - who were listening to the debate with me in another place last Wednesday are a representative sample of the group (PCG), we should be fighting tooth and nail to keep them in this country, and not treat them like unwanted raffle prizes."

Lord Jenkin spoke about the great shame of the Government giving with one hand and taking away with the other and driving contractors overseas.

Lord Higgins (leading for the Opposition) called for an undertaking that the Government would consult with people who are affected and again outlined objections to the proposals.

Lord McIntosh for the Government congratulated the PCG and its members - and then dismissed our concerns. "The second congratulations are due to the Professional Contractors Group. I have never encountered such a literate, persuasive series of letters. Ministers have had something like 2,000 letters. I have received many dozens. The noble Lord, Lord Jenkin, has received a number. They are literate, well spelt, well argued, persuasive letters - and wrong."

McIntosh assured the House that 'we are consulting with the PCG on guidance for its members so that the proposals can be made as clear as possible'.

However, in keeping with the Parliamentary convention that the Lords do not continue to defy the elected chamber, the issue was not put to a vote and therefore remained in the Bill and the legislation.

Lord McIntosh's quote was quite a rhetorical one. He'd said:

> "I have never encountered such a literate, persuasive series of letters. Ministers have had something like 2,000 letters. I have received many dozens. They are literate, well spelt, well argued, persuasive letters **- and wrong.**"

We thought it was all a bit smug and thought why don't we just guillotine the end of the quote and use it for own purposes.

"I have never encountered such a literate, persuasive series of letters. Ministers have had something like 2,000 letters. I have received many dozens. They are literate, well spelt, well argued, persuasive letters"

So we did, adding it to literature, saying it now I am almost a bit embarrassed but we weren't there to play by their rules.

So was it all over now, the legislation for IR35 had passed through Parliament? Next year it would automatically appear as a part of the Finance Bill and would come into effect in the April. Was that it, was it over? Was there anything else we could do?

I asked Susie, David and Andy what next? JR, they replied.

What's that?

A Judicial Review.

# Part 3 – Judicial Review

# Chapter 1

## What has just happened?

I sat around after Contractor Wednesday and tried to make sense of what had happened and where we were. Had we won? Were we really now defeated? Was it downhill from here on?

What was true was that in eight months we'd managed to create a movement for contractors. From nothing we had used the power of the Internet as it had never been used before. Four thousand contractors were now paying members of the PCG which gave us resources of some £400,000. The engineerjob.com site and others had provided us with an email list of over 10,000 subscribers.

We had made it onto the front page of the national papers; we'd been debated in Parliament. Andy White had been fêted by the Conservative Opposition. We held a huge mass lobby of Parliament motivating around 1,000 contractors to come to Westminster, some of them had even flown in from Scotland for the day.

The trade press was full of our exploits, though other national media struggled to get an understanding of what was happening and so our exploits, to a large extent, flew under their radar as IR35 wasn't easy to explain.

Lord Weatherill, the former speaker of the House of Commons, had backed our campaign and become our patron. Other members of the Lords had become seriously impressed by the individual contractors they had met. Over 2,000 letters had flown into the House of Lords on the subject. Even our bitter enemy Lord McIntosh had been impressed.

Brown and Primarolo had been embarrassed at the Labour Conference and the harder they worked to ignore it or put it down the stronger the movement became. Every pronouncement by Dawn Primarolo was simply petrol on the flames for us. I suggested to Susie that we needed to get Dawn to say more.

The Government's handling of the whole affair had been exposed for the farce it was. Here was a tax that they would later claim would raise £900m a year that didn't even get a mention in the budget statement. It was missed out of the Bill's Regulatory Impact Assessment then hastily added only for the figures to be openly ridiculed. Eventually they would have to issue a new one. Too late to sex it up, all they could do was try and hide the figures.

In Parliament they showed such distain for the tax that they couldn't really be bothered to debate it properly.

For the first time since the time of Henry VIII they pushed all the power to decide how it should be implemented to the Civil Service thus denying Parliament the chance to discuss it again. They asked Parliament for a mandate to carry out consultations only during the consultations to tell the PCG that they now had a mandate from Parliament to implement it, a sort of catch-22 scenario for us.

Iain Duncan Smith MP had said:

> The new clause is breath-taking. I have never seen anything quite like it. It moves from being a Henry XIII clause to being a Louis XIV clause--absolute power to the absolute monarch--before any consultation.
>
> "The Minister quietly slipped out the fact that the regulations will subsequently be subject to the negative procedure of the House. There will not be even a limited ability to debate them. As my right hon. Friend said, the most breathtaking part is new subsection 9, which states that
>
> "the Treasury may with the concurrence of the Secretary of State"—
>
> "by order make such modifications of the preceding provisions of this section as the Treasury think appropriate for that purpose."
>
> So there we have it. The Treasury can tear up the new clause any time it likes by order. They do not have to come back to the House. The whole thing is appalling.

The consultation was a sham. Half of those attending were looking for business opportunities and a chance to say to their clients that they were representing them.

All major industry bodies rejected the new proposals and Stephen Timms admitted in Parliament what we all knew that it was the big IT companies who were behind the tax:

> "The problem at the moment is that there is an uneven playing field, which is disadvantageous to major organisations"

We had got into the DTI and made our case although it was clear then how powerful the Treasury was. Our lobbying and letter writing campaign started to pay off, even Labour MPs started to question the tax.

The Government then held secret meetings, presumably with the sponsors of the legislation, to try and salvage it but unfortunately for them we learnt about the secret meetings and exposed them.

For appearances sake they then held meetings with contractor groups and reluctantly invite the PCG. However, the Government spin machine was having an off day and gets its timing wrong and during this so-called consultation meeting an embarrassed official came in and explained that the new reformed proposals had been released already. The farce that is the consultation meeting comes to an end.

The PCG team was fantastic with Andy's leadership, Susie's press skills, David Ramsden's knowledge of Parliament and Kevin Miller's accountancy skills but more importantly behind them they had woken up the contracting movement and thousands of contractors embarked on an articulate letter writing and email campaign.

Out of the ranks of the contractors rose some great figures bringing skills to the fore. For instance, Gareth Williams brought his previous experience as a parliamentary researcher and Jane Akshar brought her irresistible charm and skills for the media and leadership.

What we can see now as perhaps the first ever 'flash mob' as a mass lobby of Parliament had occurred.

Had we saved contracting? Well, the original unworkable proposals for contractor registration and a control and supervision test had been ditched in favour of self-employment tests. We had turned the PCG from being just a network or campaign group into a proper permanent body. The revolution was truly in full flow. We had our first great journée [39] when we lobbied Parliament

I am constantly drawing parallels between what was happening with the PCG and a revolution because it was one and was following a similar course.

The PCG had grown on the Internet and its democratic home was its on-line forums. After each event and everyday members would have to go on the forums and make their case and answer their critics. It was like the National Assembly or a Parliament but open 24 hours and everyone had a say. It was direct democracy.

For a long time it had been a source of strength for the PCG, but it would also prove a point of weakness. The debate never stopped. It was relentless. Time needed to be spent not just in fighting against IR35 and the Government's other plans but in managing the revolution and the PCG. The members could be like a mob and were hungry for action and some could be fickle. Many French revolutionaries used to sleep in their committee rooms in fear of the relentless movement of events. I could appreciate this.

The members would need to be placated and involved. I make this analysis now but at the time there was no chance for real reflection, events moved on a daily basis and we had to keep on top of them.

The PCG had asserted itself as the main representative body for contractors having sometimes brutally pushed out the agency and accountancy bodies who had previously tried to do that.

There were two new realities, firstly IR35 was going to become law in April and secondly, we now stood alone. The agency groups like ATSCo now deserted the cause; it didn't affect them so they stood back from the fight.

---

[39] Journée's were pivotal days during the French revolutions. For instance Bastille day, and when the Monarchy was abolished and others times when the masses from Paris would come out in force

Our task was to equip and educate contractors on how the new tests would work. We needed to continue to argue against the tax with agents, clients and accountants. I and a few others felt that we should go to war against agencies. We had thousands of contractors on our books now so why not set up a contractor led agency or create the environment where people could go direct more easily. We should have pursued this idea but it fell onto the back burner, should we be opening up a second front against agencies when we were still at war with the Inland Revenue? We needed to focus on IR35 and come back to agencies later[40]. We never did and the moment was lost.

### Judicial Review

The big card we could play next would be to challenge the Government's tax in the High Court. Our PCG executive team was basically the old Sunday Trading team who had fought a long and protracted case in the courts. Andy White's business solicitors were Bond Pearce and they, then under the name of Hepherd, Winstanley and Pugh, had been the solicitors for the Sunday Trading group and knew David and Susie.

The team were convinced that a case could be mounted and won and took legal advice to that affect. We would need funding though; the costs could be in the region of £500,000 if we lost so we would have to ask contractors to put their hands in their pockets again and convince them that they could win.

There was also a feeling that we shouldn't give up - and I'm not sure the membership of PCG at that point would have allowed it. There have been many criticisms levelled at us in recent years that at that time we were maverick, reckless, out-of-control, in fact the opposite was true, the PCG leadership team considered every action and its consequences. We spent a considerable amount of time explaining to members why we would not sanction or take more extreme measures and were pilloried on the forums for holding back.

My view was that it would also keep the momentum of the PCG going, give people a feeling that we wouldn't give up. I felt if we could raise the money that we should fight it. I also saw it as democracy in action, people pulling together morally and financially.

---

[40] The PCG did setup a business to business portal service

# Chapter 2

### Revenue Issues Guidance

The first real manifestation that the proposals had been passed by Parliament was that the Inland Revenue now issued guidance on how they should be interpreted.[41] This was basically a list of case studies about what sort of work would get caught and what work wouldn't. Basically lots of infeasible situations for fictional characters called Gordon, Henry and Charlotte. Gordon was the nasty IT contractor and would be caught by the new rules, Henry (not Harry), as a consulting engineer would be outside the rules and Charlotte would be engaged as an IT contractor, but not in a way familiar to anyone reading it and so would not be caught by the rules.

It all sounded reasonable on the page but bore no real relation to the workplace, this wasn't how contractors worked. Maybe of course that was the point, they had got us now.

Interestingly enough there was no case study for kitchen or bathroom fitters, so I am not sure what they did.

The guidelines were sent to us, we now officially had a seat on the table which meant that despite all the rhetoric we were now acknowledged as a bona-fide organisation that would represent contractors. Wisely Andy despatched Kevin Miller to do these meetings. Kevin is an accountant and not political at all and to be fair, built up a good fair and working relationship with the people at the Inland Revenue.

The other recognised bodies were Anne Redston - Chartered Institute of Taxation; Mike Cullen - Independent Computer Contractors Group; Brian Keegan - IR35 Consultation Group; Ian Sutherland - The Institution of Analysts and Programmers; Paul Daniels - Forum 2000; Tim Warr - IR35 Consultation Group; Kevin Miller - Professional Contractors Group; Barry Roback - Forum 35; Peter Flaherty - Association of Technology Staffing Companies; Christine Little - The Federation of Recruitment & Employment Services; Robert Maas - The Institute of Chartered Accountants in England & Wales; Ron Downhill - The Law Society; John Whiting - The Association of Temporary & Interim Executive Services; Richard Baron - Institute of Directors; Chris Baker - Computer Services and Software Association; Peter Kirk – CBI and Simon Sweetman - Federation of Small Businesses.

We reported to members that:

The PCG has been accepted as a representative body and Kevin Miller will be leading the PCG team in negotiations with the Revenue. The devil will be in the detail. We would ask that you study these guidelines, specifically the three examples given. We

---

[41] http://www.hmrc.gov.uk/ir35/draftgn.pdf

will be carrying out a survey shortly to aid the discussions with the Revenue. We believe that many Contractors will be in the borderline area and if so this will cause massive uncertainty.

Next year, the Finance Bill is currently being drafted and will be published in spring 2000, when it will have to pass through Parliament in order for the IR35 provisions to be fully enacted. The Opposition has made it clear that they will continue to push the arguments against IR35.

The issue has become - and will remain - political. It seems clear that the Conservatives are going to attack the Government primarily on its economic policy and particularly what they have dubbed 'stealth taxes'. They believe that, along with many others, IR35 falls into this category and will therefore remain on the political agenda.

However, for the next few months, the Revenue officials are the key proponents of this, as they will be working on the guidelines. It would seem clear that they are as committed as their political masters to pushing this measure through - and some quarters believe it is being driven more by the mandarins than the Ministers.

We believe that these rules are fundamentally unfair, anti-competitive and will have a serious impact on the UK economy and we will continue to consult, educate and lobby with Ministers, officials, MPs and the media. It is important to appreciate that this is delegated legislation and therefore can be changed.

## Raising the Profile with Presentations

The strategy now was to get word out to clients, accountants and agencies as to how this new legislation would work and to try to influence them in engaging with the contractors' cause sympathetically. There was still a mass of confusion out there as to how it would work and while accountants were mystified as to how it would work, clients were concerned that it might have legal or employment implications for them. Agencies had similar concerns too and they also wanted to be able to field questions from the contractors on their books.

On 9th November Andy White gave a presentation to about 80 accountants at the Institute of Chartered Accountants. He outlined the work of the PCG and the background to the proposals. Francesca Lagerberg from the ICAEW explained the complexities of the implementation of the proposals as they stand. The accountants then debated and disagreed with each other on a number of points until one accountant in exasperation said: "This is all Alice in Wonderland stuff. The only winners are the accountants, solicitors and liquidators"

On 12th November Susie Hughes gave a presentation on behalf of PCG to an open meeting of contractors at Blackpool. She explained the work of PCG, the campaign to date and called on contractors to join up. Accountant Tim Warr also spoke and called on the Government to rethink IR35 in the context of an overhaul of the tax/NI treatment with a salary/dividend split for all businesses. Michael Jack, the local Conservative MP, was supportive of the campaign and offered his assistance.

## Going abroad and Fast Track visa

One of the charges made against previous Labour Governments in the 1970's was that they had created a brain drain because of their tax policies. We had mentioned this in our briefings against IR35 and the Tories had picked it up and used it too. It was one of those double edged sword things. I had remembered laughing in May 1997, after Labour had won the general elections, at all the celebrities who had said that they would leave. Paul Daniels had promised to leave if Labour had won and some radio DJ's made a point of ringing him up and asking him which flight he was on. The right wing had always said if you don't like it go and live in communist Russia, so it was good to get our own back.

Perhaps I was out of touch but with my own home and family (I had a two year old and another child due), I thought it would have to be really awful for me to leave, I couldn't just up sticks and go, if you were single perhaps, but not me. Were all IT contractors single twenty-something? Or were they in their 30's and 40's and now contracting out of the ten or so years' experience they have?

That was certainly true for me but the surveys came back and in them 30% of contractors in April had said they would move abroad because of IR35. I thought that was rubbish. Polls during Major and Thatcher's time would ask are you willing to pay more tax for the NHS Everyone said yes, but they then went into the polling booths and voted Tory anyway.

Andy said in his newsletter:

"The survey carried out back in April indicated that some 30% of Contractors surveyed would move overseas at the first opportunity as a result of IR 35. Many are no longer waiting for IR 35 to take effect. The way the consultation process has been handled, the frustration that the Government says one thing, but actually does the opposite and the uncertainty surrounding planning for the future are causing real anger and undermining the confidence of a highly-skilled and mobile workforce in the future of the UK. The undoubted effect will be to drive many of the most highly educated, talented and hard working members of our society, overseas."

The PCG would follow this path on the going abroad scenario and many contractors did go abroad. Holland had once offered favourable rates for IT contractors to go and work there. (They were offering a 35% tax break).

One IT contractor even bumped into Treasury Minister Andy Smith on a train to the airport, pointing to his suitcases told him that he was an IT contractor and he was leaving the country.

For such a strategy to work we needed thousands of contractors to up sticks and leave and I never thought that was going to happen. Regardless of this a middle-aged contractor and active PCG member, Brian Curnow, and others with experience of working abroad helped to put together fact sheets for working in other countries. Of course prior to IR35 the UK had been a great place to be self-employed, by accident not design. In other European countries the regulations were so complicated to work self-employed in this way that UK professionals often found themselves working freelance in Frankfurt because it was harder for the Germans to work as freelancers. The famed TV series 'Auf Wiedersehen Pet' where UK builders were working in Germany is part proof of this.

Dawn Primarolo had allegedly heard of the plans so she hit back by announcing a special fast track visa scheme to bring qualified foreign IT workers into the country to address the risk. Peter Hain went to India and built up links with IT companies. These badly thought out actions would have disastrous consequences for the UK's skill base as it opened the doors for projects and jobs to flow abroad.

Dawn Primarolo said:

> "However this government recognises that there is a more general skills shortage in engineering and in particular the IT sector.
>
> This is inflating wage costs and harming the competitiveness of British industry. The government has put in place training initiatives and is investing in higher education but it will take some time to reap the benefits of this investment.
>
> To address current demands the Home Secretary is looking at a *fast track visa scheme* for qualified applicants from Eastern Europe, Africa and India.
>
> We recognise that recruiting in these areas is difficult; the Foreign Office is looking at ways for British embassies and consulates to assist in this process. This will be in partnership and funded by industry and we are talking with leading UK recruitment specialists to help in this process."

Now not only were they going to tax IT workers more, they had plans to reduce the wages and bring in foreign workers so it seemed that the new IR35 tax would be used to fund the recruitment of foreign workers. It was incredible. Talk about taking it badly, the Government wanted to get their own back. It was Dawn's Parthian shot at contractors.[42]

Though a slow burner, the policy would become an even greater threat to the contracting model. As one contractor would later remark, 'IR35 was about whether I could afford to be a contractor, Fast Track Visas were about whether I could get work'.

## Unpicking the new Proposals

Gareth Williams, who would later become the PCG's chairman and remains to this day an active PCG member, wrote an analysis of the new tax. Gareth had previously been an MP's researcher and had written some fantastic briefing notes for the members of the House of Lords.

---

[42] The ancient Parthians were expert horse riders and were famed for firing arrows while retreating

Andy commented that:

> He [Gareth] makes some very salient points. A key conclusion is "that the independent consultancy (failing the self employment tests) will be more heavily taxed than any other way of providing an equivalent service. It would be cheaper for the consultant to work for any company but his own. It is unclear why the Government should seek to tax independent consultants in this punitive way, or what they expect to achieve by it."

Kevin Miller and others got to work putting together some new draft contracts that would clearly put contractors outside of IR35, but it was becoming clear that the Inland Revenue would also be looking at the Agency-Client contracts too and these could well catch contractors in IR35. The irony was that contractors weren't party to these contracts and could never see them, but the Agencies, now they weren't going to be affected by this, didn't care. Despite that we sent the new contracts out for consultation:

> "This draft contract has now been issued to members and other Representative bodies for their input. It describes a business relationship to meet the criteria set down for self employment. It is important to realise that whilst this describes the form of the relationship the actual substance of the relationship must also match up. We aim to gather input on the draft agreement up to Christmas. Following this we will issue the final document together with detailed guidance for members

Andy had this great belief in the idea of the wisdom of crowds. In the French revolution there was a belief in the general will, it had been created by a common movement and together they must have common wisdom and will. He felt that we had thousands of literate contractors who would all examine in detail any idea or proposal that we put together and could add some much positive critical feedback and scrutiny. He was right although the feedback all needed careful management and sometimes there was so much of it took time to absorb. In fact we could put documents or policies together and then feed them out to members to then get instant feedback. The downside was that we could spend twice as long analysing the feedback as we had in preparing the stuff in the first place. The lesson was that though we could ask for feedback we still had to provide leadership and make the decision on what to do next; we couldn't always go with the consensus. The crowd idea was amazing and gave such value to everything we did, but there was a line or a point where the crowd would become a mob and instead of leading it you would be carried by it or, at worst, trampled by it.

## Legal opinion – there is no case law

In Whitehall and in Parliament Dawn Primarolo and the Inland Revenue were insisting that case law worked for the rest of the population and everyone else, so why wouldn't it work for us? To date we had relied on the informed opinions of leading tax and industry figures, but we chose now to research real detail at existing case law into self-employment tests and their precedence in the knowledge-based sector. We engaged a team of lawyers to do the work and found as expected, that none existed.

Tony Askham of Bond Pearce, who conducted the research said:

> "It supports the argument conclusively that there are no knowledge-based industries involved in this test."

The PCG also had a case conference with a leading tax barrister. In his written submission, he concluded that:

> "The fundamental problem with the IR35 proposals is the use of the case law test for employment/self employment. This will cause a great deal of uncertainty."

# Chapter 3

### First ever e-Petition

It was nearly a month since Contractor Wednesday and our contractor 'sans-culottes[43]' were getting restless and were in need of another revolutionary journée.

They needn't have been restless since the tax was far from dropping out of the news or off Parliament's agenda.

On the 17th November William Hague told Parliament:

> "The truth behind the Government's policies on Europe and on the economy is that they think that a highly regulated and highly taxed super state is the future. The rest of us can see that it is the past.
>
> That is why they are presenting a needlessly complicated Bill on e-commerce, which will tell business how it should license itself. Only one part of the Bill is necessary or desirable.
>
> That is also why they are imposing a heavy new tax on information technology businesses—the IR35—which, the Professional Contractors Group says—
>
> Labour Members should listen to what the Professional Contractors Group had to say. It said that IR35 'shows an astonishing naivety of the knowledge based entrepreneurial sector ... that will kill the enterprise culture.'
>
> The Government's Financial Services and Markets Bill threaten to load more costs and bureaucracy on the financial services industry and we shall seek further concessions on that Bill during this Session. Only a Government who have lost all sense of self-awareness could possibly celebrate two years of introducing red tape and burdens on business by promising a deregulation Bill."

Frances Maude, the shadow chancellor, told the House on the 24th November that:

> ""The next part of the great Labour lie is enterprise. Within days of announcing to the CBI tax cuts said to be worth £40 million to entrepreneurs, the Chancellor confirmed his plan to rake in £500 million under his IR35 proposals. It is a bit of a shame that he did not speak first to Mr. Peach from Aberdeen, who wrote to his local Member of Parliament.
>
> Mr. Peach said: 'I promised to let you know how IR35 would affect me.' 'I am pleased to say that it will, in fact, have no effect as I have obtained a contract with

---

[43] In the French Revolution, the sans culottes were the radical militants of the lower class, common people not part of the aristocracy or royal family. They played a large role in the French Revolution. They were typical urban labourers and even though they weren't well equipped, they were the ones who made up the mass of the revolutionary army during the first years of the French Revolution

> a top Internet solutions company in New York, for which I must thank the Government—without IR35 I would never have been looking...
>
> Given your Government's professed declarations of support for Information Technology and, in particular, internet technologies, I wonder if my skills are really the sort that you want to drive away from the UK.''As my family will be emigrating with me, you will lose my wife's taxes as well as my own...last tax year we paid some £26,000 in Corporation Tax, Income Tax and National Insurance...and for the current year... I would estimate a net loss...of £30,000".' Is the Chancellor proud of that?
>
> The Paymaster General may come to regret her arrogant assertion that claims of a vast exodus are irresponsible and do not bear a moment's scrutiny. The fact is that the Government are hitting not only their old heartlands but the very people they persuaded to trust them before the election."

He also added:

> "It is very interesting that the hon. Gentleman, like his right hon. and hon. Friends, has no answer to the problem of IR35. We said that it would drive people abroad and it is already doing so. The economy, the country and the new technologies will all suffer from that ill-judged measure."

However, we needed to do something a bit spectacular to get the members involved, to get the ball rolling again. I am not sure where the idea came from, though I think Brian Curnow had a great hand in it, but the idea was put forward to arrange for an e-Petition to present to Parliament, the idea being that people could email in and sign it. Today of course there are e-Petitions on the Downing Street website but back in 1999 it hadn't been tried before.

### Alan Duncan helps with e-Petition

The shadow e-Minister Alan Duncan was game and gave us the right advice so David Ramsden sent out 10,000 emails and asked people to sign it by simply emailing in with a certain subject header.

Our suggestion to people was as follows:

Alan Duncan MP (Conservative Shadow E-Minister) will be carrying out a press call on Monday 29th November and will be signing this electronically. It will be the first time that a Parliamentary petition has been signed electronically.

Text of Petition

SUPPLEMENT TO THE VOTES AND PROCEEDINGS

ELECTRONIC PETITION FROM THE PROFESSIONAL CONTRACTORS GROUP (PCG)

29th November 1999

To the Honourable the Commons of the United Kingdom of Great Britain and Northern Ireland in Parliament assembled.

The Humble Petition of those members of the Professional Contractors Group and others of like disposition.

Sheweth.

That Her Majesty's Treasury and the E-Minister should give consideration to the plight of those businesses in the IT and engineering industry, whose livelihoods will be threatened by the proposals for the treatment of personal service companies, with the effect that many thousands of these workers may be forced to cease their activities or work abroad.

Wherefore your Petitioners pray that your honourable House shall urge Her Majesty's Treasury and the E-Minister to consider the plight of those members of the PCG and others similarly affected, and to reconsider IR35.

And your Petitioners, as duty bound, will ever pray, &c.

If in agreement please send email message to alanduncan@tory.org or alan.duncan@tory.org.uk

Subject: [ir35update] IR35 Petition

You must include your name and address in the body of the email. No other text is required.

Many thanks
David Ramsden

We decided to launch the e-Petition with a press conference, so with a computer screen as backdrop Alan Duncan did a press call. In 48 hours it got three thousand signatures and made it as a story on the BBC website. At one point during the press call e-mails were arriving at the rate of one every 5 seconds.

In a debate on the e-commerce Bill Alan Duncan MP questioned Labour's commitment to IT. In what turned out to be a heated exchange of words, Alan Duncan MP criticised the Government on its supposed Pro-IT stance. He questioned the validity of their commitment to IT and its capability when introducing new technology to its departments and noted its latest IT fiasco, (this one involving passports!)

Mr Duncan stated that the Government pretended "that they favour IT and the great Internet revolution, but they planned to introduce IR35" which would cripple those who were responsible for the growth and advances in that sector, forcing many to consider moving abroad. He suggested that the Government was "kicking people out" of Britain through unfair discrimination against entrepreneurs but giving visa exemptions to people from overseas.

Of course we weren't a trendy group presenting a petition so it got only a passing mention in the national press and the parliamentary authorities questioned whether they could truly accept it as a petition, but it totally wrong footed the e-Minister Patricia Hewitt. She wanted to promote e-Government and the Internet revolution but had to spend most of her time defending one of Gordon Brown's stealth taxes. Years later in the twilight hours of the Labour Government she tried to bring Brown down but failed.

The BBC ran a couple of news stories on their website, one about the e-Petition story and another a position piece by Francis Maude in which he published a lot of comments from Andy and Susie and noted too that "Even the Labour-dominated DTI select committee has said that Labour's policies on small business constitute loosely connected and apparently uncoordinated policy initiatives shooting off in all directions, generating noise and interest, but not commensurate light".[44]

### Sunday Times cover IR35

An interesting article appeared in The Sunday Times (28/11/99). The article on IR35 came under the wing of The Sunday Times' attack on Red Tape Britain. Quoting from a PCG member it clearly described the detrimental effects the proposed policy would have on their business. The news item explained to the reader the full extent of damage that would occur to self-employed contractors and small businesses should IR35 be implemented.

Ian Peters, deputy director-general of the British Chambers of Commerce, was scathing in his view of what IR35 would do to British entrepreneurs. He was quoted in The Sunday Times article as saying:

> "It is an attack on enterprise, entrepreneurship and business flexibility". He went on to state, "What is really worrying is this red tape, but more than that it is stifling enterprise."

---

[44] http://news.bbc.co.uk/1/hi/uk_politics/479087.stm

# Chapter 4

## Agencies don't care about IR35

We had all had enough of the agencies, in particular ATSCo, as far as they were concerned everything was ok now and we should all shut up. I suspect that they represented us to Government as this maverick organisation.

As for the agencies, Andy had nothing but scorn for them (even though he was a founder and major shareholder of one of the largest agencies on the South coast at the time), commenting on Gareth's IR35 analysis he said:

> This is apparently in contradiction to the viewpoint from the Agency and Contractors Accountants. Many of them seem to have given up the fight and are briefing Contractors that if they fail the self employment test they would still be advised to continue to trade through their Ltd Company.
>
> This may ensure that the Agency can reduce "employment" liabilities and the Contractor Accountants continue to charge fees, but from Gareth's analysis the only reason you would want to continue trading through your Ltd Company is if you pass the self employment tests.
>
> Contractors Accountants may work closely with Agents, but it is becoming clear that if we cannot pass the self employment tests then there seems little point in continuing to trade as a Ltd Company.
>
> As such, both Agents who cannot provide this service and Contractors Accountants will find themselves losing significant business.

Later in December Andy wrote:

**'It'll be alright on the night', claim some agencies**

At the moment, the ink is not even wet on the detail of these proposals, yet some agents and their partner "contractor accountants" appear to have folded their tent and given up. However, during the week they were 'striking camp', the PCG was in direct discussions with the Paymaster General - an indication that the game is still very much on as far as PCG is concerned.

At the second Revenue meeting held recently, Simon Sweetman of the FSB reported in his minutes (available on filestore) that "Sarah Walker of the Revenue said that they had looked at the standard agency contracts and felt that these largely had the characteristics of employment. The agencies have said they have no intention of changing them."

So even if you felt you were able to pass the self employment tests as they currently stand, the agents' contracts seem to present a danger that you would not. ATSCo did not attend either of the two IR "public consultation meetings", but asked the Revenue for its own meeting, so the assumption is that this statement has come from them or some of their members.

ATSCo, in a submission to the Inland Revenue have stated that with some minor changes on expenses IR 35 'should not present any fundamental problems for IT contractors'. The PCG rejects that view.

On the ATSCo website they state. "ATSCo was formed with 16 founder members, representing over two Billion pounds of turnover, each bringing an individual corporate style plus a shared vision for an industry respected for its quality, service and results." We would question with their present approach to their clients (the contractor) how much longer that turnover will be "over two Billion pounds".

Chairman of PCG, Andy White, wrote to Peter Searle of Computer People and ATSCo back in September of this year. He concluded: "I feel it important that contractors and agents work together on this important issue. We are certainly working closely with FRES and we would welcome more direct contact with your group. Perhaps you could call me to discuss this further after you have studied and discussed with your colleagues at ATSCo." We followed up with a call to Ann Swain (CEO of ATSCo) to chase this, but no reply has been received. Hardly surprising with what they had planned.

If choosing your next agent you may wish to note the 16 founder members of ATSCo: Abraxas, Alexander Mean Group, Apex Computer, Recruitment, Computer Futures, Computer People, Elan, Glotel, Harvey Nash, Hutchinsons Smith, Lorien, Manpower, Modis International, MSB International, Parity Resources, QA Myriad and Spring IT Personnel. See http://www.atsco.org for more information.

Ian Sutherland of 360 Group. A firm of "Contractor Accountant" who apparently work in partnership with a number of agencies including ATSCo members states "What is the Current Position on IR35?" he answer his own question with "Contracting via a Limited Company will still remain the most viable option for Contractors who wish to maximise their income."

Contractors should be wary of taking this at face value. The PCG has always believed - as have the vast majority of its members - that contracting via a limited company is the most viable option for contractors who wish to build and develop their businesses.

For contractors who pass the IR35 tests - in whatever form they eventually emerge - that will be the case. But for those contractors who fail the IR35 high jump or choose to become an employee of their client, remaining as a limited company has a serious downside.

PCG's own accountant, Kevin Miller, has done a detailed analysis of pre and post IR35 and shows that for those contractors who do not consider themselves employees of the client that failing the IR35 tests will effectively put them out of business as they would be forced into a loss. (See File store for report)

For those contractors who consider themselves employees of their client, but maybe were persuaded to leave permanent employment and set up their own PSC, then as a typical IT contractor, they are going to see a drop in take home pay of around 10,000 pounds (ten thousand pounds sterling). Of course if they continue through the PSC, as both the agent and contractor accountant would like, then they will probably not have access to any of the benefits afforded to a real employee of the client. "All the pain and no gain" as they say.

Andy White, PCG's Chairman, said: "From the beginning, we have been trying to engage in a positive and constructive dialogue with agents in order that they can become involved in assisting contractors in their battle against the disproportionate and damaging efforts of IR35.

"We are delighted that some of the small and medium sized agencies have joined PCG as associate members and are adding weight to the campaign. However, it would appear that some agencies are giving advice which is irresponsible, duplicitous and self-serving."

"Perhaps there was an assumption that in the days when contractors did not have their own representative body, there was scope for this advice. However, those days are now numbered."

Many contractors are choosing not to extend their contracts beyond April because of the uncertainty surrounding IR35 and the implications for the future. Many contractors are also starting to question the advice they have been getting. When talking to agents or their partner "contractor accountants" many report that consultants are telling them not to worry as someone senior in their company has access to 'sources close to the Government' or 'has influence in high quarters'.

They will often not mention the PCG and give every impression that matters are under control. There is a strong whiff of French cattle-feed coming out from these companies. Contractors brought up on the classic "there is going to be to be unlimited hours" have a fine nose for this BS and the result has been an upsurge in membership of the PCG.

### Comparison with nurses

The Government has made much of the comparison between the NI paid by a nurse and that of an IT contractor. Much along the lines of the evil IT contractor not paying their fair share whereas the poor nurse was cleaning up hospital wards and caring for our loved ones and was having to pay more tax than us. All this must have sounded good to the government spin doctors who, having lost the basic argument, now decided to play the sympathy card or rather read the chapter that said if you can't win the argument smear your opponent.

Meanwhile Dawn was reported to have dismissed contractors as just being 'fast typists'. This was an echo of Thatcher's criticism of the ambulance paramedics' strike when she had said they were just 'fast drivers'.

Unfortunately for the Government they hadn't thought their argument through. Lots of nurses in the NHS were agency nurses, they worked through agencies or through what is called the nursing bank. Many nurses were able to work as self-employed and there was a wealth of case law that backed this up. So a nurse could turn up at the hospital and operate the heart and lung machine programming it for patient care and would be acknowledged as self-employed, whereas a contract programmer at the factory who would be designing and programming it would not be.

Similarly, Canary Wharf was full of building workers, electrical engineers and software engineers. Electrical engineers were laying down cabling for the new networks. According to case law they were clearly self-employed as they use their own spanners, screwdrivers and hammers. However, the software engineers who turned up to configure the new networks and set up the necessary software were not self-employed according to case law.

They weren't using their own keyboards and as it wasn't their own software they were installing they were clearly 'disguised employees'. This and similar case studies were the anecdotal evidence arriving from contractors all over the country.

Perhaps if contractors had turned up in their own white van things would have been different? This was one of the key issues, it was accepted that spanners, vans and hammers would wear out or depreciate in value but what about knowledge and skills? I had knowledge of COBOL which became a bit rusty as it was not in demand so I needed to reinvest in a new skill, surely as a knowledge based worker this could be accepted as depreciation?

With regards to the sample case studies provided by the Inland Revenue the PCG conducted a survey amongst its members which, provisionally, showed that 50 per cent of businesses would fall into the 'Charlotte' (Fictitious name given to Revenue example) Grey area and the other 50 per cent would be forced into 'employment' when they have been operating as businesses.

Going forward the strategy would have to be either to deliver more certainty for contractors or produce new case law and failing that provide some insurance or support for contractors who fell foul of the tax. Of course the final option and that preferred by the Revenue was that we would all just accept the tax and pay it.

### PCG Grows and Defines more clearly what it does

By December we'd had a few clear days to think about what we did and who we were.

### BACKGROUND INFORMATION

The Professional Contractors Group (PCG) was formed in May 1999 and is one of the fastest growing Representative Groups in the UK. Membership is invited from Contractors in the Knowledge based sector (mainly IT and Engineering).

Initially formed to Campaign on the issues raised by IR 35, the scope has now been broadened following an Internet ballot of members and the annual subscription of 100 pounds is used to fund a non-profit making organisation run by a Committee of unpaid volunteers drawn from the membership. They in turn are supported by an

Executive team comprising of Legal, Accounting, PR, Lobbying, Internet and Office administration personnel who work within agreed, published, Budgets.

These experts are drawn from outside existing Industry suppliers to ensure impartiality and a high degree of independent advice. This advice is imparted via the members file store and also through an on-line discussion forum. This also allows the rapid dissemination of information concerning issues affecting Contractors. Key issues are voted upon via an Internet ballot system of all members ensuring a high degree of accountability. As a result it is recommended that Contractors considering joining should have Internet access and they must have an email address.

Associate membership is also available to Clients, Agents, Accountants and representative bodies who would support the aims of the PCG. The subscription of 250 pounds allows access to the Filestore. No further advertising (including banner adverts) is allowed and the only differentiation is the date the Associate Member joined. The earlier the membership the nearest the top of the list. Members will shortly be able to review a list of the Associate Membership together with contact details and future development is planned to add services for the mutual benefit of both classes of Membership.

Associate Membership does not carry voting rights and the funds raised from Associate subscriptions will be used for the development of these mutual services and to establish a legal "fighting fund". It will not be used to fund the core organisation, to ensure that the PCG can be fully funded by Contractors only, guaranteeing complete independence.

You can join the PCG (use the online joining form) at http://www.pcgroup.org.uk/join.html. We can accept credit card payment on line via our secure server. This allows immediate access. Alternatively you can pay by Cheque, but this will not allow access until funds are cleared. We reserve the right to refuse membership for any reason and may carry out random checks of membership applications. Full terms and conditions are available on the site for review.

# Chapter 5

## PCG Meeting the Paymaster General

PCG Chairman, Andy White and PCG member, Philip Ross, were invited to a meeting with the Paymaster General, Dawn Primarolo, on Thursday (December 9). The meeting, which overran by 20 minutes, gave PCG the opportunity to explain the working of the knowledge-based economy and the problems associated with trying to apply the self-employment tests to a sector which has never operated in this manner.

During the meeting, there was a 'full and frank exchange of views' and it concluded with a promise that PCG would submit its proposals on IR35 to Ms Primarolo. The notes of the meeting are available to PCG members in the filestore

It had been a long time coming, we had tried for ages to get a meeting with Dawn Primarolo, the Paymaster General. It is one of the things I could never quite work out – when the campaign had begun had Andy and David written to Dawn to get a meeting? I have always assumed that they had. Regardless of that she was not an easy person to see. What was supposed to be an appendix tax in the budget was now proving a major embarrassment. It should have been easy, contractors were independent, by their very nature they weren't organised and should have been an easy target. Two years earlier it would probably have been the case but now the Internet was here and it created the opportunity to coordinate a nationwide organisation and action, the Government had targeted probably the only group of people who knew, at that stage, how to use it effectively for this purpose. The organisation had come together without anyone ever having actually met in person and by the action of the press of a button a nationwide letter writing campaign could be initiated, and as we had seen, a mass lobby of Parliament organised.

I was told by a parliamentary contact that the Treasury and others felt that the PCG were punching 'above their weight'. 'What does that mean?' I asked. 'So what if we are, that is a good thing as far as I am concerned, just because we don't follow the rules and the paths that more traditional and established organisation do, maybe we are writing our own rules. The only way to stop us punching is to start listening to us. I am not going to fall for that old trick of if we shut up you will listen, we will shut up when you start listening'.

I had entered into email and postal correspondence with both Dawn Primarolo and Patricia Hewitt on my return from conference. They were obviously in touch with each other though I could sense that they weren't in the same political camps. The PCG had contact with Patricia and we, though probably me, had said that we welcomed the fact that the original IR35 proposals had been reformed but felt that the changes hadn't gone far enough.

We then had Lord McIntosh quoting us in the Lords as welcoming the new proposals:

> Before I turn to the arguments put forward by the noble Lord, Lord Goodhart, it is necessary for me to quote from the response of the Professional Contractors Group

to the press release of 23rd September. It said, first, that the removal of registration is to be welcomed; it would have been an administrative burden. That we did, and it is not in contest.

Secondly, the group said that the move from a single test of supervision, direction and control is to be welcomed. That we have done; it has not been contested.

Thirdly, on the transfer of a responsibility for accounting for tax and NIC from the client to the service company, it said that it is **"very welcome indeed"**. That is not much support for the arguments put forward by noble Lords opposite.

To say I was upset by this would have been an understatement. Later in the PCG's existence this failure would have been enough to send me to the metaphorical guillotine but at this stage we were just annoyed. Andy said that we should never use the word '*welcome*' again as they had spun it against us. We blamed the special advisor at the DTI for sending it across. Politics has to be conducted with a certain amount of goodwill and protocol but it seemed that every time we gave an inch they took it as a weakness.

I had been in correspondence with Dawn since my return from the conference; I posted, faxed and emailed every letter. I sent through a number of case studies, criticised the consultation and attacked ATSCo for being unrepresentative. I said just because they have thousands of contractors on their books doesn't mean that they can speak for them, which she seemed to accept in her reply though there was a significant gap in correspondence, partly because I had to deal with a compliance visit from the Inland Revenue, I just hope that was a coincidence.

The contention between us was that I'd said I didn't think the Schedule D employment tests would work for the knowledge based sector as there was no case law.

I occupied this sort of in-between land, I was both Labour and PCG and could campaign as PCG on the laws and could also proffer my own opinion.

I wrote to her with a proposal that 'it should be possible to retain profits in the company in order to grow it and that the self-employment tests should be modernized to take into account this new way of working'. What I wanted was some tiny shift on the position they currently held, a tiny chink of light that we could work with. I hoped that she could be a flexible friend, not the inflexible friend Prof. John Burton had suggested.

In a letter to me on the 10$^{th}$ November she told me 'I believe your worries are exaggerated'.

My hopes were dashed when she said in her letter to me on the 18$^{th}$ November 1999:

'I believe that the fairest way to distinguish between "disguised employees" and "business people" is to use the same tests which are currently used throughout the economy for people who do not have limited companies. I do not accept that these tests are not applicable to IT contractors or any other specialist group"

The only chink of light we had now was that the Inland Revenue had been empowered by Parliament to interpret the rules as it saw fit in its guidance.

## The meeting

I don't know how much notice Andy or the PCG had about the meeting with Dawn Primarolo but I had very little about a day, I think the original plan was for David Ramsden to go to the meeting but Andy thought that as I was Labour and had met Dawn before that they would have been better off with me.

The reason the meeting had come about was that basically Dawn got fed up with fending off questions in Parliament about when she was going to meet with contractor representatives and saying she had met with ATSCo or Forum2000 or the CSSA was no longer going to wash. She had to meet with us to shut up her critics if nothing else.

So on the 9$^{th}$ December 1999, I met Andy White at the Red Lion across the road from the Treasury. I was too nervous to have a drink. We had very little to go on other than that the Paymaster General would see us. Was she going to negotiate? Was she going to congratulate us on our campaign thus far? Was she going to concede some ground?

Not a chance. No negotiation, no new announcement, it was to be just a formality but it would mean the one and only time that Dawn and Andy would formally meet together.

At conference Dawn didn't seem to like Andy much and blamed him personally for all the nasty letters that came to both her office and that of the lead civil servant on IR35 - Sarah Walker. One contractor had sent in a death threat to Sarah Walker. Instead of opening a back channel with us to talk about it they leaked the information to The Financial Times who called Susie and asked her to defend the indefensible. Though a tricky conversation with a journalist ready to seize on any pause or hesitation, Susie had been clear in her denouncement of it and that it had nothing to do with the PCG. I don't think it made it out as a story.

Andy and I signed in at the lobby, put on our visitor badges and spent a few uncomfortable minutes waiting to be collected. Eventually who should turn up to collect us, none other than Sarah Walker herself. We exchanged pleasantries and walked through into the inner sanctum of the Treasury building. Andy remarked that it was similar to a colonial building he had been to in India. Sarah was friendly and indulged us when we paused to look at things of architectural interest during our passage through. We made a few deliberate stops to look and made conversation. It was in part a power play, I wanted some control and wanted the Paymaster General to have to wait for us, but it was mainly out of nerves.

When we arrived at Dawn's office we found a very traditional layout. My memory may be playing tricks on me but I remember it as being dimly lit with a standard lamp, a traditional desk and a leather arm chair. Ticking regularly in the background was a large grandfather clock. If this was the heartbeat of the Treasury it wasn't a digital or modern setting, but a largely old-fashion one representing their largely old fashion view of the economy.

Dawn greeted Andy cordially as he came through the door and remarked that it was nice to now finally meet up. I was a few steps behind Andy and came in smiling saying 'Hello Dawn'. My greeting wasn't so cordial, but was something along the lines of 'oh god, not you, I might have known'. She ignored my offer of a hand shake leaving my hand hanging in the air as she turned her back on me. She invited Andy to sit down, no such offer was made to me and I had to find a chair and drag it over. Sarah Walker sat slightly behind Dawn in advisor mode. I adopted a similar position with Andy. Dawn and Andy could go head to head. She had succeeded in creating an atmosphere of intimidation; she completed it now by looking at us with sharp disinterest and saying 'you asked for a meeting, so you have got one. What do you want?' She was a real professional.

I found my composure enough to mutter across the table 'well lucky us…' Dawn ignored me but Sarah caught my eye and the thick tension mounted in the room. Andy wasn't here to play games; he had his prepared script and was going to stick to it.

'Paymaster General, thank you for asking us to come here today…'

She enjoyed the formality and nodded at him to continue.

He proceeded to explain the history of the PCG, his own background and why he had set it up. He talked about the PCG and the concerns of members and how he was trying to address them. Dawn would occasionally tut at something, mutter something or shake her head in a discrete way. Andy was focused on his script and papers and missed this body language. I let the first couple of tuts go and then interrupted Andy mid-flow.

'…and that's why we need to build a level playing field for both contractors in IT and Oil and Gas…' said Andy

TUT.

'You tutted then…' I interrupted

Fiery eyes turned on me.

'You tutted then, why did you tut?'

Her eyes said 'I am the Minister of State, how dare you interrupt me like this'.

Mine lit brightest blue and replied 'well behave like one then',

Back in the physical world she said

'I didn't' she said.

Andy looked up from his script and stopped mid sentence.

'Yes you did, I just heard you' I said. 'Don't you think these are important points?', then I said to Sarah Walker, 'She did tut didn't she?'

Sarah remained loyal and said that she didn't think that there was any tutting,

'Are you sure?' I insisted

So I offered a half-baked apology about the tutting but as I did so an infectious smile spread across my lips and caused Andy to issue a half laugh and it flashed through the Paymaster General before she could suppress it and through her operations director. Dawn's atmosphere had been broken.

'I apologise', I smiled, 'I thought that Dawn was disagreeing with what you had to say, I now realise that she wasn't and I am sorry' I said with my subtext suggesting she did agree with us.

There had been a large effort to ignore me at the meeting and pretend that I didn't exist and I had now shown that I did.

'I didn't say I agreed with the points...' said the Paymaster General

Now I felt guilty at this point, because I had interrupted Andy's presentation. (When I say presentation, there were no PowerPoint slides; Andy was just reading out his notes)[45]. Andy had approached it from a business perspective; he would make a business presentation, in effect pitch his ideas but I wasn't convinced that this was a business environment and thought that although the words were coming out, they weren't listening. I didn't know how long we had for the meeting but felt we needed to cut to the chase. It was clear that Dawn was simply just going through the motions in having the meeting and we needed to engage her, or at least give her a hard time.

'Look', I said leaning forward, 'we do appreciate you having this meeting with us'

'You asked for it...'

'I know and we got it. We are here to speak for our members who do have genuine concerns...'

'Oh, we've seen the things your members have to say...' she added in a sinister way,

---

[45] I still wonder how it would have turned out if I had let Andy finish, he hadn't pre-briefed me so I didn't know what sort of argument or case he building

'Where?'

'On your site for instance'

'Have you seen them?'

'Not personally' she admitted

'Where on the site, because most of the content is in a secure area for members only?'[46]

'We've been told' said Sarah

We weren't getting anywhere.

'Look, we have our differences but there is common ground between us, we want this tax to work but not to affect genuine businesses and I hope you do too…'

'Our position is simple' Dawn stated, 'these measures are necessary to prevent avoidance of tax and national insurance contributions by workers using personal service companies. We can't have people setting up companies as vehicles to avoid paying national insurance'

'We aren't here to support tax avoidance' said Andy, 'but to speak up for genuine businesses who freelance for a living'

'If they are genuine businesses then they should have nothing to fear' Dawn interjected and Sarah Walker nodded in support.

'But that is the thing' said Andy, 'we don't think that the self-employment tests work for the knowledge based sector'

'They work for everyone else, what makes you so special?'

'We are not special; it is just that the case law doesn't exist yet for knowledge based workers'

Andy proceeded to talk about the Agencies Act that forced contractors to work through agencies as limited companies. All this seemed to be new to Dawn as if she had never heard of it. She persisted in arguing that we didn't need to work through limited companies believing that we only did it so that we could avoid paying national insurance. The example of the former head of the BBC who had set up a shell company to do that came up as an example. The discussion moved forward until at one point Dawn exclaimed with supporting noises from Sarah Walker that:

---

[46] We suspected that the Inland Revenue had a spoof membership of PCG to read the forums

'Our experts tell us that there is no reason why case law can't be effectively applied to this sort of work'

'What experts are those?' I asked.

Now the discussions had been going quite well up until this point, in fact it was discussion and not an argument.

'Our experts' she reiterated.

'Where are they from?'

Dawn deferred to Sarah Walker who explained that they were the Inland Revenue experts.

'Ah, so the same people who drew up the tax tell you now that it will work, it's like the Police Complaints Authority. There are no surprises there then.... because' I continued, 'our independent experts tell us the opposite, they say that it won't work because the necessary case law hasn't yet been established'

'What independent experts?'

'We asked a team of lawyers to look into it for us'

'Well Philip, they are hardly independent then if you have paid them' said Dawn.

'We asked for independent legal opinion' said Andy, 'there is nothing wrong with that, besides ask the opinion of the ICAEW, CIOT, the CBI and others'.

We managed now to focus on case law and the differences between limited company contractors and the self-employed and case law. We ran over our allotted time but by now Dawn was engaged and told Sarah she wanted to carry on, we did so for a further twenty minutes.

At one point we talked about benefits from national insurance. I pointed out that when I was between contracts I couldn't go and claim unemployment benefit even though I had paid the national insurance. Dawn stuttered on this point and Sarah Walker claimed that we could claim 'laid off' benefits. Later I tried that at the job centre later and they laughed in my face. I have always thought that one key argument about IR35 put forward at the highest level by the Inland Revenue has turned out to be wrong or I was tricked by the Letchworth Job Centre staff or both.

Andy engaged Dawn effectively on the case studies and rules and I took a back seat. He talked about larger consultancies and contractors working next to people from body shops and also contractors often moved from assignment to assignment. She talked of carpenters and plumbers as knowledge based workers and refused to see any distinction between them and software or other engineers who used new technology.

The arguments Andy put forward were strong, cohesive and logical but they didn't win over the Paymaster General who stubbornly clung to her opinions, although she did listen and engage a little. At the end she said how much she had enjoyed our strong and frank discussion and that it was very welcomed and not all her meetings were liked that. We concluded it with a promise that we would submit our own proposals on IR35 to her.

As we left I talked to her in passing about the Internet and how good the PCG web site was and she said they were trying to make improvements to the Revenue site. She said that she didn't go on the Internet much herself. I offered to come back and see her again but she suggested that we just spoke to Sarah if we had any issues, which is what happened.

In summary there was no meeting of minds, Dawn wasn't convinced and what is more didn't want to be convinced. We knew more about the topic than her and I was shocked at her lack of understanding as to why we all used limited companies. She really thought that we just did it to avoid tax. Andy liked Dawn, respected her, and the lessons I'd learnt from our previous encounters was that the only thing she respected was a hard fight. If you stood up for yourself then you won some respect from her. I left the meeting disappointed and tired, I knew that we hadn't won but we had fought so hard.

I look back on the meeting now and can't really imagine that many ministerial meetings are like that. Perhaps I should have been a bit more respectful like Andy was. He always addressed her as minister where as I showed almost totally unreciprocated familiarity.[47] I interrupted and was perhaps a little rude, but in my defence I would say that I reciprocated the same rudeness and interruptions that we were subjected to. Years later I was told that the 'new PCG' was run by grownups not mavericks, people who knew their place and were respectful. It depends what you want. We were bolshie Jacobins who, instead of waiting to be asked to a meeting, force them to have one with us. Metaphorically we seized our place at the table, we didn't wait for it to be offered. We fought for concessions and changes, we weren't grateful recipients, but those would also be the charges against us later, not that we didn't fight hard enough but that we fought too hard for the PCG.

### Dawn's version of events to Parliament

When asked about what had happened at our meeting this is what she told Parliament on the 9th March 2000. In short, in a veiled complement on the success of our campaign, she accused us of scare mongering about the IR35 and called us 'tax cheats'. We weren't scare mongering at all, we were just highlighting the opinions of the thousands of small businesses and of established bodies like the ICAEW and the CIOT.

---

[47] On a couple of occasions she called me by first name

The Paymaster General (Dawn Primarolo): I met representatives of the professional contractors group in December. I explained to them why the Government believe that it is necessary to prevent avoidance of tax and national insurance contributions by workers using personal service companies.

Dr. Cable: What advice has the Minister received from the Prime Minister's adviser on e-commerce, who has publicly expressed his disquiet about the impact of the tax on our knowledge-based industry? How does the Inland Revenue propose to treat the tens of thousands of IT contractors, who are honest and do not avoid taxation, but have great difficulty in distinguishing between employed and self-employed status, as they are now required to do, because of the complexities of IT contracts?

Dawn Primarolo: First, it is not true that the e-commerce envoy has been making representations to the Treasury about relaxing the rules. He made it clear that he supports the Government's policy of stopping unfair tax and national insurance avoidance.

Secondly, IR35 deals with avoidance in cases in which one employee in a company avoids tax and national insurance. That means that such employees do not pay tax and national insurance, which are paid by other people who are self-employed or on pay-as-you-earn pay. The hon. Gentleman should explain why he is prepared to support a group of workers whose companies their own advisers describe as tax havens. Why should they be allowed to continue to cheat honest taxpayers?

Ms Julia Drown (South Swindon): A small IT business in my constituency has told me that it fears that it will not be able to survive and continue to prosper under the new IR35 rules. Will my hon. Friend liaise with colleagues in the Government to ensure that the Inland Revenue and the Small Business Service work with such companies to ensure that they can continue to be successful?

Dawn Primarolo: Frightening and undermining the legitimacy of the many hundreds of thousands of legitimate companies that operate as service companies is part of the scare tactics of those who seek to avoid tax by using service companies. The Inland Revenue continues to advise those companies that will be caught by the rules through a helpline and a comprehensive website. We are ensuring that honest taxpayers will be strengthened by the rules, not undermined, and that people compete on skills, not by using the rules only for tax advantage, as the few are doing.

Mr. Richard Ottaway (Croydon, South): Is it not clear from yesterday's written answers that the Minister has absolutely no idea of the damage that IR35 is causing to the knowledge-driven economy? The Government's manifesto at the last election said that they would Give Britain's entrepreneurs and small businesses the backing they deserve.

Instead, we have IR35--a stealth tax introduced by the back door. The result is uncertainty over self-employed status, a lot of competitiveness and a brain drain to more stable tax systems. Did not the biggest gaffe come from the Minister for Small Business and E-Commerce, who said that she would use a recent visit to the United States to try to woo back British expats? Looking at the chaos caused by IR35, who in his right mind would come back to this mess? It is pain without gain.

Dawn Primarolo: Perhaps the hon. Gentleman needs to be reminded of everything that the Government have done for small businesses: the small business company rate cut; the new 10p corporation tax starting rate; first-year capital allowances; enterprise management incentives; and help through the Small Business Service. He still has not told the House why his party supports a few workers who use their companies to avoid paying tax when millions of others pay their tax. I direct him to Computer Contractor magazine of October 1999. Under the headline "Make hay while the sun shines", it said:

Beg, borrow or steal to avoid paying higher tax rates this year. Next year you will not be able to avoid it. You should recognise that your company . . . is a tax haven.

He has to realise that, as we have rules in the system for self-employed and PAYE employees, it is not unreasonable to expect those few who are avoiding the rules to comply with them.

## Our final response

We'd had a frank exchange with Dawn on IR35. We said that we would send in our own proposals but when it was discussed on the forums no one had any faith in the Government actually listening to us still. It was felt that it would form just part of a box ticking exercise with the Government. If we put in new proposals perhaps the Revenue would use it as 'proof' that it has consulted and listened.

At the end of December Susie wrote to members to explain why we wouldn't send anything in.[48] Perhaps that was a mistake, perhaps we should have submitted something but at the time our conclusion was not to.

> 'Regular readers' will recall that the last newsletter contained information about the recent meeting with Paymaster General, Dawn Primarolo and Andy White and Philip Ross from PCG. The PCG said it would return to the Paymaster General with further comments.
>
> PCG and our members felt we would not go down the road of submitting yet another flawed half way house to the Government which, from past experience of other's proposals, would be rejected out of hand and used as evidence of 'consultation'.
>
> The Government has stated its commitment to the knowledge-based sector and small businesses, but its actions have consistently belied its words. Therefore, the PCG will not attempt to make a bad job better, when the fundamental basis is fatally flawed.
>
> PCG is in a unique position to understand what the future holds because it is its members with the support of the PCG who will make this happen. As a result, the

---

[48] http://www.shout99.com /contractors/showarticle.pl?n=&id=38&p=1

PCG has clearly laid out what options lay before the Government at this late stage and what the subsequent action will be.

We then laid out what the future would hold for the IT contractors depending on the choice of actions open to the Government at that time.

# Chapter 6

## The Stephen Timms fiasco

Now I liked Stephen Timms MP, I felt sorry for him having to implement IR35. Also as a Labour person he was the only other IT person I knew with a similar deep interest in politics but also because years later I am also indebted to him. In 2003 I was working in Parliament for Tony McWalter MP and walking through the Palace and crossed an internal road which I never realised had traffic. In a day dream I stepped into the road and as a hand pulled me back a car whisked past just missing me, had I not been stopped I may have been seriously injured. The person who saved me was Stephen Timms MP.

In December 1999, someone uncovered the fact that Stephen Timms used to work for the IT consultancy company OVUM and he held some shares. It was suggested that as larger consultancy companies would benefit from IR35 that he had breached parliamentary protocol. I knew nothing about this until I saw it in the press. I thought it was a very tenuous connection. Also, given the amount of brilliant stuff we had done – e-Petition, mass lobby, House of Lords win – why was it this that made it as a big story?

I thought it was pretty crappy to have done it. I think you should always fight on the facts not against people and their personal lives and personalities, but I suspect I was in a minority of one on this. Everyone else was angry with the Government and ready to fight and hurt them wherever they could.

On the basis of a few nasty headlines about a decent man I felt that we had damaged our relations with the Government and Labour. I know they may have been nasty to us, but that's them, not us but it happened and this is what was published on Christmas Eve, not a nice Christmas present.

This is what the PCG had to say about it in the press:

"At the last General Election, the majority of the membership of PCG voted for New Labour. They were attracted by the bright new vision for Britain portrayed by Tony Blair and fed up with the constant revelation of sleaze by Old Tory. This latest revelation indicates that New Labour are no better.

"We believe that IR35, which will damage if not destroy many small IT and engineering consultancies, has been lobbied for by big business, like Ovum.

"Faced with the Internet revolution these companies can see that tomorrow's competitor is the small knowledge based company leveraging their skills through the Internet. With high fixed costs the larger conventional consultancy runs the risk of being blown away. After all, it is not if these higher costs bring a better result; look at fiascos with the Passport Agency and the new air traffic control for proof of this.

"These bigger companies are fighting back to prevent this. It is clear that a major factor in their armoury is their influence with this Government.

"These stories confirm this, and our members who put their trust in Tony Blair at the last election, will wonder is there any party in this country that can Govern for the interests of the majority rather than the narrow self serving interests of their 'cronies'.

"Is it any wonder that many of our members are taking their knowledge and boarding planes never to return?"

Though it was revealed that his shares had been placed in some sort of trust which too many of us sounded like some sort of tax avoidance scheme. Do as I say, not as I do?

# Chapter 7

I won't pretend that after our meeting with the Paymaster General that we had built up any special rapport nor had a special relationship but if we had after the Stephen Timms story it would be broken, at least in the short term. The PCG team and the members seemed to think they could launch these rocket attacks at the Government's camp and there wouldn't be any consequences, in politics you reap what you sow.

I raised objections at the time which were listened to thoughtfully by Andy and Susie but among the membership my criticism of the policy was held up by some as reasons why I couldn't be trusted, that I was a Labour supporter in disguise. That wasn't true, there was no disguise. I was a Labour supporter but opposed to IR35.

## Seminars... spreading the word

We had been split on what to do next, a number of people wanted to focus our attention on unpicking the agency model. Now that a group of contractors had got together in the PCG surely we could build our own agency model and run them into the dirt. ATSCo was generally hated and a group of contractors formed a spoof organisation called ATSCO (Association of Technology and Software Consultants) as opposed to Association of Technology Staffing Companies. The contractors bought the .org.uk whereas the agency one was ATSCO.org. (They are now called APSCO Association of Professional Staffing Companies). I wasn't part of this and rolled my eyes when I had heard what they had done, but I did think that we should have gone after the agency model but the consensus was to try and bring agencies onside and persuade clients to be amenable to IR35 friendly contracts.

As the first step in this process a series of IR35 information seminars were organised. Susie, Andy, Kevin and a few others traipsed around the country explaining to contractors, clients, agents and accountants what IR35 meant. I went to the one at Regents College.

In an effort to be nice Andy wrote a personal note to Dawn Primarolo telling her that they were holding a seminar in Bristol, her constituency. Andy meant it in a kindly way thinking that perhaps he was following some sort of parliamentary protocol. Dawn I suspect, didn't see it like that at all and instead thought he was sticking two fingers up. She was married to a senior UNISON official (Ian Ducat, a regional secretary) and with the details of the seminar to hand they arranged for a UNISON picket of the event. Lots of aging UNISON activists and shop stewards paraded outside the meeting room with banners and leaflets condemning them as tax dodgers in an attempt to intimidate them.

Contractors never forgot this and in 2011 I came across an Internet posting about it[49]:

> Next time a UNISON member whines about getting a bad deal from Government, expecting the private sector employees to pick up the tab for their excessive pensions, I shall show them the solidarity they showed to me and other 'worker' contractors

Andy was furious about it, when I saw him at Regents College he showed me a copy of their flyer and told me of the link between Dawn and Unison. I suggested that there must have been some pillow talk about it and we should take it as a compliment. Lots of PCG members wrote to UNISON HQ to complain. Unison tended to write confused letters back as they thought the PCG was about 'Primary Care Groups', this being the same UNISON who had raised no complaint about excessive pay for senior council executives nor did I see them condemn the use of personal services companies by public sector executives.

Tuesday, 01 February 2000

IR35 INFORMATION SEMINARS

The Professional Contractors Group is holding a series of IR35 information seminars around the country for contractors, agents, clients and other interested groups.

IR35 is a controversial proposal by the Government which would force independent contractors - mainly from IT and engineering - into an 'employee status for tax and NI purposes. The result will be that tens of thousands of small businesses are forced to close down, while many highly-skilled people take their expertise overseas.

The purpose of these seminars is to give contractors and others an explanation of IR35 as it currently stands; the role of the PCG; and the future options available to contractors. The seminars also allow for a detailed question and answer session with the country's leading experts in this field.

The panel will include PCG's chairman Andy White, director David Ramsden, accountant Kevin Miller and lawyers and tax experts.

PCG chairman, Andy White said: "The Government is proposing to introduce this measure in April, despite losing every logical argument as to the damage it will do to individuals and the knowledge-based economy.

"PCG has been at the forefront of the campaign against IR35 since April. We are aware of the need for information about this issue and our panel of experts has collectively unparalleled experience and knowledge of the issue. Together, they are in a position to explain the detail of the proposals and look to the future alternatives available to contractors."

---

[49] http://www.housepricecrash.co.uk/forum/index.php?showtopic=160866&st=105

There will be two two-hour seminars at each venue - an afternoon session (2pm) and an evening session (7pm). Initially the seminars were restricted to members of the PCG. However, such was the demand for places that additional seminars have been added to the programme in order to allow non-members to attend.

Anyone wishing to attend should register

It will cost £25 to attend and booking is carried out completely on-line. The venues and dates are:

Feb 9 (Wed) - Eastleigh Posthouse, Southampton

Feb 15 (Tues) - Stakis Treetops, Aberdeen

Feb 16 (Wed) - Kelvin Park Lorne Hotel, Glasgow

Feb 17 (Thurs) - Holiday Inn, Newcastle

Feb 22 (Tues) - Renaissance Hotel, Manchester

Feb 23(Wed) - Moat House Hotel, Birmingham

Feb 24 (Thurs) - Watershed Media, Bristol
<<<<< picketed by unison>>>>

Feb 28 (Mon) - Regents College, London

Mar 1 (Wed) - Regents College, London

Mar 2 (Thurs) - Chilford Halls, Cambridge

## Andy's New Year's Campaign Review

In January 2000, now with 5,000 members in the PCG, Andy was fired up after his Christmas break and wrote to members his views on the way ahead. He would be damning about Dawn's view of contractors and criticise accountants who were conning their clients that they could get them round IR35. The FSB had told him that the Revenue had been looking at agency contracts and that these all clearly pointed to contractors being caught by IR35. With ATSCo and other agencies having now abandoned the IR35 cause, we stood alone. [50]

We noted that:

> The clear objective of the Revenue is to force you to work as a "temp". They want you working on PAYE, which does not cost as much to collect as other forms of tax. The possible impact on the enterprise culture and the loss of opportunity for you to build a business is a foreign language to them. They

---

[50] http://www.shout99.com /contractors/showarticle.pl?n=&id=41&p=1

work for a Paymaster General who considers that any one earning more than a nurse is a lifelong Tory voter and deserves all that is coming to them.

## Campaign Review by PCG Chairman

On March 12th 1999, five days after the Budget, I started a web site which led to the formation of the PCG and a full time (unpaid) campaigning job for me. Nine months on and at the start of the New Year I thought it useful to review the situation.

When we started PCG no-one gave us a chance. Against all the odds we have achieved significant movement from the original, unworkable proposals. At the same time we have created the fastest growing representative group ever and one that, for the first time, gives contractors a real voice.

Members now know that they have 5000 fellow members who can support and back them up if they get grief from the Government, Agents, Accountant or Clients.

So nine months on is it enough? The answer is a resounding NO. As in March I hear people saying that "this Government has got a massive majority and will not change". "It is a waste of time trying"; "You will need a miracle". It is not "Constructive"

Many of those who question our need or ability to influence events further are those whose businesses have not been put at risk by the proposals. Some of those who live off the back of contractors have even welcomed the proposals!

The Government has changed its position once and it can do it again. Nothing is yet cast in stone. Our members are convinced that if the Government truly understood the situation they would modify their proposals once again.

My view is we need to continue to explain ourselves, our position and our concerns to those politicians whose opinions count and who have not yet understood the full impact of what is proposed.

The PCG now has members in 9 out of 10 constituencies. They are eager to educate their MP. We have members going to MPs surgeries, visiting Ministers and contacting civil servants deep in the bowels of Whitehall. If it moves, has a pulse and has a passing interest in IR 35 it gets an email.

Our views are spelt out in more detail in my letter to Gordon Brown. This is a follow up to a meeting that a member had with the Chancellor of the Exchequer. (See link at end of this email)

## What can you do to help?

I guess it is important to first understand why you need to help.

The objective of the Government is to remove the tax advantage of providing your services through a Ltd Company or partnership "in circumstances where an individual worker would otherwise be an employee of the client" (from IR website)

If you are a Ltd Company contractor working on a client's site ask yourself the following question. Do I consider myself an employee of my client? (If the answer is yes and you have been forced into working through a service company then we would like to hear from you.)

Now ask your client "Do you consider I am an employee? (If they answer yes ask them "can I have access to all the perks that you give your permanent staff?)

My guess is that in 99.9 per cent of cases the answers to both questions will be NO. If this is the case then clearly you are not employees of your client. Again, if I am wrong e-mail me, I want to know.

The Government does not consider a simple question of you and your client's motives to be the best way of checking this out. To prove that you are not an employee they wish you to consider if you pass the self employment tests. They say that everybody else can pass these so you should be able to. No problem. These are the tests that, for example, a carpenter will use - and who, incidentally, the Paymaster General considers to be a knowledge based worker.

But here is the problem. Check this out from the minutes of the recent Revenue meeting and as reported by Simon Sweetman of the Federation of Small Businesses (FSB.)

"Sarah Walker of the Revenue said that they had looked at the standard agency contracts and felt that these largely had the characteristics of employment. The agencies have said they have no intention of changing them."

In other words you may not consider yourself to be an employee of the client, but the Contract between your Agent and the Client will say that you are and allow the Revenue to tax you as an employee. (Many of you will not even have sight of this contract)

To then check out how really unfair this is go and ask your client (or Agent) if it is possible for you to contract with them as a "self employed" (sole trader), knowledge based worker. As you have both agreed you are not employed it means you must be "self employed". The added advantage is that you will not have the hassle and expense of running a Ltd company.

I would be interested to receive emails on this. I expect that your clients will tell you that the tests for self employment are uncertain and they cannot take the risk of tax penalties of getting it wrong. As such they will only deal with incorporated companies. For the same reason your agent will have asked for a copy of your certificate of incorporation.

As I say to Gordon Brown in my letter "The problem is this: if self-employment status had provided certainty we would already have been using this method. The simple fact is that due to the way we work in the knowledge based sector, clients will not contract with us if we are 'self employed' rather than' incorporated businesses' because of the uncertainty arising from these outdated tests. (There are additional benefits of incorporation for a knowledge based business which include limited liability, retention of IPR and ability to build up equity value, but a fundamental reason for trading as a Ltd Company is because we have to, not because of the supposed tax advantages)"

**Now consider the role of Agencies and Clients.**

We have received reports of an Agent and their partner Accountant briefing clients that the impact on contractors will be limited and therefore there will be no impact on Clients - business as usual. Our source said the client "breathed a huge sigh of relief when he heard this"

We disagree. Contractors who are forced into "circumstances where an individual worker would otherwise be an employee of the client" and taxed accordingly will want access to the same rights as employees. How about share options? Farfetched? In the USA contract workers seeking such employee benefits have just won a court case against Microsoft for this - even though they were working through an Agency. PCG will be making clear that our members who are forced by legislation into "disguised employment" will use legislation to gain these rights and have engaged legal opinion to support this.

Then we come to the question of what it will cost the Contractor. If you fail IR 35 your company will never make a profit, in fact the pathetic 5 per cent for expenses will probably mean that you will make losses and will never be able to retain earnings to provide for periods between Contracts. Unlike the real permanent employee you will have to pay for training, down time, secretarial support etc from taxed earnings. The result is likely to be reduction of up to 25 per cent in your post tax income. An analysis carried out by Accountant, Kevin Miller, shows that to make this up, rates to your Client will need to increase by 37 per cent (see link at end of this email).

We suspect that many contractors believe there will be a loophole. One Agent told our researcher "do not worry, our accountants are working on a loophole round the problem" Wrong. This is delegated legislation. This means that after April 5th the Revenue can take action without going back to Parliament. Offshore trusts, Composites, you name them they will have limited shelf life. From leaks within the Revenue we hear that the first tweak is already in the pipeline. Those who fail IR 35 will be required to pay tax and NI monthly to prevent overseas based contractors from absconding without paying. After all you are "employees" now and employees pay monthly.

The clear objective of the Revenue is to force you to work as a "temp". They want you working on PAYE, which does not cost as much to collect as other forms of tax. The possible impact on the enterprise culture and the loss of opportunity for you to build a business is a foreign language to them. They work for a Paymaster General who considers that any one earning more than a nurse is a lifelong Tory voter and deserves all that is coming to them. She in turn works for a Chancellor who is probably the most powerful in history, working within a Government with a huge majority.

Good. Nothing worthwhile comes easy. Our challenge is to work within these constraints and effect change. The PCG has drawn a line in the sand on this issue. Our members are genuine businesses and should be taxed accordingly.

You can help by clearly stating to your Agent that if IR 35 comes in as presently proposed you will not renew your Contract past April 5th this year.

Help them explain this problem to your client by copying both your agent and your client the letter to Gordon Brown and the briefing document prepared by Kevin Miller.

Get them to inform their MP and Industry association. Ask them to join the PCG as an Associate member to ensure they keep fully briefed on this key issue.

Finally if you have not already joined the PCG, help us to help you by joining up.

Kind regards

Andy White
Chairman PCG

### Opening up new fronts

While Dawn had been concentrating her efforts in persuading her husband to get UNISON shop stewards to picket PCG information meetings, PCG members and the PCG team had focused their attention in a more productive fashion. Andy's New Year thesis and call to arms did the trick. Fresh letters flowed into MPs inboxes. We made particular efforts to target Labour MPs in marginal seats (and Lib Dems too). The off-shore oil and gas people were making a lot of noise and Lib Dem MPs like Robert Smith were leading the charge. Even Anne Begg, the Labour MP for Aberdeen South, was paying attention. While she was initially sympathetic to some of the issues Ann Begg told me that she had received some nasty and personal letters which were basically counterproductive to the cause; a case of the messengers damaging the message.

Andy, I and other leading PCG focused our attention on the new e-Envoy Alex Allen and the e-Minister Patricia Hewitt.

### Dawn comes under pressure from her own MPs

Following large postbags on this issue Labour MPs had asked for a meeting with Dawn Primarolo to discuss their constituents concerns directly which is common practise in Parliament for contentious legislation. One of the largest concentrated groups lobbying their MP has not been IT but the offshore oil consultants centred on Aberdeen, suffering rate cuts imposed by the clients IR 35 is a further blow to their livelihoods. David Ramsden reported on the forum that:

> "A largish group went to see Dawn Primarolo. According to my informant, who was there, they were treated with disdain and arrogance. DP made a longish presentation and then gave each MP time to ask one question. They were not allowed to ask more than one."

"My sources told me that she was furiously angry with the campaign and tried to tell MPs that they had all been misled."

In a letter to the FT in reply to a PCG member's letter, the Paymaster General volunteered this interesting insight:

> "Under current legislation, some employees may be persuaded, against their own interests, to give up their rights as employees and set up personal service companies in order to benefit from substantial savings on tax and National Insurance Contributions."

> "Our proposals will take away these savings. It is unlikely that employees will be tempted to give up their employee status if they would be no better off. We see no reason to expect this practice to continue once the new legislation is in force."

She just didn't get it.

## William Hague increases the pressure

Tory leader William Hague drew his line in the sand with a speech to the Institute of Civil Engineers. In this speech he mentioned IR35 directly. William didn't need to fully get it; he knew it was a great bat to continually hit the Government with. It helped to illustrate stealth taxes, a lack of consultation, a failure of joined up Government and poured cold water on the Government's entire e-Government and e-Commerce policies.

> "The technology consultants and software engineers who should be driving Britain's new economy are being driven out of the country by new stealth taxes known only as IR35, because they were sneaked out in Inland Revenue Press Release Number 35 on Budget Day. IR35 is contributing to a brain drain not seen here since the 1970s. The drain will become a flood if the Government gets its way, with European tax harmonisation exposing us to tax increases of up to 20 per cent.

> This isn't 'modernising' the British economy, this is destroying it. In the age of the Internet, where businesses can locate anywhere in the world, it will be the low-tax, lightly-regulated countries that thrive and attract business. Whereas high taxes and heavy regulation will simply drive businesses and jobs away because they simply cannot exist in that uncompetitive climate."

## Pressure on e-Minister increases

Reuters reported from the FT:

> The Treasury is under pressure to reverse a decision to make freelance information technology (IT) consultants pay National Insurance Contributions, the Financial Times reports. The report said IT minister Patricia Hewitt had brought the issue before the Treasury after a study in Computer magazine said about 18 percent of IT freelancers would leave the country because of the changed tax rule.

## E-Envoy adds his voice

CNN reported: U.K. fears cyber brain-drain

LONDON - Britain's most senior e-commerce officials are urging the U.K. Treasury to soften new tax rules that increased the effective tax rate for freelance technology consultants, fearing the change could prompt an exodus of cyber-savvy workers from the country, according to a newspaper report Friday. Alex Allan, the U.K. e-commerce chief, and his government colleague, information technology minister Patricia Hewitt, expressed their concerns to Prime Minister Tony Blair that the tax change could hamper the growth of e-commerce in Britain.

Computer Weekly also ran it as a story on the 20$^{th}$ January. They noted that:

> The Government's e-envoy, Alex Allen, is in discussions with the Treasury regarding the IR35 proposals.
>
> He recently expressed concerns about the proposals, and is said to be worried that the tax change could stunt the growth of the e-commerce industry.
>
> A spokeswoman for Allen's office said,
>
> "Alex Allen has certainly not criticised Government policy. At a conference he said that he was aware of concerns in the IT industry about the impact of the Inland Revenue's proposals and his office was discussing this with the Treasury.
>
> But he made it clear that policy on this was for the Treasury to decide, and that the Treasury has to balance these concerns against the need to protect the tax system against abuse."

While Dawn had got the PCG's meeting in Bristol picketed by her husband's friends in UNISON, we had successfully got the Treasury picketed by Labour MPs, Tony Blair's e-Envoy Alex Allen and the DTI's e-Commerce Minister Patricia Hewitt.

Dawn needed some new friends so she turned to ATSCo, who were happy to oblige.

### Treasury under Siege

You can skip this part if you want; I want to paint a picture of what the situation was like. The citadel that was the Treasury was under siege. Their neighbouring allies at the DTI and the Cabinet Office urged them to sue for peace and questioned their tactics and cause. Inside the citadel the palace guards that were the Labour MPs were jittery and were ready to lower the draw bridge. Outside the PCG's peasant army had the place surrounded with the Federation of Small Business providing the cavalry. The artillery was manned by big hitters from the CIOT, the CBI and the ICAEW. Completing the circle stood reluctant aristocrats from ATSCo and the big agencies.

Inside the citadel the dark Lord of the Treasury brooded grimly at how events had unravelled. Diplomacy had failed, his attempts at getting help from the King had gone unheard and unheeded, he had lost the argument and his so-called allies were deserting him. The only card left to play was that of treachery and deceit. If there was a weakness in the contractors' cause, perhaps flattery and maybe bribery could exploit it from within the 'outsiders', but that is what happened, the centre piece of the anti-IR35 argument was that it would damage Britain's competitiveness and could risk a new brain drain. It was all based on anecdotal evidence, in particular many contractors sending Dawn Primarolo post cards from abroad saying they had moved. Her response was to say that there were no addresses on the post cards for her to write back to them.

Ann Swain from ATSCo was persuaded to burst this balloon with her own anecdotal evidence that people weren't moving abroad. Perhaps it had no more credence than the argument that they were going abroad. The betrayal wasn't in what she said, but the fact that she said it in comments to The Times newspaper.

## ATSCo in the Times

Andy reported to members how ATSCo and their Chief Executive Ann Swain were anxious to curry favour with the Government or was easily flattered. He wrote to members about ATSCo's comments to The Times:

> Following thousands of man hours of effort and millions of pounds in lost opportunity cost, PCG members were entitled to feel that progress was being made. This was being confirmed in private briefings. The campaign then received a hammer blow. Ann Swain of ATSCo (an association of large Agents mainly in IT.) made the following comments in the Times
>
> "Ms Swain says her members, the country's largest IT recruitment firms, have seen little evidence that contractors are fleeing the UK in droves."
>
> "For most contractors, it is a question of whether to leave a highly paid sector to avoid an extra tax burden of about 10 per cent. Alternatively they can take an average 50 per cent cut in net pay and move to permanent IT employment, with the commensurate rise in job security and benefits"
>
> "Ms Swain believes the vast majority will stay in the country."
>
> "Ann Swain, chief executive of the new Association of Technology Staffing Companies (ATSCo), has been actively involved in the issue and says the debate should now turn to helping contractors to prepare for the tax changes."
>
> Members are not aware of any contact by ATSCo to formally assess their plans and the relationship between them is such that the only way an ATSCo member will know that a contractor is overseas will be when they get the unobtainable tone the next time they try and call the Contractor for work!

Andy saved his fury to the end of the report when he recorded the possible consequences of Ann Swain's intervention.

> This offhand quote at this critical juncture will have allowed Treasury to throw doubt on the documented and independently verified research; that a large number of Contractors will leave the UK. The RIA, that has not been challenged, shows this will result in a net loss to the Treasury. The significance of these quotes

should not be underestimated as a matter of days later the Revenue issued the final guidelines.

## 2nd February – Final Guidance issued by Revenue

It was true, despite the Treasury being under a virtual state of siege from their MPs, e-Envoys and DTI ministers, relief came as ATSCo turned their coats and in effect broke the siege and gave relief to the Treasury, enough for them to push out the final guidance for IR35 with the pretence that it had some industry backing.

> The PCG today received the final version of the guidelines. Kevin Miller is at present studying the detail and will incorporate details into the IR 35 Manual shortly to be issued to members. The information will also be incorporated into the material for the IR 35 seminars about to take place around the country. The guidelines will be published next week, but members can view the copy received by PCG on the members file store. A significant change from the original version is the following statement.
>
> "The terms of contracts used by service company workers who obtain engagements through agencies tend to be of a standard form. Such contracts typically require the worker to work on the client's premises, use the client's equipment, work standard hours, be paid at an hourly rate and be subject to a high level of control. In such cases, the opinion of the IR about the engagement is likely to be that it would be employment.
>
> "Where a worker is engaged on this type of contract for a period of one month or more, and cannot demonstrate a recent history of work including engagements which have the characteristics of self-employment then we will say that the engagement would have been employment and therefore be covered by the new rules. Where the contract is for less than a month, then, although the engagement may still have been one of employment, the status position will be considered on a case by case basis."

Basically, any contract under a month's duration and you are not caught by IR35, anything over and you have no history of self-employment then you will be caught.

### Ground laid for a legal battle

I'd never expected us to win with regards to the guidance that was being issued on IR35 but the guidance did represent a 'get out of jail' card for the Government if they had wanted to water down IR35. Some enlightened guidance on what sort of engagements would have been caught by IR35 would have taken the heat out of the issue. Everyone could have calmed down but the Treasury seemed to be in no mood to compromise and among the members of the PCG there was no mood for compromise either.

The brain-drain issue had nearly got some results as pressure had clearly been on the Treasury from all sides, but ATSCo had helped to scupper it. The only real way forward now was to make a legal challenge against the tax, it's what had been done for the Sunday Trading campaign and is what would be done now for IR35.

A QC - again from the Sunday Trading team - had been found and the PCG were in the process of costing out what a possible legal challenge could be.

On the 20th February Andy wrote to members giving them a fresh campaign update and noted that:

> The writing is clearly on the wall and the time is right to focus more of our activities on the areas we have been researching for some time.
>
> When PCG was formed in May 1999, it was clear that, while our initial push had to be political, we should have contingency plans for a legal challenge. Bond Pearce, a legal firm with considerable experience of the European Court, was engaged - and has been on a continuous basis - from day one to explore all routes open for challenge in the courts. As it became clear that the legal side was likely to become important, we increased our legal team by retaining the services of a second top firm, Bevan Ashford. Both firms are analysing all options open to us - and have been for some time.

Andy noted that they had been in touch with a QC:

> At the end of January, we met leading QC, Gerald Barling, who has had considerable experience of taking cases to the European Court, including cases involving the Government. At this point, it is worth repeating for some people, that this case would involve taking on HMG, and to try to proceed without having done these months of research would be foolish in the extreme and doomed to failure.

We then prepared members for the fact that there could be a further call for funds.

> This necessary preparation has been funded to date from existing PCG resources as it has always been our intention to explore the legal avenues to the full. This has been carried on without detracting from the main activity in Westminster and Whitehall. We knew we could go this far within existing resources - and thereafter should a legal challenge be necessary and a real possibility - we would establish a separate fund. We are now in the process of doing that.
>
> When we had prepared the groundwork, it is our intention is share our knowledge with other groups and call on them to join us in the main legal push. We had started this building of alliances, believing that a concerted effort through one channel was the best way forward - That offer is still on the table for groups who want to pool resources on this issue.

# Chapter 8

## The Phoney War Begins

The final guidance for IR35 had been issued and the final parliamentary battle is drawing to a close, all that remained was for IR35 to come into force in April. The only card left in the PCG's hand was to make a legal challenge against the tax. The alternative was to stop the fight at this point and just focus on a case law strategy. The process of turning the PCG into a trade association neared completion and the internal focus would be on approving the new constitution and appointing directors. Andy White, at his own suggestion, was ready to stand aside and let contractors run their own show.

Contractors wanted to fight on with a legal challenge against the tax. The mob itself generated high expectations for the challenge, I genuinely couldn't see it myself but saw the legal challenge as a way of sustaining the PCG and it needed momentum to carry it on. It needed continued focus. In other revolutions a similar thing has happened, during the French Revolution when the Gironist forced a declaration of war against Hapsburg, Austria in the belief that it was the only way to consolidate the revolution. In the PCG others believed that a fight against the Government was needed for similar reasons.

If you had read this far you will realise that the Government was already antagonistic towards contractors. The judicial review had nothing to do with it, the Paymaster General had already described us as 'tax cheats' in Parliament and they had been general attempts to rubbish our organisation and its message. Attempts to build consensus between the PCG and Government hadn't been very successful as noted PCG members would fire rockets at the Government who would then respond in a disproportionate fashion. This didn't help us at all.

Later some of those arguing no doubt for the legal challenge and pushing hard against the Government would see it all differently, for instance one accountant later wrote of:

> The ill-judged attempt to have the legislation killed off by the judicial review process appeared to be ego-driven and raised far too many unrealistic hopes for contractors. We have consistently urged for co-operation and not confrontation with the Government.

Regardless of this, the time between the final guidance being issued and the announcement of Judicial Review proceedings against the Government I can only describe as the phoney war.

During this phoney war the PCG would get itself organised as a new trade association, it would get its contracts approved by the Inland Revenue and would create the circumstances for a few extra Journée's against the Government. Some would be created by the PCG leadership team and others would just appear from within the membership and create their own momentum. Remember that at the end of the day the PCG Executive team were just standing in front of the fury filled sans-culotte contractors; to say that we were leading them would be generous indeed.

### Revenue Approves PCG contract

The PCG had a team of tax and employment lawyers and accountants working away to create model contracts. Until this time no one had really ever looked at contracts from this perspective. Agency lawyers had written contracts to protect their interests, clients had written contracts to protect their interests and contractors... they had to take what they were given.

Now here was an organisation that pooled resources of the contractor community together and had experts working for us. Draft contracts were written for the contractor-agency relationship and also for the agency-client relationship.

*Shout99.com* reported that

The Inland Revenue has approved the first non-IR35 contract submitted to them based on the Professional Contractors Group contract.

The contract, drafted by PCG solicitors Bevan Ashford is available - free of charge to members - from the PCG web site. A number of contracts to suit different circumstances are provided, and the range is being extended.

This version - contractor to agent contract - was submitted to the Revenue after being personalised by a PCG member. The Revenue reviewed the contract and concluded that, if the written terms accurately reflected the practical nature of the arrangement, then the contract 'would not be subject' to the proposed IR35 legislation.

Were the Inland Revenue suddenly being helpful and friendly? Or were contractors using the force of the law to win their point? Their approval was worded in a Sir Humphrey-style, but it was as good as we were going to get.

### $2^{nd}$ April – PCG Growth Figures Revealed

Membership had grown by 1,300 that week, no doubt helped by the approval of the PCG's draft contract and then by taking up the High Court challenge. Contractors were literally flocking to the standard. If nothing else the action was keeping the movement alive and the momentum going. A strong PCG capable of fighting the Government over the coming years for case law and other issues would be as important as the High Court case itself.

The newly constituted PCG felt that not only did the organisation need to fight the Government but it needed to provide the facilities for contractors to defend themselves from attack by the Inland Revenue, so the PCG could claim that its £100 membership would offer the following benefits:

- free access to the contracts;
- free tax investigation insurance;

- access to free legal advice;

- comprehensive information on all aspects of IR35, including legal, accounting, lobbying and business;

- contractors online forum where information can be shared;

By now we had 6,000 members. This gave us an annual income of over £600,000. Much of it was already spent though on the tax investigation insurance and in paying our suppliers – David Ramsden and Susie Hughes as well as operating the website and services which Andy's company, Webtastic, provided.

### Andy White hands over the PCG to its members

Andy had founded the PCG. He had put up the original capital to run it and he had given up a year of his life in running it. When you read through the newsletters and emails from the time it becomes clear how intense this had been. He had put his own dot.com ambitions on hold. He had created Britain's first online trade association and done things that previously may have seemed impossible. He had harnessed the power of the Internet and focused it and the members on IR35 to great effect. However, its original purpose and intention had been a single focus, that of IR35. In fact at the outset, when the battle was won or lost, Andy had pledged to wind up the organisation and devote whatever funds were still in the pot to a charity of the members' choice, but now the PCG had a life of its own beyond the IR35 campaign.

Andy could have run it as a 'benevolent dictator' as was suggested to him by some of the membership, but as a point of principle he felt that in order for the PCG to survive and have credibility he had to hand it over to its members and for them to run it. There were three steps in this process, firstly the one creating the PCG as a trade association and the second creating a new constitution and the final one, elections based on that constitution.

The PCG's new constitution had been designed by Gareth Williams and was put to members. The organisation would now move on from being owned and run by Andy and David, it would be a member owned organisation and it would elect a consultative committee which in turn would elect a board of directors. On a day to day basis it was suggested that the PCG would be run by an executive team. Each member of the PCG would become a shareholder.

Having been at the helm for nearly a year Andy was ready to stand back and let a new team take control. He was happy to continue to supply executive and IT services. Many of the contractors who had approached him when he started the PCG had now formed into a standalone company to provide services to the PCG. He called this company Webtastic. Andy felt that he couldn't be both the chairman and service provider at the same time so he planned to stand down from any formal role within the PCG organisation. Don't forget that this was an organisation that he had created, funded and devoted a year's worth of time to. He wrote and said:

I devoted most of the past year to chairing the PCG "pro bono" and leading the campaign against IR35. It was both enjoyable because of the large number of contractors I met who were determined to 'Make a Difference' and frustrating because of the blinkered and narrow-minded approach adopted by the politicians who refused to see what was staring them in the face.

The members though would clamber for him to stay on and he would be persuaded to stand for election to the Consultative Council but would not put himself forward for election to the board of directors. I would also stand as would many of the great members.

I declined the invitation to stand for chairman; I felt that as a Labour supporting member I wouldn't be able to carry the rest of the membership. I also had ambitions to become a parliamentary candidate for Labour and I saw the two positions as being inconsistent with each other. Also we were expecting a baby in June/July and I was unsure how I could balance my Labour ambitions, the PCG campaign and fatherhood.[51] However, I did stand for election as the External Affairs Director and was elected by the entire council with the exception of a couple of objections because of my Labour links.[52]

Contractors found themselves in positions of responsibility where many had enthusiasm but not necessarily experience. Gareth Williams was elected as Chairman. Jane Akshar was in charge of public relations, Ian Durrant took responsibility for the website, Pamela Edwards focused on membership services, Simon Griffiths was to look at the business-to-business website portal, I had the campaign and Neil Wilson would look after the legal issues. In practise almost all the roles overlapped and they mapped out to suppliers carrying out the services for us in the Executive team and in Webtastic. At the first Board Meeting the PCG tendered for the contract to run the organisation and it was ultimately awarded to Webtastic. It seemed right that the PCG would be run as a contracting organisation, the directors could remain as contractors and there would be no full time employees. The directors would oversee the direction and the suppliers, namely Webtastic, and others would do the day-to-day work.

After becoming the new director it was a little bit uncomfortable when David Ramsden came and asked me what my instructions were. I explained that I could not offer him any as he was clearly more experienced than I.

### *Shout99.com* Launched – Mouthpiece for Contractors

The revolution needed its own mouth piece, its own Pravda if you like. Andy had handed over the PCG as a campaigning organisation to its members but he still saw a potential to engage with them. *Shout99.com* would always be independent of the

---

[51] Gareth Williams who became chairman managed this with 8 children, though I don't think his wife worked

[52] My friend Brian Curnow objected.

PCG but could seek to articulate policies and opinions in a way that was hard for the PCG to do. Of the 17,000 contractors who had subscribed to his engineerjob site some 6,000 had joined the PCG, but there was a list of some 11,000 contractors not covered by the PCG and there was still a need to engage with them. Besides, through advertising and other services the site could become profitable in its own right and wouldn't cost contractors anything. Susie and Andy ran *Shout99.com* and soon they would bring in Richard Powell as a journalist on the site.

> Clearly there is a need for independent, impartial news content of a high quality and that is what I will be providing through *Shout99.com* over the coming months, while working closely with the PCG.

> *Shout99.com* takes its name from the codeword used during the British Lions tour against an aggressive South African team in 1974. The Lions Captain; Willie John McBride, instigated the shout of 99 when one of his team was 'under threat'. On cue, every member of the team would 'get their retaliation in first'. The South Africans soon learnt not to play dirty and the Lions went on to be win the Test series undefeated and became recognised as the epitome of teamwork and camaraderie.

> That is the spirit I hope to recreate with *Shout99.com* .It will provide an information and news resource for contractors and provide a powerful network of like-minded individuals who are all prepared to say 'Stuff You' when their livelihoods are threatened.

> This is a site for shared information and intelligence, which will allow the small entrepreneurial contractor to gain a competitive edge in the market place.

After one week in operation it appeared a success, leading Susie to comment:

> Having launched this site a week ago, contractors have been hitting it with force - convincing us - if we needed it - that there is a need for a news and information site for contractors.

# Chapter 9

## Budget 2000 – No joy for contractors

12 months on and we have a body representing contractors engaged in a bitter war of words with the Treasury. In his 2000 Budget Gordon Brown would try to get into step with the new dot-com boom taking place. So he offered tax breaks to 'proper' small businesses to help them buy computers and other IT equipment as support for training, unless you already worked in IT as a freelancer in which case such offers would not be open to you. A contractor told *Shout99.com* that:

> 'The fact that the Chancellor thinks that he can solve the e-commerce issue by putting computers in offices shows how little he understands about this. It's pointless having hardware if the people who develop the cutting-edge software programmes are leaving the country in droves or closing down their businesses.'

The Tories knew all about IR35 now and it was a bonus really that Gordon Brown was not prepared to budge on it. This meant that in their budget response here was one issue they could pre-prepare confident in the knowledge that it would not be changed.

William Hague described Mr Brown's performance as a mugger who grabs your money and then wants you to thank him for giving you your bus-fare home.

Mr Hague demonstrated this in detail by using the example of IR35 - the 'stealth tax on the self-employed contractors'. He said:

> This is a £475 million tax on our future, driving many high-technology businesses abroad. He quoted extensively from a letter from a contractor who was in the process of closing his business because of IR35. Hague predicted that it would lead to the first brain drain since Lord Healey's time.

In the follow-up budget material, Shadow Secretary of State for DTI, Angela Browning, reinforced the point by quoting Andy White:

> Labour claim to want to help small business take advantage of the Internet revolution but at the same time is introducing a stealth tax, IR35, on entrepreneurs working in key industries of the new economy. This is already causing a brain drain. Andy White of the Professional Contractors' Group - which represents thousands of IT experts - has said that Labour's tax plans will 'kill the enterprise culture in this key sector.'

## IR35 estimates doubled to £900m

After the budget was published Susie had a look in the Treasury's 'Red Book' that provided the detailed figures behind the budget statement and there was an entry about IR35. Amazingly it detailed that the tax take for the tax would now be £900m not the £475m previously mentioned in the RIA though even that had been scaled down. Where this new £900m had come from, nobody knew.

On the 22<sup>nd</sup> March the Shadow Paymaster General, Richard Ottoway MP, asked Dawn Primarolo to explain why the costs of IR35 have been doubled by the Red Book from £475 million in 1999 to £900 million this year? He said:

> "Nearly £1 Billion out of the pockets of the self-employed is serious money. The brain drain could develop into a mass emigration. The Red Book shows that, as a result of IR35, the burden has this year leapt from £475 million to £900 million. That is one heck of a chunk to take from the self-employed." [53]

Dawn Primarolo did not provide an answer, so we all remain none the wiser.

## FTVs gathers pace

While publicly stating that there was no brain drain, Ann Swain and ATSCo had help assuring them of that. The Government decided to prepare for the worst and so relaxed the restrictions on work permits so as to allow overseas (non-EU) workers to come to Britain. The result of this would be workers coming to Britain but it would help open the doors so that projects would be done overseas, including Government projects paid for by the British tax payer.

## Agency Misinformation

Even though PCG membership was growing a number of contractors still felt that it wasn't necessary to join up. Some believed that their accountants were going to 'fix' it for them but the Revenue had quite rightly wised up to some of these fixes, such as allowing a chain of contract arrangements such as a contractor working Schedule E for an intermediate firm. When I worked at CitiGroup one contractor was running such a scheme. However, accountants weren't the only ones misleading contractors, agents were too. Some were telling contractors that their contracts were IR35 proof and would then suggest that the client-agency contract had nothing to do with it.

> My agent has just contacted me and is just about to send out a new contract to me and surprise, surprise the contract is supposed to be IR 35 proof. I did enquire what the state of play was with regards to the contract between the agent and client, his reply was 'That contract between agent and client was irrelevant, and as far as he was concerned the Inland Revenue had no right to look beyond the contract that existed between the agent and contractor. I am getting suspicious.
>
> Here is what the Revenue says
>
> The employment/self-employment test which is to be used to decide which contracts are caught by the new rules will look at the relationship between you and the client. The decision will not be affected by the presence of an agency in the arrangements.

---

[53] http://hansard.millbanksystems.com/commons/2000/mar/22/Budget-resolutions-and-economic-situation#S6CV0346P0_20000322_HOC_360

No surprise that agents had no idea what the whole thing was really about. No doubt these were the same agents who in 2000 were asking for IT people with 5-6 years experience of Windows 98.

In June the Revenue must have heard about this trash being peddled by agents and updated its guidance on IR35 to say:

> You can't look at a contract between an agency and a client if the worker is not party to it.
>
> The legislation says that the IR35 rules apply if the circumstances are such that, if the worker had contracted directly with the client, the relationship would have been one of employment. Those circumstances include all the agreements which define that relationship: contracts signed by the client are just as important as contracts signed by the worker or the intermediary.
>
> In particular, a right of substitution will only be effective if both the worker and the intermediary have agreed to it, and the Inland Revenue will need to see evidence of this. The Revenue can require the production of the contract by the client or agency if necessary to establish the facts.

What this did mean, so I was told, was that the Revenue would look at the contract between the agency and the client when determining the IR35 status of the contractor. The contractor wasn't a party to this contract and usually was unable to see it as it contained commercially sensitive information. So you could be 'convicted' of IR35 based on evidence you weren't even allowed to see. Madness.

# Chapter 10

## IR35 - See you in court

Susie understood the news and media and how it works. To create a story you need a hook to hang it on. That is an event that has happened, you can manufacture such events or you can wait for one to happen. If you play your cards right then your reaction to an event can become bigger than the event itself.

The event coming up was the formal release of the new Inland Revenue rules for IR35, the day that the legislation came into force and was of course the beginning of the new tax year. On the day that the Inland Revenue smirked at the contracting community as the legislation came into force, Susie walked forward with the news that the PCG would formally challenge the new rules in the High Court. This was now the big story. The story wasn't contractors defeated as Revenue rules come into force but the bigger news that the Revenue, and indeed the UK Government, faced a further and potentially harder fight from contractors to have the legislation struck out as it was unlawful under European law.

*Shout99.com* explained that:

> As a member of the EU, the UK laws have to comply with European legislation. If they do not, they are invalid and will be struck down. A recent example is Lunn Poly who, using the same QC as the PCG challenged the Finance Act 1997 as being contrary to European law and won the case on the basis that the tax differential part of the Act was unfair and invalid.

The new PCG chairman Gareth Williams said:

> "It is an indication of the strength of feeling and injustice that a group of 8,000 individuals - the majority of whom voted for New Labour - are now forced to take the Government to court to protect their livelihoods".

## Inland Revenue spin doctors go to Newsnight

Perhaps slightly wrong footed the Inland Revenue decided, no doubt with political pushing, that it was time to destroy these pesky contractors once and for all. Where else better to discredit their argument than in front of the whole nation? So they sent a fleet of spin doctors down to the Newsnight studio and briefed them on IR35 and what a bunch of 'tax cheats' contractors all were.

Now Newsnight and other BBC shows had shown almost universal disinterest in IR35 from our perspective, but now with a little bit of prodding from Government they would run it as a feature article on the show.

The piece was presented by Evan Davis and it made a 'comparison' of the tax position of an employee and a Personal Service Company (PSC/their one man limited company), suggesting that top employees pay 52% tax (40% income and 12% NI) compared to Ltd Companies that pay just 10% corporation tax.

This is what they had been told by the Inland Revenue. Was this what the Revenue had really thought? Is this how they thought contractors worked?

It bore no relation to how an individual could take money from the company; we were all still taxed at 40% when taking out money out. The 10% corporation tax only referred to profits, not income.

But what could we do about it?

*Shout99.com* reported the anger in contractor community.

Independent contractors were outraged by the misleading coverage of IR35 on Newsnight the flagship BBC news program. Many felt that the BBC was being manipulated by the Treasury and were spinning the story to show PSCs as tax dodgers.

*Shout99.com* **tocsin bell rings!**

Back in March Andy had explained to *Shout99.com* readers that "a contractor wrote in asking that contractors email Granada TV requesting that the Dimbleby show invites Dawn Primarolo to explain the reasons behind IR35. 24 hours later the Granada IT director phoned up to say that the server had melted and I was to stop these emails."

Andy added that "I was hoping he was going to say he was about to send the police round so I could use my favourite Willie John McBride story. On the Lions tour of South Africa in '74 the team were being 'boisterous' in the hotel. The Manager got hold of Willie to say he was about to call the police. Willie looked up at the Manager and said "So, how many police will be coming round then?""

What this incident had demonstrated was the power behind contractor movement whether in the PCG or with SHOUT. The old French revolutionaries had rung the tocsin bell when their 'patrie' was in danger, contractors would issue a 'Shout99' to call people together to do the same for them. As previously mentioned, a call of 'Shout99' brought contractors together where the outcome was greater than the sum of the individual parts.

**Newsnight Affair – The tocsin bell rings**

As soon as the Newsnight story went out emails flew around among the contractor community. The story had to be challenged and was being challenged. We rang the tocsin bell of *Shout99.com* and even more contractors had started flooding the BBC with outraged emails.

*Shout99.com* explained that:

> The BBC was contacted by contractors and Newsnight swiftly posted an apology on their website with a promise of further coverage on the story on the evening of Friday 7th April. Newsnight editors explained the story as a misunderstanding between them and the Inland Revenue.

Newsnight said of the economic editor, Evan Davis:

> Yes, we did get it wrong last night. Our Economic Editor completely misunderstood something he was told by the Inland Revenue and thought there were some people who did face a 52% versus 10% tax benefit from making themselves a small company. He is busy writing a thousand lines as we speak, and will correct it on tonight's programme.

So the next night there was something of a qualified apology on Newsnight from Evan Davis.

However, many felt that the apology was a bit lame with the economics editor shown writing lines. Newsnight fixed the blame squarely on the shoulders of the Inland Revenue who had seen the misleading figures quoted in the previous show. Nevertheless, the BBC's economic editor had issued on on-air apology - we thought it was unprecedented, though we were never the BBC's or Evan Davis 'favourite people' again, we had made a mark and they treated us with a little more respect, or caution, in the future.

Shout 99 reported that a Westminster based PR professional, who had nothing to do with IR35, was amazed by what the contractors had achieved:

> A rather sheepish looking economics editor appeared just 24 hours later to answer the question, "How did we get it so wrong?" This is Newsnight and the BBC NEVER apologise. This is a real victory for the contractors.

However, many contractors felt that the apology failed to hit the mark and those in Scotland and Wales didn't even see the appearance of Evan Davis. Contractors were again disappointed that the second IR35 article failed to give the issue proper coverage and failed to mention the difference between small personal service companies (PSCs) and the large consultancies. Perhaps just as worrying is that the figures cited were still misleading.

*Shout99.com* explained that

> Mr Davis claimed to have discussed both articles with officers from the Inland Revenue and had been told by the Revenue that what he said was fine.

This was another example of a failure to deliver a clear and concise tax law from the Inland Revenue. It was and is complicated law, badly written and badly implemented so much so that not even the BBC's economic editor could understand it! What chance did we have?

We had won a minor PR battle and we later found out that the Treasury officials did have a sneaking respect for the way we handled it. They let it be known to Susie that should she ever want to change sides, any application to be their press officer would be favourably considered.

The downside for us I am told was that Evan Davies never forgave contractors for this and this would cause us some problems in the future when we would try to highlight the issue of fast track visas.

## IR35 confuses at Prime Ministers Question Time

The Newsnight affair came after confusion reigned during PM's Question Time on Wednesday. Opposition leader William Hague challenged Tony Blair to explain why 50,000 IT consultants are emigrating or thinking of emigrating.

Mr Blair declined to answer the question directly and spoke instead of a strong economy and the recent reductions in corporation tax.

## Lucky Aussies drop IR35 equivalent

Meanwhile it turned out that in Australia they had, as the Government had been suggesting, been looking at legislation similar to IR35 but there the Government managed to see sense and withdrew it as *Shout99.com* reported in April 2000.

*Shout99.com* reported that the u-turn had come about after strong lobbying by traditional contracting sectors, such as construction, as well as those in the new economy. The original proposals have been softened considerably to protect fledgling dot-com start-ups and businesses in the IT field. Also there had been concern that the Tax office would not be able to cope with the flood of status requests.

The Australian government had evidently listened to the voting public and acted in the best interests of those who made up the working economy. They were obviously looking to avoid closing businesses and forcing contractors overseas. The difference seemed to be that they appeared to have understood that in the global economy the IT sector needs to be nurtured, not nailed.

*Shout99.com* suggested that "Perhaps New Labour could take a leaf out of the Aussie book."

### Aussies get lucky

by Susie Hughes at 11:08 13/04/00 (*Shout99.com*)

Australians will often tell you what a great country they live in: the climate, beaches and sporting culture. Many UK knowledge based contractors, who up until now have not given a XXXX about Australia, may suddenly change their views on the country of amber nectar and honey. For at the last minute, the Australian Treasurer has scrapped proposed regulations similar to IR35, aimed at preventing workers claiming business deductions under the guise of being contractors.

Originally the Australian government planned to raise $500m (£185m) a year with the crackdown, aimed at slowing the growth of contracting – where workers set-up as contractors to avoid PAYE. Sensibly, instead of casting a net to catch all contractors, as has been done in the UK, the Australian proposals meant that any contractor who earned more than 80% of their income from one source, would have to obtain a special ruling from the Tax Office. So whilst not all contractors were caught in the original proposals, even these have been scrapped!

After lobbying by the IT and building industries as well as backbenchers, the Treasurer has now gone on record saying,

(Originally the proposals aimed) to set up a system whereby people who are really employees couldn't pretend that they were contractors and walk out of the PAYE system, but you had to protect genuine contractors who really are in business. And what we are trying to do here is protect genuine contractors....those people who have always been recognised as contractors continue to be recognised as contractors and treated as people in business.

To avoid having to have a special ruling by the tax office, contractors would need to satisfy only one of four special criteria:

- Have business premises

- Have two or more related clients

- Satisfy the Tax office that the business is not loss making and that equipment is supplied, such as a laptop

- Have one or more employees who perform at least 20% of the work.

New businesses have also been given a two year grace period from the above.

# Chapter 11

## The final parliamentary battle

*She's a model and she's looking....*

While the IR35 spotlight has been primarily on IT and engineers another potential target group emerged - the fashion model. Dawn was asked questions in the House about the impact on this industry.

Conservative MP for Guildford, Nick St. Aubyn, who has been following IR35 closely, tabled two parliamentary questions relating to the fashion modelling industry's involvement in IR35.

He asked in what ways the fashion modelling industry will benefit from the changes proposed under IR35 and what was the estimate of the impact of the proposals on the avoidance of tax and national insurance payments in the fashion modelling industry.

Paymaster General, Dawn Primarolo, replied:

> "All sectors of industry will benefit from the changes we propose. IR35 will ensure that measures designed to support small businesses are properly targeted, and do not go to people who are really the same as employees. The legislation will stop the use of personal service companies and similar intermediaries to avoid PAYE tax and National Insurance Contributions in all industries."

Perhaps if Kate Moss had complained directly it could have been changed?

## Hague and Portillo keep enterprise on the agenda

The two leading figures in the Conservative Party sent a broad-side to the Government about the damage they are doing to the enterprise economy. Portillo mentioned IR35 in an article and argued that the Labour Government was moving away from the lightly regulated economy inherited from the Tories toward a more regulated European model. He noted that "new/Old Labour still has the chance to remove this potential thorn in their side by delaying the measure for another year and allow proper consultation as laid down in the Revenue Guidelines".

## 12th June 2000 - Final parliamentary fight

### Finance Bill - First Committee Stage

*by Susie Hughes at 21:07 10/06/00 (Shout99.com)*

The Finance Bill, containing the IR35 provisions took a step nearer becoming law when it passed through the Committee Stage of the legislative process. We summarise the first session of the debate.

The Finance Bill Committee debated the detailed provisions within Schedule 12 'Provision of services through an intermediary'. Richard Ottoway MP, as Shadow

Paymaster General lead for the Conservatives, while Paymaster General, Dawn Primarolo, defended the Government's position.

She outlined the comparison between an employee paying 35 per cent tax and a person doing the same job through a personal service company and paying 21 per cent tax.

She said: "There are 90,000 individuals working through service companies. Their average annual earnings are £50,000 and they pay, on average, 21 per cent in tax and national insurance. If we compare that with someone in an identical employment relationship in terms of where the work is carried out, how it is carried out and who supervises it but who is an employee, that person pays 35 per cent tax and national insurance through pay-as-you-earn. The only difference between the two workers is the interposing of a service company, which adds nothing and does not change the terms and conditions or the nature of the work. Later in the debate there was some unresolved dispute about what this 21 per cent included and whether it also included corporation tax.

She also said that the Revenue had examined 1,200 contracts and found that they were reasonably evenly split. She saw no reason why IT contractors could not follow the same rules as everyone else.

She stressed that the proposals were not to change or define employment status, but to ensure that people could not choose whether to pay tax as an employee or a self-employed person, as that decision should be based on case law. She continued: "If he is an employee and the only difference is that he seeks to interpose a service company to route money through, the definitions in case law mean that we will expect and require him to pay tax and national insurance in the same terms as though he were employed directly by the company. Really, he is employed directly by the company, as demonstrated by the terms and conditions."

Ottoway, together with the Lib Dems tabled amendments to the proposals, some of which were defeated and others were not pushed to the vote. The next stage is that the legislation will return to the full House for 'Report Stage' possibly at the end of June or beginning of July, which will be one of the last opportunities for Parliament to reject or amend IR35.

The Committee Stage debate gave all political parties an opportunity to clarify their positions - and, in the case of the Labour, reiterate many of the points which contractors have argued against for many months. Some of the noteworthy points of the first Committee Stage debate on Schedule 12 were:

**Competitiveness and small businesses**

Ottoway pointed out that Revenue figures predicted that 66,000 small businesses would be affected although other commentators thought there could be more. He cited the example of how a large company could sell its workers' knowledge to a client, but the same workers couldn't then start their own companies and sell their own knowledge without being unfairly taxed.

Ottoway reminded the Government that its 1997 manifesto has said: " A new Labour Government will give Britain's entrepreneurs and small businesses the backing they deserve." and queried how this would sit with IR35. Ottoway referred to the ICA's Tax Faculty report which gave a 'resounding raspberry' to IR35 including zero out of ten for competitiveness. However, Primarolo dismissed the Tax Faculty report: "The Institute is wrong -obviously it can account for itself - because it agrees with us that there is avoidance, but it does not have a proposition to deal with it."

Edward Davey MP supported the anti-competitive point. He said: "Many of the large IT companies that bid for the contracts, along with large engineering and oil companies, will not be affected. Those companies were worried about competition from smaller companies-whether personal service companies, the small contractor or the one-man band-and therefore support the proposed legislation. The measure will ensure that those small businesses that are nipping at their heels, driving down prices and promoting competition, cannot compete with the large players. It is anti-competitive, and anti small business, in a key and growing part of the economy, in which small business and innovators are needed. That is why the measure is so damaging. The sectors that will be hit by the legislation are those that need small business more than any others. They are the most innovative sectors, which will ensure that Britain remains at the leading edge of technology, whether in the oil industry or the IT industry.

Primarolo denied that the Bill was advantageous to large companies and put smaller ones at a disadvantage. She said: "In truth, large companies could not interpose a service company-there are tens of thousands of legitimate ones-between themselves and the employee when the only purpose of the service company is to reduce tax liability. It is not to change or influence the terms and conditions of that employment......... we are not giving larger contractors an advantage over smaller ones. Instead, we are levelling the playing field for all contractors, so that those who trade fairly and comply with definitions of "self-employed" and "employed" will not be undermined by those who avoid using the correct definitions.

## Legitimacy of service companies and IT

Primarolo spent some time explaining that IT should not be treated exceptionally and that personal service companies could continue - as it was only 'disguised employment' via a service company which was under threat.

She said: "Service companies can exist and are legitimate-it is the relationship with those service companies and their clients that we are trying to deal with. The idea that our IT industry can make progress only by the presence of such a tax-driven arrangement does not bear scrutiny. It has repeatedly been said that the IT industry can flourish only if we allow that relationship to continue. However, that is not what is being said by people in the IT industry, who work through their service companies as employees of those companies and have regularised their tax position. She quoted from a letter from a Mr Brian Hughes, who has 27 years experience in the IT industry and described contractors as 'hired hands'.

## Contracts

Ottoway queried the bureaucratic difficulties of examining so many contracts and in some cases, having to examine the same person on several occasions, taking into account substitution, length of contract, fixed fee and other factors.

Ottoway felt that the right of substitution would take contractors outside IR35 and the Revenue would not, therefore, raise the anticipated fees.

Kali Mountford MP queried why intelligent IT contractors couldn't work it out while her brother, a builder, could determine his status?

Dawn Primarolo confirmed again that "the vast majority work on standard contract terms that clearly represent employment…….The involvement of an agency in setting up a relationship between a worker and a client will, in most cases, have no relevance to the nature of the relationship, in relation to the employment test. Most contractors in the IT industry work through agencies on standard contract terms. Those terms include an obligation to work set hours for an agreed hourly rate; to work on the client's premises under the client's control; and to perform the work personally, not send a substitute. One does not have to be familiar with case law to recognise that that bears all the hallmarks of employment.

She explained that the Revenue has already looked at contracts with service companies with an element of employment rather than being 'straightforward self-employment, legitimate companies that fall outside IR35'. "So far, the Inland Revenue has been asked to examine 1,200 contracts to ascertain whether they involve employees or self-employed people. That is a reasonable sample. Of that sample, 53 per cent were found to be within IR35, and 47 per cent were found not to be within IR35, and would therefore not be caught by the current employment tests that work throughout the tax system. At no point this morning has anyone-nor did the Professional Contractors Group-explained why, of all the millions of employees who pay tax and national insurance and can determine whether they are self-employed or are employees, those in the IT industry are different……. The figures that I gave demonstrated that a significant proportion of service companies already operate as self-employed companies and IR35 will not therefore affect them. The idea that it will somehow damage flexibility is incorrect."

## Overseas

Ottoway said that Australia and America has abandoned similar proposals to IR35 and that the US was fast-tracking 200,000 visas for high technology workers to meet the skills shortfall. Primarolo disputed that Australia was repealing its legislation

## Employment v. self-employment

Ottoway argued that the legislation was a fundamental shift in attempting to redefine the existing boundary between employment and self-employment to the detriment of the economy.

He explained that the Revenue web-site pointed out that although IR35 would tax people as if they were employed they would not receive the benefits which went with employment.

Michael Jack MP raised several case law examples which, he believed, would be used in determining status. Primarolo did not accept any assertions that existing case law was unsuitable to the IT profession.

Primarolo dismissed the argument that contractors would suffer through a lack of statutory benefits that went with employee status. She said: "Frankly, the intelligent people who negotiate these contracts are perfectly capable of ensuring that terms and conditions, including pay, reflect their remuneration. In participating in this debate, we would be a little disingenuous were we not to admit that, often, such contracts carry a higher price to compensate for differences between employee and self-employed in terms of sickness pay and holiday pay. It is not credible to suggest that IT workers are poor little mites who cannot calculate a good return for their labour."

She also confirmed that nothing in the legislation would alter the relationship between contractor and client in terms of 'employee' and client as the contractor would remain an employee of his or her service company. She said: "If a worker is currently an employee of a service company, not of the client, that will remain the case under the Bill. It does not determine anyone's employment status. One of the misleading rumours that is being spread about the Bill is that it deems that a service company worker will be an employee of his or her client. It has been suggested to clients that that would mean that they would be vulnerable to claims under employment law-for example, for unfair dismissal. However, nothing in the Bill supports that claim. If the person is employed by the service company, their employer is the service company. The fact that their service company has a contract with a client does not make the client liable."

## The Conservative's position

Recently, the Conservatives have been criticised for not announcing that they would repeal IR35, despite explanations that they would not firm up on any of their tax provisions this distance before an election.

Ottoway tried to clarify the position by explaining that previous Conservative Governments had rejected the proposal on several occasions between 1979 and 1997 because it was felt that it would destroy flexibility in the markets.

He said: "When the Conservative party wins the next election we shall give serious consideration to the matter. We shall have had at least a year to see how the measure is working, and we shall implement fundamental reform as appropriate. Such reform will stimulate entrepreneurial activity, not dampen it, as has occurred. "When pressed to make a further statement, he said: "I am saying that we shall give the matter close consideration and implement whatever reform we regard as appropriate."

## Personal experience

Several members of the Committee referred to letters they had received from constituents, who explained in detail how IR35 would adversely affect them, their businesses, other people and businesses which relied on them; the skill-shortage in the UK and the knowledge based economy and flexible workforce.

## 5% debate

### Government says 'no' to increase on five per cent

*by Susie Hughes at 11:34 20/06/00 (Shout99.com)*

In the early days of the IR35 some organisations supported the idea of a salary/dividend split. The Revenue gave it to them: 95 per cent/five per cent and called it an expense allowance. Recently in Parliament, there were unsuccessful moves to allow a more realistic level for business expenses.

During the Committee Stage of the Finance Bill, Shadow Paymaster General, Richard Ottoway (Conservative MP for Croydon South) supported amendments which would 'replace that arbitrary figure of five per cent with the genuine costs for the intermediary.'

He said: "We are dealing with a sector that works extensively through intermediaries and private service companies, who incur substantial expenditure and disbursements in the course of their duties. There are accounting costs, legal costs, training costs, the cost of supplying support staff and, importantly, the cost of the equipment that will allow the worker to provide the services and maintain the necessary skills at home. There are travel costs, including the cost of motor cars. Those are the normal, day-to-day business expenses of the typical self-employed person. Imposing the figure of five per cent may make the Inland Revenue's burden lighter, but it is grossly unfair on the individuals concerned."

He also pointed out the iniquitous situation, as outlined earlier in Shout99, which would allow large companies to be exempt from this measure as they are taxed on company profits, while the small independent provider is taxed on company income. Also he drew the comparison that it was 'okay to sell things, but not knowledge'.

Edward Davey (Lib Dem MP for Kingston and Surbiton) supported Ottoway, stating that this figure had been 'plucked from the air with no particular rationale'.

He said: "If those who run personal service companies are employed, there is no case for a five per cent figure, but if they are self-employed, five per cent. is almost certainly too low. In IT, there are no one-off training courses and accreditations that last an entire career. Training in IT is on-going, and incurs much higher costs than in many other industries. Moreover, there are the equipment costs to which reference has been made. Therefore, the Paymaster General must give a better explanation of why the figure is only five per cent.

The Paymaster General, Dawn Primarolo, described the five per cent as 'straightforward and fair', denying that it had been 'plucked out of the air'.

She explained: "We are not saying that all service companies can have only five per cent of their running costs taken into consideration. The five per cent will apply to the proportion of a service company's contracts that relate to people in an employee relationship. Those contracts that clearly relate to self-employment - as determined by case law - will have access to the normal arrangements relating to the self-employed or to businesses."

The Paymaster General explained that a Revenue survey of accounts of service companies shows that, on average, they spend two per cent of turnover on 'associated costs', such as accountants' fees and Companies House registration charges. The additional three per cent on top of the average costs made it a 'generous formula'.

Ms Primarolo said: "Even if such companies have to spend a little more in future to ensure that they comply with the legislation, the five per cent that we are allowing is well within their current costs, and will allow further room for manoeuvre. The same service companies that are spending two per cent of turnover are saying that the five per cent that we propose to give them is not enough."

The issue of training costs provoked a heated debate as Conservative MPs pointed out that an employee's training costs would be paid for by the employers, whereas a contractor would have to meet his or her own expenses.

Ms Primarolo said: "It is important to consider how employees and the self-employed are treated under the tax system in relation to training costs, and to consider who is entitled to deductions. The Bill seeks to ensure that an employee will get the same deductions as any other employee. For instance, employees can claim some deductions for training expenses, through fairly restrictive rules. Why should someone employed in a company who decides that they want to improve their position by taking a training course be treated differently?

"Some people (Richard Ottoway) says that the employers pay. Precisely. If a person has an employee relationship with their service company, that raises other issues. I am talking about a person who is employed by a client, and interposes the service company only for tax purposes so as to disguise his true employment status."

Despite the lengthy debate, Ms Primarolo held the position that the five per cent was a generous allocation, as it only applied to employee-deemed contracts and the normal rules will apply to contracts that are deemed to be self-employed contracts where there will be no limits on deductible expenses.

She said: "There is no justification for raising the five per cent. We have gone through the matter logically - we have examined the current costs for companies, increased the amount that they pay and ensured that if employees are involved, they are taxed as such. If a company or a self-employed person is involved, they should be taxed as such, according to their status."

The question of increasing the five per cent was put to a vote and defeated by 17 votes to nine. Regular readers of *Shout99.com* may recall a recent article about some MPs' wishes in relation to their own expenses.

Ms Primarolo also reiterated her opinion that IR35 would not prevent people from being self-employed. She said: "The provisions are designed to protect the status of the self-employed and to stop employees trying to access reliefs in the tax system that are designated either for small companies or for the self-employed. The tax rules for small companies were never meant to apply to employees. The Government's position is that the provision affects income only from engagements that would have constituted employment if the person in question had entered into a direct relationship with the client. The Bill seeks to ensure that people in that employee relationship have access only to tax reliefs to which other employees are entitled."

# Chapter 12

## Professional bodies all come out to say it is no good

We had been saying that IR35 was not only the wrong tax for contractors and the economy but it had also been badly written, but as far as the Government was concerned we would say that wouldn't we?

Even Evan Davies, the BBC's top economics expert couldn't understand it, yet Dawn continued to insist in Parliament that it was easy to understand and that we were just creating a lot of trouble because deep down we were 'tax cheats'. In fact the deep down bit is something I have added through poetic license, I don't think she felt it was deep down.

At our meeting with Dawn it seemed to us that she didn't really understand IR35 and I am not sure if Sarah Walker did either, or maybe she was just keeping quiet to be polite. In Parliament Dawn had suggested that because contractors had bought 'off the shelf' companies that they must be tax cheats. This sort of evidence went down well with lots of murmuring MPs who had never worked for themselves, but almost everyone who sets up a company then bought an off the shelf one, it was just so much easier to do.

With the ink dry on the final details the chartered tax and accounting bodies were starting to have a closer look at the measure, it wasn't to make good reading for the Paymaster General and her supporters.

On the 14$^{th}$ May at a meeting of the Chartered Institute of Taxation the Institute reported feedback from a respected tax barrister, Graham Aaronson, QC who stated:

> "I really do prefer naivety or even foolishness in politicians to hypocrisy and deception. Dawn Primarolo seemed to be very pleasant, and clearly fell within the first pair rather than the second. I was particularly amused by the way in which she sincerely believed that the Budget measures would simplify matters and lead to a fairer and more efficient tax system. While I might have thought that someone with the several years experience in the job that she had would have realised the silliness of such statements, she seemed entirely at ease with her consciousness in making them."

Then on the 22$^{nd}$ May the highly respected Tax Faculty of the Institute of Chartered Accountants report, 'Towards a Better Tax System', analysed the 10 tenets required to make good tax legislation. These tenets were then applied against IR35 with the Government scoring a miserly 30 out of 100. If that had been one of my GCSEs then it would have been marked as 'U' unclassified, total fail. 'Were you listening at all? Have you learnt nothing?'

Hot on the heels of the accountants' broadside came a similar message from e-business when a survey by Internet World UK 2000 showed that 93 per cent of e-movers and shakers didn't think the Government was communicating effectively with British business on e-commerce.

Even the CBI's President gave the Prime Minster a slap on the wrist regarding his policies towards the business community citing in particular changes in UK employment laws as 'the biggest and most damaging overhaul of labour market regulation for 20 years'.

Then, having had a clear 'could do better' message from the practitioners and businesses, one of the trade associations joined the condemnation. The CSSA, which represented many of the large software houses who to date had been generally supportive of the Government, also told the Government that its policies were driving highly skilled workers overseas and making the UK an unattractive place to do e-business.

The following week the accountancy body the Association of Chartered Certified Accountants (ACCA) joined in.

Chas Roy-Chowdhury, Head of Taxation at ACCA, said:

> "The whole point with IR35 is that it is based on a lack of understanding of how small businesses work. They do not work like this for an NIC wheeze. There is a lot of risk involved for the self employed - if there is no business, you go out of business. If these people take the risks they are entitled to the rewards.
>
> "The Finance Bill is still in Parliament and this is the last chance to do something about this. It's not about the detail within the legislation - the whole thing should be scrapped."

Mr Roy-Chowdhury concluded:

> "Not only is this measure unfair, it also discriminates against wealth-creators who are adding value to the economy. The Government is seriously mistaken on the issue and should reverse its decision."

One of our Conservative supporters, Francis Maude MP, had reported in a BBC article that "Even the Labour-dominated DTI select committee has said that Labour's policies on small business constitute "loosely connected and apparently uncoordinated policy initiatives shooting off in all directions, generating noise and interest, but not commensurate light""

## Accountants slam the Government over IR 35

*Shout99.com* reported that the Tax Faculty believes that the IR35 proposals are fundamentally unfair and could have been resolved in another fashion.

> "We believe the rules affecting personal service companies are unnecessary.

They added that:

> 'Disguised employment' seems to us an irrational concept. There are many types of business organisation and these have different tax consequences. If a person chooses to provide his services as an employee of a limited company we can see

no rational reason why the natural tax consequences of that choice should not apply.

The Revenue itself has often taken the view that there is no reason why two people carrying on the same activity in the same way should suffer an identical tax burden when one has chosen one type of business organisation and other has chosen a different type. This is a valid principle.

The IR35 rules undermine that principle in relation to an ill-defined group of taxpayers.

The Revenue is entitled to look through a sham transaction and tax the real transaction. However, there are no reported cases of the Revenue using the existing law to take this stance. **Instead we are being faced with new sledgehammer provisions to tackle an issue that we believe could have been resolved in another fashion.**

References to 'disguised employment' imply that a person who is in reality an employee is treated as self-employed. But that is not the case. The worker is already taxed as an employee of his service company

We believe that these proposals are likely to impose an enormous additional burden on small businesses. Many taxpayers affected will not be able to cope with the IR35 rules without professional assistance. A tax that forces people to incur heavy professional fees in order to calculate their liability is not good law.

**It appears that what the Chancellor told the House is not what the legislation is actually primarily aimed at.** It is aimed at the avoidance of national insurance and whilst it will catch the Friday/Monday worker it will catch a great many other people as well that the Chancellor did not allude to. "

## The ICAEW Score Card

The most damning analysis of all the assessments was that by the ICAEW which score carded the tax and gave it just 30/100, a clear failure. This was the article that appeared in *Shout99.com* in 16$^{th}$ May 2000:

The Institute of Chartered Accountants (ICAEW) have slammed the Government over IR35, in a hard hitting report just issued. Francesca Lagerberg from the Tax Faculty of the ICAEW has contributed the following article.

Today's taxation is far too complex, is full of anomalies and is spinning out of democratic control. Individual taxpayers are left bemused, often unable to ascertain what they are bound to pay; businesses are burdened with added inefficiencies and complexities. Tax proposals are often designed for the convenience of the authorities and not the citizen. The result is a tax system that is inaccessible to far too many and lacking in proper Parliamentary scrutiny.

Last year, the Institute of Chartered Accountants launched our 'Ten tenets for a better tax system'. We aimed to generate debate about reform. Our proposals attracted widespread support.

Today we take these proposals a stage further, involving a wider cross-section of opinion. And, to illustrate our point, we have judged one of the Government's most recent proposals – the taxation of personal service companies (IR 35) – against the 10 tenets.

IR 35 is a key part of this year's Finance Bill. Our conclusion? The authorities could certainly do better.

## Tenet 1: legislation should be enacted by statute, with proper Parliamentary scrutiny

The proposals are written into primary legislation, though it may be possible to amend some PAYE regulations in ways that will affect them. Sadly, though, it has become clear that the Chancellor's intention is broader than he first stated. The real reasons behind a proposal should be explained by ministers from the outset.

7 out of 10

## Tenet 2: in almost all circumstances, the application of rules should be certain.

These proposals are widely drawn, then reduced by exceptions. This leads to anomalies and there is uncertainty about the dividing line between who is an employee and who is self-employed. These proposals will create real uncertainty if taxpayers are unsure of their status.

3 out of 10

## Tenet 3: tax rules should aim to be simple, understandable and clear in their objectives

The objective behind these proposals is still uncertain, so it is difficult to judge whether the complexity of the rules is necessary. Positively, the rules use the style developed by the Tax Law Rewrite Project, but strangely they do not follow this consistently and there is a contradiction with other legislation that is designed to encourage employee share-holding.

2 out of 10

## Tenet 4: tax should be easy to collect and to calculate

Collection is straightforward and will be through the PAYE system. Calculation is complicated by the uncertainties as to which contracts are caught and there will be problems calculating liabilities in time for when payment to the Revenue is due. The Revenue suggests taxpayers do the calculation twice – once as an estimate and again for the final figures.

5 out of 10

## Tenet 5: tax should be properly targeted

Many people will be caught by these rules when there were probably not intended to be and there is an exemption for partnerships where no partner has more than 60% of the profits. This seems to leave open a clear route to avoiding the new provisions.

5 out of 10

### Tenet 6: changes to the underlying rules of tax should be kept to a minimum

The proposals represent a major sea-change in the UK tax system. They will impact on many people in long-standing commercial arrangements, where the ground rules will now be altered. Like many other tax changes, this one appears to have been introduced to counter the unintended impact of previous policy changes; no doubt a further change will be needed at some point soon. Taxpayers are entitled to greater constancy.

1 out of 10

### Tenet 7: all proposals should be subject to proper consultation

The proposal was briefly mentioned in the March 1999 Budget. Subsequently, there was no formal discussion paper or consultation document. The Government's Regulatory Impact Assessment (RIA) was not available until June 1999. When wider discussions did take place, they were confined to problems of implementation, excluding the principles behind the reform. When draft legislation was posted on the Revenue's website, it was marked "for information only".

2 out of 10

### Tenet 8: tax rules should be subject to regular review

It is too early to judge this, but IR 35 could have been an opportunity to build in an automatic timetable for a review.

5 out of ten

### Tenet 9: Tax should be fair and reasonable, with a right of appeal to an independent tribunal

The new rules are both unfair and unreasonable. Unfair because they take a select group of people and treat them in a new way without making it clear how to determine who is and who is not implicated, or why, and unreasonable because in an age of self-assessment they require large amounts of subjective judgement which can be open to dispute.

0 out of 10

### Tenet 10: tax should be framed to encourage investment, capital and trade in and with the UK

These rules do not encourage healthy tax competition. They will distort business decisions and may make some businesses uncompetitive. Some will now be attracted to more welcoming tax regimes in continental Europe. Ironically, given the Government's enthusiasms, the information technology and e-communications industries could be particularly harmed.

0 out of 10

Judged against these 10 tenets, we have awarded the new personal service company rules a score of **30 out of 100**. This is a poor result. But imagine how some of our older tax legislation could fare.

There is now a clear need to review all tax legislation against modern principles. We can't think of a better way to start the new century.

*Francesca Lagerberg*

*ICAEW*

# Chapter 13

## IR35 is not the only fruit

### RIP Bill

Alongside the progress of IR35 were a number of other Government plans that could have an effect on the livelihoods of freelancers and small business. One was the Regulation of Investigatory Powers Bill. This Bill, also called the snoopers charter, would later be used by local councils to snoop on children to check where they lived in case they were attending schools outside their catchment areas and as a method of dealing with perceived 'trouble makers'/taxpayers by council CEO's throughout the country.

In terms of IT this meant that Internet Service Providers (ISP's) would have to keep access logs from their servers, the cost of which threatened to price all small firms out of the market.

Just as IR35 was a totally tax raising issue with little regard to enterprise (until it had all gone), the aptly named RIP Bill was focused entirely on security issues and not enterprise. Contractor expert on this issue, Simon Burns, said:

Jack Straw's letter to the FT on 14th June states that "This Bill is about law enforcement." What he didn't seem to realise (or chose to overlook) was that it is also about e-commerce, whether he liked it or not.

In this arena it is the British Chamber of Commerce who have disputed the Government's figures and with tactics eerily similar to those employed against IR35, ministers set out to rubbish the figures.

Commenting on Jack Straw's Letter to the Financial Times, 13th June 2000 .Simon Burns said:

> Having read the BCC's report, it is unclear in any event how the £46 Billion figure is arrived at ... Out of nowhere the loss next year from the Bill is estimated at £2 Billion. Yet the total contribution of e-commerce to the UK's economy is estimated at around 0.6% of Gross Domestic Product, or about £5 Billion.

> You might expect the Home Secretary to repudiate the figures by producing his own calculations, or do something to indicate why the British Chambers of Commerce report is "quite literally incredible". As it is, we just have to take his word for it.

Charles Clarke's Letter to the Guardian, 14th June 2000, said 'Your editorial ("Kick this legislation out," 12 June 2000) could do far more to drive e-commerce overseas than you allege the Regulation of Investigatory Powers (RIP) Bill would.'

It is extraordinary that Mr Clarke seeks to place the blame for any damage with the newspapers that are analysing this legislation, while at the same time denying that the Bill itself will cause any damage.

Simon noted that he went on to write about the "myths and misunderstandings pedalled by those who know they are untrue".

> "These pedlars of lies include the British Chambers of Commerce, London School of Economics, The Times, The Financial Times, The Guardian, The Independent, Richard Stallman, Foundation for Information Policy Research, the STAND website and, of course, *Shout99.com* . Given the political diversity of these groups and people, it's amazing that they agree on one thing: the RIP Bill is bad news. "

## Fast Track Visas

The PCG had upped the ante about people leaving the country due to IR35. The Government's response while denying that this was the case was to make it easier for non-EU nationals to come to the UK to work. As noted Dawn Primarolo had helped to launch this special fast track visa.

*Shout99.com* reported that

> The Prime Minister's office has provided more details of the Government scheme to make up the losses caused by IR 35 (and to drive down salaries and contract rates in the IT sector). Shout99, in an exclusive report, reveals that EDS chaired the Task Force that made the recommendations concerning the need to bring in IT workers from overseas. Unsurprisingly one of the measures proposed is a pilot scheme to allow Multi National Companies to Self Certify the immigration forms which will be 'rubber stamped' by Government officials. Other commercial organisations present on the Task Force include Spring Group, the IT Recruitment agency which has strong links to New Labour

Later on *Shout99.com* would write further on the topic as it became clear that large firms would be using both IR35 and fast track visas to firstly out-price the independent competition and then secondly to replace them altogether. Moves ahead would be to allow agencies to issue visas if they felt they were needed. Which in practise would mean they find a foreign national willing to accept a lower rate and hence a higher margin for the agency.

In June an Evening Standard article entitled "Tax loophole is helping foreign IT contractors" Ross Davies stated: "Treasury Minister Dawn Primarolo is backing visa fast-tracking in the Finance Bill now going through Parliament. Independent contractors object neither to immigrants nor to their earning low wages but they do object to foreign contracting firms getting a tax break which allows them to charge British clients less than British contractors do."

## Agency legislation

Down the road at the DTI they were consulting on a new Agencies Bill, unfortunately for the agency bodies the DTI was not a Brownite organisation and we believed that any alleged promises made over IR35 to ATSCo and others were not going to be honoured by the DTI, but this Act would be the agency equivalent of IR35 and soon the agencies would be keen for our help.

# Chapter 14

## Office of Fair Trading (OFT)

The OFT had opened up a consultation on 'competition restriction for professions'. The PCG started to gather evidence and I suspect that there was some spamming of the OFT by contractors who were pointing out the issues with IR35. This resulted in the OFT 'moving the goal posts' and declaring that IR35 was off limits for this consultation partly in an attempt to stop the harassment from contractors and partly to stop their whole consultation being sabotaged by the IR35.

We discussed it as a group and there was a view that perhaps we shouldn't be upsetting such an important group. My view was that they had clearly been 'got at' and we should carry on regardless, they can't tell us what we can or can't say. The whole issue was that we are professions (contractors) and here is another attempt to say that we aren't and to disregard us. In the end we agreed that Kevin Miller would make the submission, which he did in June 2000.

His well thought out argument concluded with the following points:

Conclusion

The introduction to your Consultative document states:

The customers of United Kingdom professions need from the professions an appropriate choice of services, provided efficiently and to a high standard. The professions must be competitive, unfettered by unnecessary restrictions and free to adopt the business structure best suited to meeting clients' needs.

The PCG believes that these aims apply in full to the provision of knowledge-based consulting/contracting services within the UK.

IR 35

- presents a barrier to entry into the knowledge-based consultancy market,
- restricts the provision of consultancy services through small independent companies,
- reduces competition and limits the choice of the clients using such services,
- represents an unnecessary, unwarranted and unfair restriction on the ability of knowledge-based workers to adopt the business structure best suited to meeting their needs and those of their clients.

## Is there anyone out there? Susie makes a desperate call

We may have had a new PCG committee, a consultative council and a board of directors, but other than that it was business as usual. Susie still did the media and David Ramsden did the public affairs. Andy White was still around though with his focus on *Shout99.com* and building his other businesses. Gareth Williams was now chairman and the PCG forums remained hot beds of activity and debate.

Susie Hughes lived and breathed the struggle and put out the following call to arms herself in shout on the 26$^{th}$ June:

When New Labour were returned at the last General Election with a huge majority and a chorus of 'things can only get better', many people believed that we had created a political utopia which would go unchallenged for the next five years. In an excellent article Susie Hughes, a former Government press officer examines whether it is worth campaigning against a Government with such a majority.

She concludes "If you want to make a difference - this is the last opportunity to tell the politicians they've got it wrong."

If you want to make a difference, the Office of Fair Trading is asking for comments on a report about competitiveness in the professions; the Finance Bill is still in Parliament and is the responsibility of the Chancellor and his Paymaster General, Dawn Primarolo; the Prime Minister is still promoting e-commerce and wanting the UK to lead the world in IT, while his Ministers push through this legislation; there is an e-Czar, Alex Allen, who initially expressed concern about IR35, but who seems to have gone quiet on the subject recently; there is a Minister for E-Commerce and Small Businesses, Patricia Hewitt, who should understand the damage this legislation will do; there is a Champion for Small Business, David Irwin and there are more than 600 constituency MPs who were elected to represent the views of their constituents - or lose their seats next time around.

The Finance Bill (and IR 35) has not yet got Royal Assent and until that happens, I do not consider this measure is "in the bank". A similar measure was stopped in 1981 at this stage, by Contractors mobilising and making a difference. I would suggest we continue to oppose it in every political arena we can find.

### Summer time

The Government wasn't very happy with the 30/100 that the ICAEW had awarded them and suggested that they 'looked at it again'. I am not sure how this 'look at it again' was framed or said as it sounds quite sinister.

To their credit the ICAEW did look again but responded with an even more critical report on the Government's performance using such words as 'fundamentally unfair', 'irrational', 'ill-defined' 'unjustifiable', 'enormous additional burden on small businesses' and 'unreasonable'.

Their press release said:

The Tax Faculty believes that the IR35 proposals are fundamentally unfair.

We believe the rules affecting personal service companies are unnecessary.

'Disguised employment' seems to us an irrational concept.

There are many types of business organisation and these have different tax consequences. If a person chooses to provide his services as an employee of a limited company we can see no rational reason why the natural tax consequences of that choice should not apply.

The Revenue itself has often taken the view that there is no reason why two people carrying on the same activity in the same way should suffer an identical tax burden when one has chosen one type of business organisation and other has chosen a different type.

This is a valid principle.

The IR35 rules undermine that principle in relation to an ill-defined group of taxpayers.

- The Revenue is entitled to look through a sham transaction and tax the real transaction. However, there are no reported cases of the Revenue using the existing law to take this stance. Instead we are being faced with new sledgehammer provisions to tackle an issue that we believe could have been resolved in another fashion.

- References to 'disguised employment' imply that a person who is in reality an employee is treated as self-employed. But that is not the case. The worker is already taxed as an employee of his service company

- We believe that these proposals are likely to impose an enormous additional burden on small businesses. Many taxpayers affected will not be able to cope with the IR35 rules without professional assistance. A tax that forces people to incur heavy professional fees in order to calculate their liability is not good law.

- It appears that what the Chancellor told the House is not what the legislation is actually primarily aimed at. It is aimed at the avoidance of National Insurance and whilst it will catch the Friday/Monday worker it will catch a great many other people as well that the Chancellor did not allude to.

Shout99's view was that 'this is the most damning expose of IR35 seen in the last 12 months. Written by the leading body for Accountants and after full consideration of comments made by the Paymaster General, it is a clear call for the Government to stop this legislation now'.

### Revenue asks agencies for contactor details

However the Government and the Revenue weren't prepared to stop and in early July they revealed plans to write to some 3,000 agencies to ask for the details of the contractors working through them. When challenged over the legitimacy of such an approach they said:

> This provision has been introduced as an extension of the powers of section 16 of the Taxes Management Act (TMA) 1970. We can bring these powers into effect under this section and therefore don't need to consult.
>
> "The TMA is about how to manage the day-to-day practical matters of the Revenue. The agencies will therefore have to comply with it in the forms."

I bet that they couldn't wait for the new RIP Bill to come into law and they could then snoop out even more opposition.

Late in August the Inland Revenue would explain that it may ask agencies for copies of agencies/client contracts in order to determine the tax status of a contractor. These would be the same contracts that the contractor would not be party to or would ever have seen but they would be judged on it nonetheless. They sent the letters out in December and Andy White noted that:

> This information will allow the Revenue to collect a definitive list of Ltd Co contractors working through agencies. They presumably will then correlate this list with returns made by those Ltd Co contractors, to draft up a list of contractors working through agencies who claim to be outside IR 35 (By continuing to draw dividends). They then have up to six years to carry out further investigations.

In early July IR35 finally went into law as a part of the Finance Act.

### There is no case law says Revenue inspector

The Paymaster General and senior officials had been insisting that contractors be subjected to the same tests as everyone else who was self-employed and there was no problem with doing this.

Then in August a contractor wrote to the Revenue about his status and in the reply back they admitted that there was no case law that would support contractors and with appeals it could be 5 years before any was established.

In the letter the inspector stated:

> "The existing rules are based on a long history of case law, but of course, none exists in relation to the new legislation. It is envisaged that IR35 will ultimately lead to new case law."

As a demonstration of how out of touch the rules are, the Inspector points out that the most common indicators of self-employment include:

> the worker supplies materials, plant and heavy equipment needed for the job.

Exactly how a knowledge based business would be able to supply "materials, plant or heavy machinery" is not explained.

It was exactly the point we had been making, the case law didn't fit the circumstances. It was round pegs and square holes. To us in the PCG it was yet another nail in the IR35 coffin, but it seemed that it didn't matter how bad it was, or how unworkable or that the Government's arguments would all be defeated, it was still going ahead. The only hope we had was some swift case law victories or to blow the whole thing out through a judicial review.

## Lord Report on e-Commerce

My focus during this time had been on the House of Lords Select Committee Report on e-Commerce. Andy and the directors all thought that this was a key area in which we should engage. I had never written a response or a call for evidence from such a distinguished group before. I wasn't quite sure how to write it, but I knew what to say.

Instead of writing in some flowery style that some suggested we use I would write it instead in conversational English putting carefully and clearly our case. I wasn't out to impress anyone, I just wanted to get our points across and hope that it would get a mention in their conclusions.

### Memorandum by the Professional Contractors Group (PCG)

The Professional Contractors Group (PCG) appreciates this opportunity to present evidence and comment on the subject of e-Commerce: Policy Development and Co-ordination in the EU.

Many of the members of the Professional Contractors Group are now engaged in the e-commerce sector providing services and skills for their own start-up companies or contracting services to other companies.

We welcome the appointment by the Government of a Minister for e-commerce and an E-Envoy and the work they are conducting in order to initiate and promote the knowledge economy and e-commerce in the UK.

However, the PCG feel that these initiatives will have been undermined by the new IR35 tax legislation announced by the Treasury which will take effect from 6 April 2000.

### 1. WHAT NEEDS TO BE DONE TO CREATE CONFIDENCE AND STIMULATE E-COMMERCE?

We believe that small companies and a flexible work force should be key factors in driving forward e-commerce in the UK. The recent growth of the "dot.com" companies is evidence of this.

IR35 will use the self-employment tests to determine the level of tax that small companies will have to pay, but there is not sufficient and clear case law in existence to allow workers in the new knowledge economy selling skills and knowledge any degree of certainty in establishing their tax treatment.

We will not rehearse all our objections to IR35 here, but will concentrate on its likely effects on e-commerce and the developing knowledge economy. Fundamentally we believe the Government has failed to understand the operation of the contract sector and is using a quite inappropriate criterion of self-employment when the real question is one of outsourcing and an unbalanced tax system.

Given the use of the employment tests in the legislation, we are particularly concerned that the Inland Revenue guidance on IR35 does not give sufficient weight to factors pointing away from employment such as the right of a small company to provide an alternative consultant, and gives unjustifiable emphasis to factors such as the length of a contract, and payment by the hour, in an apparent attempt to bring as much of the IT contract sector under IR35 as possible.

As a consequence many small businesses working in the knowledge-based sector that do not satisfy any reasonable definition of "disguised employment" risk falling foul of the new IR35 legislation. This will have the following impact on these small businesses:

— They will suffer a proportionately much higher tax burden that their larger competitors;

— Companies will not be able to fund research and development projects nor employ extra staff using revenue raised from contracts that fail the IR35 legislation;

— Companies will not be able to undergo expansion using any retained profit;

— Companies will not be able to build upon or develop any equity in their business;

— Companies will not be able to claim the same business expenses as their larger competitors; and

— IR35 legislation will discourage potential entrepreneurs within the UK and the EU from starting up a business.

The PCG thinks that the huge implications brought about by this ill-conceived legislation will severely hamper the future growth of e-commerce in the UK and that this will likewise damage the ability of the UK to compete within the EU.

## The Importance of Outsourcing

The developing sector of e-commerce demonstrates the importance of outsourcing to the knowledge economy. Businesses with little experience of IT will have to engage external consultants to provide e-commerce solutions. These consultants require the flexibility to work closely with their client over a period of months to fully understand their client's businesses and needs and to integrate the most appropriate e-commerce solution with the client's existing operations. This is exactly the kind of engagement which (when carried out by a small business where the employees each own more than 5 per cent of the shares) risks being classified as "disguised employment" under IR35.

## Lack of Certainty

All businesses need to know with certainty what their likely tax position will be before they start to trade. The IR35 legislation means that after 18 months at least, or at worst, six years could elapse before the Revenue challenges the status of that contract under IR35. Companies starting a new e-commerce business will not want to run this risk.

**Loss of Skilled Workers**

The impending effects of IR35 legislation have affected the viability of the contract market over the last three months in the UK.

Many IT contractors have already left the UK, a significant number of individuals will leave in the coming tax year, and many more will leave in a continuing stream such that the replacement of key individuals who have left or not returned to the UK will take decades to recover from.

The recent announcement from the Home Office that fast track visas are to be provided for skilled IT workers from underdeveloped countries shows that the Government expects an exodus of skilled workers from the UK and this is presumably the only way of making up the short fall.

A skills shortage in the UK will hamper "start-up" companies because they will find it difficult to hire specialist knowledge and skilled workers for short-term contracts.

**Increased Costs**

If the effect of IR35 is to reduce the number of small independent IT consultancies, this will force increased reliance on the large international consultancies (which will not be hit by IR35 since their staff do not own 5 per cent of the companies' shares) which charge considerably higher rates. The cost to business of taking up e-commerce will increase, and the take-up rate will therefore be slowed.

**Summary**

IR35 will not deliver the Government's vision of enterprise and expansion of the UK's fledgling e-commerce businesses into a global economy but will unfortunately discriminate against small businesses.

The PCG aims to support individuals that are willing to form and develop their own businesses, in many cases employing staff and diversifying. IR35 will prevent and hinder this process. The uncertainty thatIR35 will create over a company's tax position will not create confidence and will hold back developments in e-commerce.

It is good and their Lordships thought so too. We had put it together as a joint piece working with the communications committee[54] that we had formed and then with help from everyone on the forums. When published in July their conclusions were:

> (paras 288/289): "IR35 is a tax regulation which was introduced to counter a situation in which in some companies employees were re-designated as self-employed sub-contractors even though the nature of their work had not changed. Unfortunately, the regulation affects the genuinely self-employed entrepreneur

---

[54] Gordon Grant, Mike Beizley, Brian Curnow, David Ramsden, Susie Hughes

too. e-Commerce depends to an increasing extent on skilled and creative practitioners. There is already a shortfall in the numbers of such people, both in Europe and in the United States. Nations are competing to attract and to hold these skilled people. The Government's imposition of IR35, which strikes directly at the self-employed IT specialist, lowers the attractiveness of the United Kingdom as a market for such skills.

"We recommend that the Government keep under review the operation of IR35 so as not to impede the development of new e-commerce companies."

Another direct hit.

## PCG launch their Gone Abroad Page

By the end of the holidays the PCG decided, against my better judgement, to launch a 'gone abroad' web page where contractors could log their details if they had left the country. I thought it was one thing to allege that people were going abroad or were planning to but to have to back it up with actual real figures would lead to disaster, but the majority of the PCG board were analytical and fact based and they believed that people were leaving so the PCG launched a webpage and quite quickly a few hundred people had logged onto it and ultimately totalled around 800, which is a lot but not quite the thousands alleged. My argument too was that if people had left could they be bothered to log it? The page backfired on the PCG as the Government instead of them were able to use it to say that thousands clearly weren't leaving.

*Shout99.com* later reported that Patricia Hewitt MP had told the Select Committee that:

> She then dismissed the idea that contractors were leaving the country in any significant numbers. She told the Committee: "It is interesting, if you look at one of the contractor's websites, you will find a monthly survey of the number of IT contractors who have left or are planning to leave the country. On the most recent one I have seen, and I think it was the early December results, there were about 78 sub-contractors who were planning to go to Germany or had already gone, there were about 48 who were planning to go to the Netherlands or had already gone, there were around the 10s or 20s in a handful of other countries.

# Chapter 15

## The e-Envoy

One person who had read the gone abroad page was the e-Envoy who was himself planning to leave the UK to go and live in Australia.

The office of the e-Envoy had been established by Tony Blair in 1999, its goal was to get Government services and departments all online so that things like renewing a driving license or tax disc or paying taxes could be done over the net. This was an ambitious project that met with some success.

The first e-Envoy was British patrician, Sir Alexander Claud Stuart Allan, KCB, or Alex Allen as he was known. We liked him because his personal website said that he had wind surfed down the Thames. He had been the principle private secretary to John Major and then to Tony Blair before having a spell as Australian High Commissioner. (Contractors were emailing him while he was still in Australia). He was appointed as the e-Envoy in 1999. To be fair he quickly grasped the problems with IR35 and made some good noises about it, so much so that Dawn Primarolo had to dispute that he had done so.

On the 9$^{th}$ March she told Parliament that

> It is not true that the e-commerce envoy has been making representations to the Treasury about relaxing the rules. He made it clear that he supports the Government's policy of stopping unfair tax and national insurance avoidance.

It was a bit late to say this as we had been telling the press the complete opposite and they were all glad to write up some disagreements, and to be fair we believed them to be true, well more than believed they were true but not officially acknowledged. The same press spokesmen were also telling us that Brown and Blair were really best friends and that any suggestion of a rift between them was pure tittle-tattle.

Computer Weekly reported on Alex Allen that:

> He recently expressed concerns about the proposals, and is said to be worried that the tax change could stunt the growth of the e-commerce industry.

A spokeswoman for Allen's office said,

> "Alex Allen has certainly not criticised Government policy. At a conference he said that he was aware of concerns in the IT industry about the impact of the Inland Revenue's proposals and his office was discussing this with the Treasury. But he made it clear that policy on this was for the Treasury to decide, and that the Treasury has to balance these concerns against the need to protect the tax system against abuse."

Or they could have said, 'he knows what a disaster IR35 will be and has done everything he can to get the Treasury to change their minds but they won't budge'.

Later in the year we got a meeting with him but by then he had handed in his notice and was going to return to Australia. His successor was Andrew Pinder who was far more compliant for the Treasury. He never met with us. The office of e-Envoy was scrapped in 2004.

## Guardian interview the e-Envoy

At the end of August the Guardian thought that it would be quite trendy to get involved with some e-democracy and so invited Alex to take part in an online chat about his role. As ever of course it was 'hijacked' by IT contractors who wanted to talk about IR35 and their businesses, not some vague liberal cause.

One of the first questions was:

rmarriott1
Mr Allen, how does it feel to be appointed e-envoy by a Government which is doing everything it can to destroy the UK's future in the developing new e-commerce economy? The following measures are doing real and lasting damage to the UK's competitiveness in the new e-business world:

1. IR35 - this vindictive tax measure is driving UK IT consultants out of the country in droves. I myself start a contract in New Jersey in October, leaving the UK precisely because of IR35. My skills - distributed database systems and the integration of large databases with the web.

2. NICs on share options - bad policy which is inhibiting investment by high tech. companies. Real examples - Veritas has halved its investment in the UK because of this measure and Cisco is rumoured to have diverted its investment plans to Eire for the same reason.

3. RIP Bill - it is simply stupid for the UK Government to attempt to go it alone in internet regulation - far better to wait for international agreement. As a consequence of RIP, four UK based ISPs have threatened to move offshore.

Mr Allen, I suggest you resign in protest at the Government making your job impossible.

AlexAllan1
rmarriott1 - as you can imagine I get more email about those three topics than almost anything else.

It got worse for him and the Guardian as more questions came in.

JosephSW
Dear Alex,

I run a small IT consultancy (I am not a disguised employee), and have a real opportunity to join a new e-Commerce company in this country.

The new company has been approached by a thriving marketing company to act as its e-Commerce partner. However, because of the new IR35 measures my existing business will not be able to afford to fund the initial start-up costs... the company profit is being taxed at 52% before it can be re-invested for growth.

Is it clear to you now that IR35 is killing new e-Commerce ventures in Britain?

jrharding

Mr Allen The danger of a _genuine_ business falling foul of IR35 is real and the penalties are horrendous (personal bankruptcy and even imprisonment) How are _genuine_ small business's supposed to thrive in this environment?

AlexAllan1
I promised to come back on IR35 and share options, though don't expect easy solutions.

On IR35, the Inland Revenue have made it clear that if someone meets the tests for self-employment, then they won't be affected. I know some contractor groups have sent in model contracts which seem to meet that test, though others seem to feel this won't help them. We'll have to monitor how that works out in practice. It's not a question of attacking entrepreneurship: there was some genuine abuse by people avoiding employee's income tax and NICs by becoming contractors even though the reality was that they were in the same position as before. The difficult bit is stopping that without hitting people who have genuinely set up businesses.

I could agree with Alex Allen and did agree with him, it was just a shame that the Treasury didn't. The problem was that IR35 *would be* hitting those who had genuinely set up in business but as far as the Government was concerned anyone who complained about was clearly not in business.

During the French Revolution Robespierre said 'only the guilty tremble' and that seemed to be the Government's approach. Certainly it was the issue if you submitted a contract for review by the Revenue, if you were so concerned or unsure as to get it reviewed, then you're probably guilty as far as they were concerned.

The e-Minister Patricia Hewitt would later declare that no sub-contractors or small businesses had ever raised IR35 with her. I thought, that is strange because we have met several times and I have raised it with you as I know have hundreds of other contractors. But of course we obviously weren't real small businesses in her eyes.

## New Statesman Award

As a political animal I had my subscription to the New Statesman and sometimes I even read it. One key point on its calendar of events was its 'New Media Awards'. A few years earlier I had noted how a friend who worked for an MP had submitted her website for an award. When I saw the awards advertised in the magazine I thought of the PCG and thought surely a new online trade association is exactly the sort of initiative that should be recognised.

I posted up a call on the PCG forums for people to nominate Andy and the PCG[55]. Though I had to fend off a number of negative comments about how it was a 'Liebour' magazine, etc. and that we should really be going to the Spectator. I persuaded people that this was indeed New Labour territory, so therefore an excellent place to embarrass the Government by winning an award for our campaign. Which I did feel was worthy of an award in any case.

As a consequence hundreds of PCG members emailed the New Statesman (with a cc to me) proposing Andy White and the PCG. So many that they couldn't be ignored.

They were nominated for four national awards for innovative communication using new technology.

PCG and Andy received a 'special mention' in the Elected Representative Section and were nominated in Advocacy, On-line Communities and Overall Merit.

The awards were presented by Cabinet Office Minister, Dr Mo Mowlam MP, and the judges included the Government's e-Envoy, Alex Allen.

Andy White said: "The power of the web allowed PCG to grow and operate so efficiently in such a short period of time. It provided the means whereby individuals could become part of a community and act with greater impact through their combined strength. And it has shown the future for lobbying and campaigning so that every voice can be heard.

"It is so ironic therefore that the measure which brought these people together, IR35, is in fact a Government move which will have severe damage on the development of e-commerce and force tens of thousands of information technology businesses to close down."

Awards moderator, Bill Thompson, said: "Andy deserved a special mention in the Elected Representative Awards. Even though this was intended for MPs, MSPs and councillors, such was the depth of support for Andy that we felt that his sterling effort to show what would happen with IR35 deserved to be recognised.

"So while he technically wasn't eligible for the category, the judges strongly felt he deserved a special award for his work in this area."

Susie, Andy and a few others went to the drinks evening and awards ceremony, I was absent instead at the hospital as my son was being born.

## Meeting with the e-Envoy

I had lobbied the office of the e-Envoy and the groups surrounding him to try and get a meeting. Initially they were interested but then became lukewarm on the

---

[55] And to copy their nominations to me

subject suggesting to us that the e-Envoy understood the issues around IR35 and didn't need a meeting. I challenged that and pursued a policy with Susie's help that everywhere he went and every new article he would appear in we would be on hand to rebut the idea that they were making Britain ready for e-Commerce. The Guardian article above was a good example but this wasn't a case of Susie Hughes and I going online ourselves, we just put out a note calling for people to jump in and on the PCG forums people put up their own calls for such things anyway. The IT press and soon the national press soon referred to us for good copy.

I wanted to get into see the e-Envoy as a DTI minister had told me that the only way of stopping the tax was going to Downing Street and getting Tony Blair to intervene. Getting to Blair was not an easy thing to do, but here was the e-Envoy who was allegedly close to him and sympathetic to our cause. At least if not sympathetic he wasn't aggressively opposed to us. Our efforts paid off and we got a meeting in early September 2000.

I had attended two meetings with Michael Wills and two meetings with Patricia Hewitt and had one formal and one informal meeting with Dawn Primarolo. I was getting better at it. Preparation seemed to be the key as well as some clear objectives. Aside from the meeting with Dawn, which was more of a parley, the main objectives were to build up a good rapport and open up channels for future meetings. These objectives were a key and a close working relationship from our delegation was essential, we were a team acting and fighting on the same side. Like the Roman army we should move as one as opposed to having individual heroics or actions.

This meeting though wasn't to prove to be our best. We took too many people to it and were ill prepared and divided. The contractor/directors who had taken over some of the senior positions wanted to be involved in more than name only with a hands-on role in areas which did not always play to their strengths or experience. Gareth Williams, Pamela Edwards, myself and I think one other attended[56]. The meeting was far too top heavy with people; two of us would have been enough. For some reason Gareth and others came down to London and stayed at the Savoy Hotel which I thought was a bit expensive, though I did enjoy going there for our pre-meeting the night before. We couldn't agree what the common line was and Pamela declared that we couldn't tell her what she could or couldn't say. Gareth was quite prepared and had lined up some quite detailed arguments to put to the Envoy. I thought at the time were too detailed, but he thought were fine. In hindsight I think Gareth was right but I was still keen to keep the meeting at a high level and even though Mr Allen had resigned from his post I was keen to build up some good feeling. Pamela wanted to use it as an opportunity to vent her spleen at the Government. I was the people person with the technocrats. My view was that once I had a feeling on the personalities I could then work on the policies. The others felt that the policies and data were all that was needed and they spoke for

---

[56] It may have been David Ramsden

themselves, there was no need to put up an argument. Pamela felt that if they weren't for us at this stage then they were clearly against us.

Pamela also questioned why I should be at the meeting, I did point out that I was the public affairs director but she felt it should be Gareth as chairman and her but I can't even remember what her role was. Through this mayhem and argument Susie Hughes worked hard with us to try and build a coherent strategy. My mistake was to suggest that I didn't think that Alex Allen would know about our gone abroad register and we decided, as it didn't have that many names on it, not to mention it.

The next day we went to the Cabinet Office for the meeting with Alex Allen. The first thing Alex said to us was to take his name off our gone abroad register[57]. (He was returning to Australia). I was embarrassed but I thanked him for his engagement on IR35 and other issues and explained that we wanted to engage positively with him. The following discussion was wide ranging and Gareth did start to focus him on the specifics of the IR35 tax issue and Alex Allen did engage. I would make positive noises and comments about Government policy and aims and objectives, only for Pamela to interject and contradict me and then make some anti-Labour statements. As a consequence the meeting was going nowhere, any suggestions I made would be contradicted by Pamela. The view of Alex Allen was that we needed to be clear on what we wanted first as a group (i.e. stop arguing among ourselves) then he could help. It was embarrassing. The meeting achieved nothing. The only saving grace was that Alex Allen was leaving his post so perhaps the episode could be forgotten though Gareth had done well and built up some rapport with him. Afterwards I dropped a note to the e-Envoy's office offering a positive spin on our discussions and received a favourable reply. Susie Hughes asked what she could tell the press, I had to say I had nothing to give her and nothing went out that I remember.

However, a few days later the e-Envoy published his annual report which suggested keeping the door open on changes to IR35, maybe we had been able to reinforce those paragraphs.

Pamela suggested to me afterwards that the meeting wasn't a place for spin and politics; I disagreed saying that was exactly what it was for. She said we shouldn't make any offers or mention anything that hadn't been previously discussed. I said that we needed to use our judgement and adapt to the situation as it changes, that is why we have been selected as directors. I said we were soldiers in battle and that we were objective driven, the tactics were down to us, not armchair generals. She reiterated her view that she didn't trust me or my judgement and felt that I had the interests of Labour more at heart than that of contractors. I pointed out that she was a card carrying member of the Conservative Party and perhaps it was those interests and personal prejudice that she had in mind.

---

[57] Someone had added it as a joke

She was older than me and from a more wealthy social class and I would experience being talked down to as the comprehensive school boy that I am. We didn't get on, though I tried and tried. We were supposed to have been on the same team but she didn't have the right skills, aptitude or personality for such meetings or negotiations. The problem was that the balance of power had shifted in the PCG. Andy was no longer in charge and though Gareth was chairman his job was to lead on IR35 technically and front the organisation. Andy still exerted great influence and authority, but in this vacuum people like Pamela were able to come to the fore with their opinionated and entrenched positions.

She had lots of energy though and was very much engaged with the fight and if we could point her in the right direction she could be a great asset, but she was not a team player and was very opinionated on this issue and others. She was perhaps a Tory version of Dawn Primarolo and my Labour Party membership and support was beyond the pale to her. My view was that she had never been that 'close to one before' (a socialist), but over the following months she would continually push for me to go and would lobby for it with other directors and those on the consultative council. Later on she would be one of the leading coup members against Andy White, but for now was good friends with Susie Hughes and I left them as they went for lunch together.

# Chapter 16

### The e-Minister

Our relationship with Dawn Primarolo wasn't the best one. By 'our' I mean both the PCG's and my own. Perhaps I had wrecked it by speaking at the Labour conference but from getting to know her I didn't think that had made any difference. The speech and my subsequent role gave me authority to fight for contractors, otherwise she would have fobbed me off as mistaken and wrong quite easily.

When Patricia Hewitt was appointed as the e-Minister I wrote her a similar letter to the one I had first sent to Dawn Primarolo pointing out that I was an IT contractor, a Labour supporter and by this time a prospective parliamentary candidate and was involved with the PCG. We exchanged letters and then as the e-Minister she sent me her private email address and we corresponded more. I didn't over do it but would send her news and information. In November 1999 she invited me to a meeting with her at the House of Commons, just me and her discussing the issues around IR35. I thought it strange at the time that it wasn't an 'official' DTI meeting with her advisors.

I took it to be an off-the-record discussion though that was never discussed, but I didn't feel that we could publish it in the press. Later on I realised that from her perspective making it unofficial meant that the Treasury didn't need to know and couldn't find out, they very much frowned on any such meetings taking place. In September 2000 we met at the Labour Conference and I asked if we could have a photograph taken together, she agreed but then expressed concern lest Dawn found out. I promised to only use it for election purposes not PCG ones. These two facts together very much colour the relationship that existed between her and the Treasury, or rather her and the Brownites. In the dying days of the Labour Government together with Geoff Hoon she would attempt a coup to get him to stand down, it was unsuccessful.

I remember the first meeting we had in part because I had the most dreadful cold and wanted to be at home in the warm with some Lemsip, but instead was navigating my way through a cold, rainy and windy November evening to the Central Lobby of the House of Commons.

Prior to meeting we had been in some communication about the issues. We met in the lobby and went through to the corner of a tea room. My aim wasn't to give her a hard time on IR35 but to educate her about it. Few of the ministers or officials we had dealt with had any experience of self-employment or running their own firms, the only exception being Michael Wills who had given us a fair hearing so my mission was to try and inform and educate. I explained how contractors had to use limited companies and that the way you bought them was often off the self. I talked about agencies, I talked about the sort of work that people did. My father had been self-employed. I talked too about the abuse that IR35 was trying to address, the fact that people paid themselves a tiny wage and then huge dividends. I said that the

IR35 solution was a sledge hammer to crack a nut, but first and foremost I worked to win her trust and friendship, which I did.

We had quite a few subsequent meetings, some long and some as short as 5-10 minutes. I kept the channel open. It was clear from discussions with her that the Treasury were totally adamant at pushing through the measure and we couldn't stop it. I sent her the news story about the ICAEW scoring IR35 at 30/100. I know that she read it because she emailed me back with an air of resigned disbelief. We discussed the issue of the self-employment and why people didn't just work as self-employed. I didn't have all the answers but said that because of the agencies legislation people needed to incorporate and suggested that perhaps they could create a sort of LTD-company-self-employment as they had done for partnerships (LLP). She asked if this was PCG policy. No I said, but I could try to raise it with them. We also discussed the 5/95% dividend split. If we weren't happy with the 5% what figure would be acceptable? I said that the whole salary/dividend split was unacceptable unless you were to move it to the 40/60 area. That wasn't going to happen, maybe we could have got it to 10-15% with her, but we would have had to have settled with IR35, I couldn't do that. At a later meeting she told me that the only way to make changes to the tax was to get it into Downing Street and with Tony Blair, but didn't offer to help us with this.

I discussed some of these issues with Susie Hughes, Andy White and Gareth Williams and noted some of them on the forum. However, a red-mist had come across the eyes of many members, 'les Enragés[58]', who were following the line drawn by Pamela Edwards that I wasn't to be trusted and was too close to Labour. It was true that I was close to Labour; that is how I had managed to get those private meetings and hold these frank discussions. However, I would have to dip into the forums regularly to defend myself and other members would email me links to let me know what was happening. Many of those who attacked me I had never met and had no idea who they were.

The self-employment idea was not going to fly, nor would a change to the 5/95% split, any change in that would be an acceptance of the legitimacy of IR35. I agreed with that, but in hindsight it would have been something.

These negotiations, I was told by the Enragés, were pointless as the judicial review would wipe the tax out and if that failed Labour would lose the 2001 election because of it.

### Hewitt dodges questions on IR35

Despite all my meetings with Patricia Hewitt I couldn't promise that she was now onside. She would be asked in the press about IR35 and would often present

---

[58] The more extreme members of the PCG. In the French Revolution they were the extremist 'sans-culottes'. It means literally 'the mad men'.

conflicting answers but if you think about it she was simply representing the Government's policy and as a minister was morally bound to support it.

Despite our relationship we continued to challenge her in the press and would despatch 'agitators' to any business functions that she, Dawn Primarolo or Alex Allen were attending with the key objective to raise IR35.

I reported earlier about the House of Lords Select Committee report on IR35 and letting her know about it. I could sense that she was finding it increasingly hard to defend the indefensible, though there was a degree of amusement with these things. I'd report them to her and she would respond in despair, but what I didn't mention was that I was the author of that report and of many of the press stories.

When she gave evidence to a DTI select committee in December 2000,

> Lindsay Hoyle, Labour MP for Chorley asked the Minister: "I wonder if you have been contacted by SMEs who are very, very concerned about IR 35 contractors going overseas, which would leave them with an IT skills shortage that they do not think can be filled? I wonder if you share their worry about what is happening?"
>
> Ms Hewitt replied: "I do not think I have had any small businesses raise IR 35 with me. I have had a couple of large businesses saying they have lost a few contractors as a result of IR 35. I recently spoke at a main session of the CBI Conference on e-commerce generally, a big panel discussion, and nobody raised IR 35."

She later said:

> "I care very deeply about small businesses, which is why I spend so much time listening to them. As I say, no small business users have raised with me the issue of IR 35. Obviously I am aware of the concerns of the Professional Contractors Group and of the judicial review. We will see what decision the court comes to, but clearly the Government will be defending that action".

I thought, well I am a small business and I have raised this with you many times. She pointed out that the question was about small firms complaining that they couldn't get contractors or had lost contractors because of IR35 and that is what she had answered. I said that it underlined the problem; we were small firms but weren't recognised as such.

On another occasion she told the press that:

> "The sub-contractors I have spoken to have been greatly reassured by the approach that the Inland Revenue has taken."

I asked her if she was serious or quoted out of context. I told her that such expressions would have a consequence as thousands of contracts deluged her official email with complaints.

I could never really tell if Patricia Hewitt was playing me or I was playing her. It didn't really matter as we both got benefits from the relationship but you needed to keep your eyes open and be aware.

### Govt Report opens a door on IR35

Saying all this, the biggest output from our lobbying of the e-Envoy and e-Minister was a joint report that they published that September.

The report stated that:

> IR35 is not aimed at IT workers specifically. It will ensure that workers, who use service companies but actually do the job of an employee for a client, will pay a fair amount of tax and NICs. Through online consultation over the e-Envoy website we have helped ensure effective two-way communication between the Inland Revenue and potentially affected contractors.

It concludes with:

> As with all legislation, the Government will monitor the effects of the IR35 changes to ensure that they achieve their objectives and do not have unexpected harmful effects on genuine business activities. This will include investigating any effect on the labour market in industries where the use of service companies is common.

Not everything we wanted by a long shot, but it left the door open to changes and that had to be a positive.

# Chapter 17

### Tories and IR35

The Conservatives embraced the campaign against IR35 with vigour. It proved to be a great example of a stealth tax, Labour's failure to understand business and of a shoddy consultation. We sensed though that they were always a little bit uneasy about it as a tax issue in case they were tarred with backing tax dodgers, but the saving grace of the issue was that Gordon Brown was never going to back down so they could always use it as a stick to hit the Government with.

Their opposition would be maintained during their years in the wilderness, despite a few blips right up to the moment when they took office when as all politicians do, moved goal posts and reneged on their promise and instead of abolishing it undertook instead to just reform the way it was operated. I had a good article published widely on the topic in March 2011. The 2011 PCG were politically out manoeuvred and failed to even call for the abolition of the tax when the Coalition Government, through the Office of Tax Simplification, did a promised consultation on the issue. With shades of French footballer Eric Cantona and his infamous seagulls and trawlers, the chairman of the PCG wrote an article about 'tuna fish and dolphins' to justify IR35 and the reason they didn't call for it to go. At least that is my take on it and I think contractors must have been the dolphins, I am not sure who the tuna fish were or whether the Inland Revenue should be using a line rather than a net?

When we were children our neighbour's dog would bark at our cat all the time and chase it when it could. One day it actually cornered the cat but was terrified itself as it didn't know what to do, so it turned and ran away scared itself.

After all our years of fighting, the blood, sweat and tears, the promises and subscriptions from members over these years, it was a real let down. It had been 12 years since the start of the campaign and 12 years until there was the first one and only real chance to get rid of it - and the PCG, the trade association that had been born with that one aim in mind, didn't even support its abolition. Instead, it left some supporters wondering what all the fuss had been about when it took the middle ground and supported an otherwise unsupported call for a new form of business tests to judge if people where inside or outside IR35. We would have been taken to the virtual guillotine if we had even suggested a compromise! Ironically, the PCG was later to learn the lesson of being careful what you wish for when the business tests became a reality to universal condemnation - including the PCG!

Mark Prisk MP, the Conservative small business minister, was an ardent campaigner for freelancers. He had run his own business before entering Parliament and so understood the issues and risks. I have great respect for him and am sure he was disappointed with the eventual outcome on IR35.

Back in 2000 people were flamed on the forums and metaphorically put in tumbrils and sent to guillotine for a lot less than what the 2011 PCG chairman had done, but times change.

In 1999 the Tories had their first wobble on IR35. When Michael Portillo returned to Parliament in a by-election and became Shadow Chancellor word slipped out that instead of promising to abolish IR35 they would now just promise to 'review' it, which is what happened in 2011.

Francis Maude had been hard line on the issue but under Portillo it was review not repeal. PCG members weren't prepared to stand for this.

Pamela Edwards was a member of the Conservatives Technology Forum, I was a member of Computing for Labour; both were networks of party supporters with this special interest. She arranged a special meeting of the forum and invited Oliver Letwin, the no.2 Shadow Treasury Minister, to speak. She opened up the meeting for all contractors to attend. So far so good, but then when reading the small print I discovered that you had to pay to attend and tickets were £25.

This was a hard one for me to deal with, I certainly wasn't going to write out a cheque for the Tory party, however, they did need lobbying and this was the perfect forum in which to do it.

I just stood back from it; I wasn't welcome in any case. Gareth Williams went as did Susie Hughes, David Ramsden, Jane Akshar and at least 50 contractors. Below is the report written by Susie Hughes for *Shout99.com*. It was clear that Oliver Letwin hadn't fully grasped what the issue was and had turned up on the basis that 'his enemy's enemy was his friend', so as a consequence he was given something of a friendly hard time over it.

Mr Letwin surprised some of the group by saying that he had some sympathy with Paymaster General Dawn Primarolo as there was a problem which needed addressing. Where he disagreed with her was the manner in which the Government had attempted to solve the problem with IR35. He was resistant to making any commitment to remove IR35 and preferred to have it revised in order to target the abuse more accurately.

However, he was unable to give a clear definition of what the 'abuse' was, citing one example of that of John Birt, the former BBC director general, he also proffered a possible 'solution' of exempting contracts which were under one year's duration.

Gareth Williams, the PCG's chairman tabled an aptly titled position paper 'We Wouldn't Start From Here' and explained that although the Conservatives understood that IR35 was a bad law, they had made a fundamental error in accepting the Government's description of the problem.

Gareth told the meeting: "It is wrong to start from the premise that people establish companies merely to avoid NIC. We do not see IR35 or anything like it as being the solution to any genuine problem. We would suggest that the Conservative Party should be sceptical not only of the Government's 'solution' in the form of IR35, but of its entire analysis of the 'problem', and its assertion that there is a major 'tax avoidance' issue to be addressed".

A sometimes heated question and answer session followed when Mr Letwin was left in no doubt that the contractors would view any 'solution' which put small companies at a disadvantage compared to their larger competitors as unacceptable.

The conclusion of the meeting was that PCG would be invited to meet again with the Treasury team, and Mr Letwin left with a much better understanding of the real problems and a message that a quick-fix Band-aid solution was not the answer.

The meeting did the trick and come February, sensing they had nothing to lose the Tories (or had already lost the general election) declared again for 'repeal' not 'reform' then the Shadow Secretary of State for Trade and Industry, Rt Hon David Heathcoat-Amory MP said:

> "IR35 was a sly measure which turned into a disastrous attack on the IT sector. In seeking to eliminate the bad it destroys so much that is good. The Government fails to understand that contracting out is a legitimate and growing practice in IT and other sectors.
>
> "Labour have been deaf to the reasonable representations from the industry. By contrast we are taking positive steps to free people who are essential to the new economy from this repressive measure."

*Shout99.com* reported that in a clear pre-election statement the Conservatives have confirmed "A future Conservative Government will repeal IR35 and replace it with legislation to address abuses."

They continue:

> "After extensive consultation with, among others, the Professional Contractors Group, the Conservatives have decided that the existing legislation will be replaced by targeted legislation to deal with any abuse of personal service companies for purely tax purposes. There will be further consultation with the industry before such replacement legislation is brought forward."

# Chapter 18

The PCG was developing as an organisation. It had grown to have around 11,000 members by the summer of 2000. Some people had joined in part to get the benefits of joint insurance, in part to get access to the sample contracts but the best of them had joined because they wanted to fight against IR35. Andy White once declared that trying to organise contractors was like trying to herd cats and it was almost impossible to get them all pointing in the same direction. Now it was getting even bigger.

Andy had founded the PCG with himself and David Ramsden as the nominal shareholders but they had passed ownership and control over to the members. Gareth had written a constitution and there had been elections for a consultative council and then subsequently for a board of directors from within the membership.

The PCG forums had been alive with debate and full of radical members, many becoming prolific posters, while others just read the content. The creation of a board and the council led to the introduction of two new forums, one for directors and one for council members as well as a general on-line forum. These new tiered forums undermined the old open democracy that had existed in the PCG but with a judicial review planned there needed to be a secure area where issues could be discussed. It was felt that the open forums were too open to leakage and people were convinced that the Inland Revenue must have a rogue or secret membership, though this was never proven. Agencies certainly had membership and in these early days of the forums we were confronted with problems over slander in postings. Mainly where people had slagged off an agency, the agency would demand it be taken down and we even had threats of court action. Susie knew people at Carter Ruck, the libel lawyers who would step in to defend us, although the whole issue of Internet libel and responsibility was in its infancy and, like IR35, a very grey area. On some occasions we had to stamp down on unreasonable behaviour by some contractors. Some of these were the 'Enragés' that I mentioned. Nasty posts could be made against politicians and we would have to get these withdrawn. A code of conduct for the forums was created to ensure that posts weren't libellous, slanderous or abusive but as with all such codes it would later be used to suppress debate, not support it.

Politically the PCG was easier to control if you controlled the board of directors, managed the consultative council and broadcasted to the members as a whole. Instead of just keeping only confidential matters in the two forums later on policy would be strictly debated in these two elite forums rather than in the general forums. Nowadays the restricted discussion forum is commonplace and the mainstay of social networking sites. However, a decade ago this was still quite revolutionary to have differing access permissions. Under Andy's 'reign', transparency had been key, now the new regime closed some of the doors to the membership masses, which ultimately led to a culture of suspicion.

Debate in the general forums would remain hot and sometimes debate would move around and almost hide in different places. In 2005 (long after I had left) I read that the new leadership sought to suppress debate and even deleted the entire archive of the 'lounge forum' [59] because of the debate that had taken place on it.

None of this should be viewed with surprise since the PCG was simply evolving along the pattern of most new groups with its forming, storming and norming. If viewed in parallel with the French revolution the similarities were uncanny.

The PCG didn't exist just as a crowd of angry voices; it was now an organisation with significant revenue and large resources. My focus was on the political and campaigning goals while others looked upon it as a corporation – a business in its own right. In the time ahead there would be challenges on not just the political goals of the contractor movement but also the corporate goals of the contractor organisation, control of its policy and control of its wealth and revenue. This battle would come to a head a few years later.

But for now factions were forming in the organisation whose objectives were not just about beating IR35 but beating their perceived opposition in the organisation.

Pamela suggested that we used the weight of the PCG to negotiate better terms on things like health insurance and the like. Some were opposed to it but I thought why not, why shouldn't contractors come together to get similar deals and benefits to their permanent counter-parts? What it did do was subtly change the focus of the PCG reinforcing the organisational side.

Many were angry that the PCG had allowed agencies to become members and were worried about the influence that they could have in the organisation. My view was we were letting them have a ticket to watch but not play, but I too was concerned about letting them in, was it watering down the PCG? How could we fight agencies if they were members? Presumably if they weren't happy they'd just leave, of course they didn't they stayed and moaned and used up our most precious resource – time.

Another faction was that of the pedants. One such pedant was a contractor who posted under the name of Quattro who was obsessed with formalism, procedure and all our regulations. He criticised letters and postings and policy and how decisions were reached suggesting that they breached this or that regulation and were therefore invalid. He had a number of supporters on the forums but he was costing us both time and resources. He would challenge decisions or letters and we would have pay for legal advice to check things over to ensure they were right, which they tended to be. Council meetings were taken up discussing such points and sorting them out. I complained to Gareth, Jane, Susie and Andy that we just didn't have time for all this, we were supposed to be fighting for contractors and against IR35 and I didn't have time for it. Some suggested that he was a Revenue spy or stooge; I didn't think that was true, I just thought he was a pain but initially I

---

59

http://www.itcontractor.com/Articles_IR35_News_Advice/view_article.asp?id_no=2294&photopage=0

thought it was useful to have someone doing such scrutiny and I even voted for him at the time.

I am not a great person for rules and regulations, to me they are simply guidelines, which is wrong I know. The result was that the resources of the PCG focused on this single contractor and keeping him happy. We had to deal with it once and for all in November 2001. The directors agreed that he should be expelled from the organisation, which was a bit harsh. Later on others would be expelled too for similar 'crimes' but here was the setting of a terrible precedent which would be used to more manage dissent than control slander. That is what happens in revolutions, small actions have consequences and there are consequences if you don't take those actions, damned if you do and damned if you don't.

## Media training course for directors

The directors wanted a hands-on role. Susie arranged for media training for the directors. Previously this had been the domain of David Ramsden, a seasoned media 'pro' under Susie's scripting but there was a High Court battle coming she felt that we needed to be able to speak to cameras, to print journalists and to radio confidently and competently. I had had some high level training in this already through the Labour Party.

It is not easy dealing with the press and it takes practise and a lot of confidence to get it right, then you can have an off day and ruin everything.

Lion's Den communication did the course and exposed all our personal flaws. Gareth was unable to succinctly explain anything; he would also drop into too much detail and there wasn't time for it in a radio or TV interview. I was doing ok spinning lots of good lines and platitudes until they exposed my weakness. They asked why I thought it was that Tony Blair had got it so wrong. I stuttered and hesitated. I wasn't used to criticising the Party and leader per se, I was happy attacking IR35 but not attacking Labour and they showed me how easy it would be to trip me up.

Pamela Edwards was also asked a few difficult questions but she turned angry and said that she wasn't prepared to answer any more stupid questions. Susie tried to explain to her that you couldn't do that in an interview, she said that Michael Heseltine did it all the time.

Pamela was less concerned with her own performance, which she thought was perfect, and more concerned with mine citing my hesitation in attacking Tony Blair to be proof as to why I was unsuitable to be in the PCG let alone on the board. Her view was that I shouldn't be talking to the press at all.

Andy made sure he couldn't be misquoted by folding his arms and answering monosyllabically to every question. Jane Akshar proved a natural, she had the ability to master a brief, say the right thing but still come across as human and professional. Susie had found her spokeswomen, but convincing Gareth to step aside from the media spotlight was never easy.

By the end of the training day we were all much improved in our awareness of handling the media.

## Joint Letter to the Financial Times

Outside of all the internal politicking of PCG we still managed to find some time to focus on the real enemy and the cause. Andy had managed to get his foot into the door of the CBI who had also become associate members of the PCG. He pushed all the way up the organisation until they managed to get Digby Jones to jointly sign a letter to The Financial Times attacking IR35 in the July. The other joint-signers were the Federation of Small Business and the PCG, Gareth as chairman.

The letter read:

> "As representatives of industry and small business, we would urge the government to reconsider the IR35 measure, currently before parliament in the Finance Bill 2000.
>
> "This legislation, which will treat small businesses as employees for tax and NIC purposes, will prove detrimental to the small business sector, the knowledge-based economy and the UK's drive to lead the world in high-technology.
>
> The legislation will also discourage entrepreneurs to remain UK-based tax payers.
>
> "While we support the government's attempts to create a fair taxation system and support measures to crack down on blatant abuse, the IR35 provision is unfair, poorly targeted and ultimately unworkable. We would call on this government to draw a halt to this, while there is still time to do so, and to consider a better way forward."

## July Forum Flaming!

Around this time I announced on the forums that I had been selected as Labour's prospective parliamentary candidate for North East Bedfordshire. I had been selected in April, it was an open secret and I didn't formally announce it on the forums, but I felt that I needed to be fully open about it in case people claimed that I was keeping it a secret. The directors and other activists knew already but now I told the forum and the members at large.

I explained how this was proving to be a useful asset in lobbying the Government but while I stood with the PCG and its membership on IR35 that didn't mean I would support every other political issue.

The forums set themselves alight as the 'Enragés' flocked on and flamed me. A definition of flaming from Wikipedia is included before.

Flaming, also known as bashing,
is hostile and insulting interaction between Internet users. Flaming usually occurs in the social context of an Internet forum, Internet Relay Chat (IRC), Usenet, by e-mail, game servers such as Xbox Live or PlayStation Network, and on video-sharing websites. It is frequently the result of the discussion of heated real-world issues such

as politics, religion, and philosophy, or of issues that polarise subpopulations, but can also be provoked by seemingly trivial differences.

Deliberate flaming, as opposed to flaming as a result of emotional discussions, is carried out by individuals known as flamers, who are specifically motivated to incite flaming. These users specialize in flaming and target specific aspects of a controversial conversation, and are usually more subtle than their counterparts. Their counterparts are known as trolls who are less "professional" and write obvious and blunt remarks to incite a flame war, as opposed to the more subtle, yet precise flamers.

It was a relentless fight against me personally, against every Labour policy and comments about how unfit I was to be representing the PCG. I responded to almost every comment and other directors, including Gareth Williams, nobly came to my aid with supporting comments. It went on for hours and was quite a traumatising event. I don't like doing such discussions anymore but after being shelled and attacked for hours on end they lacked the ability to charge forward and defeat me. I had stood my ground and won.

I was seriously annoyed, especially since I had already thought about stepping down. This was because I was still a contractor working in my day job for Salomon Smith Barney, I did the work for the PCG and alongside this I was a parliamentary candidate; our son Harry had been born in the July and we had moved house two weeks later. Something would have to give; I couldn't find the time to cope with all these things. I had to let the dust settle on the flaming and have to wait longer than planned but was resolved to leave. What I couldn't bare was the idea of Pamela Edwards and her opinionated Enragés taking over. I resolved to hold on till after the PCG's first annual conference.

## October – High Court agrees that PCG has a case

We were stepping our way towards the High Court. Gareth and the other directors focused intently on it and in October the High Court held a preliminary hearing. Basically we would present our outline argument for a case and the Revenue would put their case and explain why ours did not add up then the Judge would decide if it was worth having a full hearing.

On the 10$^{th}$ October in the Administrative Court Mr Justice Gibbs "gave permission to the Professional Contractors' Group to Judicially Review the IR35 provisions. PCG had maintained that it had a case which was fit for further consideration by the Court at a full hearing, and that its case was clearly arguable"

Our argument was that the IR35 provisions should be 'set aside' on the basis that:

- they constitute a prohibited State Aid in that large and small consultancies in the sector are treated differently for tax purposes
- they create obstacles to the free movement of workers and the right to provide services within the European Community

- they infringe the European Convention on Human Rights (EHCR) now enforceable in England via the Human Rights Act

The Inland Revenue contended that the measure could not be a State Aid as it did not confer an advantage on large companies because IR35 does not provide for taxation of companies at all. Mr Justice Gibbs indicated that it was artificial to suggest the legislation has no effect on the companies who are members of PCG. It was to go forward to a probable three day hearing and we were told that this wouldn't be before February, but we explained that it needed to be before the end of the tax year because if IR35 was deemed illegal no one would pay the tax.

Patricia Hewitt, the e-Minister's response was 'The Inland Revenue is tightening its definitions to exclude bona fide consultants from being treated as employees'. Maybe she got confused because what was happening was that 'The Inland Revenue is tightening its definitions to treat bona fide consultants as employees'

## Account of the proceedings

We were challenging the UK Government over its tax policy in one of the highest courts in the land - and we didn't even have an office. Susie improvised and with the help of a friendly landlord we set up shop, or more accurately a communications centre, in a pub across the road from the courts, the George. Armed with laptops, mobile, modems and an arsenal of battery charges - (this is pre Wi-Fi days!) we let it be known to contractors, television, radio and the press in general that 'we were briefing and open for business'.

The Court hearing was held in Court 57. Inside the court room for the PCG sat Susie, Gareth, Neil Wilson, David Ramsden, Tony Askam and our legal team led by Gerald Barling.

On the other side of the hall sat the Revenue's team lead by their QC, Richard Plender, and their officials.

Justice Gibbs listened as Barling laid out the PCG's case for a full hearing. He explained the three points that we thought a case should be brought under - state aid, obstacle to free movement and infringement of human rights.

His talk illustrated the reasons why all these issues were valid and even used the famous Bosman football case as an illustration.

Contractoruk reported that "The PCG claim that IR35 effectively deprives the shareholders of a limited company of the benefits of owning the company. It prevents a legally constituted company from operating as a company because of the 5% restriction of expenses against tax and the ability to make a legitimate profit. If there is no profit the shareholders are deprived of that and that is, therefore, effectively interference by the State of the peaceful enjoyment of one's possessions".

Richard Plender QC for the Inland Revenue tried to show that the 'limited company' was simply a tax avoidance device. He explained that a low salary could be taken along with high dividends, thereby avoiding National Insurance Contributions.

He added their usual argument that the use of a limited company in this context was simply a vehicle for tax avoidance and to the Inland Revenue this was 'disguised employment'.

He repeated that the declared objective of IR35 was to counter this tax avoidance, and that this was in-line with the Government's objective that everyone should pay fair taxes.

Those who had hoped for answers on the day were to be disappointed; it was going to run into a second day, perhaps the judge needed to sleep on it.

Simon Juden, who wrote an account that was published by *Shout99.com,* said that 'Like everyone, I was hoping for a result on the day. The first indication that this was unlikely came shortly after the start (delayed from 10.30 to around 12); when the stenographer was dismissed until 3 (the stenographer only records the actual judgement, although the proceedings are videotaped)'.

Generally it seemed to be going well. When Barling spoke Juden said that the opposition appeared restless and it is true that the opposition never like to hear the case that is being made and this was also true of the Revenue, who Juden reports as not 'taking Gerald's speech very well at all'. To most contractors it looked like a solid case and people wondered what on earth the Revenue could say in their defence as Barling even covered some of what he thought would be the Revenue's argument and stated how unsound it was.

The next morning Judge Gibbs ruled on the issue. The Inland Revenue had stated that freelancers did not have to use a limited company structure and instead they could opt to take up employment with a larger company and that the choice to be 'employed' or self-employed is tax and national insurance neutral. (That is what they said anyway).

I don't agree with that and nor did Justice Gibbs, because as the PCG said the reason that a limited company was used was not to evade tax but was to be entrepreneurial. Technically, Barling said that the effect of IR35 would be to distort competition under 'Article 87 and give state aid under Article 88'.

It proved enough to convince Justice Gibbs that it should go to a full hearing; he said that 'both the anecdotal and the academic evidence were highly compelling'. He noted that the Revenue could not 'disprove that IR35 impedes the fundamental freedoms of the EC Treaty'.

He felt that there was 'substantial argument for a judicial review on all three issues and that the issues should be heard in full'. We had won the right to a full hearing on all three counts.

It was a good first outing; all our team had been impressive. Juden said:

> Something that came over very, very strongly for me was the extremely high quality of our team. Gareth was simply superb in his interviews, and delivered some devastating lines to the Sky cameras after the judgements. Neil (who unfortunately had to miss the second day) and the rest of the legal team have clearly done an amazing job of assembling and choreographing evidence.

He was also complementary about Susie:

> Susie works the press better than anyone I've ever seen (and I've seen quite a few do it) -when you see us plastered all over the Mirror and the rest of the papers tomorrow, don't for one second think it happened by accident, it happened by Susie.

## Media is mad for IR35

The media did go mad for it. Suddenly we had made a break-through and here was a story about an unfair tax that had legs. A judge had said that we had a legitimate case, so despite Dawn's Unison pickets of PCG meetings and her accusations that we were 'tax cheats' who employed our wives and husbands and paid ourselves an array of expenses[60], the judge said it wasn't as clear cut as this. Basically, he waved a green flag to other bodies to say this is a legitimate area for discussion; it is not about tax avoidance or dodging.

The Evening Standard was first out of the blocks and Dawn, to her credit, was ready with a standard letter attacking contractors similar to the one she had written to the IT press before the parliamentary vote.

## The Evening standard

Anthony Hilton, respected City Editor of the Evening Standard, wrote damning indictments of the Government in the News and City section. This is some of what he said:

Among the mass of information sent in by readers incensed about IR35, the Inland Revenue's measure against IT professionals who set themselves up as companies, was a copy of a letter from Dawn Primarolo, the Paymaster General, admitting it could possibly harm the competitive position of British workers by putting their costs up. But, she added, that was a price to be paid. It was more important to be fair to all those taxpayers who did not have the advantage of corporate status.

Primarolo was known as Red Dawn before she became a minister so the comment is in character. It is more of a surprise to see Patricia Hewitt, the minister whose brief it is to foster e-business, leaping into the battle on the Revenue's side. She of all the Government should understand that arguing about the share of the cake is much less sensible than working together to make the cake bigger.

---

[60] Though in retrospect such a description fits the MPs expenses scandal as much as it does contractors

It is not as if she can't know what is going on, or how acute the shortage is. Serious academic studies predict Europe's economic growth could be cut by 3% in 2003 because of the damping effect on productivity and the difficulty of moving small and medium-sized companies into the internet age without skilled help.

One study estimated Europe-wide demand this year for skilled IT workers and e-business specialists in Europe at 14.5 million. There was a shortage of 1.2 million IT specialists and 660,000 e-business experts. Separately, Brussels is looking at proposals to put to governments for them to develop immigration policies that favour IT skills. Yet the IR35 policy Hewitt is backing drives them abroad.

I also came across an old cutting from last year which told how the CBI was urging the Chancellor Gordon Brown to drop National Insurance on share option schemes so that young small companies did not suffer a huge tax hit when employees exercised their options. Brown subsequently went some way towards conceding this, although in terms of fairness there was absolutely no reason why small fast-growing companies should be treated differently from those in the mainstream. There were very strong pragmatic reasons to do what he did, though, because the NI tax on options does real financial damage.

We should not be surprised that politicians understand fairness, or what they think of as fairness, far more than they understand business and globalisation. But what they have to grasp if they are to be an effective government is that capitalism is intrinsically unfair in the short term but out of that comes wealth creation which makes even the unfairly-treated better off than they would otherwise have been.

The primary job of government is to grow the economy because if it fails to create the conditions where that happens, everything else it wants to do become impossible.

This is why Primarolo's comment is so depressing. Having understood how damaging IR35 could be to Britain, why does she think it is good government to persist with the measure?

### The Times wrote...

The Times covered the Judicial Review result with a hard hitting commentary from Patience Wheatcroft, the City editor

GORDON BROWN must be realising that tax changes are best made after consulting those who are going to be affected by them, even if the Inland Revenue prefers to ignore its clients.

Big business was stunned by his original proposals for hitting overseas dividends and some speedy back-tracking was required. Now his plans to clobber professional contractors face a full-scale legal challenge.

The Chancellor of the Exchequer probably had no inkling of the upsurge of fury that would greet IR35, the legislative move that would change the status of many workers from independent operators to employees. Now he knows that many thousands of people view the move as a threat to their livelihoods. They are aggrieved that their efforts to be entrepreneurial have been met with legislation that they believe will curtail their work. For, whatever the suspicions of the Inland Revenue, these contractors are not, on the whole, tax dodgers so much as people trying to make a living in a tough market.

Then in reference to our campaign she added:

One look at the e-mails that have bombarded this office from contractors determined to fight IR35 and Mr Brown would see the extent of the anger he has unleashed. We publish a typical example on page 31 today. Now they have won the first hurdle in their battle to have the legislation repealed. Mr Justice Gibbs was persuaded that IR35 might be contrary to EU regulations.

Whatever the outcome of the case, the contractors have demonstrated an admirable degree of organisation and effectiveness.

## York AGM and Conference

We organised our first ever conference and decided to hold it in York. This was in part to allow contractors from Scotland to attend. It was held over a weekend and attendance of a few hundred was really good. We were a virtual organisation so it was quite strange to actually meet people behind their forum names. We all wore name badges with our 'real' names as well as our forum names. I didn't quite get it at the start when I had registered on the forum so I was 'Philip Ross' and 'PhilipRoss', whereas others could be 'Bill Johnson' and 'SuperKnigh73' or something. For some on the forums it was easy to see their true identities but others remained almost permanently anonymous. In London various drinks parties (so-called RLMs - 'Real Life Meetings') and the like had been held so some of us now knew each other quite well.

They had done a good job in organising the conference, as well as contractors a number of accountants and tax advisors also attended. My wife attended with my three year old daughter Olivia and three month old Harry. Gareth's wife also attended with her new born too.

It was very good with much talks and discussions. Initially people were a little hesitant in getting to know each other but it worked. Gareth gave a presentation and then I took the platform. I thought of conferences as being like party conferences that it should be political and about banging the drum for the PCG and the contractors cause whereas everyone else saw it on a more corporate level. It needed a mix of both so I took the platform and gave a rousing speech in favour of contracting and praising their efforts at the Mass Lobby and on the e-petition and against Newsnight. I said that a lot had been done but there was a lot left to do. It went down very well with everyone except for Pamela who told me that it would be over her 'dead body' that I got involved in stuff like EURIM[61] and representing contractors elsewhere.

In the audience was Sir John Harvey-Jones who had been invited as our guest speaker. He turned up early, met contractors and had been chatting hoping to learn more about the subject. He said that he had enjoyed my speech and that we had achieved some great things. I was very flattered. Gareth looked after him and later he addressed the conference and delivered a great speech that talked about the importance of small firms and how great contractors were. He also gave some very interesting anecdotes to a very attentive audience.

He said:

> "I'm a very strong admirer of what you have done and I am very keen to see you do even more in the immediate future."

I said to Jane and Gareth that it was fantastic how did you manage to get him to agree to come? Gareth explained that he hadn't taken that much persuasion as he was interested in business and excited by what we had been doing. Jane noted that of course we were paying for him.

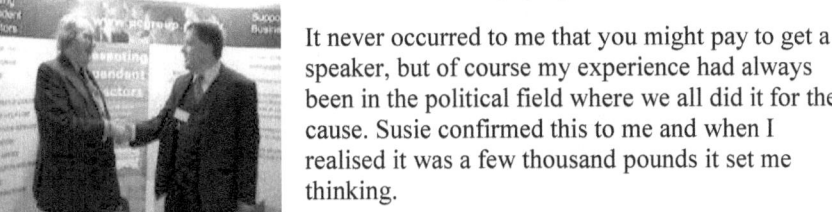

It never occurred to me that you might pay to get a speaker, but of course my experience had always been in the political field where we all did it for the cause. Susie confirmed this to me and when I realised it was a few thousand pounds it set me thinking.

I wanted to get our monies worth and Sir John was clearly game and keen on what we were doing. I rushed Susie, Gareth and Jane to an impromptu meeting and said that we needed lots of photographs with Sir John. Why not let every contractor have their photo taken with him? Then they could then send it off along with a model press release to all their local papers, so that is what we did. Some technical wizardry was setup and over 200 contractors walked onto the stage and had a photo with Sir John. After the conference they could pick them up off the website and send them with a model press release to their local papers. It was a cheeky thing to have asked of Sir John but as he pointed out it was entrepreneurial thinking and he liked it.

To be even cheekier I suggested to Gareth that we invite him to become a patron of the PCG along with Lord Weatherill, Sir John agreed.

It had been a successful conference and as these contractors left York on a high with their judicial review pending they felt that, like the Bolsheviks, they could "storm any fortress and that any doubt was treason".

---

[61] EURIM is a parliamentary body

## Sir John Harvey-Jones on Sky News

Sir John was good to his word and in January 2001 he was interviewed by Sky News explaining why he had become associated with the members of PCG, he said:

> "I think they are an extremely important force for the future and for change. They are by and large much more experimental and have a much broader view of the business than the large contracting companies.
>
> "I think unfortunately the Inland Revenue has it wrong. They think the reason people go freelance is they want to indulge in some sort of tax fiddle. The reason people want to go freelance is because more and more businesses want to employ part-time specialists in particular areas. That's the way business is going."

Sir John praised the actions of the PCG and the speed with which the Group has grown in a short period of time. He said:

> "They have got leave to have a judicial review so I don't think the Inland Revenue are necessarily going to be able to bulldoze this through."

Asked what he could do personally to help increase fairness for the contractor and small business, Sir John rounded off the interview by saying:

> "I'm a very old, retired, old fart. I can't do very much about it except add my voice. I do deplore the bullying of small people and the future of our country depends very largely with small businesses. So anything I can do to help I will."

## December – ATSCo fight with Jobserve

The IT market was changing and the agencies were worried. Not only had the Internet allowed contractors to get organised now the web was challenging the agencies business model. People went to agencies because they had people on their books and could supply them. But now internet website like Jobserve had come along and in theory these allowed prospective clients and employers to just post up their own job vacancies and access the same market.

In part with was why ATSCO the top 16 IT agencies had got together to protect their market. They didn't like the threats to their business model from Jobserve. In December 2000 it started to turn nasty. ATSCO decided to go into competition with their own jobs board (in partnership with silicon.com) but when Jobserve suggested that in that case they wouldn't take jobs from ATSCO members on their side, the response from ATSCO was a court injunction.

*Shout99.com* reported that

It is an indication of the concern that they might lose access to Jobserve and thus create competitive advantage for non members, that ATSCo are resorting to legal threats to force a competitor to do business with them! Presumably they hope that they can continue to access IT contractors and candidates through Jobserve, whilst they build up their own site. Robbie Cowling would appear to want the battle now, rather than have to suffer death by a thousand cuts.

With increasing use of preferred supplier agreements agents will often receive the same job requirement at the same time and the race is then on to get the CV's in front of the client. To lose access to the No 1 source for IT contractors and candidates could be disastrous for ATSCo members.

ATSCo will be aware that Robbie Cowling has fought off a similar attempt in the past, by agents grouping together, to put him out of business. He has developed a simple, but very effective job site which IT contractors use in preference to all others. He has only accepted agency advertising and has provided a level playing field, independent of any agency and refusing to favour any agency over another.

In the interview with Shout99, Robbie Cowling also indicated, in addition to refusing business from his new competitor (ATSCo members) he might also open up the site to direct advertising from clients.

This latest development appears to be an attempt to create a unique selling proposition (USP) for ATSCo, but could end up costing their members significant business. They presumably are confident that they can "face down" Jobserve, but if they are wrong (and Jobserve's response should not have come as a surprise) then ATSCo members will start to question the value of belonging to an Association that costs them business.

To make matters worse for ATSCo, following the news that they had welcomed IR 35 as "a very good result for our members" (FT 24/9/1999), many Contractors informed ATSCo that they would not contract with their members. It would appear that Jobserve are about to provide a certain capability to ensure that you will not be working through an ATSCo member.

The ATSCO jobsite, you have probably never heard of it, I haven't[62]. Later on *Shout99.com* also reported suggestions that ATSCO was over-stating the number of jobs on its website.

In a letter email to *Shout99.com* Robbie Cowling of Jobserve stated:

> They have claimed I am using a market dominant position to threaten these agencies and monopolies the recruitment market place.
>
> Jobserve has always supported the agencies and has expected a bit of support from them in return. For this reason we have chosen not to do business with an agency if it becomes a competitor.

---

[62] The website states that it is under maintenance

> With the ATSCO site we were planning on taking a similar approach, though not because of the betrayal, but because I believe it is fundamentally wrong for a group of agencies to run a job board and I question their motives for doing so.

We watched as independent observers and my conclusion was that there was nothing personal in the way ATSCO treated us, it was just their arrogant nature, because here they were treating another group with similar distain.

## ATSCO interview Sarah Walker

With their new jobsite up and running and a fresh court injunction in their pocket and contractors subdued under IR35 it is time for the Axis powers to get together and celebrate. Which is sort of what happened. To promote the ATSCO jobsite silicon.com broadcast an interview between Ann Swain, ATSCO CEO and Sarah Walker from the Inland Revenue.

Writing for *Shout99.com* Andy White talked of an "an interview style that brings to mind Denis Healey's comment on Geoffrey Howe (It is like being savaged by a dead sheep!) Ann Swain, the CEO of ATSCo offered Sarah Walker, what many contractors will consider an "open goal" to put the Government position."

ATSCO claimed in the interview 'For example, we were active and successful in direct discussions with Government which led to radical revisions to their original IR 35 proposals.'

Which was a surprise to the rest of us, as Andy noted :-

> I suspect that PCG, ICAEW, CBI, IOD, CIOT, FSB etc who all agreed to ask for consultation and not offer solutions, were all disappointed that ATSCo (represented at the meeting, which agreed this strategy, by the 360 group) decided to offer solutions to the Government. Many feel that this allowed the Government to demonstrate that consultation had taken place.
>
> In fact the suggestion by ATSCo/360 group to adopt a salary/dividend split was rejected out of hand by the Government.

## Downing Street Forums close down

To try and get to grips with the internet Tony Blair set up a number of discussion forums on the Downing Street website, but as we moved towards the end of the year, Downing Street realised that its discussion forums weren't working. Or rather weren't working as they wanted them to do. People weren't coming to discuss policies or offer new ideas but to moan about Government policies. The Oppositions' supporters loved it as did contractors who filled them with anti-IR35 rhetoric. So in a way freelancers did manage to get into Downing Street, in a virtual fashion. When they realised that the breach had happened they close down the forums.

In a message from Tony Blair he stated:

> Over the last year, the discussion forums on the No 10 website have proved a fascinating insight into the issues that concern you most.

He continued

> The discussions have always been lively and the range of subjects explored extremely wide.
>
> I hope now that the discussion forums are being moved to a new home on the Citizen Portal, that you'll continue to use the opportunity to make your views known and to enter into debate.
>
> It isn't possible to transfer the large volume of old postings but my office is investigating depositing the archive in the Public Records Office.

*Shout99.com* correctly suggested that cynics would offer the view, that to have the No 10 website hosting such lively debate with an upcoming election, was a hostage to fortune.

Susie added that in terms of debate the exercise has been somewhat futile. With thousands of posts there has not been one recorded incidence of a Minister responding to the "issues that concern you most". It was a good example of the policy for the web, if you can't control it close it. A lesson that everyone is ten years later learning the hard way with social media.

In Parliament Dawn wasn't helping matters when she told lib Dem MP Andrew Stunell that

> "It is estimated that 90,000 companies will be affected by the introduction of the new legislation to tackle avoidance of tax and National Insurance Contributions through the use of personal service companies. Information on the number of persons or taxpayers affected is not available."

This was more than the 66,000 mentioned before, perhaps it was more windy when they put their finger in the air?

Dawn Primarolo refused to be drawn on the cost of the review suggesting that it would be depend on the outcome. Ie who won. Which is actually correct, if you lose the case then you have to pay the costs of the winner, sometimes but not always. Hence the PCG war chest had to cover the costs of losing the case.

# Chapter 19

## January 2001 – I stand down from PCG board

I stood down as a director of the PCG at the end of October, I was exhausted and short of time. I had spent a long time fighting for the PCG and now with the judicial review a few months away the battle lines were being set. Little was going to happen on the political front, I suspected that the Government would continue to rubbish the contractor cause and this wasn't such a terrible thing as it would keep the issue in the news. Letters continued to flow to the papers and Evening Standard who had 'got it' from the early days, seemed to mention it every night. Elsewhere contractors were becoming concerned about the fast track visas scheme and the new agency regulations.

The few overtures I made to Ministers were rebuffed on the basis that the High Court case was imminent. They were worried about saying anything lest it affected the case. The same was true with the Inland Revenue itself.

My prime focus was my role as Labour's Prospective Parliamentary candidate. Ironically I landed myself a two week contract working at Labour HQ processing their electoral registers. The fact that I now had two clients at the same time improved my own prospects of being outside IR35. I had worked freelance for the Labour Party for several years I always took two weeks off a year to go to them and wrote it into my other contract and organised a substitute to cover me if needed.

I remained in the PCG and I remained as a consultative council member but was no longer a director but still very much involved. The main difference was that I just didn't have to read the forums every day.

This what I wrote to the other board members at the time :

> I don't believe that the PCG should be party political at all. I have tried to campaign against IR35 from inside the party. I don't just believe that it is wrong but that it goes against my socialist principles and will be a disaster for business and the country. I also think that it could lead to many good Labour MPs losing their seats at the next election.
>
> However I don't believe that just because they are wrong on IR35 they are wrong on everything else which sometimes is the impression one gets from the forums. I can understand this though I use to think that the Tories were wrong on everything and I was suspicious of everything they did.
>
> I have been selected as a Prospective Parliamentary for the Labour Party. I don't have the luxury of time to be Campaign Director of the PCG and do this as well. With great reluctance I therefore tender my resignation as Campaign Director. I am happy to stay on until a suitable replacement can be found. I am also prepared to undertake specific tasks (e.g. Agency legislation) but I do not have the time to be the eyes and ears co-ordinate the campaigning as a whole. I cannot do the role justice.

# FI offers £1,000 bounty on contractors

At the start of the new year a big news story about contractors was broken by the Mail on Sunday.

Computer services company, the FI group were caught out offering a £1,000 bounty to their staff to shop a contractor and replace them with a cheaper worker from the Indian sub-continent. The PCG forced them to withdraw the offer though they claimed that had done nothing wrong. They weren't the only company to have done such a thing, others including one I later worked for in Dunstable were very eager to use the scheme to rid themselves of UK contractors and replace them with foreign non-EU workers.

To us, the fast track visa system was part of an assault on contracting by the Government, the PCG said that Government was helping large companies introduce a 'corporate blood money scheme'. (That put it in tougher terms than I would have).

*Shout99.com* reported it as

The accusation follows an investigation by The Mail on Sunday (December 24) which revealed that computer-services company, FI Group, is offering its employees a £1,000 bounty to nominate UK contractors with the company who could be replaced by cheaper workers from the Indian sub-continent.

The PCG represents the interests of more than 11,000 contractors and has been warning that the Government's controversial IR35 proposal is a charter to destroy the small entrepreneurial business.

PCG's Chairman, Gareth Williams, said: "This shameful move by FI shows that the Government's 'fast track' visa scheme contains a massive loophole. While it would be illegal to replace employees with workers from overseas, there is nothing to prevent independent contractors being treated in this way. These are the same independent contractors the Government wants to treat as 'employees' when it comes to tax purposes, rather than let them operate legitimate businesses they want to be.

"Far from halting the skills shortage, this scheme is now being used for short-term cost saving by short-sighted companies, to the detriment of the UK's small businesses and the country's long term economic prospects. And it is the Government's legislation which has enabled them to do this.

"Companies like FI will discover to their cost that it is not so easy to force out highly skilled contractors and try to replace their years of experience with cheaper imported labour. They will pay for their greed with slipped deadlines and spiraling costs, and they will find the homegrown engineers with the knowledge and experience to fix the problems have moved abroad and are helping the development of projects in the US, Germany and Holland.

"In the long term this will run down the UK's skills base and train up our competitors, who will return home taking the experience they have gained here with them.

"This comes in the wake of the IR35 legislation which treats independent contractors as 'disguised employees', preventing them acting as businesses and disallowing their legitimate business expenses. Yet this demonstrates once again that contractors are not employees and have none of the rights of benefits of employees.

"The Government is complicit in this scheme by choosing FI Group to act as a pilot in self-regulating its own visa applications. By supporting this measure, the Government has shown the foolishness and nonsense of its own legislation.

"Every member of this Government who is associated with this should hang his or her head in shame that they have created a scheme which puts a bounty of £1,000 on the head of a small business in the UK and, at the same time, encourages a form of high-tech slave labour."

FI Group was run by millionaire Hilary Cropper. In 2004 they changed their name to Xansa. However Ms Cropper was rewarded for her efforts by being made a Dame to go along with her CBE. The Guardian reported that she considered herself to be an advocate of 'equality in the work place'.[63] But many female contractors felt betrayed by Cropper as they worked freelance in part because of the flexibility that it brought but here was Cropper actually undermining them.

On the 28th December the bounty offer was withdrawn. Once again we had had to play hard ball, but it demonstrated that the PCG wasn't going to let contractors be pushed around. The profitability and viability of contracting was under threat by IR35 but fast track visas and schemes and offers like these threatened the very possibility of UK contracting. The fast track visa scheme and the opening up of the UK to Indian multi-nationals were damaging the UK's IT infrastructure and skill base rather than supporting and improving it.

### Dawn says that contractor who are leaving are silly

If Ministers and the Revenue were staying tight lipped with us on IR35, they would find it harder in Parliament as lots of Parliamentary questions were put down.

On the 25th January 2001, during Treasury Questions Ruchard Ottaway said

> Can we now have a straight answer to the question asked by my hon. Friend the Member for Guildford (Mr. St. Aubyn)? Will the Paymaster General admit that IR35 represents everything that is damaging about the Government? It adds to the regulatory burden; it is a stealth tax and an attack on innovation and enterprise; it is an attack on the genuine wealth creators of this country; and it is driving our finest people overseas. In short, it is the politics of envy.

---

[63] http://www.guardian.co.uk/business/2005/jan/07/guardianobituaries.obituaries

He still didn't get a straight answer, just an assertion that it wasn't driving people abroad. She told Nick St Aubyn that :

> ...that IR35 hits IT workers, is not true; and secondly, that it discourages entrepreneurs, is not true because the Government's policy has encouraged them. It ensures that those people working in the same conditions are subject to the same tax. It is not a stealth tax; it ensures that people pay the tax that they should have been paying all along.

As a Parliamentary candidate I raised the issue with Labour's head office and they insisted that it wasn't a big issue. Presumably it wouldn't affect the seats Labour needed to win. But it would hurt in the Hertfordshire and Bedfordshire marginals that I knew. Also in the 'unwinnables' like the true-blue Tory seat I was fighting it did come up as an issue a lot. Unfortunately people weren't prepared to listen to my views they just saw the red rosette and shut the door.

## Final Justifications

In a letter leaked to Shout99, Paymaster General Dawn Primarolo made the new claim that "IR35 is an essential part of our policy of encouraging small business, enterprise and wealth creation." It had been sent to an MP in 2000. In a letter sought to address the fears of one his constituents who was particularly concerned about the effects IR35 would have on his business.

> "I'm afraid that he has misunderstood what this legislation is all about," Dawn wrote, speaking of the MPs troubled constituent. "In fact, 'IR35' is an essential part of our policy of encouraging small business, enterprise and wealth creation.

> "The tax system distinguishes between the self-employed, who invest, take financial risks, create wealth and employment and employees, who are paid a wage for their work and take less risk. This distinction allows Governments to introduce tax policies which encourage and support small business - such as the 10% Corporation Tax rate we introduced in 1999. But we were faced with a situation where people who were not small businesses in the accepted sense, but were in fact little different from employees, were able to benefit from the tax treatment intended for entrepreneurs simply by buying an off-the-shelf limited company".

She continued:

> "Our legislation applies to people who work for a client in a way which would mean that they were taxed as an employee, but for the fact that they had to set up their own contracts using a limited company or partnership as an intermediary. Individuals who sell their skills and knowledge to a client on contracts which do not carry the characteristics of employment will not be affected."

Attempting to allay the constituent's fears that the legislation is driving skilled contractors out of the country, she added:

> "Any measure which removes a tax loophole will result in some people paying more tax. But there is no evidence that significant numbers are being driven

overseas - and no reason why that should happen, since the tax regime here still compares favourably with that in most other countries."

Finally, defending the measures as being in the interests of protecting genuine business, she concluded:

> "There is nothing in the legislation which will undermine the workings of genuine small businesses. The rules will simply ensure that our raft of measures designed to support small business are properly targeted and do not go to people who are really the same as employees. If we did not take such actions, then we would not be in a position to target support for genuine businesses effectively. There are no plans to amend or repeal the legislation."

Gordon Brown's Treasury were in this entrenched position and could not be persuaded to move. This had as much to do with the state of mind of Gordon Brown and his group. In the November of 1999, they had also announced that pensions would only rise by 75p, which was another huge own goal. Gordon Brown refused to budge and it was Tony Blair who would ultimately apologise for it. Years later they would do the same again when they abolished the 10p tax rate. On that occasion they did change their minds but it was too late to avoid the political damage that it had done.

My point is that the intransience with IR35 had more to do with the personality of Gordon Brown and the culture inherent in the Treasury than in how we had lobbied them during our campaign.

# Chapter 20

## March 2001 – Judicial Review

Almost two years on from the day that IR35 had been announced we now had a full fledged trade association with over 11,000 members. It had evolved to become a member run organisation and now those members as well as paying an annual membership of £100 had raised over £500,000 between them to take the Government to the High Court to challenge the legality of IR35.

The £500,000 had been raised from within its membership. It remains an astonishing figure. Yet the Government suggested that it had been easily raised and considered it not worth the comment. Simple maths will tell you that the mean average donation only needed to be about £45 per contractor in the PCG yet I gave substantially more and I know others did too as did some agencies and accounting firms. Yet contractors who I worked with that hadn't joined the PCG and hadn't contributed followed the whole issue with considerable interest. The irony was that while they didn't contribute to the PCG's membership or fighting fund they probably paid more to their accountants to try to 'fix it'.

We had tried persuasion and diplomacy. Parliament had rejected the clause once in the House of Lords. Senior and established business, tax and accounting bodies all said the same thing, that it was a bad and unworkable tax and would be bad for Britain. We had suggested that it would drive contractors abroad and Government's response had been to introduce the fast track visa system to bring in foreign cheaper labour to undermine contracting further.

We had met the Paymaster General, the e-Minister, the e-Envoy and various Treasury and DTI officials. Even tax inspectors themselves had revealed that the new tax had no case law and it would take time to establish it.

It had proven hard to manage contractors, some of whom were desperate for a fight and felt that the battle (like that of the miners) would not just win this cause but would help to bring down the Government. Andy White suggested that it was like herding cats.

The Government's response had been mixed. Some like Alex Allen seemed to grasp the issue and understood the problems that contractors faced, others like Patricia Hewitt struggled to understand but appeared sympathetic whereas others such as Dawn Primarolo under the watchful eye of Gordon Brown saw it as almost a class battle and belligerently held their ground. She labelled contractors as 'tax cheats' in Parliament, the main evidence she cited for such an accusation was that they had bought their limited companies 'off the shelf'. They tried to compare the tax take for contractors with that of nurses and plumbers, to which the PCG had responded by pointing out that many nurses worked through the bank and had self-employment case law that covered, the same was true for plumbers.

Contractors argued for a level playing field with their larger competitors whereas the Inland Revenue argued for a level playing field between contractors and employees. We were talking up for small business and freelancing and they seemed to be talking it down. Here in this was the argument, what constituted an employee and a business? It was debated many times on the forums of the PCG and on *Shout99.com*. It was *the* defining issue. Would we be able to explain it clearly enough to our barrister to get it through to a judge?

## What is a judicial review?

A judicial review is the legal procedure where the courts ensure that public bodies such as local authorities, ministers, Departments of State, regulatory bodies and, to some extent Parliament, operate within the law when making decisions.

A judicial review will deal with the process and the legality of the decisions of public bodies while the UK Parliament has a right to introduce laws it must ensure that they do not contravene European legislation. If UK laws are contrary to European measures, the European law will prevail and the UK law can be struck down by the Courts by way of a judicial review. The PCG was claiming that IR35 contravened European law. The PCG team had used a similar method when they were the Sunday trading team - and the attendant confusion and disruption had ultimately led to the end of the prohibitions on Sunday trading. But IR35 and Sunday shopping were different creatures, not least because we didn't have the deep pockets of the national retailing chains that had bankrolled their campaign.

A judicial review will not examine the 'good' or 'bad' of a measure or consider if a minister or Department of State might have acted differently, the court will only concern itself with the lawfulness of that measure.

The European Communities Act 1972 provides that where European Union law applies, EU law overrides UK law.

## The legal process

The first stage of the judicial review process is to seek the permission of the High Court to proceed with the judicial review. Both parties have an opportunity to present an outline of their case and the judge will decide whether there is sufficient merit to proceed. (That had happened in the October).

The decision can be appealed.

If permission is granted, a date is set for a full hearing.

The court could at any stage decide there are issues on which the advice of the European Court of Justice (ECJ) is required and refer those issues to the ECJ.

## The PCG's Case

In legal terms we were asking for the provisions of the Welfare Reforms and Pensions Act (1999) and the Finance Act (2000) that related to the new tax rules that related to the provision of services through an intermediary (IR35) to be judicially reviewed.

We believed that the provisions were incompatible with European law and hence unenforceable because:

- IR35 is an illegal provision of state aid to larger competitors;
- IR35 is in breach of the fundamental EC right - known as the right of establishment;
- IR35 is in breach of the fundamental right protected by the European Convention on Human Rights in that it amounts to a confiscation of property contrary to Article 1, Protocol 1 of the Convention. With effect from October 2 2000, it is a breach of the Human Rights Act 1998.

We were one of the first groups to make a challenge on the new Human Rights Act, which didn't make the more conservative elements of the PCG that happy. These elements are explained below from an article in *Shout99.com*.

**Illegal Provision of State Aid**

The EC Treaty prohibits state aid, which is granted by Member States or through state resources; and which distorts competition by favouring certain undertakings; and affects trade between Members' States. Differential tax rates affecting a specific sector have been held to constitute an illegal state aid.

PCG's case was that IR35 is a state aid, which will distort competition by taxing small knowledge based contractors in a materially harsher way than their competitors. As a result, many independent contractors will cease to trade. Given the nature of the IT industry it is inevitable that interstate trade will be affected.

**Breach of the Right of Establishment**

The EC Treaty provides that a Member State ('the host state') must not impose restrictions on the freedom of a national of another Member State to establish himself in the host state. Neither may the Member State restrict the provisions of services in 'the host state' from an establishment in another Member State.

PCG's evidence shows that IR35 discourages EU (non-UK) knowledge based contractors from trading in the UK because of the lack of certainty as to the tax to which they will be subject or the substantial tax disadvantages that they will incur. Nine IT contractors (both UK and non-UK nationals) have provided evidence, which shows they have or may cease trading in the UK as a direct result of IR35. Two of these contractors are joint applicants in this case.

PCG's evidence shows that the legislation cannot be objectively justified and is disproportionate to its stated aims.

**De Facto Confiscation of Property**

The Human Rights Act, which came into force on October 2, requires UK laws to comply with the provisions of the European Convention on Human Rights. IR35 represents a de facto confiscation of property because it prevents a legally constituted limited company from operating as such, allowing its expenses against tax and making a legitimate profit, and therefore prevents its shareholders from enjoying the benefits of owning the company.

To support our case we had gathered a number of case studies from members and also carried out surveys of the membership. We had also arranged for Dr Leslie Willcocks of Templeton College Oxford to be an expert witness for us.

Batting for us in court would be Mr Gerald Barling QC and Miss Kelyn Bacon both of Brick Court Chambers. They were instructed by our solicitors Tony Askham from Bond Pearce. Barling was a specialist 'competition and technology barrister'[64].

Batting for the Inland Revenue would be Mr Richard Plender[65] QC of Essex Street Chambers and Mr Rabinger Singh from Matrix Chambers. They were of course instructed by solicitors from the Inland Revenue. I was surprised as I thought the Inland Revenue would have had their in-house barrister rather than contracting it out.

What we had to remember was (and to get the media and members focused on) that the case wasn't about whether IR35 was fair or good legislation, we knew it was neither fair nor good, but whether it was lawful.

> A judicial review will not examine the 'good' or 'bad' of a measure or consider if a minister or Department of State might have acted differently - the court will only concern itself with the lawfulness of that measure.

Many felt that because it was unfair we would win. Those weren't the rules. The lesson from Sunday Trading was that although they had lost the case the judgement was so damning that reform followed anyway.

We weren't in such a good position, in part because IR35 had ceased to be just a tax issue and had become an emotive and political issue for both us and the Government. In the same way that fox hunting issue wasn't about the control of foxes but about the hunt itself. Now it was about what constituted a legitimate business model.

---

[64] http://www.thelawyer.com/a-hard-man-to-find-new-cat-president-steps-up-to-the-challenge/130110.article

[65] Years later in 2008 I lost a permission High Court hearing (though won the eventual case hands down) when the High Court judge was a Justice Plender.

# Tuesday 13th May 2001 – Morning Session

It begins. Close to a hundred PCG members and supporters made it down to the High Court to cheer on the legal team challenging IR35.

The Register recorded the feeling outside the courts of justice when they said:

> PCG Chairman Gareth Williams was available for comment but before we could speak to the unassuming man he was dragged back and forth around the High Court for the best photo. He was also distinctly uneasy when asked to walk down the road in faux conversation for the classic walking-down-the-road-in-conversation set-piece for TV news.
>
> However, when it comes to explaining his position, Mr Williams is far more confident. "The IR35 legislation is unworkable in practice," he told us. "In many ways, if the Inland Revenue were to lose here, it would be a lucky escape for them." Why? "Because if this stands, the government will be inundated by thousands of individuals bringing separate cases." Does he really believe that will happen? "Yes. Every contract will have to be assessed on its own merits - it's not a case of being caught or not being caught [in the legislation]."
>
> Will he win the case? "We have a good case."
>
> And if he loses? "We are looking at the possibility of an appeal if we lose the case."

Picture is of Gareth Williams PCG Chairman at the High Court

The Court hearing was being held in Court 28. Once again on one side of the hall sat the PCG's supporters and their legal team and on the other the side the Revenue's team lead by their QC Richard Plender and their officials.

Justice Burton opened the day by saying he had only received the evidence the day before and therefore had only read the skeleton arguments. (This may sound terrible but I have been to other High Court cases and this seems to be the usual form). He said that he believed the main question to be "what is the effect of the legislation?"

Rebecca Seeley-Harris writing for contractoruk.com said that 'It was quite clear from the outset that Mr Justice Burton had not done his homework vis-à-vis the fundamental basis for the test in case law' but she added that 'Mr Justice Burton seems to be a rather curious judge, very sharp and apparently witty.'

Barling (for the PCG) started by saying IR35 would have a detrimental effect on small businesses in the knowledge based sector, to which Plender (for the Inland Revenue) responded that it would affect everyone not just small companies and not just the knowledge based sector. Some commentators thought he was really saying it will be bad for everyone not just freelancers.

Judge Burton started by questioning Mr Barling on the 'employment status test' demonstrating a view of a typical layman, e.g., stating such arguments as 'control', having equipment, being in business, etc.'. It was clear that PCG would have to explain the nature of contracting and then the law before they could attack IR35 and the Revenue's attitude, whereas the Revenue could just focus on attacking our arguments and look for holes in it.

One example was the 5% allowance, Justice Burton couldn't understand why 5% was not enough and said "If 5% was not enough why didn't you just ask the Revenue for 10%?" If only it could have been that easy.

Seeley-Harris said that "Barling had walked into a huge elephant trap by stating that IT contractors set up their Ltd companies because they would not get the 'premium fees' as an employee. Burton jumped on this, stating, 'if one gets more then surely one should pay more tax?'"

She also reported that "Burton stated that the position of the IR was merely to remind people that there are some jolly nice benefits to being employed. If however, people decide not to pay heed to the IR they will make damn sure that they will not reap the benefits. From this Burton concluded for Mr Barling that actually what they are doing is discouraging entrepreneurs".

The afternoon session proved interesting too. It looked at how the IT industry operated with the use of contractors and why companies were willing to pay more to 'intermediaries' than to an employee. The answer being that they were paying for the absence of risk in that they would have no responsibility for employee rights. The judge acknowledged that it is therefore a reality that both client and contractor benefit from the flexibility of the pre-IR35 working practice."

They then discussed the fictional figures in the Revenue's case studies. In the first instance they discussed 'Charlotte' who the Revenue had suggested would pass IR35 because she was a genuine entrepreneur as opposed to the "fakes".

Harris noted that "Barling was very quick to point out the obvious; the situation where entrepreneurs start out on their own! Burton then provided the analogy of a car that goes from 0-20 mph as opposed to the car that goes from 0-60 mph, to his own enjoyment."

She added that "An interesting point was discovered that in fact the Inland Revenue 'employment status' manual on one particular point conflicts with their Charlotte example. Of course the conflicting advice goes to more uncertainty. Score one for the PCG."

The issue of certainty was discussed and it felt as though we were making headway when Burton said:

> "What you are saying then is that in IR35 one cannot arrange one's affairs with any certainty. One can arrange one's affairs and then anticipate year on year and contract upon contract a fight with the Revenue. That would indeed be uncertainty. That seems to conflict with what the Revenue are seeking to argue."

The judge asked Barling if the measure was targeted just at the knowledge based sector and Barling said that he thought that was the target. The judge enquired also about pop and sports stars and made reference to Elton John and Barling said they could be, though he suggested that it was more likely to affect sports tars than entertainers due to the short duration of their engagements.

Juden's notes published by S*hout99.com* noted that "the judge asked if IR35 could apply to big companies and Barling said in principle yes but not in reality (excluding the construction industry). The judge concluded that IR35 only applies to big companies where people are not paid through PAYE but via dividends on different classes of share".

There was further discussion about the expenses and the 5%. Barling said that the average expense figure was 16.6%, though the Judge did dispute this noting some of the expenses were still permitted under Schedule E, though Barling countered that no other companies were artificially restricted to 5%. He talked about contractors having one hand tied behind their back by IR35 and this affected their competitiveness.

When Barling told the Judge that contractors were assessed on a contract by contract basis and not on their overall activity for the year Juden noted that he "seemed taken aback, he had assumed it would be a once-a-year assessment." Juden noted that "Barling pressed the point: this is a key element of the uncertainty engendered by IR35. He also mentioned the issue of back-to-back contracts, pointing out to agreement from the judge that a contractor had no right (nor should have a need) to know what was in any contract between an agency and a client."

Before lunch Barling said IR35 was really about competition between big and small companies whereas the Revenue argued that it was between permanent employees and contractors. The judge disagreed and then Barling gave an example of body-shop workers working alongside contractors. He had made a strong point. Juden said 'the clang as the penny hit the floor could be heard from the back of the court'.

### JR 2: Judge 'sympathetic only to uncertainty over IR35'

*by Richard Powell at 19:26 13/03/01 (shout99.com)*

At the start of the afternoon session of PCG's first day in the judicial review, its QC Gerald Barling, ran through the issues underlying the uncertainty behind the operation of the legislation and its effect on competition.

The evidence included a number of case studies detailing the counter-measures that successful limited companies had chosen to take to cope in the climate of uncertainty surrounding the legislation. The Judge duly acknowledged this, stressing to Mr Barling, 'I don't think I am sympathetic about anything other than the uncertainty caused'.

However, the Judge's required clarification of the case study of the contractor Marc Deveaux, now based in the US, led him to suggest that the example was actually 'working against' the case until Mr Barling led him to the correct definition of a 'sole-trader' as regarding the operations of a contractor in the knowledge-based sector. The Judge had attempted to suggest that Mr Deveaux, 'proves that a contractor can be successful through 12 years of uncertainty'.

Justice Burton received guidance from the PCG's counsel to understand the finer points of why a contractor would want to remain a contractor and the desire they have to be able to grow a business using innovation and entrepreneurship.

At one point of the hearing Justice Burton asked whether an IT contractor would take a screwdriver with him to work as he attempted to link a contractor's need to take tools to work with him in the same manner as a builder or plumber. 'Am I right in thinking they only take their brains?' he asked Mr. Barling rhetorically. 'You can't justify this sort of situation by adding the letters Ltd. after your name and having a clever accountant.'

Mr Barling QC also presented to the court, the Institute of Chartered Accountants for England and Wales' (ICAEW) report in which IR35 was awarded a total of 0 out of 10 for fairness and 3 out of 10 overall. They were additionally presented with evidence backing up the fact that half of all contractors fell into the grey 'Charlotte' area where the Revenue's assessment of whether they fall under IR35 could lead them to decide 'either way'.

'If there is a real tax dodge then the Revenue should have targeted it specifically rather than shooting everyone down' Mr Barling told the court. According to Frontier's expert evidence for the PCG, 24 per cent of a contractor's income is paid as salary and subject to PAYE and NIC'. 'What of the other 72% the judge asked Mr Barling. 'It goes into expenses, investment, re-investment and dividends like any other business' Mr Barling replied.

At the conclusion of the first day, it was felt that the Judge had taken on board a number of important issues. He appeared to recognise the inherent unfairness of contractors being tax as employees without receiving the benefits of employment from their 'disguised employer'. He also appeared to be concerned that the focus of IR35 seemed to have changed significantly since its initial inception as a measure that was designed to protect employees from being forced into service companies by employers to one that was focused on perceived tax avoidance.

At the end of the afternoon, he appeared to be in full agreement that contractors working through their service companies were bound to be in competition with their larger body-shop competitor.

At the close of the first day of play PCG Chairman Gareth Williams said "The judge came in having not read the papers. I think he has accepted some of our points and think he understands the situation a bit better now. I'm positive after today's session and he seemed to accept the points of competition and the questions raised regarding uncertainty'.

# Judicial Review Session Three – Wednesday 14 March 2001

The third session began and the judge still didn't seem to be up to speed. He explained that he had read some more of the submissions but still hadn't read the 'expert' evidence. However, on a positive note he explained that he now understood what a contractor was. According to Simon Juden - who wrote an account published by *shout99.com* - he now understood 'contractor' to mean the personal service company, not the director of the company. It was only session 3 and at last he understood what we meant by 'contractor'! On the plus side he seemed to be getting the hang of it.

He was still confused about the margin that an agency took out of the fee (which most contractors know can be 10-20% or even higher), he asked if this was caught under IR35. Plender said 'no' and explained that the 'deemed salary' calculations were net of this charge.

The judge had read Sarah Walker's submission which had said that the Revenue provided service on advice for contracts had been 'spurned' by contractors. (I thought did they really think a service where people could ring up and ask if they are guilty would work?) We had 'spurned' it and also the service was only available for signed contracts, which didn't really help with certainty. Plender had to explain that it was true opinions were only provided on signed contracts, but 'advice' was available pre-signing.

Further discussions followed on SSP and SMP payments and whether they were available on the 'deemed' or actual salary and this was followed by a discussion about unemployment benefit, basically that contractors can't get it because they are deemed to be an employee of their service company. The complexities and fairness of these benefits were discussed in a contractor context as they played around with the idea of 'deemed' and actual salary. Though I had thought it was academic because if you were caught then by IR35 then you might as well pay it all as actual salary.

They then discussed the issue of multiple clients and how having several clients (one after another) was a pointer to self employment, though Barling pointed out that contractors were turning down contract extensions because of this.

Next the judge turned to Gareth Williams' statement. It sounded as though Gareth had complained about the fairness of the tax and whether it was politically acceptable because the judge said that it wasn't for him to decide on any such matters, his opinions would be limited to issues of legality.

This was something we knew, but a lot of contractors still felt that as it was unfair and badly constructed the tax could be thrown out. The judge clarified this point but saying that it is always good to include in court documents such arguments as they effectively go into the public domain and it can annoy the opposition.

Next they discussed State Aid and what it was. PCG contended that IR35 was State Aid to larger companies as it gave them an unfair advantage. Barling used a previous case involving Lunn Poly - the travel agent - to illustrate our point. There was discussion about whether IR35 was an anti-avoidance scheme or not. Barling pointed to the original justification of the scheme, the kitchen fitters, who left on Friday as salaried employees and returned on Monday morning working through their PSCs.

Juden reports him as saying 'that in this regard it is wholly disproportionate'. Rebecca Seeley-Harris writing for contractoruk explained that Barling presented evidence from PCG contractor Kevin Peacock. He had explained how a client had engaged a large body-shop but had subsequently replaced them with the services of a contractor because they were less expensive. Harris said that it provided evidence that contractors could compete with the likes of EDS.

The judge then started to give Barling some advice, according to Seeley-Harris he suggested that he went for an argument that IR35 was an 'obstacle' as there is no discrimination or movement involved in the legal argument. He suggested that the burden of proof would then shift to Plender who would have to come up with an objectively justifiable reason for IR35. She said that if it was either on social grounds or if on 'tax avoidance' it would only be valid if it wasn't closing a loophole or 'restructuring the company to limit the advantages given'. She went on to report that Plender would then have to 'prove the measure was proportionate and not 'a sledge hammer to crack a nut'".

Next up was the issue of Freedom of Movement. The PCG line was that IR35 was forcing IT contractors to seek employment outside the UK, a claim that had been strongly denied by the Inland Revenue. Barling sought to explain his reasoning behind it, but the Judge didn't seem to be convinced.

Juden reported that the Judge said "this line seemed very narrow and he was worried about elevating Freedom of Movement to the level where anything and everything other than the varying rates of direct taxation or harmonisation of indirect taxation could be viewed as a ground".

For Human Rights Barling argued how someone could have spent years building up a business and a brand only to now have it all trampled upon by IR35. He cited the RIA which talked of 60,000 businesses closing down and all the general uncertainty that IR35 was bringing because of the way it had been implemented - by looking at engagement by engagement rather than a view of the whole year.

The judge seemed to think that the standard agency contracts which were not IR35 friendly would wither away over time to be replaced by more favourable contracts. Barling said that this wouldn't necessarily happen since agencies 'don't care, as they are not directly affected by IR35'.

The judge talked a lot about this per-engagement issue, he didn't seem to like it at all and said that in the event the PCG lose the case he was minded to issue guidance with the authority of the High Court. The judge was also highly critical of the Inland Revenue's guidance. He suggested that if contractors could show a 'willingness' and "intention" to work for multiple clients, they should be outside of IR35

The PCG team later issued a statement saying that this alone would make it "much easier for members of the contracting community to place their businesses outside of IR35".

As for length of contract for assessing such an arrangement he talked of a year, Barling pointed out that EDS had just signed a ten year agreement with the Inland Revenue and asked why should they be able to have such a deal and why a small firm shouldn't?

The judge then said he thought our case on Human Rights was weak, (which it was) but Barling countered by saying that when viewed in conjunction with State Aid and Freedom of Movement it had value.

Next off contractors had a laugh when the judge was presented with evidence that the same contract had been submitted to the Inland Revenue twice, on one occasion they said it passed IR35 and then on the other they said it was caught. "The same contract, same company, same circumstances but deemed 'outside IR35' – by the same Tax Office".

There were red faces all round on the Revenue bench but Barling was gracious in saying that it wasn't the staff's fault it was the fault of this "wolly" legislation and was clear evidence that even Inland Revenue inspectors have no idea how to decide IR35 status.

Contractors had also had a laugh when Barling had gone through the Institute of Chartered Accountants review of the tax which had given it a mere 30/100, a clear fail.

The judge said he was 'troubled' by the legislation's history because it didn't start off being aimed at a 'disguised employee'. Juden reported that he said that it might be 'hard to shake the origins of the thing off'. Barling, Juden records, said that there were many other options that could have achieved the Revenue's stated aim in a 'more reasonable and proportionate way'. The examples he gave were of raising NICs on dividends or having a rule about the proportion of income a closed company can declare as dividend etc. The fairness of the tax was discussed further in the context of a paper presented by Frontier Economics and the judge said that if we had a socialist government (and 'some say we do') it might want to punish entrepreneurs, but if that was the case it still wasn't his place to stop them. Contractoruk reported that the gallery of PCG members seemed delighted by this remark.

In another ray of light the judge talked further about Gareth William's evidence which explained why contractors had to use limited companies rather than be sole traders (because of the agency legislation). Plender didn't contest this point even if our erstwhile Paymaster General would continue to do so.

The judge acknowledged that a caught company would now be less competitive than one not caught and Barling said that caught ones would have to put up their prices, but then a stupid discussion ensued around the point that contractors were cheaper than bigger consultancies and could therefore pay it. As far as the State Aid argument was concerned Barling asserted that the test was not that a measure 'does distort the market, merely that it has the potential to do so'.

The judge seemed to be getting it now. He said that there two different mindsets - that of contractors as outsourced employees and of contractors as small consultancies. Juden said that the judge still had to decide which mindset he agreed with and Juden felt that this would decide the case.

When Plender stood up to make the case for the Inland Revenue he stated that that their position on IR35 hadn't changed. Seeley-Harris reported him as saying "It was and still is a tax avoidance measure and it is designed to stop the interposition of an intermediary as a vehicle to gain a tax advantage". She said that "they are not disputing that IR35 is a tax avoidance measure, this being the point which Barling has lain out before the court for the last two days".

She noted that "In Plender's statement, therefore, and bearing in mind what has been discussed previously on the legal issues the Revenue will simply have to justify the tax avoidance measure. Well when I say simply, I don't mean at is going to be simple. Judging by the rest of the case it will be far from that."

She hoped that Plender would get a hard time off the judge, since Barling had.

At the end of the third day it was looking a lot better. Commentators felt that the judge seemed to be more respectful towards the PCG's case - now he had read it. I am not sure if that was the case, but optimism was rising.

## Who was who in court?

For the Inland Revenue there was Richard Plender QC and Rabinder Singh, Sarah Walker - Assistant Tax Director, IR and Peter Seedhouse - IR Employment status expert and his assistants.

For the PCG there was Gerald Barling QC and Kelyn Bacon, Gareth Williams - Chairman of the PCG, Kevin Miller - PCG Finance Director and David Ramsden - PCG Political Director.

In the gallery Gary Mackley-Smith – AccountingWeb, Anne Redston - Ernst & Young, Diana Galpin - Ascot Drummond, John Antell - PCG Employment Status Lawyer, Members of the PCG, Rebecca Seeley Harris - contractoruk and Richard Powell – *Shout99.com*

## The War Room – PCG take over the Cheshire Cheese

On the eve of the hearing the Inland Revenue contacted news organisations and invited them to a pre-JR briefing. Richard Powell of *Shout99.com* revealed that *Shout99.com* had its name on the list for a briefing but was informed - at the same time others journalists were being 'cold-called' and invited in - that there were no spaces available for the contractors' own news-site.

Across the road from the High Court is a pub called the Cheshire Cheese. On contractor Wednesday we found that taking over the Red Lion had proved very successful. We'd also 'set up shop' in the George on our first visit to the High Court so on this occasion we hired out a room at the Cheshire Cheese as our own media and communications room, though on this occasion it had less to do with having a drink and more so to act as a focal point for contractors and as a 'war room'.

Susie had contacted all her press contacts and even the BBC had run it as a story. We invited interested press and media to come to the Cheshire Cheese where we would be happy to provide commentary and give interviews.

Gareth Williams and others populated the spectator seats in the court room itself. (Which despite the grand outside, isn't very grand inside, it is just a lecture theatre). Susie and Andy asked if I could come in and help with the press side, which is what I did. I spent my time trying to explain to various journalists what IR35 was all about and why we thought it was so important. It was hard work from phone calls to hard meetings. The open house mentality encouraged our friends from the other trade associations to pop in as well as hundreds of contractors who populated the place at lunch time and just wanted to feel 'part of it'. Something that was very much encouraged.

Rebecca Seeley-Harris wrote some excellent articles for contractoruk.com though because they were impartial (or not partisan enough) they upset the Enragés and a thread was started on the PCG Forums called 'Burn the Witch'. Maybe they all thought it was just a 'laugh' but I am not sure that others viewed it like that. To them even to doubt or question the case, the cause or its execution was treason. More acceptable to them was Simon Juden who wrote some court sketches which were published on *Shout99.com* and on the PCG forums and went out as emails with encouragement for people to distribute them far and wide.

To deal with the huge amount of Internet traffic *Shout99.com* even set up an alternative website called ir35update.co.uk. This was in part to try and help the PCG's server because on the last day of PCG's evidence the website took nearly 1 million hits - at one point taking 25 hits per second.

In the pre-Wi-Fi days it was a remarkable achievement as we operated from a pub with laptops, mobile phones and very dodgy modem connections. We also had some of the country's leading edge technology experts who solved our communication problems by climbing on chairs and positioning mobiles in the optimum place to keep our Internet connections live for as long as possible! Anyone with a mobile phone with battery life was seconded in to help.

It was a huge operation, but good hearted. I saw PCG campaigner Collete Mason working on her laptop while in session she had managed to develop and deploy a website for the pub itself by way of a thank-you to our cheery landlord who didn't have a clue what we were all about, but as someone who ran a small business was right behind us taking on the Inland Revenue.

Les Enragés were also there and I had to put up with a few comments along the lines of that 'I was going to lose'. I said I thought we were going to win and then they explained that my team was not the PCG but the Government.

At one point Susie introduced me to a 'special guest' who had literally walked in off the street. He was the son of Rudi Viz, the Labour MP for Finchley, (Thatcher's old seat). He worked in IT and came to offer his support and expressed his concern that his father could lose his seat at the coming election because of IR35. Of course we got on very well and spent time talking about IR35 and clearly framing it and the right to self-employment in Labour principles and values.

Each evening we would review the results of the day's proceedings and there would be lots of chatter on the forums. It was exhausting stuff. On the legal side I had left it to the barristers and solicitors to deal with and they had been managed by Gareth and others.

PCG IT director Ian Durrant told *Shout99.com* that "A few hours as an observer in the War Room is an illustration of why PCG has achieved so much in so little time. We have a team of 12,000 committed people who are working together to save their businesses. The country cannot afford to lose people of this calibre."

Susie summarised the first three days on Shout99:

JR - The Story So Far
=====================

The majority of the three days has been devoted to outlining the PCG's case. While it would be inappropriate to predict the outcome at this stage or
raise hopes, there have been several occasions which have been positive for the contracting community.

Here are some of the highlights from the PCG's case:

Multiple clients
****************
- if the PCG loses, the judge indicated that he would consider issuing guidance with the authority of High Court which would indicate that seeking work opportunities from multiple clients would put a company outside IR35.

Nuclear option
**************
- the judge, who sits on Employment Appeals Tribunal, said that he thought there was a strong case for employment rights for those caught under IR35.

Beyond the nuclear option
*************************

- the court also indicated that the employment rights issue could extend to employees of body-shops selling them into clients.

### Freedom of movement

- the judge indicated that the freedom of movement issue is potentially an easier hurdle to cross - doesn't depend on sector or competition.

### Evidence of competition

- there was a strong argument of a competition element in IT and the judge asked for additional evidence of other sectors. Engineering evidence was provided to demonstrate the point.

### Same contract, different opinion

- the example of one contract which received a 'yes' and a 'no' from different IR offices. It took 4-5 months to get a decision (28 day limit) and the 'inside IR35' was an obvious cut and paste job which showed that the assessor hadn't read the content. Judge was highly critical of this and the
Inland Revenue's QC, Richard Plender, apologised.

### Mutuality of obligation

- the court recognised that if there was no mutuality of obligation, then that would be an indicator that it was outside IR35. The Revenue's QC agreed.

### Consolation prize

- there was an early indication from the judge that - if the PCG loses - there could be some declaration which would make the application of IR35 less restrictive.

### Tax mitigation

- discussion about the difference between tax mitigation (i.e. making arrangements in accordance with tax regime after you've set up a business for other reasons) and tax avoidance (i.e. setting up a business/arranging your affairs in order to maximise tax benefits). Judge indicated there was nothing wrong with setting up companies and using them to mitigate tax. Contractors could fall into that category.

### Emotive language in press release

- the judge was critical of the use of emotive language, such as 'disguised employee' in the original IR35 press release.

### Friday to Monday

- judge indicated that there should be no prejudice in the assessment procedure because the first client of the contractor had previously been an employee.

Expert competition evidence
***************************

- judge indicated that he could see the force of argument when supported by PCG's expert evidence, and that the IR were relying on assertions not supported by evidence.

Freedom of Movement
**********************

- IR must show that there is an overriding reason of public interest - which cannot be an 'economic one'.

Proportionality
***************

- judge indicated that if the objective was Friday-to-Monday, it was a sledgehammer to crack a nut.

Incorporation
*************

- the judge indicated that there was nothing critical in terms of people taking advantage of laws allowing them to incorporate.

Implementation
**************

- the judge was critical of the manner in which the IR was going about implementation in practice and, should the PCG lose, he would have more to say on that point.

## Thursday 15th March

On the Thursday the PCG continued to outline its case, thus denying Plender his real chance and the press started to suggest we were deliberately dragging out the case. I wouldn't have thought that was true, we were all contractors and needed to get back to work.

PCG said that "The case is overrunning because of the detailed nature of the judge's questions to counsel".

### JR4: Judge recognises nuclear option

*by The Editor at 12:58 15/03/01 (shout99.com)*

As the Professional Contractors Group's judicial review entered its third day, the judge indicated that the Revenue couldn't have it both ways regarding employment rights.

Mr Justice Burton said that if the IR35 laws were allowed to stand it would mean that where the Inland Revenue decided that employment tests applied and that a worker was caught by IR35 then the worker would have a very good case to claim employment rights against the client.

The issue of the double-standards – taxed as an employee but none of the employee benefits – has been identified by the PCG as one of the many inconsistent and unfair aspects of the law. The 'employee rights issues' has already caused legal cases in the US where the so-called 'permatemps' have taken their 'client' to court and have won various rights.

He also indicated that he didn't see why, in some cases, the employees of large service providers should not be treated as employees of their client. As an employment law specialist, he view is particularly significant.

PCG's Chairman Gareth Williams said: "It is encouraging to see that so many of the anomalies and inconsistencies of IR35 have been identified and understood by the court. Despite the unfairness and, what we believe to be the illegality of the law, we always firmly believed that it was a fundamentally flawed piece of legislation which would not work in practise anyway."

This follows yesterday's opinion that businesses seeking work from many clients would appear to fall outside IR35.

## Morning of Monday 19th March

The Inland Revenue had outlined their case on the Wednesday afternoon. It now continued.

*by Richard Powell at 15:25 19/03/01 (shout99.com)*

This morning's session (Monday March 19) of the PCG's judicial review began as the judge declared he had a series of 8 questions to put to both the Inland Revenue and the PCG having spent the weekend reading through the evidence both parties had supplied him with.

The Judge's questions were as follows:

1/. Is the effect and intent of IR35 to eliminate the avoidance of tax and NICs?

2/. Will many workers with personal service companies be required to pay more to the Revenue?

3/. Roughly 80% of PSCs are in the sectors referred to in the relief sought

4/. PCSs will experience uncertainty as a result of confusion as to what will and won't fall under IR35

5/. PSCs will be in competition with those larger companies which remain unaffected by IR35

6/. Those unaffected by IR35 have an advantage in tax flexibility and time

7/. IR35 will make some of those PSCs leave the country and will stop others wanting to set up in the country

8/. IR35 may have effects on interstate trade.

Mr Plender QC acting on behalf of the Revenue answered 1/.Yes, 2/.Yes, 3/.No, 4/.No, 5/.No, 6/. Yes, 7/.Yes (some) and 8/. Yes (comparable to previous findings).

Mr Barling QC for the PCG answered 'Yes' to all of the questions.

Mr Justice Burton announced that he believed Mr Plender would try to argue that the differences between them were factual but that he 'did not see it as such'. He also spoke for sometime about the Human Rights part of the PCGs case against IR35 but there was no conclusion to this argument and this is expected to be concluded over the next two days. The judge also said that IR35 attacked intermediaries who pay greater amounts of tax than if they were directly employed by the intermediary. The Judge also made the proclamation that 'independent contractors' was not a relevant term for those the court was discussing and expressed his wish for them to be henceforth referred to as 'service contractors'.

There was also some debate over the findings of the Regulatory Impact Assessments. Looking to Mr Plender QC and the Revenue bench in general, he asked them "What was the deciding factor between your first draft in which you more or less stated that 'those to be hit by IR35 will all die and good riddance' and the second draft that said 'many of these companies will choose to stay in business and good luck to them'?" At this stage there was no fundamental defence from the Inland Revenue of how this had come to pass.

The Judge went so far as to suggest an imaginary case study himself, asking Mr Plender about the possibility that IBM might one day decide to hire someone and have to make a choice between a service company and a bigger, IR35 immune company. "It doesn't need to be disputed that the two will be in competition," the Judge said, "but the fact is that the contract for the service company could come under IR35. If you make it more difficult for the service company then they will not be able to operate properly against their competitors." Mr Plender attempted to construct an imaginary situation in which he argued he would not be in competition with a big legal firm if a Greek Telecoms company approached him for legal advice but it ended up showing there would be a competition element. "With operating a service company under IR35, you do so with an uncertainty no-one can really be sure of and that's a conclusion you ought to be accepting," the Judge told Mr Plender.

The judge finished by announcing that he would like to be furnished with more information concerning the definition of 'negative state aid' and 'selectivity' as is concerned by the case

### The Judicial Review – Day 4 – Monday 19th March[66]

The fourth day of PCG's judicial review began with Counsel for the Inland Revenue, Richard Plender QC, continuing with his arguments against the PCG case.

---

[66] Also see http://www.contractoruk.com/news/00340.html for a good account of proceedings

The morning session focused mainly on arguments of fact with the judge spending his time asking Plender to clarify this, that and the other and in particular points over competition and freedom of movement.

He seemed surprised that contractors couldn't see the client-agency agreement and suggested that they should be able to and said that perhaps there could be an industry-wide "non-IR35" contract brought into use.

Barling had done his job well in the previous sessions and the judge was critical of Inland Revenue's internal guidance manual that is used by inspectors to assess IR35 status. He was concerned that while the legislation and indeed the Revenue's own submissions to court said that all circumstances for a contractor should be taken into account, the guidance manuals said to just use the contracts. Plender made no response to this criticism.

Despite Plender's assertions to the contrary, Justice Burton seems satisfied that competition did exist between contractors and the larger consultancy firms.

Plender dismissed the Institute of Chartered Accountants of England and Wales (ICAEW) report into IR35, that was highly critical of the legislation (it would later turn out that they had Batman on their side who was all for it).

But for all this Plender did land some blows. The PCG reported to its members that he made the case that "IR35 may be damaging and unfair, but this does not make it illegal".

He insisted that IR35 was a general measure. He insisted that it was not a specific piece of targeted legislation, that it didn't favour one industry sector or individual company over another as it did not name a particular industry sector. He said it was not State Aid to a sector or a company.

This aside he then used examples from European law to show that it wasn't an illegal law. He said it was a tax avoidance measure and was aimed at all companies with an 'employee like relation'. It wasn't there to help big companies and it wasn't done to undermine contractors and therefore… it wasn't illegal.

*Shout99.com* reported that "the judge seemed to agree and drew a parallel with "green" legislation. Carbon tax is not seen as State Aid to non-polluting companies, because it is "intended" to help the environment. The fact that it raises lots of money for the Treasury and may put laundrettes out of business is immaterial".

The day ended and it was noted it was becoming clear that the "onus is on the PCG to prove that IR35 is illegal under European law".

Day 5 – Tuesday 20$^{th}$ – Final Day

The Tuesday saw more laughter as the Inland Revenue desperate to find some industry support for its measures quoted remarks posted on a website by an individual called 'Adam West' that had supported their measures. The PCG pointed out that this 'Adam West' was distinguished by the email address of purplepants@capedcrusader.com and so perhaps it was really Batman[67]. (Perhaps Mickey Mouse had helped to write the legislation in the first place?) This wasn't without precedent - it turned out that Dawn Primarolo had quoted the caped crusader in Parliament the previous May.

Plender tried to convince the judge that contracting and larger companies did not compete with each other and that despite the assertions of Mr Barling that the Inland Revenue's IR35 Guidance Manual was a solid document.

Shout99 reported that "Plender spent the morning discussing the finer points of European law regarding Freedom of Movement. One of the main justifications for IR35 from the point of view of the Inland Revenue is that it is a general tax measure. They maintain that IR35 is not targeted at discouraging foreign businesses from coming to the UK. It may *discourage* companies from coming here because the business climate is less favourable, but this does not have a disproportional effect on foreign businesses seeking to come to the UK, therefore, IR35 is not illegal. For example, Swedish income tax is comparatively high, but this is a feature of the Swedish tax system, not a deliberate barrier to discourage people from moving there. Therefore, this cannot be an obstacle to Freedom of Movement".

The judge was well aware of how intensively the case was being reported and discussed on the Internet, not just by the PCG but by shout99.com and contractoruk and others, so when Plender said he had to leave the court early to catch a plane the judge told him 'you'll have to pick up what's happened on the Internet'.

In his absence Barling gave the PCG's responses to the Inland Revenue's evidence. With their boss gone it was reported that the 'Inland Revenue team now consisted only of the solicitors, who trickled away one by one during the course of the afternoon'

The Judge had given Plender permission to submit his response in writing by midday Friday 23 March. Shout99 reported that "The judge would like to give a judgement sometime next week. Before leaving, Plender indicated that the Inland Revenue are not seeking referral to Europe as they would not want to prolong the uncertainty for contractors".

Barling said that if the judge was uncertain about certain points, he could consider referring to Europe.

Waiting for the ruling

Then it was over, the judge indicated that he would go away and think about it. Already from his pronouncements at the hearing, he wasn't happy with the way

---

[67] Adam West had been the actor who played Batman in the TV show

IR35 had been implemented and he would make some clarification comments about that, particularly with regards to contractors who had multiple clients. If we didn't win we could also hope for some changes to the guidance and the case studies published of 'Charlotte, Gordon and Henry'.

The Inland Revenue's contract review system had been opened to ridicule when somebody submitted the same contract twice. It was dealt with by different offices, one passed it as clear of IR35 and the other rejected it.

It was noted to the court that it took 4-5 months to get a decision on IR35 (despite a 28 day limit) and the 'inside IR35' text that they included in letters was an obvious cut and paste job which showed that the assessor hadn't read the content. The Judge was highly critical of this and the Inland Revenue's QC, Richard Plender, apologised.

The issue of employment rights had come up; if you pay tax as an employee then surely you should have the rights of an employee? Contractors called it the nuclear option because if activated it would both destroy IR35 and contractors together. No one would hire contractors if they risked having to employ them permanently on such high rates. (Though it was the sign of the times, in 2001 rates were still high but would soon be suffering a fall).

Justice Burton was critical of the language in the original IR35 press release where businesses were described as 'disguised employees' and rejected the Paymaster General's assertion that because there was nothing critical in terms of people taking advantage of laws allowing them to incorporate. (Thus dispelling Dawn's argument that we were all tax cheats because we had bought off the shelf companies). Finally he didn't like the way that IR35 was being implemented by the Inland Revenue.

All of this sounded great, yet it was all about the fairness of the tax, nothing here suggested that the tax was in fact illegal and as we suggested, benefited larger companies. There had been a big concern as their case had proceed as to whether the judge fully understood knowledge based sector and much of our barrister Barling's work had been in explaining this, whereas Plender for the Inland Revenue could spend most of his time just firing off shots at contractors.

Waiting for the judge's decision Andy wrote to *Shout99.com* members that:

> It is difficult to predict an outcome, but one thing appears certain that the parties are not considering a straight win or lose situation. It has been clear from the events within the court, that while PCG has been vindicated on many of the contentious issues of fact which have been under dispute with the Revenue for the past two years, such as the right to be viewed as businesses in competition with larger companies; the concern about the uncertainty and confusion of the Revenue guidelines; the fact that people will not set up businesses in the UK, the PCG still has to clear the 'legal' hurdles.

## Taking a last political shot

Labour had been slow to say anything official about IR35 but with the General Election just round the corner and uncertainty about the High Court case they felt they had to say something, but to persuade candidates and supporters instead of talking about it as a tax issue they described it as an employment issue.

> IR35 means that companies cannot employ people as contractors when they should be treating them as employees.'

> 'This does not penalise self-employed people. It simply means that people who would otherwise be employed do not lose entitlement to benefits such as paid holidays, pensions, sick leave, redundancy entitlement and payment of their national insurance contributions. It also means that companies have to compete on a level playing field, employing their staff on the appropriate basis.'

> 'People who are self-employed and undertake work for a variety of clients or from their own office, among others, are not affected by these rules.'

It finished by linking to a document simultaneously released by the Inland Revenue explaining the detailed workings of IR35 and how to calculate your payment should you be eligible to do so, which I thought it was an outrageous way to spin it to their own people, so to get my own back during this lull in the fighting I published my own article on *Shout99.com* as a Labour candidate attacking the Government on IR35. I never received any criticism from Labour HQ because of it.

**Government should listen to Contractors**

by PhilipRoss at 12:56 21/03/01 (*Shout99.com* - Political News)

Philip Ross, Labour's prospective parliamentary candidate for North East Bedfordshire (also the PCG's first Campaign Director), calls afresh for the Government to engage in proper consultation to create 'a better targeted and fairer piece of legislation that is more suited to the 21st Century and modern working practises'.

At the 1999 Labour Party Conference, I delivered a speech during the debate on Economy attacking the new revised IR35 proposals. Gordon Brown had delivered his key note speech a few minutes earlier on the theme of 'Enterprise for All'. I re-titled my speech at the time as 'Enterprise for all and IR35'. I supported then and support now what Gordon had to say on the economy and the steps that he has taken to deliver a sound economy and I fully support the idea of 'Enterprise for all'. However I have always felt that there was a contradiction and that it was IR35.

I said then that:

'[IR35] fails to understand that knowledge and skills are commodities that are traded today just as manufactured goods have been traded in the past".

"For example these plans imply that a small company that invests in a van is a genuine business but one that invests in knowledge is a disguised employee! This can't be right."

"Under these rules, small companies will NOT be able to retain profits to grow their business. Small companies will NOT be able to claim the same expenses as their larger competitors"

"These plans betray the principle, ' that the Workers should have the Right to reap the fruits of their own labour by hand or by brain'. These plans imply that I cannot work for myself ".

I stand by these comments again now and urge the Government in the letter below to consider their position carefully as we await the judgement from the High Court.

**Letter**

Win or lose the judicial review currently being heard at the High Court the Government needs to listen carefully to the arguments that the Professional Contractors Group have put forward. IR35 is an unfair tax that treats IT contractors and others operating in a similar way as 'disguised employees' and taxes them as employees and not as businesses. It does not allow them to retain any money to grow their business, for training or to cover sickness or holidays. The law has been badly drafted and can lead to contractors paying tax on the same money twice. So if the Government should win or lose the hearing, instead of allowing it to go to appeal by either side, I would urge them instead to start again and consult fully with the contractors to create a better targeted and fairer piece of legislation that is more suited to the 21st Century and modern working practises.

Yours

Philip Ross

Labour's Prospective Parliamentary Candidate

The 2001 election was fought on a platform of opposing cuts of £16bn by the Conservatives. The Tories claimed that it would only be £8bn of cuts, which writing in 2012 seems like peanuts given the financial crisis and bank bail outs.

For IR35 Labour alleged that abolishing it would cost the country £700m, which was double the original estimate but now less than the £900m they had suggested after the last budget.

### Andy's view

Andy, who despite not being a director of the PCG anymore, remained one of the best fighters for contractors and sent an impassioned message out to contractors on *Shout99.com* on the eve of the High Court result.

> Two years ago I felt strongly enough about IR35 to get on the modern equivalent of the soapbox and try to effect some change. Contracting through my own limited

company had given me the chance to build my other businesses and I considered that if IR35 had been in force when I started I might not have done so well.

I consider that the tax loss caused by any so-called abuse is more than outweighed by the tax increases resulting from allowing people to build their own businesses. IR35 places an uncertain barrier to those who want to make the first steps into business and drives people, used to the certainty of mathematical exactitude, to give up their ambitions of being in business on their own account.

I, together with 13,000 other members of the PCG, have been trying for the last two years to engage the Government in proper consultation to ensure that they are fully aware of the damage they are causing to the knowledge-based sector.

We have been ignored, called 'tax cheats' by a Paymaster General who should know better and generally had our eyes opened to a Government, that many of us voted for, who do not appear to 'walk the talk'.

Our own Government refused to listen to us so we ended up paying for our own consultation. It is called a Judicial Review. An experienced, intelligent and independent Judge with evidence presented by skilled advocates has given us the consultation we requested 18 months ago.

## The Register's View

The Register is an IT based news website; their report on the hearing was that:

> And so it looks as though the PCG has won its case on the impracticability of IR35. This, however, is very different from finding the measure illegal and having it struck down. The decision over whether IR35 is legal will be based on seemingly obscure points of law. It is far from clear that the PCG has proved its case in this respect, and the judge will be naturally wary of striking any legislation passed by Parliament.
>
> PCG spokeswoman Susie Hughes summed up the PCG's feeling: "We are very pleased that we have been allowed to put this case to the High Court. We are also pleased that the Judge has recognised our concerns and made several findings of fact in our favour. Now it is a question of points of law."
>
> The case has certainly provided some plenty of copy. The group contesting the law, the PCG - has had a member taking extensive notes of the whole case and posting them on the Internet.
>
> In fact, the case and the PCG in general has shown the great power of the Internet when it comes to allow people to communicate and share information. The judge even made mention of the Internet reports on the last day - suggesting that the Inland Revenue's QC check them to see what he had missed (he had had to leave at 4pm to catch a plane).

## The Ruling

Judgement day was announced and we were first out of the blocks to make sure the press knew how to reach us. The war room was set up again. Susie drafted three advance versions of a press notice and kept them under lock and key but we had our statements ready to hand out depending if a) we won, b) we lost well, or c) we lost badly - and invited the press to hear our reaction regardless of the outcome.

OPERATIONAL NOTE: HIGH COURT RULING IN PCG'S JUDICIAL REVIEW

The High Court judgement in the judicial review which the Professional Contractors Group brought against the Government will be given at 10.30am on Monday, April 2, 2001. This note outlines the PCG's operational arrangements for the day.

PCG, which represents more than 12,500 small businesses, brought the legal action against the Government over the controversial 'stealth tax on small businesses', IR35, in the High Court from March 13-15 and 19-20, 2001.

The five-day case claimed that IR35 contravenes European legislation on three counts (state aid; freedom of movement and Human Rights) and therefore should be removed from the Statute Books. The PCG won the permission hearing on all counts last October after the Revenue was defeated in its attempt to prevent the case being heard.

Immediately after the decision on Monday April 2, representatives from the PCG will be available for brief comments outside the High Court, The Strand, London. WC2. Thereafter, the PCG will also be operating a communications and press office in the upstairs floor of the Cheshire Cheese, 5 Little Essex Street, London WC2 - opposite the High Court from 11.30am to 7pm. (PLEASE NOTE: This is NOT Ye Olde Cheshire Cheese in Fleet Street). Journalists and photographers are invited to attend the Cheshire Cheese for one-to-one interviews, briefings or photographs throughout the day with the PCG chairman, directors and members.

There is a comprehensive briefing on the background to the case and the PCG on the PCG's web-site http://www.pcg.org.uk. Updates and comments on the Court's decision will be available on PCG's dedicated news-site http://www.ir35update.co.uk throughout the day.

IR35 was announced in a press notice after the March 1999 Budget. It treats small businesses in the knowledge-based sector as 'disguised employees' for tax and NI purposes, thereby preventing them from operating on similar terms to their larger competitors.

Case dismissed. We had lost.

We had lost but we had lost 'well', so well in fact that the Revenue press office was ringing round journalists to correct reports that we'd actually won but despite our 'spin', the reality was that IR35, the legislation that sought to eliminate the avoidance of income tax and national insurance contributions by the use of service companies, did not infringe the human rights of service contractors nor was it incompatible with provisions of the EC Treaty

(i) We had lost on all three counts.

(ii) The Revenue was awarded costs.

(iii) We were refused leave to appeal.

We'd won the argument on fairness and implementation but we'd lost it on the grounds on which we challenged it.

Judge Burton also published a 50 page ruling and this summary:

Application to challenge the legality of the composite legislation, contained in s.75 and s.76 Welfare Reform and Pensions Act 1999 and in s.60 and Sched.12 Finance Act, known as IR35, which sought to eliminate the avoidance of income tax and national insurance contributions ('NICs') by the use of service companies as recipients for payments in respect of services provided by contractors who, in the opinion of the Revenue, were de facto employees.

The essential thrust of IR35 was that those payments should be treated not as company revenue, but as deemed salary to the service contractor whose services the company provided, thereby subjecting the service contractor to Schedule E income tax and Class 1 NICs.

The grounds of challenge were that IR35:

(1) was incompatible with the service contractors' right to protection of property under Protocol 1 Art.1 European Convention on Human Rights and Fundamental Freedoms 1950;

(2) constituted unlawful state aid, contrary to Art.87 and Art.88 EC Treaty; and

(3) infringed Art.39 (freedom for workers), Art.43 (freedom of establishment) and Art.49 (freedom for services) of the Treaty.

The following facts were agreed, assumed or found by the court:

(i) the purpose of IR35 was as set out above;

(ii) because of IR35, a substantial proportion of all service contractors, of the order of two-thirds, would have to pay more tax and/or National Insurance and earlier to the Revenue;

(iii) IR35 introduced greater uncertainty than had prevailed under the previous arrangements;

(iv) those affected by IR35 would face competition from those who were unaffected by it, with the latter enjoying greater fiscal and commercial advantages;

(v) some service contractors would either close their existing UK business or would not start a contemplated UK business; and

(vi) IR35 would thus have an effect on trade between EU member states.

HELD:

(1) The impact of IR35 was not even arguably so severe as to amount to a de facto confiscation of service contractors' property, to a fundamental interference with their financial position or an abuse of the UK's right to levy taxes. Subjecting service contractors to the common law of employment did not interfere with their human rights.

(2) IR35 did not give rise to an unnotified state aid as no one could be specifically identified as the recipient of any such aid. (R v Commissioners of Customs and Excise ex parte (1) Lunn Poly Ltd (2) Bishopsgate Insurance Ltd (1998) TLR 11/3/99 considered).

(3) The court was satisfied that the imposition of IR35 could be said to be an impediment to mobility, in the sense that a positive incentive for service contractors to come to the UK had been removed. However, any such impediment was justified by reference to tax reform, the prevention of tax avoidance and the protection of the Revenue.

Application dismissed.

# Chapter 21

## Revenue says Pay Up!

Shortly after the finale of the judicial review an Inland Revenue spokesman in Somerset House told Richard Powell of Shout99: "The Government is glad the court has confirmed what it believed all along. We maintained what was in accordance with the law so we're happy to see it has come out the way it has."

Asked if it represented a victory for the Inland Revenue, the spokesman replied: "We don't really want to talk 'victories or defeats' at the moment."

As for the question of how much impact the guidance handed down would have on IR35, he said,

> "We'll take everything on board and see what amendments need to be made. We hear what the judge is saying and we'll make the Employment Status Manual more user-friendly. Looking at the judge's comments and the outcome of the case our policy people will look at what changes now need to be made."

When asked what consultation the Inland Revenue will be conducting with regards to the amendments it mentioned, the spokesman replied,

> "There is no mention here of any consultation."

An internal briefing paper from the Inland Revenue's press office obtained by *Shout99.com* directly after the session had closed reads as follows:

Restricted- Policy Press Briefing

Government wins Judicial Review of IR35

### Statement

The Government is glad that the Court has confirmed that the IR35 legislation is not contrary to EC and Human Rights law, and that the uncertainty caused by this case can now come to an end. The legislation was necessary to ensure fair taxation of all workers, whether or not they use a limited company to arrange their contracts.

### What happens now?

The IR35 legislation is the law of the land, as enacted by Parliament and upheld by the Court. Individuals affected by it will need to make sure they take the necessary actions to ensure they comply with their obligations under this law.

### What do workers affected by IR35 need to do now?

Workers affected by IR35 will need to:

- calculate the tax and NICs due under the legislation by 5 April; and

- pay the tax and NICs due (or at least a provisional amount) by 19 April.

## PCG's Response

Andy liaised with the PCG directors and issued the following note via shout99:

> PCG has three legal options: appeal (despite Judge Burton's comments) a European challenge or a case law challenge.
>
> In addition to the legal options, all contractors should now feel more comfortable challenging IR35 and the dreaded Inland Revenue on a commercial footing. The Judge openly criticized the approach and guidance of the Revenue. On this point, he agreed with PCG - that the IR net was caste inappropriately wide and that their guidance was unclear, unhelpful and created uncertainty.
>
> Both contractors and Revenue inspectors should understand the comments made by the Judge (who sits on employment tribunals). He is perhaps the best-placed expert so far to pass comment on how IR35 will be viewed in a case law situation

Losing is one thing; the crowing of the victors is another. We needed to be able to fight back immediately. As a reader of history I expressed that this shouldn't be some sort of Culloden[68] or Waterloo, we should continue to fight. The judge had tried to rule out an appeal but Susie explained that we could get round this. What was at stake was not just the fight against IR35 but the future of the contractors group. Would it all fall away or would people stay together? What we did now would determine that future. Defeat would have recriminations, especially in an organisation like the PCG full of enthusiastic as well as angry members because as in Revolutionary France and Russia to be a general and to lose a battle was a dangerous thing.

## PCG Press Statement

So we put out an upbeat press statement. We had been successful in many key areas and any Government with some common sense would surely react to it and change its plans, as had happened for Sunday Trading. My view was that they would do what they had to, nothing more, which came down to changing the guidance and I was proved correct. The Inland Revenue had suggested to *Shout99.com* that there would be no further consultation on the guidance, they would do what they had to, nothing more. There was no reason why they couldn't have consulted.

As for the ruling the key pieces were as noted:

> 'on every finding of fact the judge concurred with the PCG including the key issue that contractors are in competition with larger consultancies and that IR35 would distort the marketplace'.

But that didn't make it illegal, even though he:

---

[68] The final defeat of Bonnie Prince Charlie in Scotland after which English soldiers went on a rampage of killing and looting

> 'was also critical of the Revenue's selective use of the employment tests to assess whether a small business fell inside or outside of IR35'.

In his final judgment he had described the Revenue's guidance as:

> inappropriate, unclear, inflexible, inaccurate and unhelpful. He also made reference to the unnecessary emotive and 'colourful' language in the original press notice which set the tone for a hostile debate

That wasn't illegal either.

Our angle on the judgement was that

'HIGH COURT ISSUES CLEARER GUIDELINES IN PCG'S JUDICIAL REVIEW'

We had lost and everyone could see that but the fight would carry on. The biggest pain was that he had said we couldn't appeal, which of course would have been the easiest response to make.

Our press notice - the 'we had lost well' version - pulled in every positive we could find from a defeat and must have had the Revenue wondering who had been the actual victors!

The High Court today criticised the Inland Revenue's tests for the stealth tax IR35 and laid down new guidance to make them more relevant to the knowledge-based sector.

The decision followed a judicial review brought by the Professional Contractors Group on behalf of its 13,000 members who operate their own small businesses, mainly in the IT and engineering sector, and whose companies were under threat because they were being wrongly classed as 'disguised employees'.

The PCG has argued for 18 months that the tests the Revenue used to assess the status of these companies were inappropriate to the modern operating practices of the knowledge-based sector and belonged to a bygone era.

PCG Chairman Gareth Williams said: "IR35 has been a catalogue of disasters from the very beginning. The most unfair aspect of it was that we had to pass a set of tests which had no relevance to our working practices.

"The High Court has been the first authoritative body to listen to our concerns and has confirmed that we were right. The Revenue got it wrong and as a result has damaged many small businesses, some of which have closed down and some have moved abroad.

"The Court has fortunately intervened to restrict further damage with a much more relevant set of guidelines which prove that IR35 was unfair, unworkable and created an uncertain climate. For example, the judgement was highly critical of the Revenue's 'inflexible stance' regarding blanket advice that standard agency contracts would be caught and he ruled that some of the uncertainty could be removed by the drafting, agreement and approval of a series of acceptable standard forms. He also found that the Revenue has been incorrect in assuming that mutuality of obligation was not a relevant issue, and he was critical of the Revenue's 'too inflexible approach' to the right of substitution. "

On every finding of fact the judge concurred with the PCG including the key issue that contractors are in competition with larger consultancies and that IR35 would distort the marketplace. He was also critical of the Revenue's selective use of the employment tests to assess whether a small business fell inside or outside of IR35. In his binding judgement, he described the Revenue's guidance as inappropriate, unclear, inflexible, inaccurate and unhelpful. He also made reference to the unnecessary emotive and 'colourful' language in the original press notice which set the tone for a hostile debate.

However, this judgement comes only days before the end of the tax year when these small businesses will have to make decisions based on Revenue guidance which has now been shown to be inaccurate and misleading.

The PCG has renewed its offer to meet with Ministers or officials at any time to assist with this transition to the new guidelines with the minimum of disruption to all parties. The PCG, representing 13,000 members mainly in the IT and engineering community, began a legal challenge to judicially review the Government's action in introducing IR35 after the Treasury and Revenue refused to engage in any constructive debate with the Group's members.

IR35 was announced in a press notice after the March 1999 Budget. It treats small businesses in the knowledge-based sector as 'disguised employees' for tax and NI purposes, thereby preventing them from operating on similar terms to their larger competitors.

**Background:**

1. The Professional Contractors Group was formed in May 1999 to lobby against the Government's IR35 proposals. It is a non-party political group and its patrons are cross-bench peer, Lord Weatherill, former Speaker of the House of Commons; and industry guru Sir John Harvey-Jones. Since its formation it has evolved into the representative body for independent contractors from many disciplines including IT and engineering on many issues affecting the knowledge-based sector. It is the fastest growing trade association in the country and now has more than 13,000 members.

2. The PCG's aim is to work for proper recognition of independent contractors as a genuine and valuable sector of the economy, generating wealth and employment, providing industry with a flexible workforce. The Internet has been the primary resource, providing fast, effective communication.

3. The PCG brought the judicial review against the Government, claiming IR35 contravenes European legislation.

4. During the actual judicial review hearing in March, the Court indicated it agreed with a number of PCG's points which had previously been contested by the Revenue. They included:

◦ Certainty many of contractors will be taken out of 'certainty' and put into a position of 'uncertainty' as to whether their contractors fall within IR35

◦ Financial flexibility Unaffected companies have greater flexibility in arranging their financial affairs than those affected by IR35

◦ Competition there was real competition between small contracting companies and larger body shops

◦ Moving overseas Some contractors will move overseas or others will be deterred from coming to the UK

◦ Multiple clients - seeking work opportunities from multiple clients would put a company outside IR35.

◦ Employment rights there was a strong case for employment rights for those caught under IR35. The employment rights issue could extend to employees of body-shops selling them into clients.

◦ Freedom of movement - the freedom of movement issue is potentially an easier hurdle to cross - doesn't depend on sector or competition.

◦ Evidence of competition - fairly convinced of a competition element in IT and asked for additional evidence of other sectors. Engineering evidence was provided to demonstrate the point.

◦ Same contract different opinion - the example of one contract which received a 'yes' and a 'no' from different IR offices. It took 4-5 months to get a decision (28 day limit) and the 'inside IR35' was an obvious cut and paste job which showed that the assessor hadn't read the content.

◦ Restrictive - the application of IR35 should be less restrictive.

◦ Tax mitigation the different between tax mitigation (i.e. making arrangements in accordance with tax regime after you've set up a business for other reasons) and tax avoidance (i.e. setting up a business/arranging your affairs in order to maximise tax benefits). Nothing wrong with setting up companies and using them to mitigate tax.

◦ Emotive language in press release - there was criticism of the use of emotive language, such as 'disguised employee' in the original IR35 press release which the judge described as 'wholly regrettable and unnecessary'

◦ Friday to Monday - there should be no prejudice in the assessment procedure because the first client of the contractor had previously been an employer.

- Expert competition evidence - judge indicated that he could see the force of argument when supported by our expert evidence, and that the IR was relying on assertions not supported by evidence.

- Freedom of Movement - IR must show that there is an overriding reason of public interest - which cannot be an 'economic one'.

- Proportionality - if the objective was to prevent Friday-to-Monday, it's a sledgehammer to crack a nut.

- Incorporation - there was nothing critical in terms of people taking advantage of laws allowing them to incorporate.

- Implementation - the judge was critical of the manner in which the IR was going about implementation in practice

## Press Reaction

Gareth gave the BBC an excellent quote which was that:

> The judgement contains a detailed and what we would say is a damning critique of IR35, and the judge has issued binding guidance which effectively rewrites the IR35 rulebook

We could live in hope. Other press reaction was mixed. Some trade sites such as SDJAccountancy were critical[69]

> During the five day Judicial Review, the judge criticised the Revenue's Employment Status guide and expressed his distaste for the emotive language of the original IR35 press notice in the 1999 Budget pack. However, Mr Justice Burton was swayed by the legal arguments marshalled by Revenue QC Mr Richard Plender. The PCG was partly hindered by their QC, Gerald Barling, who did not always appear on top of his brief.

The Daily Telegraphs headlined it as 'Judge criticizes Revenue but upholds IR35'[70]

> Although Mr Justice Burton decided that IR35 was compatible with European free trade laws and the Human Rights Act, he said the Inland Revenue's approach to IR35 had been "inflexible" and issued guidelines on how better to put the new regime into practice.
>
> Despite having its case thrown out, the Professional Contractors Group, which took the Inland Revenue to judicial review over IR35, claimed victory on the grounds that the High Court had recognised some of its concerns. Jane Akshar, one of the group's directors, said: "OK, IR35 is not illegal, but the High Court

---

[69] http://www.sjdaccountancy.com/cgi-bin/item.cgi?id=5815&d=101&h=160&f=127

[70] http://www.telegraph.co.uk/finance/4487965/Judge-criticises-Revenue-but-upholds-IR35.html

admitted it is unfair. The court has said that all our facts are right and heavily criticised the Inland Revenue's [IR35 compliance] tests."

The group looked forward to working with the Inland Revenue on the new IR35 guidelines, she said. A spokesman for the Inland Revenue said that although "IR35 remains the law of the land", the Revenue would "study the judgment and see if there were any lessons to be learned for the future".

They reported too that Anne Redston, a partner at Ernst & Young and an IR35 expert, said the group "would be better advised to take test cases [against IR35] through the UK courts." She said: The judge agreed with some of the facts, but not enough to make the legal case."

Good advice, but the next steps weren't to just be about fighting IR35 but about keeping the PCG afloat and its momentum going.

Mail on Sunday

The Mail on Sunday went one better and in an article entitled 'Court leaves tax rebels in limbo' by Jo Thornhill it stated:

> 'Thousands of hi-tech contract workers have been forced to play a waiting game after a High Court judgment on a controversial tax rule that could have pushed many of them out of business or forced them abroad.'

This seriously annoyed the Inland Revenue who thought the war was now over and that contractors should shut up and pay up. So the Head of the Inland Revenue - Nick Montagu - made the following formal response and complaint to the Mail on Sunday. It read as follows:

> "It is misleading for Jo Thornhill to suggest (MoS 8 April) that there is any remaining uncertainty over IR35. The High Court has confirmed unequivocally that it is valid in law, and people must now comply with the obligations which it imposes.
>
> "We will be looking at whether we need to improve the guidance which we give the public and our own people, in the light of the judge's remarks. But the basic tests for determining whether someone is employed or self-employed for tax and national insurance purposes remain unchanged. Everyone affected by IR35 needs to work out how much tax and national insurance they owe us and pay it by 19 April."

### Dawn responds in Parliament

In Parliament Paymaster General, Dawn Primarolo, responded to parliamentary questions regarding IR35 saying the Treasury was now ready to consult with the Professional Contractors Group.

Former Conservative IT Minister, Mr Ian Taylor (Esher and Walton), opened his questioning of the legislation by saying: "I have some comments on something that is close to the heart of the Paymaster General: IR35. Perhaps it is close to some other part of her anatomy, but if it is not her heart, I do not want to speculate too much."

He then went on to accuse IR35 as being a 'blight on the landscape' adding that it was causing 'damage' and 'confusion' in the IT sector.

He told the House:

> "The court case last week may have pleased the Inland Revenue in some ways, but it certainly added to the confusion. It took an 88-page document from the High Court to try to clarify the existing position."

Dawn Primarolo replied by saying:

> "The court ruled in favour of the Inland Revenue on every count and leave to appeal was refused. It is important that proper dialogue now takes place. We have already written to the main body, the Professional Contractors Group. IR35 is the law of the land, but discussions about its implementation and the advice that is given would benefit enormously from the positive engagement of those who are still unhappy with it."

(We are now the main body, recognition at last!)

Mr Taylor responded, saying:

> "I hope the PCG takes up her offer. There is definitely a need, however, to achieve a clearer understanding, in all circumstances, of what constitutes an employee. Accepting that IR35 is the law of the land, it would none-the-less be better if we could obtain that clarification.
>
> There is frustration out there in what are broadly described as the knowledge-based industries that IR35 is still a problem. I have heard the Government referred to as a 'sales prevention agency', they are certainly a 'job confusion industry' when it comes to IR35.
>
> "Many skilled workers in this country think that it might be easier to get jobs abroad. I stress that, even if the court was clear on the matter, some of the applications of IR35 regulations are less clear to people working in the industry. The Paymaster General should continue to be concerned about that."

I wasn't involved enough now so I have no idea what the response was to her letter, but no further formal meetings with her ever took place.

### Sarah Walker Speaks

After the case had finished but before the judgement was released we learnt that Ms Walker had recently started a new job within the Revenue which removed her from having responsibility for IR35. The day after her final court appearance on the Revenue benches she gave *Shout99.com* an interview to explain her Department's motivation and justification for the measure and possible future action in the light of the JR outcomes.

Ms Walker began by explaining the motivation behind the creation of the legislation itself.

She said: "Ministers were concerned that there were people working in certain situations which were clearly the same as employees but were able to pay significantly less in tax and National Insurance than they would if they were employed directly by their clients by using a service company. They didn't think that was fair, and thought there was a problem with fairness between those that were directly employed and paid National Insurance and tax. Those that were using service companies had arranged their affairs to pay considerably less."

A frequently-used term within the Government's thinking has been that 'genuine businesses' would be unaffected, however there has been no clear definition of what constitutes a 'genuine business'.

She explained the terminology: "I think the distinction that is made in the tax system is between an employee and a self-employed person, that a self-employed person has to make an investment in their business and take financial risks and provide substantial amounts of materials and equipment, and a genuine part of the financial risk is that they work for a fixed price for a project rather than an hourly rate. They will have much more control over the way they work whether they work on the client's premises or whether they work on their own premises.

"Those sorts of things correspond generally to a common sense view and certainly to the view the courts have taken as to what the difference is between someone who is in business and is a self-employed person and someone that is an employee and is clearly dependent on their employer for their work."

Judging from the comments from Ministers during the past two years and the case presented during the judicial review, it was questionable whether the 'service companies', who were members of the PCG, could be counted among these 'genuine businesses'.

Ms Walker said: "That depends very much on the circumstances. The fact of having a company doesn't make you a genuine business. We have to look at the way in which you behave and so we're applying those same tests to people with service companies as are applied to people without service companies.

"The Ministers have made clear that they consider IR35 is not just consistent with encouraging growth and innovation but is actually important to ensure that the tax system is able to encourage growth and innovation because it is ensuring that the tax treatment that is made to go to genuine businesses who are taking risks, who are creating wealth, who are creating employment in the economy isn't actually also available to people who are basically the same as employees. If you can't make that separation, then you can't target measures that are intended for genuine small businesses.

"That's not to say that people in the IT industry can't also set up small businesses in their spare time, be innovative, invent all sorts of things at work and when they are doing that kind of work, they will get the benefit of the treatment that is available to small businesses and they will get all the expense deductions and all the tax treatment that go with that. If someone who has been working either as an employee or as a contractor who has been caught by IR35 goes on to set up a small business then they will get all the encouragement thought the tax system that any other small business will.

"If a service company, a limited company, is working in a way that falls within the definition of 'a small business', of the definition of 'a self-employed person' they could also be entitled to the benefits.

"If you're working on a standard 9-5, 40 hour per week contract, but in the evenings or at the weekends, you're developing a software product or a website or something comparable, and you incur expenses in doing that or you make an investment in doing that- all of that will be treated as self-employed income. Not only will that not be subject to the expenses limit, but any sort of surplus expenses that you incur in relation to the IR35 court contract can be set against that income. Any money that you invest in order to pursue that business can be fully set against the profits of that business when they materialise."

One of the main areas of concern among these companies has been the limit of five per cent expenses, which could prevent development of other business streams or prevent investment in hardware, reinvestment or training.

When asked to justify this limit, Ms Walker said: "If somebody needs to buy an expensive PC or hardware in order to fulfil a contract - that contract is less likely to be caught by IR35. Contracts that are caught by IR35 are generally those that involve working on a client's premises and working on a client's equipment so when you are in that sort of situation, you won't get a deduction for buying an expensive PC at home any more than an employee would because it is not necessary for that employment."

On the subject of competitiveness, it has been disputed by the Revenue that the small companies actually competed with the larger body-shops. However, the High Court heard considerable evidence this week to show that in many and diverse areas the small companies not only compete with the large body-shop, but in some cases tender and win the contracts. It appeared, at one point, that the court had accepted this as fact.

Ms Walker said: "I think what the judge was saying was that people who were equivalent to employees who met the employment test were not in competition with other businesses. There were people who genuinely would have been self-employed if they hadn't been working through a service company, who are the 'Charlotte' example. There will be some people there who, genuinely, would have been in competition with larger companies and they won't be caught by IR35, but those are people using service companies in competition with the larger companies. That is not the case that the PCG were putting, which is that everybody hit by IR35 is in competition with a bigger company and I don't think the judge accepted that."

"For example, Microsoft wrote a product that they went on to sell. Somebody doing that will not be affected by IR35.

"It's possible for someone to have two occupations at once, they can be employed in a day job and they can be setting up their own business in the evening. If you're literally employed in a day job, you don't get to set all of the expenses of your project you are working on in the evenings against the income from your day job and that's exactly what we're doing for IR35 people."

Later in the article

Early on in the judicial review the judge, who also sits on Employment Appeals Tribunals, signalled that he saw the case where someone taxed as an employee could have a case to claim benefits as an employee - and potentially an employee of a body-shop could have a claim for rights against the client. The Financial Times reported this could result in a £2 Billion Bill for British industry.

Ms Walker said: "I don't think the judge or the Financial Times was saying that that was as a result of IR35. Whether a worker can claim employment law rights against the person he's working for depends on the facts of the case - whether he, under employment law, will be counted as an employee. Our advice up until now has been that somebody with a service company that is clearly an employee of that service company can't claim employment law rights against his client. We've heard what the judge said; he is clearly an employment rights expert and will be taken seriously by the people who deal with these things. There may well be cases where people using service companies may try to claim employee benefits, but it is more a matter for the DTI as it would be tested in the courts under employment law.

"There is no suggestion in any case law, here or abroad, that somebody who is clearly an employee of a service company can claim rights against a client. If that were to be the case then people clearly would have the right to make those claims and it would be between them and their employers- on what basis those employers or those clients wanted to take them on, but really it is a matter between the worker and the client."

The PCG has long contended that the consultation process was a 'sham' considering it was invited in to a meeting to be told of the announcement which was due to be made the following day. Also the Revenue has stated, including in the court case that the PCG 'welcomed the revised IR35', when the PCG's press notice at the time described the move as replacing the 'unworkable with the illogical'.

She said: "The PCG wrote in as part of the process. They came to a meeting here at Somerset House and there were various conversations with representatives of the PCG. The PCG was certainly involved in our consultation.

"Their input contributed to Ministers' understanding of how the industry works and, as you know, there were changes that resulted from that consultation which were welcomed by the PCG.

"I don't think that the PCG have said that they didn't welcome them. I know they think they didn't go far enough and that's very clear but the PCG thought they were improvements and they said so in their evidence in the judicial review."

Although the outcome of the judicial review is unknown, *Shout99.com* asked if the Revenue would be prepared to meet with the PCG after the court ruling.

Ms Walker said: "Ministers have said that they are not prepared to amend the legislation. Clearly we need to wait and see what the result of the judicial review is. The Revenue is prepared to talk to the PCG at any time and we have said that all along. It will be for Ministers whether they want to amend IR35 but at the moment their position is that they don't want to - they have defended it very strongly in the judicial review and elsewhere and they don't see any need for any amendment."

At one point in the hearing the PCG's QC, Mr. Barling, held up a contract that received two opposing replies after a 5 month wait, when there is a supposed 28 day turnaround, from the IR35 contract reviews department. Despite the time delay, one of the decisions was within IR35 and one was outside - despite the fact that they were the same contract. It was also apparent that the contract which the IR had deemed to fall within IR35 had been judged on a 'cut and paste' reply where the actual submitted contract had not been considered.

The Revenue's QC, Dr Richard Plender apologised for the situation.

Ms Walker explained: "It was a mistake - we're dealing with thousands of pieces of post everyday and clearly mistakes happen. We have apologised for that. What happened was that the case came in and was inadvertently copied and sent to two different offices, and those offices looking at a contract that was clearly one that was written deliberately to be ambiguous, the people at the time looked at it and gave different answers.

"We keep the procedures under review all the time and we try and make sure that they are working properly. People may be uncertain as to whether they will be caught or not. The Revenue has provided a service of giving opinions to give people certainty so if they have submitted a contract for an opinion- we've given an opinion- that will be binding on us, they should no longer be uncertain."

The only clear 'justification' for IR35 goes back to the Revenue's original 35th press notice which outline a desire to prevent to so-called Friday to Monday scenario, whereby an 'employee' quit his job on a Friday and continued the same 'job' on a Monday, but this time in a self-employed or limited company status. However, the IR35 legislation, in its finished version would not have prevented this perceived 'abuse' anyway.

Ms Walker said: "Some people have tried to say that 'where somebody who leaves an employer and comes back to the same employer straight away through a service company- that's avoidance', but 'if they leave one employer who goes back and does an identical job with the employer next door, that's not tax avoidance'- that doesn't seem to me to be a valid distinction. It doesn't seem to make a lot of sense to Ministers and I don't think that's something we could have legislated for.

"What we've done, and I think this is something that the judge recognised, is to look at anybody who using the existing common law test to identify an employee, would fall clearly within that definition if it hadn't been for the fact that they were using a limited company. All those people will pay tax on the same basis as employees who are directly employed."

And as to the future, if the Revenue where to lose the judicial review?

"If we lose the case, it will depend on the terms of the judgment. If the effect of the judgment is that the scope of European Law is so much wider than we were expecting it to be - that it prevents the Government from taking this kind of action, then I think we would expect to appeal - but clearly it depends on the terms of the judgment.

"We're just as confident as we were before the case, we and Ministers are confident that this is fair and proportionate and consistent with all of our European obligations."

### PCG offers discounted tax insurance

Around this time there were also subtle shifts within the PCG and its internal structure, although not significant at the time they were later to be used in a leadership 'coup'.

Andy's company, Webtastic, was providing the 'back office' network for the PCG on a contracted-out basis. He had also convinced Kevin Miller, PCG's accountant and Finance Director, to join him. Kevin had provided some of the detailed IR35 technical papers. Simon Banton and later Hugo van der Sanden, were highly respected members of the open source programming community and PCG members and came on board in that capacity. The PCG was Webtastic's main client - but not their only one. Susie had never been employed directly by the PCG or Webtastic; she was an employee of a London-based PR consultancy, Vane Percy and Associates. However, when it was known that she planned to leave, Andy encouraged her to set up her own consultancy with PCG as a client - and a few others from her previous consultancy work. Consequently, most of the original team who had come to the PCG from various roads became connected in offering PCG support. The PCG Board were, at the time, just happy to keep the original team in place - and requested that Kevin stay as a PCG Board member given his financial expertise.

Andy's commercial background and Kevin's financial grasp soon led to enhanced deals and offerings for PCG members - including tax investigation insurance.

*Shout99.com* Thursday, 24 May 2001

Contractors faced with the uncertainty surrounding the implementation of the controversial IR35 tax can now insure against the risk that the Inland Revenue will disagree with their assessment of their own company's status.

The Professional Contractors Group, working in conjunction with tax and VAT consultants Qdos, has launched 'Tax Liability Cover 35' (TLC35) a fully insured policy which insures PCG members tax liabilities and penalties that might arise if they were to be 'caught' under IR35 by an Inland Revenue challenge.

Previously the PCG had offered 'tax investigation' insurance which covered the costs of an investigation, but now members could insure against any of the IR35 costs if they were investigated by the Inland Revenue. Obviously they would have to meet certain criteria, but it was a leap forward in arming contractors in the fight against IR35.

# Chapter 22

## June 2001 - General election

IR35 turns out not to be the decisive issue.

The General Election came and went and Labour was returned with a similar majority as it had been before. The Tories had made no real progress, though their existing seats all seem to be bluer, though the red seats are as red as they were before.

IR35 had come up on the doorstep and despite having being a huge advocate for the fight against it didn't do me any good at the ballot box. If you were anti-IR35 you didn't vote Labour. My message to contractors was that it was a vote for me, not for fighting IR35, though I suspect they decided it would be safer to vote Conservative.

I'd come second in North East Bedfordshire against Alistair Burt and managed to record a respectable 14,000+ votes. Alistair and I got on well and discussed IR35. He had initially asked me if I knew anything about it as they were putting it on their leaflets. I told him of my role in the PCG and so I suppose I managed to neuter the issue as I don't think they used it in the end.

## Aftermath

After the judicial review and with the General Election running I had lost touch with the PCG. Jane Akshar became chairman, taking over from Gareth Williams who had done an excellent job fronting the organisation. A new team of appointees took over, or rather I should say shuffled around. Andy took a back seat role and had stepped out for a while. He also dropped off the Consultative Council.[71]

It was suggested that the new PCG should be more moderate and consolatory and less revolutionary. Besides, the Jacobins[72] who had led the initial charge were now on the side lines. The defeat in the High Court did lead to some recriminations, but I wasn't there to witness them. The so called 'corporatists or 'thermidorians' took control on the assumption that the revolution was over, that the PCG could now become just a trade organisation and could focus on those organisational aspects. The removal of the Jacobins, (myself, Andy and his supporters), would demonstrate to the Revenue and Treasury that the PCG had changed, that it was now a more moderate and consolatory and less revolutionary organisation. Though neither of us had been directors for some time I could understand this reasoning.

In some dark places the blame for the defeat was laid with the strategy of fighting the Government, it was suggested that we had fought too hard and should have

---

[71] From memory

[72] The Jacobins were the radical group that initially led the French revolution

been more conciliatory. Ironically this was the suggestion of those arguing for the judicial review in the first place but they now sought to deflect the blame elsewhere. Those thoughts would be put on hold though.

I am told that suddenly all these arguments came to a halt when the PCG decided to push for an appeal after all. This had less to do with the Directors but as much to do with the members who weren't prepared to accept defeat so the PCG had to try and raise funds afresh and also find grounds under which to appeal, which they managed to do in the June. The war against IR35 wasn't over. Some thought we should push with the judicial review, others thought our time and money would be better spent in driving forward case law by challenging every possible case - others still wanted to fight a political battle. Lines were being drawn and not only over the PCG's direction and policy - but who controlled it.

While all this was going on the Revenue had updated its guidance on IR35 but this wasn't the major rewrite that we had hoped for.

Around the corner were fresh challenges. The Government had introduced a fast track visa system to tackle skills shortages and out of fear that contractors were going abroad, but by the time it had been implemented the demand for contractors had fallen and firms then used the scheme to terminate UK workers and to replace them with foreign workers. At the same time the DTI had issued a consultation on new agency regulations which threatened to consider all contractors to be temporary workers in terms of rights. In a way it made sense, if you got taxed as an employee you should get employee rights, but in reality it would mean that firms would avoid using contractors. The two issues together with the draconian IR35 were coming together to threaten the very business model of contracting.

Fortunately contractors were prepared, they were organised and they had a voice and were ready to defend their rights.

That fight is the next story.

# Appendix

# Nominations for the New Statesman Award

*As collected at the time by email and noted in my box file. This may not be a complete list but is indicative of the strong feelings and warm regard contractors and observers had.*

"10,000 new members last year! Great support organisation" Alan.

"A classic example of the power of the Internet. From 0 to 10000 members in a year, with some of the most effective lobbying of MPs ever seen from such a group" Ian Cargill

"A brilliant example of what can be achieved using Internet technology. What has been achieved would have been impossible until recently. 11,000 (and rising) people who have mostly never met more than a handful of other site users, have mobilised against a deeply unfair and unpopular new government tax initiative (IR35). The new Internet technology means that information and messages are available immediately to all members. Further it means that fighting funds can be raised with tremendous speed and efficiency. The PCG can be incredibly quick on its feet in response to government actions and misrepresentations. As a side effect the site provides support and help to contractors generally. For the first time contractors have national voice instead of being little people struggling against the cruel outside world all on their own. The government until recently could pick contractors off one at time and bully them generally. Now they have a real high profile fight on their hands" Dave Richardson

"A great online site representing the contracting industry" Simon Fitze Horswell

"A group fighting for the rights of small businesses, and the repeal of discriminatory legislation" Jim Hughes

"A group that started with 0 at the beginning of the year 1999 and now has over 5000 members one year later all done through the web. They now have one of the highest percentage representations of the population they represent. The group was formed to represent the interests of engineering and IT contractors who will be badly affected by new Inland Revenue legislation called IR35 which will unfairly tax the contractor's companies compared to other small businesses. The group has been involved in a number of other firsts, including the first mass e-mail petition and the organising of over 700 contractors at 3 days notice to arrive at the House of Commons and green card their MPs. Such was the turn-out that the HoC could not cope with such a high turn-out, possibly the first time this has happened in the history of the HoC" Jon Axtell

"A pathfinder for how society may be able to explore and debate complex issues in the future" Pat McEvoy

"A superb example of this media being used to promote debate and political pressure" Jon Clark

"A web-based organisation whose membership has grown from 0 to over 10,000 in less than a year. Formed to fight the new draconian, illogical and wholly unfair tax laws (IR35) which specifically target the knowledge based consulting sector and have forced many of the most intelligent workers in the country to overseas competitors. The first organisation to create a web-based petition. An organisation which has become a real community with its members helping, communicating and offering each other help and support under a common cause" Paul Nolan

"Amazing to mobilise over 2000 complete strangers, from diverse disciplines, within weeks (since risen to over 4000 within one year), solely using the Internet. The achievements over the past 9 months are nothing short of staggering" Brett Wing

"Andy has been exceptional in promoting the cause of the PCG, fast becoming a force to be reckoned with" Simon Wiehe

"Andy planted the seed that became the Professional Contractors Group, which is not only a successful lobbying group for Professional Service Providers, but also, when that had taken off, created Shout99, an Internet news and discussion site for contractors. See also http://www.*Shout99.com*" James Dodds

"Andy White came from nowhere in April 1999; within 12 months he had built an organisation of some 10,000 members to represent UK contractor's interests. And he did this free of charge. Seldom can there have been such a significant contributor" Andrew McKay

"Andy's site made thousands of us aware of the fact that we have an active part to play in the politics of how this country is governed. Truly an eye-opener" Paul Hennebry

"Any group that goes from 0 to around 11000 members in the space of only 12 months must be doing something right!" Bernard Rushton

"As someone who has managed to unite a fragmented industry sector (and therefore easy govt. target) into a representative body of 10,000 and rising by using the online environment, and thus providing the sector with an authoritive voice, Mr. White deserves this recognition" Eric Ahlers

"Everything's been said, a great organisation pulling together 5000+ small businesses to provide a single voice" Simon Fitze Horswell

"excellent web site" Melanie Haylock

"Fantastic!" David Morrison

"Fighting the illogical IR35 rules" Mike Aubury

"First e-petition to parliament. Use of web and e-mail to organise opposition to changes in legislation on small companies. Use of web to organise members to go to Westminster to meet their MPs". Douglas Reid

For all of the reasons already mentioned - from an idea, through inception, to a force to be reckoned with, in nine months (what a baby!). Bob Smith

For creating the PCG and bringing over 10,000 small businesses together. Marc Deveaux

For its outstandingly professional approach in advocating the rights of IT contractors, who are being unfairly attacked, by the Inland Revenue & HMG. Keith Hassan

For its use of the internet as a powerful lobbying tool Jonathan Russell

For the first truly internet organised mass lobbying group. Derek Bergin

For their total use of the web for their campaign against the IR35 legislation, this also included the first e-petition to parliament. They recruited over 2,000 subscribtion paying members within a week and have 5000 members now. Lord McIntosh said of the PCG in the House of Lords :- "The second congratulations are due to the Professional Contractors Group. I have never encountered such a literate, persuasive series of letters. Ministers have received something like 2,000 letters. I have received many dozens. The noble Lord, Lord Jenkin, has received a number. They are literate, well spelt, well argued, persuasive letters" Paul Gallagher

For use of the Net to run a new style of campaigning and building community of common interests out of a notoriously individualistic group of small contracting businesses Malcolm Cowen

"Founder and organiser of the Professional Contractors Group; dedicated to advancing the cause of small knowledge-based businesses. Campaigning against IR35 and the damage it will cause the UK" Dr James S. Albinson

"From a standing start the PCG has organised thousands of contractors against the crazy IR35 legislation. It has demonstrated to the Government that with a huge majority comes a huge responsibility not to misuse that power" Neil Wilson

"From a start up group to oppose one bad piece of legislation this organisation now has "grown up" to be an effective voice for all Professional Service Providers in the country" James Dodds

"From one man's attempt to inform the general public about an inconsistent, unfair, illogical piece of legislation, this site has grown to become a focal point for over 10,000 individuals who exchange information and suggestions for ways to change the law" Christopher Boote

"Group to stop 'New' Labour turning into the North Korean Communist Party" Stephen Simpson

"Has grown from nothing to 5000 paid members since April 99. Helped organise the first ever e-petition in parliament. Used the power of email to organise a mass lobby of parliament (800 people) within 3 days. Surely the most technically advanced, and motivated lobby group in the UK" Kevin Peacock

"I nominate the PCG for giving us a glimpse of how true democracy might work in the future" Roger Tilbury

"I nominate the PCG for their total use of the web for their campaign against the IR35 legislation; this also included the first e-petition to parliament. They also used email to motivate some 800 people to attend parliament with three days notice, to lobby and green card their MPs. The campaign was setup on the web, a call put out for subscription to fund a campaign. They recruited over 2,000 subscription paying members within a week. Lord McIntosh said of the PCG in the House of Lords: "The second congratulations are due to the Professional Contractors Group. I have never encountered such a literate, persuasive series of letters. Ministers have received something like 2,000 letters. I have received many dozens. The noble Lord, Lord Jenkin, has received a number. They are literate, well spelt, well argued, persuasive letters"" Mike Spencer

"I nominate the PCG, as an organisation which has been formed entirely through the Internet and, in the space of 7 months has grown from nothing to an extremely powerful lobbying and representation group with a membership of 5000 and growing" John Peach

"I nominate the Professional Contractors Group (PCG) for their total use of the web for their campaign against the IR35 legislation; this also included the first e-petition to parliament. Also they used email to motivate 800 people to come to parliament with three days notice to lobby and green card their MPs. Normally the Commons expects about 25-50 people to green card their MPs, so this was unprecedented. The campaign was setup on the web, a call put out for subscription to fund a campaign. They recruited over 2,000 subscription paying members within a week. They now have upwards of 5,000 members and are still growing. They have made tops news stories in both the national and trade press. Since being founded in March they have also been invited in to meet Ministers at both the DTI and the Treasury. Lord McIntosh said of the PCG in the House of Lords: "The second congratulations are due to the Professional Contractors Group. I have never encountered such a literate, persuasive series of letters. Ministers have received something like 2,000 letters. I have received many dozens. The noble Lord, Lord Jenkin, has received a number. They are literate, well spelt, well argued, persuasive letters" Philip Ross

"I nominate the Professional Contractors Group (PCG) for their total use of the web for their campaign against the IR35 legislation; this also included the first e-petition to parliament. Also they used email to motivate 800 people to come to parliament with three days notice to lobby and green card their MPs. The campaign was setup on the web, a call put out for subscription to fund a campaign. They recruited over 2,000 subscription paying members within a week" Lee Dryburgh

"I would like to nominate Andy White, for his skill in drawing attention to IR35 and mobilising the Contractor/Consultant/Self Employed sector into doing something about it. Thank you Andy" Marc Deveaux

"I would like to nominate the Professional Contractors group for this award as they have used the new media of the Internet in new ways to lobby and raise awareness of the issue that they are concerned with. Through the use of their web site all members are quickly aware of what is happening, what is being said and new issues are constantly being discussed. Through their web site they have been able to organise an 800-strong lobby of Parliament within a few days and inform members of an e-petition within hours of it being raised. This use of the Internet has changed forever the way in which lobbying will be carried out on issues that affect British Citizens" Ian Watkins

"I would like to nominate the web site of the professional contractors group for their tireless work linking the now nearly 10,000 professional consultants in a campaign against the new labour stealth tax IR35. Without the use of this new technology it would be difficult for this number of people to communicate effectively about such a disastrous issue. The use of the web in this situation is a forerunner for new styles of communication and empowerment, which is probably why new labour are trying so hard to legislate against independent entrepreneurs as we do not fit into the labour sheep mould" Stuart Ranson

"In one year this group has grown to 10,000 members, effectively representing their interests to the Press, Government and the general public. Using the Internet and email enables its members to quickly react to events, and provide assistance to its members" Stephen Chalkley

"It was Andy White who started it all. Well done that man!" Bernard Rushton

"Managed to bring together a group of IT professionals who had never before been represented by one body. Has gone from zero to nearly 10,000 members in just over a year. A remarkable achievement" Douglas Reid

"My vote is based on the meteoric rise in membership through the medium of the Internet to associate more than 5000 professionals in less than one year. Also participated on the first e-Petition to be presented to Parliament" David A. McKelvie

"Organised a 5000 member pressure group, based purely on the Internet. 2000 members within a month. Now recognised (6 months later) as the only official group to represent engineering and IT contractors" Manuella Phillips

"Organised the first ever electronic petitions to the House of Commons. Has become (in 6 months) the group recognised as the only one representing the views of engineering and IT contractors" Manuella Phillips

"PCG has blazed a new trail in this category. Formed only a year ago it has grown into an incredible online community with electronic elections, the first electronic petition to parliament, and thousands of people able to talk to each other on a daily basis about a multitude of issues concerning them. The online 'Forums' are something to be seen to be believed. Help is always at hand, and news spreads across the community in minutes. It's quite remarkable and undoubtedly unique" Richard Whittington

"PCG was formed on the web. In less than 1 year it has grown to over 5,000 members and now has Associate members that include CBI, ICAW, etc. I was formed to fight the Inland Revenue proposal IR35 to tax small IT companies differently to large IT companies. It is now recognised as a significant body of opinion by all 3 major political parties" Bob Connell

"Superb and informative 'pressure group' with a superb and informative web site. Nuff said" Peter Mabe

"The first effective Internet lobbying group, with the first email petition" Richard Lambourne

"The first Internet lobby group and the fastest growing" Jack Gibson

"The group has used the Web to campaign very effectively against the IR35 regulations. Despite being called unrepresentative Dawn Primorola has on a number of occasions responded very forcefully and directly to arguments raised by the PCG. This indicates very effective lobbying. If the group was truly unrepresentative then it would just be ignored by Government. From a start in March 1999 the group has grown to 5000 members" Fred Weil

"The only organisation created for and by the "average" computer consultant. The website is brilliantly organised and the contributors are intelligent and articulate. The most useful website and organisation I've found" Mike Hattemore

"The PCG came from a standing start to being recognised as the voice of contracting in less than 12 months. Repeatedly mentioned in the House of Commons by senior figures on all sides. An outstandingly successful organisation" Alex Cosser

"The PCG has amassed an 11000+ membership in the space of only 12 months, and although was initially a single-issue body (the removal of the ill-conceived piece of legislation known as IR35), has now evolved into a properly-functioning representative body" Bernard Rushton

"The PCG has performed a remarkable feat in organising the campaign against the illogical IR35 tax. The ability to collate and share information speedily using the Internet has enabled it to highlight Government & Inland Revenue incompetence, evasion and half truths on a national scale. Raising the money for a Judicial Review and for a case to the European Court was achieved in a just over a day! Not bad for an organisation barely a year old. The Revenue will never be able to raise taxes whilst relying on intimidation, misrepresentation of the law and the ignorance of its victims again" C Sheriff

"The PCG has used the Internet to great effect in its lobbying of Govt on the IR35 issue" Abdulhai Patel

"The PCG have been able to consistently wrong foot the government by reacting quickly to spin by publishing the facts, via the medium of the Internet. Their ability to rally support continues to confuse and disturb a Labour Party that trumpets the Internet whilst consistently underestimating its power. What the PCG has created will, in the near future, decimate the position of spin doctors in politics. They could become as obsolete as the government would like to make contractors" Geoff Robbins

"The PCG was formed to fight the illogicality of ir35 which means that information contractors are worried sick about how to continue to run their businesses. The stress that this has put on the most able within our independent knowledge contractors is incalculable. But the PCG is there to share, inform, encourage and help" E Woolfenden

"The PCG was founded less than a year ago to represent independent IT and Engineering contractors in the fight against the government's IR35 tax legislation. Within 2 weeks of setting up it had 2000 members, and now has in excess of 5,000. All communications are performed over the Internet, via their website and e-mail. They also helped in organising the very first e-petition of parliament, and used their website and e-mail to organise, at very short notice, a lobby of Parliament by over 800 members. Their use of the web enables contractors all over the world to keep up to date with the latest developments in the fight against this legislation at any time of the day and night, and has proved invaluable to me in keeping me up to date, and enabling me to fully see the effects of this legislation on the future direction of my business" Kevin Callaghan

"The PGC is a shining beacon to all. Advocacy and lobbying at its very best" Adam Baldwin

"The previous comments speak volumes. I won't waste your time making another" Dillon Spring

"The Professional Contractors Group has run a highly original and professional web based campaign on behalf of freelance consultants. We have heard much in recent years of the power of the Internet. I would contend that the Professional Contractors Group is the first professional body to exploit and demonstrate that power to the full, having achieved over 10,000 fully paid up members within one year of inception. Richard Marriott

"The Professional Contractors Group setup an Internet site to allow Computer and Engineering contractors the chance to discuss and share information on the recent IR35 tax changes. The PCG subscribing members, around 10,000 and growing fast is an indication of the value and quality of the site" Brian Wojtowycz

"They've certainly impressed me!" Mike Pattison

"They have created a true sense of belonging and purpose in a very short space of time on an excellent website and email basis" Peter Mabe

"This group has succeeded by using the Internet to mobilise large numbers in opposition to an ill-conceived & illogical piece of discriminatory legislation. It uses the same medium to advise & inform its members. The PCG has shown the way for lobbying groups in the future" Robin Monks

"This has to be a great demonstration of the power of the internet. A lobbying group that has grown to 5000 people in 8 months all through the Internet. It has had enough impact to be mentioned in Parliament and to attract considerable media attention" Jane Akshar

"This site has revolutionised the way an organisation of individuals (or companies) can operate. Andy set up PCG as an Internet based organisation, and has developed it to the point where the members, who are located all over the UK, communicate better than if they were living in the same street. As a group, they can support each other in a way never possible before, and can respond at incredible speed. This is real people power; the days when organisations and Governments played "Divide and Rule" are truly over" Mike Parris

"To become the one body that advocates from all interested parties turn to for real information and true reason (as opposed to "spin" or hearsay), even when they are trying to formulate rules to cripple that body's members in a situation of their own creation (the Inland Revenue), is a tribute indeed. And the members have had a scary and uplifting glimpse of the feeling ("buzz", as my MP expressed it) of power that politics brings. But THIS is the democracy of here and now, the Internet: its ability to expose the truth and to give power to the people is something that our existing politicians and officials simply cannot grasp or accept. Their future is endangered by the merciless truth that the freedom of expression and information of this medium brings. This is the model for a true democracy" Roger Cole

"Uses the full power of the Internet to co-ordinate, inform and campaign for IT business" Richard Fryer

"With over 10,000 members, the PCG are cohesively and actively fighting for the survival of their business sector using e-Technology to its advantage" David A. McKelvie

"Within 12 months have become powerful advocates for 10,000 members" Richard Whittington

"What more can I say that hasn't already been said?" Anne Smith

# Glossary of Organisations

| | |
|---|---|
| Professional Contractors Group | Now just called the PCG |
| IR – Inland Revenue | Now part of HMRC |
| ATSCo | Trade association representing the biggest IT recruitment agencies. Ran by Ann Swain as CEO. Now known as APSCo |
| Shout99.com | News website founded by Andy White and Susie Hughes. Still run by Susie Hughes and provides an independent view on contracting issues |
| DTI | Department of Trade and Industry. Included the office of the minister for small business and ecommerce. |
| ICAEW | Institute of Chartered Accountants for England and Wales |
| CIOT | Chartered Institute of Taxation |
| FSB | Federation of Small Business |
| itcontractor.com | News website founded by Gerry McLaughlin in 1999 as NamesFacesPlaces changing its name in 2005 |
| Silicon.com | News site and an affiliate member of ATSCo |
| Jobserve.com | Online jobs website |
| REC (FRES) | General trade association for recruitment agencies. Grew from FRES. |
| BCS | British Computer Society, chartered body for IT professionals and academics |
| ICCG | Independent Computer Contractors Group, sub group of the BCS, led by Mike Cullen |
| ATIES | Association of Temporary and Interim Executive Services |

# Glossary of terms

| IR35 | Short hand for the tax on contractors supplying their services via an intermediary. Named after press release 35 of the 1999 Budget. |
|---|---|
| Agency Regulations | Reform of the agency regulations from 2000-2004 |
| FTV – Fast track visas | The PCG's name for the Work Permits scheme for IT workers. |
| DTI | Department of Trade and Industry |
| Sans culottes | During the French revolution the sans culottes were the workers and tradesman from the poorer districts of Paris and elsewhere. They would be the engine of the revolution, the mass army that would propel it forward.<br><br>I use this term to describe the thousands of contractors in the PCG and *Shout99.com*. I use it as a term of endearment as it was the scrutiny and energy of the members that formed the PCG and allowed us to challenge the Government. |
| Les Enragés | The more extreme members of the PCG. Also from the French Revolution extremist 'sans-culottes', means literally 'the mad men'. I use it to describe those against me and who felt we should be attacking the Government more |
| Jacobins | The leading revolutionaries during the French revolution. Comprising of such figures as Danton, Robespierre, Desmoulins, Carnot and others. History records them as being the radical element in the revolution. After their fall from power the revolution's momentum ceased leading to the dictatorship of Napoleon. After they had lost power they were blamed for everything that had gone wrong. |

| | |
|---|---|
| EURIM | EURIM is the expert group for Internet and information society policy in Parliament.<br><br>It brings together industry experts, observers from the civil service, professional bodies, charities and trade associations to help identify solutions to policy, regulatory and legislative problems impacting UK competitiveness and to help ensure taxpayers' money is spent efficiently |
| PSC | Personal Service Company. Another name for the limited company that a single contractor may use. |

# Index

360 Accounting Group, 33, 44, 45, 48, 97, 101, 167, 202, 260
Adam Smith Institute, 97, 100, 105
AEEU (union), 35, 112, 118
Akshar, Jane (PCG Director), 60, 154, 199, 245, 249, 299, 308, 317
Allen, Alex (e-Envoy), 93, 190, 192, 226, 233, 235, 236, 238, 242, 267
Askam, Tony, 252
Association of Chartered Certified Accountants (ACCA), 218
Association of Temporary & Interim Executive Services (ATIES), 90, 98, 101, 319
ATSCO, 184, 258, 259, 260
Banton, Simon, 55, 64, 68, 306
Barling, Gerald (QC for the PCG), 195, 252, 253, 270, 271, 272, 273, 274, 275, 276, 277, 278, 284, 285, 286, 287, 299, 305
BBC News, 99, 120, 164, 165, 176, 204, 205, 206, 217, 218, 245, 279, 299
Begg, Anne (MP), 190
Birt, John, 70, 120, 245
Blair, Tony (MP, Prime Minister), 21, 28, 61, 62, 64, 72, 98, 99, 106, 119, 122, 124, 130, 142, 143, 146, 182, 192, 207, 233, 237, 241, 249, 260, 266
Bond Pearce (solicitors), 49, 52, 155, 161, 195, 270
British Chamber of Commerce, 223
British Computer Society, 18, 31, 33, 34, 35, 36, 43, 44, 54, 56, 319
Brown, Gordon (MP, Chancellor of the Exchequer), 21, 27, 28, 38, 39, 51, 62, 64, 66, 88, 90, 92, 98, 104, 107, 109, 117, 120, 129, 165, 187, 188, 190, 201, 244, 255, 266, 267, 288
Burton, John (Prof - Adam Smith Inst.), 97, 98, 105, 172
Cable, Vince (MP, Lib Dem Treasury\DTi), 76, 79
Carey, Elaine (Inland Revenue), 24, 39, 47, 48, 63
CIOT, Chartered Institute of Taxation, 35, 82, 83, 84, 85, 97, 98, 101, 177, 178, 192, 260, 319

Computing for Labour, 79, 245
Confederation of British Industry (CBI), 43, 48, 85, 101, 116, 156, 162, 177, 192, 218, 242, 250, 255, 260, 315
Cropper, Hilary (CEO FI Group), 264
Cullen, Mike (BCS ICCG), 18, 32, 33, 42, 44, 45, 85, 90, 156, 319
Curnow, Brian (PCG member), 158, 163, 199, 231
Darling, Alistair (MP and Welfare Minister), 64, 72, 95
Davis, Evan (Newsnight, Economics Editor), 204, 206
Deveaux, Mark (PCG member), 273, 313, 314
DTI, 44, 46, 55, 66, 67, 70, 72, 98, 102, 153, 165, 172, 192, 194, 201, 218, 224, 237, 240, 242, 267, 304, 309, 314, 319, 320
Duncan Smith, Iain (MP), 79, 80, 153
Duncan, Alan (MP), 163, 164
Durrant, Ian (PCG Director), 199, 280
Edwards, Pamela (PCG Director), 199, 237, 241, 245, 249, 251
e-petition, 13, 256, 312, 313, 314, 315, 317
Evening Standard, 129, 224, 254, 262
Fast Track Visas (FTVs), 12, 15, 159, 202, 224, 320
Federation of Recruitment and Employment Services, 18, 25, 43, 44, 49, 85, 97, 98, 101, 167, 319
Federation of Small Business (FSB), 85, 89, 90, 97, 98, 101, 156, 166, 186, 188, 192, 250, 260, 319
Finance Act, 82, 204, 228, 268, 292
Forth, Eric (MP), 78
Gould, Joyce (Baroness - Computing for Labour), 62
Griffiths, Simon (PCG Director), 199
Guardian, The, 28, 81, 143, 223, 224, 234, 237, 264

Hague, William (MP, Leader of Conservative Party), 14, 119, 143, 146, 148, 162, 191, 201, 207
Harvey-Jones, John (Sir - Patron of PCG), 3, 257, 258, 297
Heathcoat-Amory, David (MP - Shadow DTI), 246
Hewitt, Patricia (e-Minister), 46, 93, 99, 123, 165, 171, 190, 191, 192, 226, 232, 235, 237, 240, 241, 242, 243, 252, 254, 255, 267
Hoggart, Simon (Guardian), 143
Hughes, Susie (PCG Press and Shout99.com), 14, 49, 55, 60, 70, 81, 86, 90, 92, 94, 95, 96, 98, 103, 104, 107, 110, 119, 125, 126, 134, 136, 139, 140, 141, 143, 144, 147, 149, 150, 152, 153, 155, 157, 165, 173, 180, 184, 198, 200, 201, 204, 206, 207, 209, 214, 225, 226, 231, 236, 237, 238, 239, 241, 245, 247, 248, 249, 252, 254, 257, 261, 279, 280, 290, 291, 295, 306, 319
ICAEW, Institute of Chartered Accounts for England and Wales, 3, 35, 74, 85, 97, 98, 101, 157, 177, 178, 192, 219, 222, 226, 241, 260, 274, 285, 319
Independent Computer Contractors Group (See also Mike Cullen), 18, 32, 33, 43, 48, 55, 56, 57, 58, 97, 102, 319
Inland Revenue, 13, 21, 23, 24, 25, 27, 29, 30, 32, 33, 38, 39, 40, 41, 42, 43, 44, 45, 47, 48, 51, 55, 57, 58, 62, 63, 65, 66, 67, 68, 70, 73, 74, 76, 78, 82, 83, 84, 85, 86, 87, 88, 89, 90, 92, 94, 96, 97, 98, 99, 100, 101, 102, 104, 105, 117, 121, 122, 123, 128, 132, 134, 144, 146, 155, 156, 157, 160, 166, 167, 169, 172, 173, 176, 177, 178, 179, 180, 186, 188, 189, 191, 192, 194, 196, 197, 202, 203, 204, 205, 206, 209, 210, 212, 213, 214, 215, 219, 220, 221, 227, 228, 230, 233, 235, 242, 243, 244, 247, 248, 251, 252, 253, 254, 255, 256, 258, 260, 262, 264, 267, 270, 271, 272, 273, 274, 275, 276, 277, 278, 280, 281, 282, 283, 284, 285, 286, 287, 288, 290, 291, 292, 293, 294, 295, 296, 297, 298, 299, 300, 301, 303, 304, 305, 306, 307, 308, 309, 311, 313, 315, 316, 318, 319
IOD, Institute of Directors, 85, 101, 260
Ireland, Chris, 66
Jacobin (revolutionaries), 14, 178, 308, 320
Jobserve.com, 258, 259, 319
Jordan, Alec (PCG member), 64
Justice Burton, 271, 272, 274, 282, 284, 285, 287, 299
Justice Gibbs, 251, 252, 253, 256
Kennedy, Charles (MP, Leader of LibDems), 99, 146
Kintore, Earl of, 92, 94, 127, 128, 149
Lagerberg, Francesca (ICAEW), 3, 157, 219, 222
Letwin, Oliver (MP), 245
Mail on Sunday, 106, 117, 118, 263, 300
Mandelson, Peter (MP), 28, 66, 106, 117
Mason, Collete (PCG member), 279
Maude, Francis (MP), 120, 141, 144, 165, 218, 245
McIntosh, Lord, 3, 92, 93, 95, 119, 127, 129, 130, 149, 152, 171, 313, 314
McWalter, Tony (MP), 15, 64, 182
Milburn, Alan (MP), 76
Miller, Andrew (MP - Computing for Labour), 62, 79
Miller, Kevin, 55, 60, 73, 93, 97, 100, 101, 104, 125, 127, 140, 147, 153, 156, 160, 167, 185, 189, 190, 194, 225, 278, 306
Newsnight, 13, 204, 205, 206, 207, 256
Oil and Gas Chapter, 94, 95, 128, 129, 147, 162, 186, 190

Ottoway, Richard (MP - Shadow Paymaster General), 202, 209, 210, 211, 212, 213, 214, 215
Page, Richard (MP), 38, 61
Paymaster General (Dawn Primarolo MP), 3, 14, 28, 29, 39, 40, 65, 66, 72, 100, 114, 134, 139, 141, 163, 166, 171, 173, 174, 175, 178, 179, 180, 184, 187, 188, 189, 191, 196, 202, 209, 210, 214, 215, 217, 226, 227, 228, 245, 254, 264, 265, 267, 277, 287, 290, 300, 301
Peacock, Kevin (PCG member), 276, 313
Plender, Richard (QC for Inland Revenue), 252, 270, 271, 275, 276, 277, 278, 281, 282, 284, 285, 286, 287, 299, 305
Portillo, Michael (MP, Shadow Chancellor), 22, 209, 245
Powell, Richard (Shout99.com), 83, 200, 273, 278, 283, 294
Primarolo, Dawn (Paymaster General), 3, 28, 30, 38, 39, 54, 62, 65, 85, 95, 96, 97, 104, 112, 114, 115, 117, 118, 119, 120, 130, 131, 133, 134, 136, 140, 142, 143, 144, 152, 159, 160, 168, 171, 172, 173, 174, 175, 176, 177, 178, 179, 180, 184, 185, 186, 190, 192, 193, 202, 205, 209, 210, 212, 214, 217, 224, 226, 233, 237, 239, 240, 242, 245, 254, 261, 264, 265, 267, 286, 287, 300, 301, 316
Prisk, Mark (MP), 85, 244
Rae, Elaine, 66
Ramsden, David (PCG Public Affairs), 49, 51, 52, 58, 60, 61, 66, 70, 80, 81, 82, 86, 90, 91, 92, 93, 94, 96, 104, 117, 119, 130, 137, 138, 139, 141, 142, 143, 153, 163, 164, 173, 185, 190, 198, 199, 225, 231, 237, 245, 247, 249, 252, 278
Recruitment & Employment Confederation, 18, 85, 319
Redston, Anne, 83, 103, 156, 278, 300

Register, the (website), 271, 290
RIA, Regulatory Impact Assessment, 60, 70, 72, 73, 81, 82, 85, 98, 124, 125, 147, 193, 201, 221, 276
Ross, Philip, 1, 2, 3, 15, 35, 86, 107, 110, 171, 180, 256, 288, 289, 314
Roy-Chowdhury, Chas (ACCA Taxation), 218
Seeley-Harris, Rebecca (Journalist), 271, 272, 276, 278, 279
Smith, Robert (Sir, MP), 64, 79, 94, 134, 135, 190
St Aubyn, Nick (MP), 265
Sutherland, Ian (360 Group), 156, 167
Swain, Ann (ATSCO CEO), 167, 193, 202, 260, 319
Tax cheats - accusation, 178, 196, 204, 217, 254, 267, 287, 290
Taylor, Ian (MP), 300
Telegraph, Daily, 60, 81, 109
Times, The, 60, 70, 193, 224, 255
Timms, Stephen (MP, Treasury Minister), 76, 77, 78, 142, 153, 182, 184
Treasury, 27, 28, 29, 47, 54, 62, 63, 66, 70, 72, 73, 74, 75, 76, 77, 79, 80, 94, 96, 98, 99, 101, 104, 105, 111, 112, 121, 123, 139, 141, 153, 158, 164, 171, 173, 174, 179, 191, 192, 193, 194, 201, 205, 206, 224, 229, 233, 234, 235, 240, 241, 245, 246, 264, 266, 267, 285, 297, 300, 308, 314
UNISON, 184, 185, 190, 192
Viz, Rudi (MP), 280
Walker, Sarah (Inland Revenue), 39, 55, 166, 173, 174, 175, 176, 177, 188, 217, 260, 275, 278, 301
Warr, Tim (Accountant), 156, 157
Watson, Tom (AEEU), 112
Weatherill (Lord - PCG Patron), 58, 59, 80, 86, 92, 152, 257, 297
Webstatic, 198, 199, 306
Welfare Reform Bill, 57, 60, 62, 64, 72, 73, 76, 77, 79, 80, 81, 89, 90,

92, 102, 127, 130, 132, 138, 141, 143, 146, 149, 268, 292

White, Andy (Founder of the PCG), 3, 14, 25, 26, 31, 38, 40, 43, 44, 48, 49, 50, 52, 54, 55, 56, 57, 62, 65, 69, 70, 73, 81, 85, 86, 87, 88, 93, 94, 95, 98, 99, 100, 102, 103, 104, 107, 110, 119, 122, 123, 124, 125, 126, 136, 140, 141, 142, 144, 145, 146, 147, 150, 152, 153, 155, 156, 157, 158, 160, 165, 166, 167, 168, 171, 172, 173, 174, 175, 176, 177, 178, 180, 184, 185, 186, 190, 193, 195, 196, 198, 199, 201, 205, 225, 228, 229, 236, 239, 241, 247, 248, 249, 250, 260, 267, 279, 287, 289, 295, 306, 308, 312, 314, 315, 318, 319

Whiting, John (ATIES), 84, 90, 156

Williams, Gareth (PCG Director), 92, 127, 154, 159, 160, 166, 198, 199, 204, 226, 237, 238, 239, 241, 245, 246, 247, 248, 249, 250, 251, 252, 254, 256, 257, 263, 271, 274, 275, 277, 278, 279, 280, 283, 296, 299, 308

Wills, Michael (MP, DTi Minister), 54, 66, 67, 70, 86, 93, 110, 237, 240

Wilson, Neil (PCG Director), 199, 252, 313

www.ingramcontent.com/pod-product-compliance
Lightning Source LLC
Chambersburg PA
CBHW020727180526
45163CB00001B/139